# THE CASE FOR COURAGE

# The Case for Courage

By WILLIAM M. KUNSTLER

Author of "Beyond A Reasonable Doubt?"

WILLIAM MORROW AND COMPANY

NEW YORK

1962

9530

Second Printing, July 1962

Library of Congress Catalog Card Number 62-12086.

*For Malvina Rothman*

# Acknowledgments

Grateful thanks are due to the following persons and institutions who helped to make this book possible: Ethel Beckwith; Arthur A. Charpentier; Earl Conrad; Morris L. Ernst; Wallace M. Exman; Simmons Fentress; Robert R. Gibson; Elizabeth Gorman; Hale & Dorr; Isadore L. Kotler, Coroner for Fairfield County, Connecticut; Michael J. Kunstler; Judge Harold R. Medina; Neil Metcalf; Joanna Miller; Michael P. Rosenthal; Holdredge M. Sinclair, County Clerk of Cayuga County, N.Y.; The American Numismatic Society; The Association of the Bar of the City of New York; The Greenwich (Conn.) Library; The New York Public Library; The Pace College Library; The Port Chester (N.Y.) Public Library; Prof. Hans Zeisel; and lastly my patient wife who now knows that the term "galley slave" is far from an anachronism.

# Contents

# Foreword

Several years ago, I attended a Twelfth Night presentation of the Association of the Bar of the City of New York. In general, these annual events are designed to satirize the careers of some of Gotham's more illustrious practitioners. The subject of the evening in question was the effervescent Morris Ernst, who bore up nobly under the slings and arrows that were hurled in his direction.

In his rebuttal, Mr. Ernst proclaimed, with some real dismay, that he was very much disturbed by the reluctance of the leaders of the legal profession to accept criminal cases more controversial than those involving evasion of income taxes, antitrust violations and Securities and Exchange Commission complaints. While I cannot claim that his critical observations on this score inspired this book, I must confess that they frequently came to mind during its writing. Like Ernst, I have long realized that lawyers, despite their addiction to conflict, share in common with the rest of mankind a natural resistance to involving themselves in situations fraught with grave consequences to their pocketbooks, their reputations and their peace of mind.

Fortunately, there have been notable exceptions. The ten cases reviewed in this book, spanning more than two hundred years, offer some proof that every generation of lawyers produces its own unique heroes. In each of them, an American attorney risked his career by involving himself, in one way or another, with one of the most explosive cases of his time and place. For some, the end result was political extinction; others suffered social ostracism, financial loss, or both. However, many not only survived the experience, but found that it did not stand in the way of future triumphs.

No claim is made that the individual lawyers selected exhaust all possible candidates for a book of this nature. For example, Georgia Governor John J. Slaton's commutation of Leo Frank's death sentence and Judge James E. Horton's setting aside of the jury's verdict after the second trial of "Scottsboro Boy" Heywood Patterson, *beau gestes* which doomed both men to political oblivion, were acts of rare courage. Even a precursory search of the trial records of the various states would reveal a significant number of instances in which lawyers fully and wholeheartedly live up to the spirit of the American Bar Association's stricture that "no fear of judicial disfavor or public unpopularity should restrain him from the full discharge of his duty."

The ten choices in this volume are the result of recommendations received from many of the country's leading law schools, coupled with my own standards of selectivity. In the main, I was interested in attorneys who, because of their professional or political stature, had much to lose by the repercussions of the controversial causes in which they participated. An act of courage, it seems to me, must be gauged in direct proportion to the risk it involves. This is not to depreciate the efforts of those who, in the last analysis, have little to lose, but to elevate to a higher prominence the shining acts of men who were willing to place full-blown careers on the block.

I realize that my selections may not win universal approval and that there are many other subjects who could have, with perfect logic, been included in this book. The responsibility for each choice is, of course, my own and I have no intention of avoiding it. I ask only that my critics bear in mind that my omissions do not in any way detract from the exploits of those whom they—and I—might have wished to see represented. Courage is where you find it, in this or any other age.

WILLIAM M. KUNSTLER

*September 15, 1961*

"The only limitation upon a right-thinking lawyer's independence is the duty which he owes to his clients, once selected, to serve them without the slightest thought to the effect which such service may have upon his own personal popularity or political fortunes. Any lawyer who surrenders this independence, or shades his duty by trimming his professional course to fit the gusts of popular opinion, in my judgment not only dishonors himself, but disparages and degrades the great profession to which he should be proud to belong."

Portion of a letter
written in 1924 by
John W. Davis to a
political supporter
who had urged him to
get rid of some of his more
controversial clients if
he hoped to win the
Democratic nomination
for President.

# THE CASE FOR COURAGE

# Andrew Hamilton

In an age when royal governors were the source of all real power, it was a rare colonial lawyer who would stand up for anyone stigmatized by official disfavor. This was particularly true in 1735 when New York was ruled by an autocratic and unscrupulous soldier who thought nothing of subverting the legal system to punish his enemies and of disbarring those few attorneys intrepid enough to defend them. Yet, in that year, despite these obvious dangers, a sick and ailing Andrew Hamilton made the tiring trip from Philadelphia to New York to represent John Peter Zenger, an impoverished printer accused of criminal libel.

It is impossible, at a distance of more than two centuries, to ascertain Hamilton's motives in risking his liberty, his health and his career for a man whom he scarcely knew. He himself always maintained that he had accepted the nonpaying assignment to further "the cause of liberty." But there were many who believed that he was prompted more by his inherent dislike of totalitarian authority, royal or otherwise, than by any high-flown philosophical considerations.

Whatever his reasons, it cannot be denied that his willingness to stand up to Governor William S. Cosby and his subservient judges took singular courage. True, he had most of the population of New York on his side, but the Governor's power was not confined to the borders of his own province.

With a timely assist from London, he could, quite possibly, have engineered the lawyer's ruin. But, when the moment of decision came, Andrew Hamilton was not one to be found wanting.

Shortly after the transcript of the Zenger trial reached London, an exuberant Member of Parliament told one of Ben Franklin's correspondents that Hamilton's arguments in favor of his client's right to print the truth were irrefutable. "If it is not the law," he said, "it is better than law, it ought to be law and will always be law wherever justice prevails." But the fact remains that it was to be many years before newspapers on both sides of the Atlantic were freed from the threat of prosecution for criticizing those in authority.

The English common law was too well ingrained to be changed overnight by the decision of a colonial court. For generations, governments had been beyond the reach of public criticism. "To punish any dangerous or offensive writings," wrote Blackstone, "which, when published, shall on a fair and impartial trial be adjudged of a pernicious tendency, is necessary for the preservation of peace and good order, of government and religion, the only solid foundations of civil liberty." Sir William was not overly concerned with the fact that judges and not juries were empowered to determine the "pernicious tendency" of a publication, and that the latter's truth or falsity had no bearing on their verdict.

Thirty years after Zenger's acquittal, England's John Wilkes, the editor of the antigovernment periodical, the *North Briton,* was expelled from the House of Commons and convicted of seditious libel for daring to suggest that George III had lied in a speech in Parliament. Six years later, Alexander McDougall, one of the founders of the Sons of Liberty in New York, was arrested for authoring two tracts which severely criticized the provincial assembly for its support of the Mutiny Act. McDougall, who was quickly hailed as "the Wilkes of America," was clapped into jail where he was destined to remain for three months until the fortuitous death of the principal witness for the prosecution forced the dismissal of the charges against him.

Although McDougall died four years before the adoption of the freedom of the press guarantee of the First Amendment to the Federal Constitution, Wilkes lived to see Hamilton's proposition that a judge could not convict a defendant solely on proof of publication become the law of England. In 1792, Parliament passed Charles James Fox's Libel Act, which gave the jury alone the power to pass on the libelous nature of an utterance. No longer could British judges, owing their allegiance to the Crown, sit in judgment on the written and spoken word.

The other half of Hamilton's thesis—that truth was a defense to a prosecution for criminal libel—did not become an accepted fact until the early nineteenth century. Although the Sedition Act of 1798 admitted the defense of truth in prosecutions brought under it, the arbitrary application of the law made it next to impossible for defendants to obtain acquittals on this ground. It was not until 1804 that Alexander Hamilton, in his defense of Harry Croswell, a Hudson Valley publisher who had been accused of libeling President Jefferson, succeeded in convincing the New York courts that his namesake's argument in the Zenger case should be the law of the state. "The liberty of the press," he urged, "is the right to publish with impunity, truth, with good motives, for justifiable ends, though reflecting on government, magistracy, or individuals."

In 1805, the New York legislature incorporated the rule of the Croswell case into a comprehensive libel statute, and, sixteen years later, it was elevated to the status of a constitutional safeguard. Other states were quick to follow New York's lead and, today, truth is a defense to libel prosecutions in most of the United States. In 1843, the British enacted legislation incorporating the American rule.

A little more than a hundred years after his death, Andrew Hamilton's interpretation of the law of criminal libel had been accepted by the English-speaking world. The arguments which he had advanced in New York's City Hall in the torrid summer of 1735 had finally become the law of both his native and his adopted countries. Newspapers were, at long last, free to print the truth, without fear that their publishers, editors or reporters would languish in jail. One man's courage and a century of reflection had created a free press.

*"It is the best cause; it is the cause of liberty!"*

## Andrew Hamilton and the trial of John Peter Zenger, August 4, 1735

IN LATE 1697, a twenty-one-year-old university graduate, who had been sympathetic to Sir George Blaylock's unsuccessful plot to assassinate William of Orange and restore the Stuarts to the British throne, sailed from Glasgow. Carried on the ship's log simply as passenger Trent, he was headed for what he later referred to as Virginia's "peaceful eastern shore." That same year, some six hundred miles to the east, a son was born to an impoverished Palatine family. Thirty-eight years later, the Scot and the German were to meet for the first time in a New York courtroom from which both were destined to march into immortality together.

New York, in the early eighteenth century, had a government modeled after the mother country and similar to those of most of the British colonies in America. The province's chief executive was a royal governor, with the legislative power vested in a council and general assembly. The former, which corresponded to the House of Lords, was composed of a dozen or so colonists, all of whom were appointed by London. The assembly, on the other hand, was an elective body whose members were chosen by the freeholders of the "several parishes or districts."

In the summer of 1731, after the death of Governor John Montgomerie, George II appointed one William S. Cosby, an Irish colonel who had just finished a rather stormy six years as the commander of the British garrison in Minorca, as his successor. Cosby, a greedy and impolitic highbinder who had brought even the peace-loving Minorcans to the brink of revolution during his tenure on the Mediterranean island, decided to take his time about reporting to his new post, and did not arrive in New York until August 1, 1732, almost thirteen months after his appointment.

In the interim, Rip Van Dam, a local merchant who was the president of the Council as well as its senior member, served as Acting Governor. A stolid Dutchman who had never mastered the English language, the seventy-year-old Van Dam proved to be a capable if unspectacular executive who managed to keep things going until Cosby ran through his Minorcan booty in England and took ship for New York. The new Governor had no sooner assumed his duties when he asked his predecessor to turn over half the salary he had received during his brief term of office. Van Dam, who was not a man to give up a pound sterling fairly earned without a fight, just as promptly refused.

The result was a lawsuit. Cosby was understandably reluctant to sue Van Dam before a provincial jury, and, by an ordinance dated December 4, 1732, took the unprecedented step of creating an equity or non-jury side of the Supreme Court of Judicature. When the case was called for trial before Chief Justice Lewis Morris and Justices Frederick Philipse and James De Lancey, Van Dam was represented by James

Alexander and William Smith, two New York barristers who could hardly be classed as fervent supporters of the Cosby administration. The two lawyers began their defense by asking the court to dismiss the suit on the grounds that the Governor had no power to give the Supreme Court equity jurisdiction but even if he did, an equity court could not entertain a simple dispute over money. This, they argued, could only be decided by a jury.

Although his colleagues, who were very much the Governor's men, saw no merit in the Smith-Alexander thesis, Morris agreed with the two attorneys and left the bench rather than decide against Van Dam. "As I take it," he declared, "the giving of a new jurisdiction in equity to an old court that never had such jurisdiction before, or erecting a new court of equity by ordinance of the Governor . . . are equally unlawful. Therefore by the Grace of God, I, as Chief Justice of this province, shall not pay any obedience to this." Cosby's suit had been effectively blocked.

In a towering rage, the Governor personally tore up the Chief Justice's commission and appointed the youthful De Lancey in his place. Van Dam had kept his money * but the province had lost its most independent and respected judge.

After several months of brooding at Morrisania, his baronial estate which spread over most of what is now New York's Bronx and Westchester counties, the fifty-seven-year-old Morris decided to return to the political wars, and announced his candidacy for the Assembly from the District of Eastchester. Despite the fact that Cosby put up his own man and tried to keep the time of the election a state secret, more than 350 of Morris' supporters showed up on the village green in front of St. Paul's Episcopal Church on October 29, 1733, to give the squire of Morrisania a resounding victory. Even the fact that

---

* Although he continued to harass Van Dam for the next two years, Cosby apparently never succeeded in extracting a shilling from his stubborn opponent.

some forty Quakers were unjustly disenfranchised for refusing to swear to their qualifications as voters, and a group of out-of-district hoodlums attempted to crash the polls, the ex-justice's margin was better than three to one.

An interested observer of the Eastchester election was a journeyman reporter for the conservative *Weekly Gazette,* New York's first and only newspaper, which had not disagreed publicly with Cosby since the Governor's arrival in the province. John Peter Zenger had been apprenticed to William Bradford, the Gazette's publisher and the province's official printer, shortly after his arrival from the German Palatine in 1710. In 1722, he had left New York for Chestertown, Maryland, returning two years later to become Bradford's partner. He had opened his own printing shop in 1726, but supplemented his meagre income by covering news stories for *The Gazette.* A fiery and courageous man, Zenger had frequently disagreed with Bradford's policy of eternal appeasement, but it was not until the publisher refused to let him print the full details of the Eastchester election that he gave his notice.

He wasn't to remain away from journalism very long. Morris, Alexander and Smith recognized a fire-eater when they saw one, and they promptly set Zenger up in business as the proprietor of a new paper, the *Weekly Journal,* whose first issue on November 5, 1733, contained a full report of the Eastchester hustings. This was only the beginning. Week after week, the *Journal* bristled with thinly veiled attacks on Cosby and most of his chief lieutenants. Zenger, with more than an occasional literary assist from his financial angels, criticized the Governor for everything from Morris' dismissal to a bold attempt to seize choice Mohawk Valley real estate for himself and his relatives.

By the fall of 1734, Cosby could stand it no longer. He ordered his new—and thoroughly compliant—Chief Justice to do everything in his power to see that the truculent editor was indicted for seditious libel. Obediently, De Lancey appeared before the Grand Jury on Tuesday morning, October 17, and exhorted its members to put Zenger behind bars where he could no longer print his scurrilous attacks on the government. "It is high time to put a stop to them," he argued, "for at the rate things are now carried on, when all order and government are endeavoured to be trampled on, and reflections are cast upon persons of all degrees, must not these things end in sedition, if not timely prevented?" He was evidently something less than persuasive because the jury, just before adjourning for lunch, refused to return a true bill.

Undaunted, Cosby turned at once to the Council and, that same afternoon, it sent a message to the Assembly which warned the lower house that Zenger was "tending to alienate the affections of the people of this province from his Majesty's Government, to raise seditions and tumults among the people of this province, and to fill their minds with a contempt of his Majesty's Government." The best way to put an end to this sort of nefarious business, the councilmen recommended, was for "the Gentlemen of this board . . . to join a committee of the House of Representatives in order to confer together, and to examine and enquire into the said papers."

The Assembly hurriedly appointed a committee which met that very evening with the gentlemen from the Council. After some preliminary discussion, the councilman "reduced to writing, what they requested of this House." Cosby's suggestion was as simple as it was dramatic. He wanted four issues of the *Journal* to "be burnt by the hands of the common hangman, as containing in them many things derogatory of the dignity of his Majesty's Government, reflecting upon the Legislature, upon the most considerable persons in the most distinguished stations in the province, and tending to raise seditions and tumults among the people thereof." Putting the torch to heretical writings had, by English custom, replaced the similar disposal of their authors.

It wasn't until October 22 that the Assembly got around

to considering the Council's request. After some debate, its members came to the conclusion "that the said papers and request lie upon the table." Eleven days later, the Council, in a curt note, asked the lower house to "return . . . the several seditious *Journals* of Zenger, No. 7, 47, 48, 49, which were delivered by a committee of that board to a committee of this house." The Assembly was only too happy to comply and the documents were delivered to Fort George by Robert Livingstone.

The Council then took matters into its own hands and ordered Zenger's four issues "to be burnt by the hands of the common hangman, or whipper, near the pillory in this city" on Wednesday, November 6. The day before the scheduled burning, the sheriff appeared before the Court of Quarter Sessions in City Hall and read a directive of the Council ordering "the Mayor and Magistrates of this city, to attend the burning of the several papers or journals." The aldermen not only refused to file the order, but many of them stated that, "if it should be entered, they would have their protest entered against it."

The sheriff was back the next morning with a demand that the Council's order be complied with. But the court was ready for him. Its clerk stood and read the unanimous opinion of its members that "this court conceives this order to be no mandatory writ warranted by law, nor knows of any law that authorizes the making of the order aforesaid; so they think themselves under no obligation to obey it; which obedience, they think, would be in them, the opening of a door for arbitrary commands, which, once opened, they know not what dangerous consequences may attend it. Wherefore, this court conceives itself bound in duty, for the preservation of the rights of this corporation, and, as much as they can, of the liberty of the press, and the people of the province, since an Assembly of the province, and several Grand Juries, have refused to meddle with the papers, when applied to by the

Council, to protest against the order aforesaid, and to forbid all the members of this corporation to pay any obedience to it, until it be shown to this court, that the same is authorized by some known law, which they neither know nor believe that it is."

As the clerk finished his reading, Francis Harrison, the city's recorder and an avowed Cosbyite, asked the court's permission to say a few words in support of the Council's order. It was no different, he insisted, from a similar one issued by the House of Lords in 1710 in which that august body had directed the Mayor and Alderman of London to attend the burning of Dr. Henry Sacheverell's sermon attacking the Whig government for its tolerant attitude toward religious dissenters. Harrison was immediately answered by one of the aldermen who observed that there was considerable difference between the House of Lords, which was "the greatest court of justice in Britain," and the provincial Council. Furthermore, as he remembered Sacheverell's case, the defendant had "had a fair hearing in defense of himself and his sermon; and after that fair hearing, he and his sermon were fairly and legally condemned."

If Mr. Recorder could produce the law books that sustained his position, the aldermen would be happy to look through them to see whether he were right. If there were sufficient precedents to justify the Council's order, "they would readily obey it, but otherwise not." Harrison looked apoplectic. He wasn't in the habit of carrying his books around with him, he snapped. In that event, the court was willing to give him time to send for them and even volunteered the services of a constable for that purpose. But the recorder had had enough. After reminding the aldermen that an anti-Catholic pastoral letter of Bishop Gilbert Burnet * had once been ordered burnt by the High Bailiff of Westminster, he stormed out of the courtroom.

* His son, William, had been Governor of New York from 1720 to 1727.

As soon as the door had closed behind him, the court decided that, since the Council's order was illegal, neither it nor the aldermen's protest should be entered in the minute book. The sheriff, a Cosby appointee, made one more attempt to do the Governor's bidding and asked the court "to direct their whipper to perform the said order." The answer was a flat no and court adjourned for the day. That afternoon, with Harrison, several officers of the garrison and a handful of curious townspeople looking on, the sheriff's Negro slave tossed Zenger's four issues into a street bonfire.

Cosby was furious at the fact that the burning had attracted no crowds, and ordered Zenger's arrest, in anticipation of which he had obtained a warrant from the Council four days earlier. According to its terms, the sheriff was directed to "forthwith take and apprehend John Peter Zenger, for printing and publishing several seditious libels . . . and, upon his taking the said John Peter Zenger, to commit him to the prison or common jail of the said city and county." On November 17, the printer was seized and thrown in the City Hall's basement dungeon where he was held incommunicado for three days.

But the prisoner was not without powerful friends. Three days after his arrest, Smith and Alexander procured a writ of habeas corpus to force Chief Justice De Lancey to set bail or release him. At a public hearing on the writ, the two attorneys argued that, pursuant to Magna Carta, the Petition of Right and the Habeas Corpus Act, Zenger was entitled to bail "according to the quality of the prisoner, and nature of the offence." To support his contention that the poor state of his finances justified a low bail, Zenger submitted an affidavit in which he swore "that he was not worth forty pounds, the tools of his trade and wearing apparel excepted." But De Lancey, more than a little aware of the Governor's interest in keeping the printer away from his obstreperous press, ordered "that he be admitted to bail, himself in 400 pounds with two sureties each in 200 pounds."

Since this was ten times more than Zenger could raise, he was remanded to prison. But the Chief Justice, with a fine sense of public relations, decided to make things a little more tolerable for his captive and, as Zenger described it in his issue of November 25, gave him pen, ink and paper as well as "the liberty of speaking through the hole of the door of the prison to my wife and servants," by virtue of which he hoped to "entertain" his subscribers "with my *Journal* as formerly." With his wife's help, he managed to publish his newspaper regularly during the ten months he was fated to remain in the city keep.

Despite monumental efforts, Attorney General Richard Bradley was unable to cajole the Grand Jury into returning an indictment against Zenger before its term expired on January 28, 1735. With Cosby breathing down his neck, he resorted to a less popular but equally effective method of making certain that Zenger would be brought to trial. On the last day of the Grand Jury's term, the Attorney General filed an information with the Supreme Court in which he accused the printer of publishing two editions of his *Journal*, specifically Numbers 13 and 23, which were "false, scandalous, malicious, and seditious." Zenger, who had begun to hope that Bradley's failure to obtain an indictment might result in his release, settled down to a prolonged stay in his tiny cell.

The following April, Smith and Alexander tried a novel tack. On Tuesday, the fifteenth, they appeared before De Lancey and Associate Justice Philipse, and moved to disqualify both judges on the ground that their commissions from Cosby were granted "during pleasure" rather than "during good behavior" as was the custom in England. "The form of the said commission," the lawyers argued, "is not founded on or warranted by the common law, or any statute of England, or of Great Britain, or any act of Assembly in this colony." De Lancey turned purple at the suggestion that his appointment as Chief Justice was illegal. "You ought well to consider the consequences of what you have offered!" he thundered at both men. When they informed him that they had, he set their motion down for argument the following morning.

As soon as court opened the next day, Smith stood up and began to elaborate on his opinion that both De Lancey and Philipse did not have the right to try Zenger. The Chief Justice interrupted him at once. As far as he was concerned, he wasn't going to permit any lawyer to challenge his commission. "You thought to have gained a great deal of applause and popularity by opposing this court," he roared, "but you have brought it to that point, that either, we must go from the Bench, or you from the Bar!" He paused a moment to let his observation sink in. "Therefore," he continued, "we exclude you and Mr. Alexander from the Bar!"

De Lancey then directed James Lyne, the court clerk, to enter an order to that effect at once. After ten minutes of feverish scribbling, Lyne handed a sheet of foolscap to the still fuming Chief Justice. De Lancey scanned it hurriedly and then asked the clerk to read it aloud. "James Alexander and William Smith," Lyne intoned in his sonorous voice, "having presumed, notwithstanding they were forewarned by the court of their displeasure if they should do it, to sign . . . and put into court, exceptions, in the name of John Peter Zenger; thereby denying the legality of the judges, their commissions, though in the usual form, and the being of this Supreme Court. It is therefore ordered, that, for the said contempt, the said James Alexander and William Smith, be excluded from any farther practice in this Court; and that their names be struck out of the Roll of Attornies of this Court." Cosby, it seems, had not forgotten the Van Dam case.

Alexander leaped to his feet. Was this also Mr. Justice

Philipse's decision? It appeared that it was. The lawyer pointed out that neither he nor his colleague had attempted to question the court itself. Our exceptions, he explained, were only addressed "to your commissions and not to the being of the Court." But De Lancey was adamant. "We conceive the exceptions were against the being of the Court," he said. Show us, the disbarred men urged, where in our motion we ever made such an assertion.

De Lancey didn't bother to answer the question. "Be gone from this Court," he growled. Alexander made no move to leave. Ever the lawyer, he wanted to know whether the court had overruled or rejected his client's objection. Sensing a semantic trap, De Lancey remarked that it didn't make much difference to him what Alexander called it. The lawyer didn't agree. "If you have rejected the exceptions," he said, "they could not appear upon the proceedings; but if you overruled them, [they] would remain as records of the Court, and ought to be entered on the record of the cause as part of the proceedings." The papers must be filed, the Chief Justice admitted, to justify what the court had done. As far as their being part of the record of this case, "you may speak to that point tomorrow."

However, it was not until two days later that De Lancey was ready to discuss the matter further. But he would not permit either Smith or Alexander to appear for Zenger. When the two lawyers protested that he had expressly authorized them to argue this point before him, the Chief Justice shook his head. What he had told them, he insisted, was that "you may get some person to speak on that point on the morrow." As far as he was concerned, both men had been disbarred and could not take part in any court proceedings in the province.

While Alexander and Smith rushed back to their offices to prepare a petition to the Assembly for reinstatement,* the

* They were both reinstated in 1737 by Cosby's successor, Governor George Clarke.

now lawyerless prisoner asked the court to order some member of the local bar to defend him. De Lancey promptly appointed the youthful John Chambers, a conservative and inexperienced attorney, whose first step was to drop his predecessors' attack on the justices' commissions because he said that it was "not proper to speak to it." After pleading his new client not guilty, he asked for a trial date and a struck jury—a special panel selected from forty-eight veniremen drawn by the clerk from the Freeholders' Book. The Chief Justice scheduled the trial for Monday, August 4, but reserved decision on the motion for a struck jury.

On July 29, Clerk Lyne entered an order stating that "Zenger was entitled to have a struck jury." At five that evening, some of the printer's friends visited Lyne's office in order to watch while he picked the forty-eight prospective jurors. However, instead of selecting them at random from the Freeholder's Book, that worthy exhibited a list he said he had prepared from it. Zenger's friends were horrified to see that many persons on the list were the Governor's supporters, employees, tradesmen or servants. To make matters even worse, some of the clerk's selections were ex-magistrates who had been driven out of office because of the *Journal's* exposure of their incompetence or corruption.

Chambers was back in court the next morning. He asked De Lancey and Philipse to order Lyne to pick his jurors in the usual manner—out of the Freeholders' Book. After some heated words, the justices directed the clerk to strike the forty-eight names "out of the Freeholders' Book as usual in the presence of the parties." With the record set straight, Zenger's friends accompanied Lyne back to his first floor cubicle where they succeeded in striking a panel by nightfall.

The trial began on Monday morning, August 4, on the dot of nine, in the tiny courtroom on the first floor of City Hall. After some haggling between Chambers and Bradley over the order in which the jurors were named, Foreman Thomas Hunt led his eleven colleagues into the box. The Attorney

General's opening statement was quiet and surprisingly re-strained. With a warning to the jurors that a libel "tends to create differences among men, ill blood among the people, and oftentimes great bloodshed between the party libelling and the party libelled," he proceeded to read the information aloud. Among other things, Zenger was accused of writing that Cosby's conduct had enslaved the citizens of the province. For example, in his issue of April 8, 1734, he had printed in large type: "WE SEE MEN'S DEEDS DESTROYED, JUDGES ARBITRAR-ILY DISPLACED, NEW COURTS ERECTED WITHOUT CONSENT OF THE LEGISLATURE BY WHICH, IT SEEMS TO ME, TRIALS BY JURIES ARE TAKEN AWAY WHEN A GOVERNOR PLEASES, MEN OF KNOWN ES-TATES DENIED THEIR VOTES, CONTRARY TO THE RECEIVED PRAC-TICE." Morris and Van Dam, who attended the trial, must have smiled at that.

After Chambers had delivered himself of a learned, but hardly inspired, exposition of the law of libel, De Lancey ordered Bradley to put his witnesses on the stand. But before the Attorney General could call his first one, a man who had been sitting in the audience rose and asked permission to ad-dress the bench. Several weeks earlier, Alexander and Smith, who had serious doubts as to both Chambers' sympathies and abilities, had made the long trip to Philadelphia where they urged Andrew Hamilton, one of the best known lawyers in the colonies, to come to New York and represent the printer.* That they had been successful was evident when the stranger, after donning his barrister's wig, walked to the front of the courtroom, announced that his name was Andrew Hamilton and that he was "concerned in this cause on the part of Mr. Zenger, the defendant."

Bradley looked dumbfounded. Like everyone else in the courtroom, he was at a loss to understand why William Penn's lawyer would make the arduous trip north to throw himself

---

* John Kinsey, their first choice, had declined, claiming that he was "cir-cumstanced at present and in the case you mention I think I cannot do it."

into the dangerous fight to keep a penniless newspaperman out of the common jail. But Hamilton, despite his burgeoning practice and his membership in the legislatures of both Delaware and Pennsylvania, was still the same man who had left Scotland some forty years earlier rather than stomach William and Mary on the British throne.

Prosperity had not denatured the spirit of the slightly pudgy lawyer whose sensitive face with its full lips and acquiline nose belied his stormy temperament. He had come a long way since 1697 when he had boarded with Reverend Francis Machemie in Accomac, Virginia. After his admission to the bar in 1705, his practice had grown so rapidly that he soon outgrew Accomac and moved to Chestertown, Pennsylvania, where the lush legal pastures of Virginia, Delaware and Pennsylvania were all within easy striking distance. In 1712, James Logan, the manager of William Penn's estates, had recommended him to Hannah Penn as "an ingenious man, and, for a lawyer, I believe, a very honest one, and of very considerable practice in these parts."

He immediately justified Logan's faith in him by outfoxing one Berkeley Codd who had tried to get out of paying his rent to the Penns by challenging the validity of their Delaware titles. As Logan exuberantly wrote to Mrs. Penn, "Codd was baffled at ye court by the dexterity of our lawyer's management, without bringing the matter to trial." His reward was a trip to London where, in addition to attempting to clear Penn's claims to Delaware's Sussex and Kent Counties, he was admitted to Gray's Inn of Court, a singular honor for a colonial barrister.

But the old fires were still burning. On October 10, 1717, he was indicted for threatening to shoot Charles Gookin, the Lieutenant Governor of Pennsylvania. "If I ever met the damn dog Gookin out of the province," he had thundered, "by the eternal God, I would pistol him; he deserves to be shot or ripped open for what he has done already." The case was dropped when, five days after the grand jury's action, Gookin suddenly took a year's leave of absence. His successor promptly named Hamilton as his Attorney General.

In 1724, the grateful Penns gave him 153 acres between Twelfth and Nineteenth Streets in Philadelphia, where he built Bush Hill, a three-story Georgian mansion. The honors came swiftly. In 1727, he became Recorder of Philadelphia, Prothonotary of the Supreme Court, Master of the Rolls, and a member of the Pennsylvania Assembly. The following year, Delaware's Kent County sent him to that province's lower house. By 1729, he had been elected speaker of both legislatures. During the more boring debates, he amused himself by drawing the plans for Philadelphia's Province House, which, some fifty years later, was to be renamed Independence Hall.

Eleven years before Zenger's trial, Logan had written to a friend that Hamilton "is a very able lawyer, very faithful to his client, and has generally refused to be concerned for any plaintiff who appeared not to have justice on his side." If the printer had ever seen this letter, his new lawyer's first move undoubtedly would have shaken his faith in Logan's flattering appraisal. As soon as De Lancey had recognized him, Hamilton proceeded to save Bradley the trouble of proving his case by conceding that his client "both printed and published the two newspapers set forth in the information." The Attorney General immediately excused Zenger's journeyman printer and his two sons, who had been called as witnesses against him.

Their exit was followed by an embarrassing silence in the packed courtroom. Finally, De Lancey jumped into the breach and asked Bradley to get on with it. "Sir," the Attorney General replied, "as Mr. Hamilton has confessed the printing and publishing these libels, I think the Jury must find a verdict for the King." Even admitting, for the sake of argument, that what Zenger printed was true, he explained, "The law says that they are not the less libellous for that; nay indeed the law says, their being true is an aggravation of the crime."

The color returned to Zenger's cheeks when Hamilton interrupted his sublimely confident adversary to remind him that "there are two words to that bargain. I hope it is not our bare printing and publishing a paper, that will make it a libel: you will have something more to do, before you make my client a libeller; for the words themselves must be libellous, that is false, scandalous, and seditious, or else we are not guilty."

If Mr. Hamilton insisted, Bradley murmured, he would show their Honors that it was quite clear that it was illegal to attack the Governor or any of his appointees in print. As far as the law was concerned, it didn't matter one whit whether what Zenger had published was true or not. If what the defendant had written was not libelous, he didn't know what was. The Governor had been most lenient in permitting the defendant to publish his newspaper for many months without prosecuting him. It was only when Zenger had transcended all bounds of decency that the administration "had directed this prosecution, to put a stop to this scandalous and wicked practice of libelling and defaming his Majesty's Government and disturbing his Majesty's peace."

After Chambers had told the jury that Bradley had failed to introduce any evidence that the two issues of the *Weekly Journal* mentioned in the information were "false, malicious or seditious," Hamilton slowly rose to his feet. First, he disposed of the cases which Bradley had used to buttress his argument that any criticism of public officials, whether justified or not, was libelous. Those decisions, he urged, were all rendered by the Star Chamber, "the most dangerous court to the liberties of the people of England that was ever known in that kingdom." * Since they had been repudiated in Great Britain, he had supposed that they no longer had any validity in the colonies.

Furthermore, most of the prosecutor's examples involved the power and prestige of the King and his judges. As far as he was concerned, there was a world of difference between George II and William S. Cosby. "I hope," he said, "that Mr. Attorney will not think it proper to apply his law cases to support the cause of his Governor which have only been judged where the King's safety or honor was concerned." What might be good law "at one time and in one place, is not so at another time and in another place." Besides, we have learned in the colonies to protect our property by fences. As he saw it, "There may be as good reason why men should take the same care to make an honest and upright conduct a fence and security against the injury of unruly tongues."

Bradley didn't like Hamilton's drift. He interrupted to remind the court that this trial had nothing whatever to do with fences. "The case before the court," he pointed out, "is whether Mr. Zenger is guilty of libelling his Excellency, the Governor of New York, and indeed the whole administration of the Government." Since Mr. Hamilton had conceded that his client had printed and published the newspapers mentioned in the information, he couldn't see why it was necessary to waste time in homey polemics. "If such papers are not libels," he repeated, "I think it may be said there can be no such thing as a libel."

In reply, Hamilton was prepared to make another concession. Since the information accused Zenger of publishing "a certain false, malicious, seditious and scandalous libel," he

* The Court of The Star Chamber, named for the gilt stars on the ceiling of the room in which it sat, was established by Henry VII in order to control powerful nobles and landowners. By the reigns of James I and Charles I, it had become an arbitrary tribunal which sat without a jury, employed torture to compel testimony, and often mutilated those whom it found guilty. It was abolished by the Long Parliament in 1641.

was willing, in order to save time for everyone concerned, to admit that the printer was guilty if Bradley proved that what he had written was untrue. The Attorney General shook his head vigorously. First of all, he didn't see how he could "prove a negative." Secondly, there was nothing in the law that said that a libel was any less a crime because it happened to be true. "Supposing all the words to be true," he argued, "yet that will not help them."

Very well, Hamilton said. If the prosecution didn't want to go to the trouble of proving a negative, the defense would assume the responsibility of showing that every word of what Zenger had written was true. When Bradley seemed at a loss for words, De Lancey came to his rescue. "You cannot be admitted, Mr. Hamilton," he stated, "to give the truth of a libel in evidence. A libel is not to be justified, for it is nevertheless a libel that is true." Despite Hamilton's protestations that the law books sustained his position, the Chief Justice was adamant. "The Court have delivered their opinion," he reminded the angry lawyer, "and we expect you will use us with good manners; you are not permitted to argue against the opinion of the Court."

MR. HAMILTON: With submission, I have seen the practice in very great courts, and never heard it unmannerly to—

MR. CHIEF JUSTICE: After the court have declared their opinion, it is not good manners to insist upon a point, in which you are overruled.

MR. HAMILTON: I will say no more at this time; the Court I see is against us in this point and that I hope I may be allowed to say.

MR. CHIEF JUSTICE: Use the court with good manners, and you shall be allowed all the liberty you can reasonably desire.

With a perfunctory "I thank your Honor," Hamilton strolled over to the jury box. Since De Lancey's decision prevented him from proving that Zenger's accusations were truthful, he had to rely on its twelve occupants as "honest and lawful men" to acquit the printer. But he hoped that, during their deliberations at the end of the case, they would remember that "the supressing of evidence ought always to be taken for the strongest evidence." Foreman Hunt smiled knowingly.

Before continuing with his argument, Hamilton wondered whether Bradley would be kind enough to let him know "what certain rule have the books laid down by which we can certainly know whether the words are malicious." The Attorney General shrugged his shoulders. As far as he was concerned, the words in Zenger's papers were capable of no misunderstanding. It was always his understanding, replied the defense attorney, that, to be libelous, the words had to be "well understood to mean only to upbraid the parties with the want of those qualities as if they had directly and expressly done so. The words are scandalous, scoffing and ironical only as they are understood."

De Lancey joined the fray. "Mr. Hamilton," he asked, "do you think it so hard to know when words are ironical or spoke in a scoffing manner?"

> MR. HAMILTON: I own it may be known; but I insist the only rule to go by is, as I do or can understand them. I have no other rule to go by, but as I understand them.
> MR. CHIEF JUSTICE: That is certain. All words are libellous or not as they are understood. Those who are to judge the words must judge for themselves whether they are scandalous or ironical, tend to breach of the peace or are seditious. There can be no doubt of it.

Hamilton saw his opening. "I thank your Honor," he said. "I am glad to find the Court of this opinion. Then it follows that these twelve men must understand the words in the information to be scandalous, that is to say false . . . and when they understand the words to be so, they will say we are guilty of publishing a false libel, and not otherwise."

The trap was sprung. De Lancey, his neck reddening, struggled to escape Hamilton's inexorable logic. "No, Mr. Hamilton," he stammered, "the jury may find that Zenger printed and published those papers and leave it to the Court to judge whether they are libellous." The Philadelphia lawyer was content to leave it at that. "I know, may it please your Honor, the jury may do so; but I do likewise know they may do otherwise."

He turned back to the amused jurors. There was no power on earth, he reminded them, that could "stop people's mouths when they feel themselves oppressed." There was another time, not so long ago, when the Court of Star Chamber punished men for speaking the truth. Yet, even in those perilous days, men dared to say that "the practice of informations for libel is a sword in the hands of a wicked king, and an arrant coward, to cut down and destroy the innocent; the one cannot, because of his high station, and the other dares not, because of his want of courage, revenge himself in another manner."

"Pray Mr. Hamilton," Bradley interrupted, "have a care what you say, do not go too far neither, I do not like those liberties." The defense attorney struggled to keep his voice calm. "All men agree," he said quietly, "that we are governed by the best of kings, and I cannot see the meaning of Mr. Attorney's caution. My well-known principles, and the sense I have of the blessings we enjoy under his present Majesty, makes it impossible for me to err, and I hope, even to be suspected, in that point of duty to my king." But, he continued, despite the respect which Mr. Attorney claims we all owe to public officials, he cannot deny that "they are not exempt from observing the rules of common justice, either in their private or public capacities."

With Bradley mollified, Hamilton plunged ahead with his plea to the jury to acquit Zenger. The nub of his argument was that public exposure was often the only way in which a misuse of official power could be corrected. "It is a right which all freemen claim, and are entitled to complain when they are hurt; they have a right publicly to remonstrate against the abuses of power in the strongest terms, to put their neighbors upon their guard against the craft or open violence of men in authority, and to assert with courage the sense they have of the blessings of liberty, the value they put upon it, and their resolution at all hazards to preserve it as one of the greatest blessings heaven can bestow."

Without mentioning Cosby by name, he observed that royal governors were not necessarily the wisest and most virtuous of men. "Power alone," he remarked wryly, "will not make a man beloved." In the last analysis, the people have to rely on the law to keep their masters in check. "For men who are not endowed with wisdom and virtue, can only be kept in bounds by the law; and by how much further they think themselves out of reach of the law, by so much the more wicked and cruel men are." As the attorney paused for breath, De Lancey ordered Lyne to stifle a smattering of applause that rippled across the crowded courtroom.

As the clerk hastened to comply, Hamilton noticed that Recorder Harrison was scowling. "I make no doubt," he reminded his listeners, "that there are those here, who are zealously concerned with the success of this prosecution." While he hoped that their number was small, he realized that men who depended on a governor for their daily bread would be very much inclined to support his policies. "I know men's interests are very near to them, and they will do much rather than forego the favor of a governor, and a livelihood at the same time; but I can with good grounds hope, even from these men, whom I will suppose to be men of honor and conscience, too, that when they see the liberty of their country in danger, either by their concurrence, or even by their silence, they will, like Englishmen, and like themselves, freely make a sacrifice of any preference or favor rather than be accessory to destroying the liberties of their country, and entailing slavery upon their posterity." Harrison's frown deepened.

If he had understood Mr. Attorney correctly, Hamilton went on, it was his position that any written criticism constituted criminal libel. Under that definition, even portions of the Bible, with a little help from the power of innuendo, would be libelous. In Isaiah, for example, the prophet had said, "The leaders of the people cause them to err, and they that are led by them are destroyed." What was to prevent Bradley from assuming that this was an indirect attack upon the Governor and punish every person who quoted the passage in public? When those in power are willing to bypass the grand jury and use the more arbitrary method of informations, there is no telling where they will stop in the pursuit of their hardiest critics.

The Philadelphian peered intently into the jury box. "The power is in your hands, gentlemen, to safeguard our liberties. If you should be of the opinion that there is no falsehood in Mr. Zenger's papers, you will, nay, you ought to say so; because you do not know whether others—I mean the Court—may be of that opinion. It is your right to do so, and there is much depending upon your resolution, as well as upon your integrity." Like Lucius Junius Brutus, who had condemned his own sons for their part in the plot to restore Tarquin to the Roman throne, you must do your utmost "to support liberty, the only bulwark against lawless power which in all ages has sacrificed to its wild lust and boundless ambition the blood of the best men that ever lived."

Hamilton had been talking for more than two hours. His voice, which had begun to quaver with fatigue, was barely audible beyond the first three rows of the spectators' benches. "You see," he explained to the jurors, "I labor under the weight of many years, and am borne down with great infirmities of body." He paused for a moment to sip from a glass of water which Zenger handed to him. "Yet old and weak as I am, I should think it my duty, if required, to go to the utmost part of the land, where my service could be of any use in assisting to quench the flame of prosecutions upon informations, set on foot by the government, to deprive a people of the right of remonstrating, and complaining of the arbitrary attempts of men in power."

"Amen," whispered a first-bench spectator.

The lawyer was almost through. "The question before the Court and you, gentlemen of the jury, is not of small or private concern; it is not the cause of a poor printer, nor of New York alone, which you are now trying. No! It may, in its consequence, affect every freeman that lives under a British government on the main of America. It is the best cause; it is the cause of liberty! And I make no doubt but your upright conduct this day will not only entitle you to the love and esteem of your fellow citizens, but every man who prefers freedom to a life of slavery will bless and honor you as men who have baffled the attempt of tyranny, and who, by an impartial and uncorrupt verdict, have laid a noble foundation for securing to ourselves, our posterity, and our neighbors, that, to which nature and the laws of our country have given us a right—the liberty—both of exposing arbitrary power, in these parts of the world at least, by speaking and writing truth."

The long oration was over, and Hamilton sank exhausted into his chair at the defense table. Whether his effort was, as William Smith later characterized it in his *History of New York,* a blatant piece of demagoguery, or, in Gouverneur Morris' words, "the morning star of the American Revolution," there was little doubt that he had stirred his listeners to their depths. It took five minutes of gavel-pounding by De Lancey before the courtroom was quiet enough for Bradley to begin his summation. The best the Attorney General could do was to remind the jury that Hamilton had skillfully avoided discussing the only issue in the case—whether the defendant had printed and published the two newspapers mentioned in the information.

Before he submitted the case to Foreman Hunt and his eleven apostles, De Lancey had a few words to say to them. Despite Mr. Hamilton's recommendation that "you should take very little notice of what I may say upon this occasion," he reminded the jurors that, as a matter of law, Zenger's words were libelous. "You are to consider," he instructed them, "whether these words I have read to you do not beget an ill opinion of the Administration of the Government." If you find that they do, he urged, you must bring in a verdict of guilty.

As the jury filed out, Hamilton decided that a little fence-mending on his part might be in order. He hoped that the Chief Justice didn't think that he had told the panel to disregard his Honor's charge. "I am very much apprehended," he said, "if you suppose what I said was so designed. You know I made an apology for the freedom I found myself under a necessity of using upon this occasion. I said there was nothing personal designed; it arose from the nature of our defense." De Lancey didn't deign to answer him.

Zenger, who had been prepared to deliver a little speech of his own if things looked black, was now so confident of victory that he decided to keep his words to himself. Minutes after it had retired, the jury returned to the courtroom. Clerk Lyne asked Hunt whether he and his fellows "were agreed . . . whether John Peter Zenger was guilty of printing and publishing the libels in the information mentioned." The foreman, with a broad grin on his face, replied that the jury's verdict was "Not Guilty." As Zenger remembered it, Hunt's pronouncement was followed by "three huzzas in the hall, which was crowded with people." Ignoring De Lancey's threats to arrest everyone in the courtroom unless the noise subsided, the cheering spectators carried Hamilton out of the building on their shoulders.

However, it was not until the next day that the printer raised the money with which to pay his food tab at the city jail. Accordingly, he had to miss the victory party that his delirious friends threw for him that night at The Black Horse Tavern on Smith Street. But Andrew Hamilton, who was never one to pass up free food and drink, stood in for him. As the festivities drew to a close, the lawyer managed to make the last toast of the evening. With his glass held high, he shouted in his high-pitched voice: "To the law—may it always prevail!" "To the toast!" roared his delighted companions. The next morning, as he left town on the Philadelphia stage, he was, as Zenger reported it, "saluted with the great guns of several ships in the harbor as a public testimony of the glorious defense he made in the cause of liberty in this province."

On Tuesday, September 16, 1735, Mayor Paul Richard called a special meeting of the common council at City Hall. He proposed that Andrew Hamilton be presented "with the freedom of this corporation," and appointed a committee of three aldermen to prepare the citation. Two weeks later, the committee finished its work. Clerk William Sharpas read the Grant of Freedom aloud, to the members of the council.

> WHEREAS honor is the just reward of virtue, and public benefits demand a public acknowledgment, we therefore, under a grateful sense of the remarkable service done to the inhabitants of this city and colony by Andrew Hamilton, Esq., of Pennsylvania, barrister at law, by his learned and generous defense of the rights of mankind and the liberty of the press, in the case of John Peter Zenger, do by these presents bear to the said Andrew Hamilton, Esq., the public thanks of the freemen of this corporation for that signal service, which he cheerfully undertook under great indisposition of body, and generously performed, refusing any fee or reward.

Alderman Stephen Bayard also reported that he had received enough contributions from grateful New Yorkers to purchase a gold box "for enclosing the seal of the said Freedom, upon the lid of which we are of the opinion should be engraved the arms of the City of New York."

Unlike Smith and Alexander, Hamilton emerged from the Zenger case unscathed. He returned to a Philadelphia that, while more restrained in its enthusiasm than its less sophisticated neighbor to the north, clearly showed that even Quaker hearts responded to the good fight. Despite his rapidly failing health, he continued to practice law until his death on the sixth anniversary of his most famous case. At his funeral, Benjamin Franklin, who had once shared a cabin with him on one of his trips to England, observed that he was "long top of his profession here." Thirty-five years later, under the caption, "Departed saints of the law with whom I have been at the Bar," an anonymous Philadelphia barrister inscribed the names of a dozen or so lawyers on the continuance docket of the Court of Common Pleas. Hamilton's name led the list.

Cosby died on March 10, 1736, after a long illness, during most of which the province was governed from his bedroom. As for Zenger, his day in the sun was over. He had served his purpose and, with Cosby out of the way, Morris, Smith and Alexander no longer felt it necessary to support a militant antigovernment newspaper. He returned to his print shop, where he eked out a precarious living, publishing his now unsubsidized *Journal* and a potpourri of tracts and pamphlets, the most memorable of which was his own account of his trial. On Monday, July 28, 1746, a week before the eleventh anniversary of his acquittal, he died in his sleep, leaving behind six children and a small but significant niche in American history.

# John Adams

In a very real sense, John Adams had a more difficult row to hoe than Hamilton. Although the latter was antagonizing New York officialdom, he at least had the support of the man in the street. Adams, on the other hand, in agreeing to defend the British soldiers charged with instigating the "Boston Massacre," was regarded by his fellow Bostonians as nothing less than a traitor and a turncoat.

On the night of the "Massacre," Adams had been attending a meeting of one of his clubs at Henderson Inches' house in Boston's South End. "About nine o'clock We were allarmed with the ringing of Bells, and supposing it to be the signal of fire, We snatched our Hats and Cloaks, broke up the Clubb, and went out. In the Street We were informed that the British Soldiers had fired on the Inhabitants, killed some and wounded others near the Town House." After inspecting the scene of the shootings, the lawyer rushed home to assure his pregnant wife Abigail that the danger had passed.

Later that evening, in the quiet of his study, he gave considerable thought to the bloodshed that had occured in front of the customhouse. "These Reflections were to me, disquieting enough. Endeavours had been systematically pursued for many Months, by certain busy Characters, to excite Quarrels, Rencounters and Combats between the Inhabitants of the lower Class and the Soldiers, and at all risques to inkindle an immortal hatred between them. I suspected that this was the Explosion, which had been intentionally wrought up by designing Men, who knew what they were aiming at better than the Instrument employed." He came to the conclusion that, if any soldiers had fired in self-defense, they should be acquitted "if Truth was respected and the Law prevailed."

Accordingly, it was not surprising to find him defending the soldiers when they were tried for murder. In the super-charged atmosphere of Boston in 1770, he was immediately suspected of donning the King's coat for a monumental legal fee. "From the first to the last," he recalled some twenty years later, "I never said a word about fees . . and I should have said nothing about them here, if Calunmies and Insinu-ations had not been propagated that I was tempted by great fees and enormous sums of Money." His total recompense was nineteen guineas* "for hazarding a Popularity very gen-eral and very hardly earned: and for incurring a Clamour and popular suspicions and prejudices, which are not yet worn out."

Yet, no power on earth, or, one would suspect, originating from any other source, could have deterred him from defend-ing the soldiers. He was determined to expose the causes of the "Massacre," even at the risk of his own career. "I very deliberately, and indeed very solemnly determined, at all events to adhere to my Principles in favor of my native Coun-try. On the other hand I never would deceive the People, con-ceal from them any essential Truth, nor especially make myself subservient to any of their Crimes, Follies or Excen-tricities."

Five years earlier, in describing the effects of the Stamp Act, Adams had confided to his diary that he considered most of Boston's lawyers too timid to oppose the oppressive legisla-

---

* A guinea was a gold coin having a fixed value of twenty-one shillings, or a little more than one pound. In 1770, a common laborer could expect to re-ceive fifteen shillings for a day's work.

tion. "The Bar seems to me," he had written, "to behave like a Flock of shot Pidgeons. The Net seems to be thrown over them, and they have scarcely courage left to flounce and to flutter. It is my opinion that by this inactivity, we discover cowardice . . ."

The "Massacre" trials gave him the opportunity to test his own mettle. Convinced that the British soldiers had been provoked into firing on his fellow Bostonians, he was determined to prevent a legal lynching, both for the sake of his clients and the American colonies. "This would be as important a Cause as ever was tryed in any Court or Country in the World," he said, "and every Lawyer must hold himself responsible not only to his Country, but to the highest and most infallible of all Tribunals."

In 1768, Governor Francis Bernard had offered Adams the lucrative post of Advocate General in the Court of Admiralty. The rising young lawyer had refused on the ground that his political opinions would not permit him to accept any Crown office. This devotion to the colonies must have been very much in the mind of one of the commanders of the British garrison in Boston when he wrote, after learning that Adams and two other colonial attorneys had agreed to represent the soldiers, "The best lawyers to be obtained here are engaged . . . and I hope they will do their duty."

He need have had no fears. John Adams may have suffered from an almost pathological persecution complex and an acute hypochondria, but he was no man to shirk his professional responsibilities. His unwelcome clients could not have had a better champion.

*"I never would deceive the People, conceal from them any essential Truth, nor especially make myself subservient to any of their Crimes, Follies or Excentricities."*

# John Adams and the trial of the Boston Massacre soldiers, November 27 to December 8, 1770

ON SEPTEMBER 29, 1768, the British frigates *Senegal* and *Duke of Cumberland* arrived in Boston Harbor from Halifax. As soon as they had weighed anchor, their longboats, loaded to the gunwales with six hundred red-coated soldiers of his Majesty's 14th and 29th Regiments of Foot, headed for Long Wharf. After assembling on the dock, the troops marched smartly up King Street to the Common where the 29th pitched its tents for the night. A representative of Governor Francis Bernard ordered the commanding officer of the 14th to quarter his men in nearby Faneuil Hall.

The regulars had been sent to Boston to protect harassed British customs officials who were trying to enforce the unpopular Townshend import duties which had replaced the abortive Stamp Act as a means of raising Crown revenues. Shortly after their arrival, the two regiments moved into permanent billets in the center of the city. The 14th was located near the Brattle Square Church, while the 29th set up housekeeping just south of King Street. The main guard was established in King Street, directly across the way from the Old State House, with a brace of cannon aimed at the front door of the building.

Although, as Sam Adams observed, his fellow Bostonians "preserved their peace and quiet," relations between the troops and the townspeople had, by the end of 1768, deteriorated rapidly. The daily parades through the city streets, the

49

shooting of deserters, the public floggings of delinquent soldiers on the Common, and the hordes of prostitutes who had
followed the regiments from Halifax were hardly calculated
to endear the lobsterbacks to an already hostile civilian population. Even the staid John Adams was moved to complain
that "My daily reflections . . . at the sight of these soldiers
before my door, were serious enough." With Hub tempers on
the rise, Sam Adams did what he could to keep the pot sim-
mering with a series of inflammatory letters in the pages of the
*Boston Gazette* reminding his fellow citizens that "the raising
and keeping of a standing army within the kingdom in the
time of peace . . . is against law."

Both John and Sam Adams, who were second cousins, had,
by this time, become firmly convinced that independence
was the only solution to the unhappy state of affairs that
existed between England and her American colonies. John,
who represented the moderate position, preferred a gradual
and peaceful separation from the mother country. On the
other hand, his fiery cousin was not adverse to a more precipi-
tous rupture. There was little doubt that the arrival of the
British troops had inclined most of Boston to the latter's
view. As one historian put it, Sam Adams "was distinctly a
man of the people, gifted with incomparable tact in banding
together the discontented, and endowed with consummate
ability in setting forth in written page the aspirations for
liberty that impelled the masses."

In May of 1769, Governor Bernard convened the General
Assembly which had been inactive for almost a year. Its first
order of business was to demand that the Governor send the
troops packing. Claiming that he lacked the power to do so,
Bernard, with a sublime disregard for the realities, escorted
the Assembly to Cambridge, where it could conduct its deliberations out of the presence of the offending soldiers. The
colonists responded by enacting a set of daring resolutions
which, in effect, declared that no British statute would have

any effect in the Commonwealth unless Massachusetts men sat in the Parliament which had enacted it.

While the legislature was in session, two additional regiments arrived in Boston. Both units were under orders to sail to Halifax, but the Governor, when he read the Assembly's resolutions in the *Gazette,* decided to hold one regiment in the city. The prospect of more soldiers was so distasteful to Sam Adams and his colleagues that they quickly capitulated by watering down their resolutions. Bernard, who was more surprised than anything else by his unexpected success, promptly released the regiment, which embarked that night for Canada.

The colonists' surrender was, in the main, a matter of pocketbook over pride. Just before the move to Cambridge, the Assembly had been asked by the Governor to vote the necessary funds to pay the salaries and keep of the British soldiers. Despite Sam Adams' brave words that "we shall never make provision for the purposes in your several messages," there was a very real fear that, under the Billeting Act, Governor Bernard had the power to make his request an order. And there was no gainsaying that two regiments were cheaper than three.

But Bernard's days in the colony were numbered. British merchants, who were beginning to feel the pinch of the non-importation agreements that their New England customers had signed shortly after the passage of the Townshend Acts, were pressing for his recall. In early spring, he was directed to return to England "for consultations" and, on July 31, with a baronetcy to ease his ouster,* he sailed out of Boston harbor to the jeers of a people he had never fully understood in the ten years he had lived among them. For a man who had bitterly opposed the Stamp Tax and given half of his library to

---

* Although he was never to return to Massachusetts, he remained the province's official governor until Major General Thomas Gage, the Commander-in-Chief of British Forces in America, succeeded him on May 13, 1774.

Harvard when the college's books were destroyed by fire in 1764, he deserved a better send-off. But Boston, in the hot, dry summer of 1769, was in no mood for the amenities, and the last sounds that assailed Bernard's ears before his ship reached open water were the catcalls that emanated from Dock Square and Pudding Street.

His place was taken temporarily by the Lieutenant Governor, Harvard-educated Thomas Hutchinson. A fifty-eight-year-old Puritan, who had held almost every significant political and judicial office in the colony, he was a literate and intelligent patrician who would have been as at home at a London levée as he was on King Street. With such a man in the Governor's mansion, English exporters were convinced that the colonists' boycott of their goods would soon be broken and, beginning in August, cargo ships bound for Boston set sail from Southhampton and Liverpool.

The Britishers' hopes were shortlived. The Boston merchants, for the most part, adhered to the nonimportation agreements, and incipient backsliders were terrorized by mobs who roamed the docks looking for any who picked up consignments of English merchandise. While the troops stood helplessly by, unclaimed shipments were impounded or destroyed, informers who had revealed to Lieutenant Governor Hutchinson that goods were being smuggled in from other colonies were tarred and feathered, and those hardy importers who dared to accept their orders were ostracized by Sam Adams' kangaroo courts.

The nonimportation agreements expired on January 1, 1770, and a handful of shopkeepers, including Hutchinson's two sons, began to sell tea again. An excited crowd immediately called on the Lieutenant Governor and asked him to prohibit any sales of Townshend Act products until all of the merchants could import enough merchandise to stand on an even footing with their better-stocked competitors. Although Hutchinson was tempted to call out the garrison—"this being as good a time as any," he later wrote—his good sense prevailed, and he reluctantly declared a moratorium on the sale of tea until every retailer had an ample supply.

But Sam Adams and his followers were determined to hew to the spirit of the nonimportation agreements until all import duties were repealed. Shortly after Hutchinson's concession, Boston went on a tea strike. Even the ladies joined in pledging themselves "to deny the drinking of foreign tea, in hope to frustrate a plan which tends to deprive a whole community of all that is valuable in life." Those importers who insisted on bringing in tea found that, in addition to losing most of their customers, they were constantly being badgered by unruly street gangs who followed them from the docks to their warehouses.

On February 22, 1770, a group of boys began tormenting a shopkeeper who had displayed a fresh shipment of tea in his window. When the boys started throwing rocks at the hapless merchant, one of his friends fired his musket at them. Eleven-year-old Christopher Snider had the dubious distinction of being the first Bostonian to give up his life to hold the tea line. At his funeral on the Common five days later, more than fifteen hundred sullen mourners stood bareheaded while young Snider was officially ushered into the next world.*

The boy's death ended the uneasy truce that had existed between the town and the troops since their arrival some seventeen months earlier. A week later, a fist fight broke out between some dock workers and a squad of the 29th Regiment near Gray's ropewalk. Before it was broken up by the local gendarmes, a half-dozen soldiers were nursing broken jaws, and several colonists were lying insensible on the blood-stained cobblestones.

Monday, March 5, was a cold, blustery day in Boston. A freezing rain had left an icy coating on the streets, and walk-

---

* On April 21, 1770, a customs employee named Ebenezer Richardson was convicted of the boy's murder. Richardson was later given a royal pardon.

ing was precarious. As the temperature dropped, the rain changed to snow and, by dusk, several inches covered the ground. The snow stopped shortly after eight P.M., and an ugly crowd quickly collected in the 14th Regiment sector. But before trouble could develop, the officer of the day ordered all soldiers off the streets. A sergeant-major, who had been struck in the eye by an ice ball, was the only casualty.

As a bright half-moon rose in the clearing sky, many of the people who had been baiting the 14th's troopers walked over to Dock Square where a tall bewigged man in a scarlet cloak was delivering an anti-British harangue. While they were listening to him, a church bell began to ring wildly, and the square quickly filled with excited townspeople who thought that a fire had broken out. Encouraged by his increased audience, the tall speaker warmed up to his task, and the crowd rewarded him with three cheers.

The 29th Regiment maintained a sentry box in front of the customhouse on King Street. Earlier that evening, the sentry on duty had boxed the ears of a barber's apprentice who had insulted one of the 14th's officers on his way back to his quarters. When the boy told his story to the overwrought crowd in Dock Square, it decided to teach the sentry a lesson. Its members marched up Royal Exchange Lane onto King Street, where the apprentice pointed out the soldier who had struck him.

The sentry took one look at clubs and stones in the hands of the excited people in front of him and, with a frantic cry for help, retreated up the steps of the locked customhouse. Seconds later, a squad of eight soldiers was dispatched by Captain Thomas Preston, the officer of the guard, from his station across the street. The troops lined up in front of the mob with their muskets at the ready. The redcoats stood their ground as the colonists pelted them with snowballs and tried to knock the guns out of their hands with their sticks.

Suddenly, a volley of shots rang out, and eleven of the attackers fell to the ground, five of them fatally wounded. As their blood began to stain the fresh snow, Preston ordered the regimental drummers to sound assembly. A few minutes later, the street was filled with soldiers who knelt facing the confused crowd, their rifles at their shoulders. Young boys scampered up into the belfries of adjacent churches, and soon the bells added their voices to the clamor that was sweeping through the town.

Merchant John Rowe, who was "much afraid for my life," left the smoke-filled street and returned to his home. There, he decided to record the events he had just witnessed in his diary. Under the heading of March fifth, he wrote: "This night the 29th Regiment on Duty. A quarrel between the soldiers and inhabitants. The bells rang—a great number assembled in King Street. A party of the 29th under the command of Captain Preston fired on the people—they killed five —wounded several others—the inhabitants are greatly enraged and not without reason."

Hutchinson, who had just finished his dinner at Province House, thought at first that the noise in the streets was the result of a fire alarm. He soon realized his error. Above the noise of the drums and the bells, he could hear strident cries of "To arms! To arms! Town-born, turn out!" From his window, he could see excited Bostonians running to King Street with rifles, swords and sticks in their hands. Throwing on his coat, he made his way to Dock Street as fast as his arthritic legs would carry him.

He could do little with the people who were milling around the square, and he decided to go to the customhouse. Because Royal Exchange Lane was blocked by an enormous throng, he ducked through a house and ran up a back alley which brought him to the beleaguered sentry box. There, he found Preston prepared to order the 29th to shoot if the menacing crowd which filled King Street attacked them again.

When he berated the captain for firing on the townspeople, Preston told him simply, "I was obliged to, to save the sentry."

There was no time to lose if a bloody battle was to be averted. Hutchinson turned on his heels and entered the Old State House. He raced up the stairs to the second floor, through the council room, and out onto the balcony that overlooked King Street. From this vantage point, he pleaded with the more than two thousand people below him to return to their homes at once. The soldiers who were responsible for the tragedy, he promised them, would be tried promptly by a civil court and, if found guilty, severely punished. He then ordered the troops to shoulder arms and return to their quarters.

After Preston and the eight soldiers who had been involved in the shooting had been arrested and confined in the Boston jail, the Lieutenant Governor remained in King Street until three A.M., interviewing eyewitnesses. The next morning, he received the town's selectmen who urged him to remove the troops if he wanted to avoid further bloodshed. Hutchinson informed his visitors that the two regiments were not under his jurisdiction and that any orders affecting them would have to come from General Gage in New York, a tack he had consistently taken since Bernard's departure.

The chagrined officials left his office and went to Faneuil Hall where Sam Adams had called an emergency meeting. After scheduling a regular town meeting for three o'clock that afternoon, Chairman Thomas Cushing appointed a committee of fifteen, which was instructed to return to the Lieutenant Governor with another request that he order the two regiments to leave Boston. When Hutchinson reiterated, for the second time in less than an hour, that he had no power to remove the troops, the disappointed committee left the State House and returned to Faneuil Hall where the town meeting was in the process of moving to the more commodious Old South Church.

However, the committee did have something new to report. Lieutenant Colonel Dalrymple, the commander of the 14th and the ranking British officer in Boston, had intimated, over Hutchinson's objections, that he might be persuaded to transfer the 29th to the harbor's Fort Castle William, in whose spacious barracks, Sam Adams had argued in the fall of 1768, all the troops should have been quartered. But even this tentative concession didn't sit well with the colonists who had wholeheartedly adopted Adams' slogan, "Both regiments or none!"

The Old South meeting didn't last long. In a little less than an hour, it adjourned, after dispatching a seven-man committee, headed by John Hancock, back to Hutchinson, who was still closeted with his council and Colonel Dalrymple on the second floor of the State House. Sam Adams, the delegation's self-appointed spokesman, was blunt and to the point. "If you or Colonel Dalrymple under you," he told the Lieutenant Governor, "have the power to remove one regiment, you have the power to remove both; and nothing short of their total removal will satisfy the people or preserve the peace of the province." At long last, Hutchinson yielded and recommended to Dalrymple that the troops be sent to Fort Castle William. The orders were issued that evening.

Earlier that day, a man named James Forrest, a prosperous merchant who was known around town as "the Irish Infant," entered John Adams' King Street law office. He had been sent, he said, by friends of Captain Preston, who wanted the pudgy attorney to defend the officer and his eight men at the trial that Hutchinson had promised the crowd in King Street after the shooting. When Forrest informed him that Josiah Quincy, Jr., a young Boston attorney, had already consented to assist him if he took the case, Adams gave in. "I had no hesitation in answering that Council ought to be the very last thing that an accused person should want in a free country."

It was a strange assignment for the thirty-four-year-old barrister who, in the two short years since he had moved to town from Braintree, had managed to build one of the best practices in the commonwealth. Not only had he played a leading role in the opposition to the Stamp Act, but he had bitterly attacked the Townshend Acts which succeeded it. As a result he had become the most popular lawyer in Massachusetts. "At this time" he wrote in 1802, "I had more Business at the Bar than any Man in the Province: My health was feeble: I was throwing away as bright prospects as any man ever had before him: and had devoted myself to endless labor and Anxiety, if not to infamy and death, and that for nothing, except, what indeed was and ought to be in all a sense of duty." *

But before he went to sleep that night, he had at least the satisfaction of knowing that he had the support of his wife Abigail, "That excellent Lady," he later recalled in his autobiography, "burst into a flood of tears." But, he added, "she was very sensible of all the Danger to her and to our Children as well as to me, but she thought I had done as I ought, she was very willing to share in all that was to come and place her trust in Providence."

During the week it took to move the 29th to the fort, Boston threw the biggest funeral in its history for four of the victims † of what Sam Adams had grandiloquently, if inaccurately, labeled "The Massacre." The hearses assembled in front of the customhouse on King Street. Then, followed by most of the town's eighteen thousand residents, they proceeded to the Granary Burying Ground where the dead men were interred in a common grave at the cemetery's northeast corner. Dr. Samuel Cooper of the Brattle Square Church,

* In 1816 Adams wrote to a friend that "A single guinea was put into my hand by the Irish Infant for a retaining fee, ten guineas were offered on the first trial and eight at the second . . . These nineteen guineas were all the fees I ever received for a whole year of distressing anxiety, and for thirteen or fourteen days of the hardest labor that I ever went through."

† The fifth, Patrick Carr, did not die until March 15th.

who conducted the graveside services, had great difficulty in making himself heard above the tolling of every steeple bell in Boston.

The Suffolk County Grand Jury met shortly after the mass funeral. It promptly indicted Thomas Preston, William Wemms, James Hartegan, William McCauley, Hugh White, Matthew Killroy, William Warren, John Carroll and Hugh Montgomery for the murders of Crispus Attucks, Samuel Gray, Samuel Maverick, James Caldwell and Patrick Carr. According to the grand jurors, the defendants were "moved and deduced by the instigation of the devil and their own wicked hearts." Warren, Hartegan, Killroy, Carroll and White were accused of firing the fatal shots and the other soldiers of "aiding, helping, abetting and assisting [them] to do and commit the felony and murder aforesaid."

In all, there were to be three trials. Captain Preston's was to be followed by that of the members of his squad. After the soldiers had been tried, four Tories, who were accused of firing into the crowd from the second story of the custom-house, were to replace them in the prisoners' dock. With all of Massachusetts reading a highly inflammatory "Short Narrative of the Horrid Massacre in Boston," which, together with ninety-four one-sided depositions, was being circulated throughout the province, John Adams and Josiah Quincy prevailed upon the more than willing Hutchinson to adjourn all the trials until the fall. Although Sam Adams tried to stampede the Superior Court judges into overriding the Lieu-tenant Governor's request, the three cases were deferred until the August term.

It was not until late in October, however, that *Rex versus Preston* appeared on the Superior Court docket. Adams, who regarded the soldiers' trial as the most important of the three, took a back seat at this one and was content to let young Quincy and Admiralty Judge Robert Auchmuty, his co-counsel, conduct most of the defense. With Attorney General

Jonathan Sewell out of town, the prosecution was handled by Solicitor General Robert Treat Paine and Josiah Quincy's older brother, Samuel. After a six-day trial, which, according to General Gage, proved "the people of Boston to be the most vile set of beings in the whole creation," Preston was acquitted and released from prison.*

The appearance of the Quincy brothers on opposite sides of the fence dramatically illustrated the division of families that had resulted from the deepening controversy between George III and his American colonies. John Adams estimated that one-third of his fellow citizens were violently opposed to British rule while an equal number remained loyal to London. The rest, who were more or less neutral, were, by 1770, beginning to drift into the former camp. Josiah, who had contributed a series of anonymous anti-British articles to the *Boston Gazette*, was one of the province's most outspoken separatists, while his brother was an equally ardent Loyalist.

The trial of the eight enlisted men, all of whom had pleaded not guilty, began on Saturday, November 27, 1770, in the Town House's first-floor courtroom, before Chief Justice Benjamin Lynde and three red-robed colleagues.† The legal line-ups were the same as in the earlier trial, except that Auchmuty had been replaced by twenty-two-year-old Sampson Salter Blowers. After it was agreed that the Quincy brothers would handle the questioning of all the witnesses for their respective sides, Lynde told the lawyers to get on with the business of picking a jury. This was no short order. Because the defense insisted on challenging every prospective juror who owned up to a Boston address, it took two tiring days to select a jury out of the more than fifty talesmen rounded up by the sheriff. Just before court adjourned on Monday after-

---

* Unfortunately, there is no verbatim record of the Preston trial. Stenographer John Hodgson's daily transcripts were immediately sent to England, where they unaccountably disappeared.

† Associate Justices John Cushing, Peter Oliver and Edmund Trowbridge.

noon, Joseph Mayo, of Roxbury, was named foreman of a panel which, that evening's *Gazette* bemoaned, did not contain a single Bostonian.

The Crown's case, which Samuel Quincy described as "grounded on the most melancholy event that has yet taken place on the continent of America," began in earnest on Tuesday morning and consisted of twenty-eight witnesses, most of whom had been in the vicinity of the customhouse on the night of March fifth. "In support of this accusation against the prisoners at the bar," Quincy told the jury, "it is incumbent on the Crown to ascertain the following things; viz. The identity of the persons charged; the fact of killing; and the circumstances attending and aggravating that fact." All that he asked of the jurors was that they would "examine into the evidence of fact without partiality or prejudice." A difficult order in Sam Adams' Boston, despite the fact that the town's cooler heads had done everything possible, including the supression of an official account of the shooting, to insure a fair trial.

The prosecution's first witness was Jonathan Austin, who had gone to King Street "on the evening of the 5th of March last [when] I heard the bells ring." He had seen "twenty or thirty men and boys" surrounding the sentry who was protecting himself by "swinging his gun and bayonet." After advising them to stop annoying the soldier, Austin had walked toward the main guard post. But he had returned to the sentry box when he noticed a noisy crowd coming up Royal Exchange Lane. By that time, Preston's squad had arrived at the customhouse. Austin had observed that McCauley, one of the troopers, "was then loading his piece."

Q. How near was you to McCauley at that time?
A. I was about four feet off. McCauley said, "Damn you, stand off!" and pushed his bayonet at me. I did so. Immediately, I heard the report of a gun.

Although he hadn't seen McCauley fire, he thought that he had noticed him reloading.

Ebenezer Bridgham had seen a "tall man" who he thought resembled William Warren "discharge his piece." But he couldn't be certain of his identification because "a few days after, I saw another man belonging to that same regiment so very like him that I doubt whether I am not mistaken with regard to him."

> Q. Was there anything thrown at the soldiers?
> A. Yes, there were many things thrown; what they were, I cannot say.

Just before the firing started, a dozen or so townspeople and sailors had "passed along the front of the soldiers, striking the soldiers' guns as they passed." He had seen rope worker Gray fall, but he was fairly certain that Warren had not shot him. "The gun that killed him," he speculated, "must have been nearer the center."

James Dodge, who had been standing near a barber shop, had heard the crowd daring the soldiers to shoot. "Several among the people said, 'Fire, damn you, fire!' but I think it was Captain Preston that gave the word to fire."

> Q. Did you see any ice or snowballs thrown at the soldiers?
> A. I saw several snowballs and pieces of ice thrown, and heard a rattling against the barrels of their guns. Whether it was sticks or what, I do not know.

No, he hadn't seen anyone throwing oyster shells.

Town watchman Edward G. Langford had another version of the incident. He had been standing next to Gray, one of the victims, when he heard someone ask, "Are you loaded? Are you all ready?" Then two guns had gone off. The witness had shouted to Killroy, "God damn you, do not fire!" but the soldier had pulled the trigger. The next thing he knew, Gray was dead at his feet.

Q. Have you any doubt in your mind that it was that gun of Killroy's that killed Gray?

A. No manner of doubt. It must have been it for there was no other gun discharged at that time.

Langford had run toward the watchhouse when Killroy "thrust his bayonet . . . through my coat and jacket." He had not seen anything thrown at the troops.

Francis Archibald was the last witness of the day. He had been in the crowd that had been involved in a fracas with the 14th Regiment some fifteen minutes before the shooting. "About ten minutes after nine," he testified, "I saw a soldier, and a mean looking fellow with him, with a cutlass in his hand. They came up to me. Somebody said, 'Put up your cutlass. It is not right to carry it at this time of night.' He said, 'Damn you, ye Yankee beggars, what's your business!' He came up to another that was with me and struck him. We beat him back, when seven or eight soldiers came out of the barracks with tongs and other weapons. One aimed a blow at a young fellow, John Hicks, who knocked the soldier down. As he attempted to rise, I struck him down again, and broke his wrist, as I heard afterwards. I went to King Street and when the guns were all fired, I saw several persons dead."

Q. Did you see any of them fire?

A. No, I was not there then.

Q. Did you see any snowballs or sticks thrown?

A. No.

It was five P.M. when Archibald stepped down and, after ordering the jury locked up for the night, Chief Justice Lynde adjourned for the day. On Wednesday morning, James Brewer was the Crown's first witness. He had seen "about twenty" teen-age boys badgering the sentry just before Preston and his squad arrived on the scene. He had told the captain, "Sir, I hope you are not going to fire, for everyone is going to their own homes." Preston had replied, "I hope they are." As the soldiers had formed into a half-circle around the sentry, Killroy "struck me with his bayonet." When the guns went off, he had seen two men fall to the ground—Christopher Monk and a "mulatto fellow." He was certain that no one had struck the soldiers or made any threatening speeches. "When I came to King Street," he declared solemnly, "it was as quiet as I ever saw it in my life."

James Bailey had joined White on the steps of the custom-house when the boys began throwing "pieces of ice big as one's fist" at the sentry. "After I first went up to him," he recalled, "they threw no more." When Preston's squad arrived, "Carroll came up to me and clapt his bayonet to my breast, and White said, 'Do not hurt him!' " Montgomery had been the first soldier to fire his musket, with Carroll right behind him.

Q. Did you see anything thrown before the firing?
A. Yes, Montgomery was knocked down with a stick, and his gun flew out of his hand, and when he recovered himself, he fired his gun.

He thought that Montgomery's shot had killed a mulatto who, armed with "a large cord-wood stick," had been leading a crowd which was running up Cornhill Street.

According to Richard Palmes, a man named Theodore Bliss had shouted to Preston, "Why do you not fire—God damn you, fire!" Palmes had stepped between the two men and pleaded with the officer not to fire on the crowd. Just as Preston assured him that he had no intention of doing so, a piece of ice struck Montgomery's rifle. "Whether it sallied him back, or he stepped one foot back, I do not know, but he recovered himself and fired immediately." As the rest of the soldiers began shooting, Montgomery "made a push at me with his bayonet. I had a stick in my hand, as I generally

walk with one. I struck him and hit his left arm, and knocked his gun down."

John Danbrooke had seen Montgomery fire two rounds into the crowd.

Q. Did you see any body fall upon his firing?
A. Yes, I saw two fall. One fell at my elbow, another about three feet from me. I did not hear the sound of another gun before they fell.

One of the fallen men had been a mulatto who, just before Montgomery had pulled the trigger, had been "leaning over a long stick he had, resting his breast upon it." The witness had been in Dock Square earlier, where he had seen a group of sailors armed with clubs heading for King Street.

When he had heard the church bells ringing at 9:15 that night, Thomas Wilkinson had left his house and gone to the main guard post. He had heard Preston cry, "Damn your bloods, turn out!" Seconds later, a squad of soldiers had emerged and followed the captain to the customhouse. When Wilkinson arrived at the customhouse, "I saw Captain Preston standing at the right of the circle. I stayed there about four minutes, when I heard the word given, 'Fire!' There was none fired then. Then I heard, 'Damn your bloods, fire!' Instantly, one gun went off; I saw the flash of every gun as they went off, one after another, like the clock striking." Nothing had been thrown at the soldiers while he was watching, and he couldn't recognize the man who had fired first.

It seemed as if every one in Boston had warned Preston to avoid bloodshed. After pleading with the captain to hold his fire, Josiah Simpson had crossed King Street on his way home. As he passed Vernon's barber shop, a voice had shouted, "Damn you, fire!" "It seemed to me," he said, "as if it came from the sentry box where I left the captain." Although he was successful in dissuading one man from hurling a club at

the troops, he saw "a white club thrown at some distance from me toward the soldiers."

Q. Did the club hit anybody?
A. I believe it hit one of the soldier's guns. I heard it strike.

After the guns went off, he had seen Attucks, Gray and Caldwell fall to the ground.

If Samuel Hemmingway was to be believed, Killroy had once told him that "he never would miss an opportunity, when he had one, to fire on the inhabitants, and that he had wanted to have an opportunity ever since he landed." When Hemmingway had cautioned the soldier about expressing such inflammatory sentiments, Killroy had replied, "I don't care." This conversation had taken place "a week or fortnight" before the King Street shooting and two other people —a housekeeper and a Negro boy—had been present.

Because he had been afraid of being insulted, Joseph Hiller had not yielded to an impulse to talk to the beleaguered sentry who, in his words, "had his gun waving as if it was to defend himself, or to exasperate people." He estimated that it was only some twenty seconds after the arrival of Preston's squad that the first shot had been fired. As he remembered it, "a little boy ran along and cried, 'Fire! Fire! Fire!' as people generally do when there is a fire. A soldier pointed his gun to him and fired, but did not hit him. He was the last but one on the left."

Q. Did you see any blows given or anything thrown?
A. No, and I was there the whole time.

Except for a cheer or two, King Street had been comparatively quiet before the shooting.

The preceding Friday, Nicholas Ferreter, a rope worker, had been coiling some cables for John Gray. One of his coworkers had asked a passing soldier if he wanted to make a few shillings. When the latter indicated that he did, he was

told to "Go clean my little house." The soldier became angry and struck Ferreter, who retaliated by punching him in the nose and relieving him of his cutlass. "He went away," Ferreter said, "and came back with a dozen soldiers with him." The rope workers drove them away with clubs but, before any further trouble could develop, Gray reported the incident to the captain of the guard, and the troops were confined to their barracks. Killroy had been one of the soldiers involved in the fracas.

When Benjamin Burdick had noticed Preston's semicircle in King Street, he had asked Private Montgomery if his gun was loaded. "Yes," was the answer. "I asked him if they were going to fire. He said, 'Yes, by the eternal God!' and pushed at me with his bayonet." Burdick, who had been carrying a Highland broad sword, managed to ward off Montgomery's gun. "If I had struck a little lower," he boasted, "I should have left a mark I could have sworn to." He had only seen one missile thrown at the soldiers, "a short stick . . . which seemed to go clear over all their heads."

Q. Did you see anybody strike the soldiers before you struck with the sword?
A. No, I had not time.

Robert Williams had been swept up by the crowd that had poured into King Street. He had just heard some one shout, "Do not press on the soldiers" when the first shot was fired. "I could not see where the gun was fired from; it made a noise like a pistol, and I imagined it was nothing but powder." It wasn't until he saw two men fall to the pavement that he realized that the soldiers were firing live rounds. As the firing continued, "the people were moving off, and the guns seemed to move as the people ran."

Q. Was there any sticks thrown?
A. No, I saw two or three snowballs which seemed to come from a distance.

Although the crowd was whistling and cheering, he had not seen anyone strike the soldiers' guns with sticks.

Nathaniel Thayer's wife had been frightened by the noise in the streets and asked her husband to find out what was happening. When Mr. Thayer went to his door, he had seen "twenty people . . . coming through Boylston's Alley. There was a terrible swearing, and they had clubs and swords and one thing and another." Then he had noticed seven coatless soldiers "driving along, swearing, cursing and damning, like wild creatures, saying 'Where are they? Cut them to pieces, slay them all!' They came up to my door. I shut the door and went in. They went around the back lane to King Street." He was unable to say whether any of the prisoners had been in the group.

Like Thayer, Nathaniel Appleton had been in his house when he heard "a considerable noise in the street." He ran to his front door and tried to find out what was happening. Finally, a passerby had told him that "the soldiers and the inhabitants were fighting." Suddenly he noticed "ten or twelve" soldiers with bayonets in their hands coming up his street. At first, he thought that they would pass his house without molesting him, but when he saw that they were heading for his door, he ran inside and threw the bolt. "They were within half a foot of it," he said. "Had it been open a second longer, they would have had command of the door." From his upstairs window, he had watched "people flying here and there like pidgeons, and the soldiers running about like mad men in a fury."

Shortly before nine o'clock, Appleton's two young sons had been sent to King Street on an errand. On their way home, they ran into "twenty soldiers with cutlasses in their hands." According to twelve-year-old John Appleton, one of the soldiers "lifted his cutlass and struck at my head, but I got the blow on my shoulder."

Q. Was the cutlass drawn?
A. I believe it was not, for it rattled on my shoulder as if it had been sheathed.

Colonel Thomas Marshall, an officer in the provincial militia, was the last witness of the day. Shortly after nine o'clock, he had walked through Dock Square where "all was quiet." Then he had strolled up Royal Exchange Lane into King Street "where he saw the sentry . . . in peace and quietness, nobody troubling." In fact, he had never seen King Street "more quiet in my life." A few minutes after he had arrived home, he heard someone outside shout, "Murder!" He had left his house and walked up King Street.

He hadn't gone more than a few paces when he saw "ten or twelve" soldiers from the main guard enter King Street. "I saw their arms glitter by the moonlight," he testified, "hallooing 'Damn them, where are they? By Jesus, let them come!' " After ordering some boys who were bothering the sentry to leave the soldier alone, Marshall returned to his house and warned his family to stay out of the streets. Several minutes later, he heard five guns go off. "I saw the people dead on the ground," he said. "I saw no opposition."

When court resumed on Thursday morning, the Crown had only a few more witnesses. Joseph Crosswell thought that he had seen blood on Killroy's bayonet just before the soldier had been arrested. James Carter, who had been standing next to Crosswell, confirmed his story. He had only been three feet away from Killroy and he was "positive" that the latter's bayonet was "covered from the point with blood." John Hill, a justice of the peace, had attempted to get the soldiers to return to their barracks but "they paid no regard to me or my orders."

The Crown's attorneys seemed more than satisfied with the testimony of their twenty-eight witnesses. As far as Samuel Quincy was concerned, he assured the jurors that they could have "no doubt but that all the prisoners at the bar were of that party of soldiers headed by Captain Preston who went down to the Custom House on the fifth of March." It was equally true, he urged, that the five dead men had been killed "by some one or other of that party." He conceded that it might be difficult, if not impossible, to determine exactly which soldier had shot each individual victim, but "it is immaterial where there are a number of persons concerned, who gave the mortal blow. All that are present are in the eyes of the law principals. You must pronounce them guilty."

His brother, Josiah, opened for the defense. He asked the jury to remember that the British soldiers had been bitterly hated from the moment they arrived in Boston. "No room was left for cordiality and friendship," he said. "Discontent was created on almost every brow. Instead of hospitality that the soldier thought himself entitled to, scorn, contempt and silent murmurs were his reception. Almost every countenance lowered with a discontented gloom and scarce an eye but flashed with indignant fire." What happened in King Street was the natural outgrowth of "heart burnings, heats and bickerings, reciprocal insults, and mutual injuries." Can we wonder, he asked, that when everything tended to some important action, the period so soon arrived?

As the first of the more than fifty witnesses called by Adams and young Quincy told their stories, it was obvious the defense was going all out to convince the jury that the soldiers had fired in self-defense. James Crawford swore that he had seen a huge crowd, armed with "pretty large cudgels," heading for King Street. Archibald Gooll, a stranger in town, had noticed "people running from all corners with sticks and instruments in their hands."

Q. What sort of sticks were they that they had?
A. Uncommon sticks, like what are pulled out of hedges.

Archibald Wilson and William Hunter, who were standing on the latter's balcony overlooking Royal Exchange Lane, had been able to get a glimpse of Dock Square where more than two hundred people were listening to a speech by an unidentified tall man dressed in a white wig and red cloak. According to Wilson, the impromptu orator had "made a considerable figure there."

Q. Could you hear what he said to them?
A. No, but after he had harangued them about three minutes, they huzzaed for the main guard.

Like his predecessors in the witness box, he had heard the clanging of the church bells and the shouts of "Fire!"

On his way home that evening, Benjamin Davis had walked through Dock Square. As he picked his way through the crowd, two young men had approached him. "Will you go and help us to fight the soldiers?" they asked him. When he told them that he had no intention of doing so, one of them took off his cloak and handed it to Davis. "If you will not go," the youth said, "hold my cloak." The witness then went to the customhouse where he "saw the sentinel standing with his back to the . . . door, and a number of people around him, boys and men. The boys were laughing and saying, 'Fire! Why do you not fire?' "

James Selkrig, another of Hunter's guests, had been watching the disturbance in the streets from one of his host's windows. "Considerable numbers of people . . . armed with sticks" were attacking the 14th Regiment's barracks. "They made attacks in the barracks," he recalled, "and were always drove back. When a fresh party came from the north part of town, they made a new attack; there were about five or six different attacks made." Later, he had heard the crowd which was listening to the tall man with the red cloak in Dock Square shouting that "they would do for the soldiers."

At 9:30 P.M., Thomas Knight saw "several companies of people" run past his front door. He had gone outside to investigate. In the bright moonlight, he could see that they were carrying "white sticks or clubs." As they headed for King Street, one man had shouted, "Damn their bloods, let us go and attack the main guard and knock them to hell first!" When he heard someone say, "Let's go back and get our guns," Knight returned to his house. Several minutes later "I heard one gun fired. In about one or two seconds, I heard another, and so on until five, six or seven were discharged."

After William Strong had testified that almost a hundred boys with clubs had been bothering the sentry, court adjourned for the day. The first witness on Friday morning was Dr. Richard Hirons, who had peered out of the front window of his locked and darkened house shortly after 8 P.M. A "little man . . . in a surtout" was having a spirited argument with "four or five officers of the 29th." "We did not send for you," the man had told the soldiers. "We will not have you here, we will get rid of you, or we will drive you away." When the officers assured him that they had done their best to keep their troops in check, the little man had turned on his heel and walked away.

A little later, Hirons had seen a soldier come out of the 14th's barracks and point his gun at a crowd which had come up Boylston's Alley. Three townsmen "immediately laid hold of him and took the musket from him, shoved him towards the barrack, and I think gave him the musket again, and charged him at his peril to come out again." Just as the bells began ringing, another soldier had emerged from the barracks, only to receive the same treatment as his predecessor. The physician was certain that the British officers had done everything in their power to keep their men off the streets.

Hirons had extracted the bullet from Samuel Maverick, a seventeen-year-old joiner's apprentice who had died several hours after the shooting. Maverick had been shot as he was walking up Royal Exchange Lane toward the Old State House. "It seems strange," Hirons mused, "how he could be killed by the firing at the customhouse. It wounded a part of the liver, stomach and intestines and lodged betwixt the lower ribs, where I cut it out. The ball must have struck some wall or something else before it struck him."

Captain John Goldfinch of the 14th Regiment had done his best to break up the fight that had developed in front of the unit's barracks. When he saw that his men were being pelted with snowballs, he ordered them confined to quarters. "The mob followed me and came to the gate of the barracks and abused the men very much indeed with bad language." As soon as the soldiers were off the streets, the "forty or fifty" people who had been taunting them had rushed off in the direction of Dock Square. "In a quarter of an hour or twenty minutes after the people had moved off, I heard some guns fire and the main guard drum beat to arms."

Benjamin Davis' son had run into Samuel Gray in Green's Lane. When Gray asked where the fire was, the boy had told him, "There is no fire, it's just the soldiers fighting." "Damn it, I'm glad of it," Gray had replied. "I will knock some of them on the head." As he watched the man run off toward the custom house, young Davis had yelled after him, "Take heed, you do not get killed in the affray yourself!"

Q. Had he a stick in his hand?
A. He had one under his arm.

Two minutes later, Gray was lying dead in King Street.

Alexander Cruckshank had watched while "twelve or fourteen lads" called the sentry "a lobster and rascal." White had told his tormentors that he intended to maintain his post "and if they offered to molest him, he would run them through, and upon his saying this, two boys made up some snowballs and threw them at the sentinel."

Q. Did they hit him?

A. I cannot say, but on their throwing snowballs the sentinel called out, "Guard, Guard!" two or three times.

Cruckshank had stepped aside as Preston's squad ran up King Street. One of the soldiers "with a bayonet or sword gave me a light stroke over my shoulder and said, 'Friend, you had better go home . . . there will be the devil to pay or bloodshed this night.'" The blow had been "very, very light."

William Davis, a private in the 29th, who was on his way to visit a friend, had run into an ugly crowd near Wentworth's wharf. When he heard someone shout, "Damn the dogs! Knock them down! We will knock down the first bloody-backed rascal we shall meet this night!" he had decided to get out of his regimentals. After he had changed his clothes in a nearby house, he started back for his barracks. As he walked through the market place, he saw "a great number of people there, knocking against the posts and tearing up the stalls, saying 'Damn the lobsters!' I heard several voices; some said, 'Let us kill that damned scoundrel of a sentry and then attack the main guard!'" When he arrived at his barracks, "there was not a man absent except some officers that quartered in the town and their servants."

Benjamin Lee had been part of the crowd that had stormed up Royal Exchange Alley from Dock Square. When he arrived at the customhouse, he had stood next to the sentry. "As I stood by the sentinel," he testified, "there was a barber's boy came up and pointed to the sentinel and said, 'There is the son of a bitch that knocked me down!' On his saying this, the people immediately cried out, 'Kill him, kill him!'" White had scrambled up the steps of the customhouse but, when he found the door locked, had shouted, "Turn out, main guard!" A few seconds later, Preston and his men were on the scene.

Andrew, Oliver Wendell's Negro servant, who, according to his employer, was "a fellow of a lively imagination," had watched the boys in front of the State House throwing oyster shells and snowballs at the main guard. Near the custom-house, he had heard one of Preston's soldiers order a man who was pressing against him to stand back. The man had retorted, "You damned lobster, bloody back, are you going to stab me?" "By God, I will," the soldier had replied. Then people began to throw "snowballs and other things which flew very thick." Finally, a stout man had attacked one of the soldiers with "a long cordwood stick." It was just after this incident that Andrew had heard the word "Fire!" and a gun shot.

> Q. Do you know who this stout man was that fell in and struck the grenadier?
> A. I thought and still think it was the mulatto who was shot.

He was certain that the soldier involved had been Killroy.

Adams and Quincy concluded their case on Saturday with some dozen witnesses, most of whom swore that the towns-people had provoked the shooting. According to William Whittington, Preston had tried to get the people in King Street to go home. They had ignored his plea and shouted back, "Fire! Fire! You dare not fire!" Thomas Symmonds, who lived near the 14th's barracks, had heard "the people . . . declare if the soldiers did not come out and fight them, they would set fire to the four corners of the barracks and burn every damned soul of them." At 8:30 P.M., William Parker, who was returning home, had rescued a Highland soldier who was being attacked by "seven or eight" boys near the market.

When the bells started to ring, Patrick Carr, who boarded with Mr. and Mrs. Field, had raced upstairs and strapped on his broadsword. Although his landlady persuaded him to leave the weapon at home, he had rushed off to the custom-

house. He had been one of the first to fall when the soldiers
fired. According to Dr. John Jeffries, his physician, Carr had
insisted, until his death ten days later, that "he really thought
they did fire to defend themselves, that he did not blame the
man, whoever he was, that shot him."

Q. When had you the last conversation with him?
A. About four o'clock in the afternoon preceding the night
in which he died, and he then particularly said he forgave
the man . . . that shot him. He was satisfied that he had
no malice but fired to defend himself.

Earlier that evening, the physician had watched the 14th
Regiment's officers ordering their troops to return to the barracks. "They begged the people would go away," he recalled,
"but they said they would not. Many persons cried, 'Let us
go home.' Others said, 'No, we shall find some soldiers in
King Street.' "

When the defense rested, the Crown called four rebuttal
witnesses. John Cox had heard three soldiers threaten to
blow up the Liberty Tree. Sentry White had intimated to
Thomas Hall that, unless the boys stopped bothering him,
"there will be something done bye and bye." According to
Henry Bass, there had not been more than fifteen people in
King Street at 9:15 P.M. "Very few for such a pleasant night,"
he added. Edward Payne, the prosecution's last witness, who
had been shot in the arm on March 5, added nothing to the
Crown's case. When he heard the boys near the sentry box
shouting, "Fire, damn you, why do you not fire?" he had
remarked to a friend "of the folly of the people in calling the
sentry to fire on them." When the last gun went off, he
"perceived I was wounded and went into the house."

The summations began on Monday morning. Josiah
Quincy led off for the defendants. As far as he was concerned, his fellow citizens had deliberately provoked the
soldiers who were harassed and insulted beyond human

endurance. "Does the law allow one member of the community to behave in this manner towards his fellow citizen," he
asked, "and then bid the injured party be calm and moderate?" This was no case in which to apply the Mosaic code
but "a law full of benignity, full of compassion, replete with
mercy." As he ended his two-hour stint, he reminded the
jurors, with an assist from Shakespeare, that

> The quality of mercy is not strained;
> It droppeth like the gentle rain from heaven—
> It is twice blessed;
> It blesses him that gives, and him that takes.

There were a few catcalls in the crowded courtroom when
John Adams stood up. His neck reddening, he looked up
from his notes. "I am for the prisoners at the bar," he said
earnestly, "and shall apologize for it only in the words of the
Marquis Beccaria: 'If I can but be the instrument of preserving one life, his blessing and tears of transport shall be
a sufficient consolation to me for the contempt of all mankind.' "

With the spectators quiet once more, he launched into a
detailed discussion of the case that was to take the better part
of two days. In the main, he took the position that the soldiers were guilty of nothing more than "killing in their own
defense." Surely, he thundered, the sentry "would be warranted in depriving those of life who were endeavoring to
deprive him of his. That is a point I would not give up for
my right hand, nay, for my life."

As for Preston and his men, they had every right to try to
protect White. Even a private citizen was entitled "to go to
the assistance of a fellow subject in distress and danger of his
life, when assaulted from a few or a multitude." No one, he
was sure, would maintain that any man lost this right merely
by enlisting in the army. But even if Foreman Mayo and his
colleagues came to the conclusion that Killroy and Mont-

gomery, the only soldiers who had been seen firing their muskets, were not justified, their crime "cannot be more than manslaughter."

Late on Tuesday afternoon, he ground to a finish. "If an assault was made to endanger their lives," he said wearily, "the law is clear they had a right to kill in their own defense. If it was not so severe as to endanger their lives, yet if they were assaulted at all, struck and abused by blows of any sort, by snowballs, oyster shells, cinders, the law reduces the offense of killing down to manslaughter, in consideration of those passions of our nature which cannot be eradicated." He paused and peered, for a long moment, into the jurors' faces. "To your candor and justice, gentlemen, I submit the prisoners and their cause."

It was almost four P.M. when Robert Treat Paine, the chief prosecutor, rose to close the Crown's case.

Naturally, he disagreed completely with Mr. Adams that the colonists had provoked the defendants into firing into the crowd which had filled King Street that unfortunate evening. As he saw it, it hadn't been the townspeople, but the soldiers who had started all the trouble. "If we will recollect the evidence," he pointed out, "a number of soldiers had come out of their barracks, armed with clubs, bayonets, cutlasses and instruments of diverse kinds, and in the most outrageous manner were ravaging the streets, assaulting everyone they met . . . and even vented their inhumanity on a little boy of twelve years of age."

Granted that many of the inhabitants had been carrying sticks, they had had good reason. "They had been fully sensible of the evil disposition and abusive behavior of many of the soldiers towards them," he explained, "and the most peaceable among them had found it necessary to arm themselves with heavy walking sticks as weapons of defense when they went abroad." That was the reason for "the appearance of sticks in the hands of many of the citizens as has been stated, and which was nothing more than might have been expected on any other night."

There was no doubt that most of Boston had been in the streets that night. But this, too, had an innocent explanation. After all, it had been a brisk, moonlit evening, "the pleasantness of which, increased by a new fallen snow, induced many persons to be walking the streets." Even those who weren't taking their evening constitutional had good reasons for not being home. First of all, many people, who had heard that the soldiers were on a rampage, had come out to see for themselves. Others had thought that the ringing of the church bells meant that there was a fire in town, and had rushed out "with bags and buckets as usual in case of fire." Still others who had been manhandled by the 14th's troops earlier that night were letting off a little steam by smashing the Dock Square market stalls.

Paine was rapidly losing his jury. As the bells of the Brattle Square Church pealed out five o'clock, several of its members were beginning to nod. The Solicitor General might have been a dull man, but he was no fool. Conceding that some of his fellow citizens might have been guilty of "threatening, rude and indecent speeches," he ended abruptly with a warning to the panel not to judge "the disposition and intention of the whole . . . from such expressions heard only from a few."

The next morning, after all four judges had taken turns in instructing the jury as to the law, Foreman Mayo led his eleven disciples into the little room behind the bench. Almost three hours later, they returned to the courtroom. Mayo read the verdicts aloud in a strident, high-pitched voice. "William Wemms, James Hartegan, William McCauley, Hugh White, William Warren and John Carroll—not guilty. Matthew Killroy and Hugh Montgomery, not guilty of murder but guilty of manslaughter."

Lynde promptly discharged the six acquitted men and they

immediately left the ominously silent courtroom. As soon as they were gone, Adams rose to his feet and urged the court to grant benefit of clergy to Killroy and Montgomery. Under English law, any convicted man who was semiliterate could ask the court to permit him to be branded on the right thumb in lieu of any further punishment. With a resigned air, the judges granted Adams' request and both defendants were immediately branded by an iron that was heated at one of the two fireplaces in the room. After they had been "burnt in the hand," the two soldiers were freed. The trial was over.

On December 12, Edward Manwaring, John Munro, Hammond Green and Thomas Greenwood, who had been accused of "aiding, abetting, comforting, assisting and maintaining . . . William Warren to do and commit the murder of Crispus Attucks," were acquitted by a jury which reached its decision without leaving the box.

A few months later, Captain Preston returned to England where, not only was he reimbursed for the money he had spent in his defense, but was given an annual pension of two hundred pounds. As Lord Barrington expressed it in a postscript to a letter to General Gage on the first anniversary of the shooting, "He is a perfectly satisfied man, which is a thing not to be found every day." The last official reference to him occurred in 1774 with the publication of his retirement from the army.

In April of 1776, Josiah Quincy died of tuberculosis while returning to Massachusetts from London, where he had been sent to plead the colony's case for more self-government. The following year, his brother Samuel sailed for England with a thousand Boston royal sympathizers who had found life intolerable in rebellious Massachusetts. On June 17, 1774, the last General Assembly that was ever to meet under royal auspices named Prosecutor Paine as one of Massachusetts' five delegates to the first Continental Congress that was to convene in Philadelphia the following September.

As for John Adams, despite the fact that he had been over-whelmingly elected on June 6, 1770 to replace the temporarily insane James Otis in the General Assembly, he retired from Boston politics and went back to Braintree the following spring. Although he was to return to the city two years later, he was determined, as he wrote in his diary on January 1, 1773, to remain "disengaged from public affairs . . . and mind my office, my clerks, and my children." He was con-vinced that his part in the Massacre trials had ended his political future.

But he never regretted his defense of Preston and his men. On Friday, March 5, 1773, the third anniversary of "The Massacre in King Street," he confided to his diary that he had attended a memorial service at the Old South Church. "I have reason to remember that fatal Night," he wrote. "The Part I took in Defence of Captain Preston and the Soldiers, procured me Anxiety, and Obloquy enough. It was, however, one of the most gallant, generous, manly and disinterested Actions of my Whole Life, and one of the best Pieces of serv-ice I ever rendered my Country. Judgment of Death against those Soldiers would have been as foul a Stain upon this Country as the Execution of the Quakers or Witches, an-ciently. As the Evidence was, the Verdict of the Jury was exactly Right."

# William Henry Seward

William Henry Seward had nothing to gain and everything to lose by his defense of William Freeman. A highly successful lawyer, a former Whig governor of New York, and the leading citizen of the upstate village of Auburn, he willingly involved himself in a case which was almost certain to cost him his friends, his clients and his political supporters. And for what? To save the life of an insane Negro who had massacred an innocent family.

Like Adams, Seward was fully aware of the difficulties he faced. Already suspect for his insanity plea in the trial of Henry G. Wyatt, another murderer, he knew that his defense of Freeman might bankrupt him. "The world are all mad with me here," he wrote to Thurlow Weed three weeks after Freeman's arrest, "because I defended Wyatt too faithfully. God help them to a better morality!"

But, despite all the risks involved, he was constitutionally unable to avoid the responsibility he felt toward a human being who needed his aid. In May of 1846, he visited Freeman in his cell. "He is deaf, deserted, ignorant, and his conduct is unexplainable, on any principle of sanity," he informed Weed several days later. "It is natural that he should turn to me to defend him. If he does, I shall do so. This will raise a storm of prejudice and passion which will try the fortitude of my friends. But I shall do my duty. I care not whether I am to be ever forgiven for it or not."

Although his partners referred to the case as "a terrible farce" and refused at first to participate in it, Seward, who was convinced that Freeman was hopelessly insane, did not hesitate to stand up for him. At his own expense, he scoured the state for medical experts to bulwark his theory that his demented client could not be held accountable for his crime. It mattered little to him that he became, for a time, a social outcast, that his law practice stagnated, or that his children were stoned on their way home from school. Duty was duty, and that was that.

But the defense of William Freeman involved more than just an opportunity for Seward to demonstrate his personal courage. Coming three years after the House of Lords had laid down what was soon to become the classic definition of criminal insanity in both England and the United States, the Negro's case represented one of the most significant American applications of the new rule. If his client was to escape the gallows, Seward would have to prove, in the language of Lord Chief Justice Tindal's opinion in M'Naghten's case in 1843, "that at the time of the committing of the act, [he] was laboring under such a defect of reason, from disease of the mind, as not to know the nature and quality of the act he was doing; or, if he did know it, that he did not know he was doing what was wrong."

In the light of today's advances in the science of psychiatry, there would be little if any public furor caused by a lawyer's attempt to save his client's life by relying on the M'Naghten Rule. But in 1846, fifty-four years before the publication of Sigmund Freud's epochal *The Interpretation of Dreams*, such a defense, particularly where a brutal crime had taken place, was sure to bring the wrath of the community down on the head of the hapless attorney who dared to plead it. Seward had already learned this lesson in the Wyatt case when he had defended an inmate of Auburn Penitentiary who had killed a fellow prisoner.

Yet even he did not anticipate the full extent of the hatred against him when he decided to invoke the M'Naghten Rule on behalf of a man who had all but wiped out one of Auburn's most respected families. But it would have made little difference to him if he had known exactly what he was letting himself in for. William Henry Seward was nobody's man but his own. "His action in the Freeman case," wrote Salmon P. Chase many years later, "considering his own personal position and circumstances [was] magnanimous in the highest degree."

*"I rise from these fruitless labors, exhausted in mind and body, covered with public reproach, stunned with protests."*

# William Henry Seward and the trial of William Freeman, July 5 to July 23, 1846

IN 1846, Auburn, New York, was chiefly known as the seat of the state penitentiary of the same name, where, sixty-seven years later, penologist Thomas Mott Osborne was to become a voluntary prisoner in order to prepare himself for his wardenship at Sing Sing. Located in the frigid Finger Lakes region of the state, the village sat astride a small stream that flowed northward from Owasco Lake, a slender body of water that stretched some dozen or so miles to the south. A beehive of antislavery activity, Auburn had attracted many Negroes who lived in a rickety settlement on the outskirts of town known locally as New Guinea.*

* The village later became the home of Harriet Tubman who, after her escape from slavery in 1849, became one of the most successful "conductors" on the Underground Railroad.

Early on the afternoon of Thursday, March 5, twenty-two-year-old William Freeman, who lived at Mrs. Newark's boardinghouse in New Guinea, walked into Joseph Morris' blacksmith shop. The slender, light-skinned Negro, who eked out a precarious living by doing odd jobs for his landlady, wanted the smith to make a knife for him. When Morris, who was busy forging a horseshoe, suggested that, in order to save time, his prospective customer whittle a model of the knife he desired, Freeman left the shop.

He returned, some thirty minutes later, with a well-carved wooden knife. Could Mr. Morris duplicate it in "good cast steel?" The smithy nodded his head. He was willing to do it, but it would cost Freeman four shillings.* The Negro hesitated for a long moment. "I think you could afford to make it for two shillings," he finally countered. When Morris insisted that he couldn't lower his price, Freeman walked to the back of the shop where, for more than an hour, he stood and silently watched Morris at work.

Shortly after three o'clock, he walked back to the forge and offered the smithy four shillings "if you grind it and put a handle on it." Morris refused. "It's more trouble to grind it than to forge it," he explained. When Freeman made no move to leave, the blacksmith, whose curiosity had been roused by the Negro's persistence, asked him why he wanted a knife. Freeman, who was quite deaf, did not appear to hear the question. A sudden thought crossed Morris' mind. "You want to kill somebody, don't you?" he asked. Freeman frowned angrily. "It's none of your business," he shouted, "so long as you get your pay for it!" When Morris persisted in his refusal to make the knife for less than his price, Freeman finally left. Four days later, he showed up at George W. Hyatt's forge on Genesee Street. This time, he was more successful. Not only would Hyatt make a knife for two shillings, but he agreed to grind it as well. Freeman was smiling

* Approximately fifty cents. British currency terms were still in common use.

broadly as he walked back to New Guinea with his purchase. Later that morning, he returned and asked Hyatt to repair a jackknife with a loose blade. The obliging smith helped him rivet the blade in place.

Freeman spent the next two days sharpening his new knife on the grindstone of Robert Simpson, a carpenter whose shop was located near the Owasco and Auburn canal dam. After he had honed both edges of the blade to razor sharpness, the Negro used Simpson's brace and bit to bore a hole in one end of a yard-long hickory club which he had brought with him. The carpenter didn't pay much attention to him, but, at one point, he noticed that his customer was attempting to push some object into the hole he had bored. After working for an hour or so, Freeman left the shop without either thanking Simpson or paying for the use of his equipment.

Thursday, March 12, was a bright, sunshiny day in Auburn, with just enough of a hint of spring in the air to raise the villagers' hopes of an early thaw. In the little town of Fleming, which nestled on the west shore of Lake Owasco, the family of John G. Van Nest was preparing for a dinner guest. Earlier that week, Mrs. Van Nest had invited Peter W. Williamson, a young bachelor who worked a small farm near Sands Beach Church, to come to supper on Thursday night. Williamson, who was flattered by an invitation from the wife of Fleming's most prominent citizen, readily accepted.

The Van Nests occupied a large, rambling house a few hundred feet away from the lake. The forty-one-year-old pater familias, who was Fleming's supervisor and justice of the peace, presided over a large household. In addition to his wife and three young children, his mother-in-law, a hired man and a serving girl lived with him. His parents occupied a small cottage, some three hundred yards away from the main house. The family's farm was one of the most prosperous in Cayuga County, and, although Van Nest was not the most gregarious of men, he was respected and admired by most of his neighbors. "A domestic, sedate and grave man," was the consensus of opinion.

After a plain but satisfying meal, Williamson and his host sat around the living room talking Whig politics until Sarah Van Nest had put the two older children to bed. Shortly before 9:30, the young farmer yielded to country custom and, after thanking the Van Nests for a delightful evening, put on his coat and left the house. His mind filled with the thought of tomorrow's chores, he had walked several hundred feet along Lake Road in the direction of his farm when he heard a series of hair-raising shrieks coming from the Van Nest house.

Thoroughly frightened, he started to run toward his home to pick up a rifle. He had almost reached the boundary of his property, when he heard the sound of a horse's hooves behind him. He had just enough time to jump to the side of the road, when a man on an unsaddled black horse brushed by him. In the bright moonlight, he could see that the rider was a wild-eyed Negro who was wearing a Webster coat and "a cap or a low-crowned hat." Williamson immediately recognized the horse as an old plug that belonged to Mrs. Peter Wyckoff, Sarah Van Nest's mother.

As soon as he reached his house, the young farmer saddled up his mare and raced back to the Van Nest's. When he entered the house, he was horrified to find that the family had been massacred. John Van Nest was lying, face down, in a pool of blood on the kitchen floor. Cornelius Van Arsdale, his man of all work, was seated on a living room chair, bleeding from multiple wounds of the chest. Near him, Williamson saw that George, the Van Nest's two-year-old son, was close to death from a stab wound that had been delivered with such ferocity that it had almost split the infant's crib. The butchered body of the baby's mother was sprawled on the floor of one of the downstairs servant's rooms.

Williamson was able to locate only two other members of the family. In one of the upstairs rooms, he found Peter and Julia, the other two Van Nest children, cowering in their beds. Although he didn't know it, Mrs. Wyckoff, dressed only in a thin nightgown and a pair of stockings, was then struggling across the fields toward the Brooks' farm, one-half mile to the south. The seventy-year-old woman, who had been stabbed in the abdomen, collapsed as she reached her destination. Young William Brooks, who had been awakened by the excitement downstairs, heard the wounded woman tell his mother that "they were all stabbed down at their home—that she was stabbed also." No sooner had Mrs. Wyckoff been put to bed than Helen Holmes, the Van Nest's maid, arrived to ask for help.

Back at the Van Nest's, Williamson realized that, if Van Arsdale and the baby were to be saved, they would have to have immediate medical aid. He mounted his mare and galloped to every farmhouse in the vicinity, spreading the news of what had happened on the lakefront. Within two hours, while most of the population of Auburn milled around the Van Nest house, several physicians attempted to save the hired man's life. As for the infant, he had died shortly after Williamson had started on his wild ride.

At one o'clock the next afternoon, an exhausted and famished William Freeman rode into Schroeppel, a tiny hamlet some forty miles north of Auburn. He stopped at the home of Abram De Puy, a relative of his sister's husband, and asked if he could rest for a while. De Puy was instantly suspicious when he saw that his mud-covered visitor had a badly cut right wrist and was riding an expensive gray horse.* When Freeman refused to answer any questions, the frightened De Puy ordered him to leave. "You can't stay here," he told him. "Take the horse and go!"

* When Mrs. Wyckoff's old horse gave out near New Guinea, Freeman had stolen George Burrington's fleet gray mare.

A short time later, Freeman pulled up in front of Gregg's Tavern, in the center of Schroeppel. There, he attempted to sell his horse to Edwin Corning, one of the farmers at the bar. When Corning began to question him as to where he had obtained such a fine gray, Freeman replied that he had "traded up" from a horse that someone had given him. The answer failed to satisfy Corning, who, after seizing the animal's halter, shouted loudly, "You stole the horse!" Suddenly eager to be on his way, Freeman tried to wrest the halter away from the farmer. In a matter of minutes, he had been subdued and arrested on suspicion of horse thievery.

Schroeppel was not large enough to boast of a jail, and the suspect was kept at the tavern. While his captors were deciding what to do with him, they gave him some dried beef to eat. He was still wolfing it down hungrily when Cayuga County Constable Alonzo Taylor entered the tavern. The moment the newcomer spotted the ravenous man, he walked swiftly over to him. "Ain't your name Freeman?" he demanded. "You damned murderer!" Explaining to the thoroughly astonished farmers that "this man just wiped out a whole family near Auburn," Taylor asked them to assist him in making sure that his new prisoner would not escape. With their aid, he shackled Freeman's feet and tied his hands behind his back.

At dawn on Saturday, the bound man was placed in a borrowed sleigh and driven toward Auburn. Eight hours later, Taylor and his captive entered the village on the North Street road, where a dozen policemen were assembled to escort them to the courthouse. A large and angry crowd, which had been waiting since noon for Freeman's return, followed the sleigh into town and milled about impatiently while Justice of the Peace James Bostwick formally charged the Negro with the murder of John Van Nest. Then the defendant was taken to the Van Nest farm where the injured

Van Arsdale identified him as the man who had stabbed him in the chest two days earlier.

By this time, there were more than two thousand infuriated Auburnians surrounding the house. As one observer noted, "The excitement of the occasion was unprecedented in this section of the state. It was thought the course of justice marked out by the law was too slow for the punishment of such an offender—that the death of the family of Van Nest must be at once avenged. The populace sought his blood, and wildly and loudly called for the victim of their fury that they might tear him to ribbons. The gibbet, rack and flame were each proposed for his immediate death. The rope and the lasso were ready for snatching him from the officers of the law. But by a diversion artfully contrived by the officers, they escaped with their prisoner and, although pursued, succeeded in lodging him in the county jail."

The "diversion" consisted of sending two constables on horseback into Auburn at full gallop twenty minutes before Freeman was taken from the Van Nest house. When most of the mob raced after the policemen, who were headed for the courthouse, the prisoner was hurried in a covered wagon to the county jail. Although the disappointed crowd broke through the fence surrounding the jailhouse when it discovered that it had been fooled, the sheriff finally managed to persuade its members to go to their homes and let the law take its slow but sure course.

At the time of the murders, William Henry Seward, Auburn's most successful lawyer and a former Whig Governor of New York, was in Albany, en route to visit his father in Orange County. He was more than mildly interested in the flamboyant accounts of the crimes which he read in the Hudson Valley newspapers. Three weeks earlier, he had defended Henry G. Wyatt, an Auburn convict who had killed a fellow prisoner whom he suspected of lying about him to the warden. During the trial, Seward had taken the novel tack that the beatings which Wyatt had received at the hands of prison guards as a result of his victim's falsehoods, had caused temporary insanity. Although Wyatt hadn't been acquitted, his jury had disagreed, and he had been returned to prison to await a new trial.

Of Welsh-Irish extraction, the forty-four-year-old Seward was a slim, slightly stooped man of medium height who was strongly addicted to snuff and good bourbon. His long face, with its thin lips, bold nose and lively blue eyes, was topped by a mass of fading auburn hair that, in its ruddier days, had become an issue in the gubernatorial campaign of 1834 when he had made his first run for New York's highest office. William L. Marcy, his successful Democratic opponent, had stumped the state referring to the youthful Whig candidate as "a red-haired young man without a record and unknown." Four years later, when Seward had been elected to the first of his two successive terms as Governor, the *New York Times* editorialized that it was grateful that the electorate had been able to see beyond the color of a man's hair.

While Seward was out of town, one of the sheriff's assistants remarked that he had seen Freeman at several sessions of the Wyatt trial. The news spread through Auburn with the supersonic speed that juicy gossip always seems to command. According to street corner rumor, it was possible— even probable—that the ex-Governor's spirited defense of Wyatt had caused the Van Nest tragedy. Judge Bowen Whiting, who had presided at the convict's trial, was so incensed by the news that Freeman had been in the courtroom that he shouted to a roomful of guests in his home, "No Seward will take this case! No Seward will defend Freeman!"

When Seward returned, he found, to his surprise, that many of his fellow villagers considered him responsible for the Van Nest massacre. But he didn't stay home long enough to catch the full fury of their resentment. On April 6, he left town for an extended trip that was to take him down the

Mississippi to New Orleans. During his absence, the Cayuga County Grand Jury charged that Freeman "feloniously, wilfully and of malice aforethought, from a premeditated design to effect the death of John G. Van Nest did kill and murder, against the peace and dignity of the State of New York." Three similar indictments accused him of the murders of Sarah Van Nest, her infant son and her mother.

David Wright and Samuel Blatchford, Seward's partners, met him when his train pulled into Auburn late in May. They told the astonished lawyer that, during his absence, his children had been stoned, and hotheads had proposed burning his home. They had calmed the townspeople by assuring them that no member of their firm would defend Freeman. Seward was furious. He hadn't authorized them to speak for him, and, as far as the indicted Negro was concerned, he would make up his own mind in good time. After urging him to think it over carefully, Wright and Blatchford accompanied him home.

Early in April, District Attorney Luman Sherwood had persuaded Governor Silas Wright to convene a special term of the Cayuga County Court to try both the Wyatt and the Freeman cases at the beginning of June. On the first day of the month, the Negro was brought before Judge Whiting to be arraigned. After Sherwood had read the first of the four indictments aloud, Whiting asked the shackled prisoner, "How do you plead?" When Freeman said nothing, the judge repeated the question. At this moment, Seward, who had been sitting back of the rail, arose and walked to the bench. "Your Honor," he said, "I plead insanity in behalf of the prisoner."

Sherwood was on his feet at once. As far as the prosecution was concerned, he informed the bench, there wasn't a shadow of a doubt as to the defendant's sanity. But Seward was persistent. If Freeman was now insane, and his own investigation had convinced the lawyer that he was, then he was excused by law from pleading to the indictment. If Whiting was open to counsel's suggestion, then he recommended that the issue of his client's present mental condition be decided before requiring him to answer the Grand Jury's charges. His Honor decided to give the suggestion some thought and adjourned the arraignment until further notice.

With Freeman back in the county jail, the way was clear for Wyatt's second trial. Its importance was underscored by the fact that Governor Wright had ordered his Attorney General, John Van Buren, to assist Sherwood. The thirty-six-year-old son of the eighth President, whose polished diction and sartorial elegance had won him the nickname of Prince John, had arrived in Auburn late in May and spent his time interviewing everyone who knew anything about Freeman or Wyatt. If any lawyer could beat Seward, the villagers said hopefully, it was Martin Van Buren's worldly, smooth-talking heir.

Wyatt's re-trial took a month. Despite Seward's request that, in view of the feeling in Auburn generated by the Van Nest murders, the defendant ought to be tried in a less tempestuous county, Judge Whiting ordered both sides to get on with the business of selecting a jury. To buttress his contention that Wyatt had been out of his mind when he knifed a fellow prisoner, Seward called a score of medical witnesses to the stand. But it was all to no avail. The jury took only thirty minutes to agree upon a verdict of guilty, and the convict was sentenced to be hanged on August 18. As Mrs. Seward wrote to her sister, "it is more than probable that Freeman, although insane at the time he perpetrated the horrid deed . . . will be another victim to satisfy popular vengeance."

On June 24, Whiting announced that he had decided to accept Seward's suggestion and try the issue of Freeman's sanity before the main trial for murder. Like the Wyatt trial, the sanity hearing took place in the commodious first-floor courtroom of the Cayuga County Courthouse, which stood on the southwest corner of Genesee and Court Streets. A stone and wood structure in the Greek revival style, which had been built in 1836, it was the pride of Auburn. Its imposing facade was supported by six Doric columns, with a colonnaded drum buttressing a dome topped by a tiny cupola. Severely damaged by fire in 1922, it was razed and replaced by the present stone block courthouse.*

It took less than a day to seat a jury which, in the words of one of its members, had "no opinion on the subject of Freeman's insanity but think, if he is insane, he ought not to hang." Before Whiting gavelled the first day's session to a close, David Wright, who had closed ranks with his partner once Seward had entered the case, opened for the defense. Freeman was, he told the jurors, more to be pitied than censured. "What is done by us, comes from no agency of his, but from the dictates of conscience and the promptings of humanity."

Seward paraded twenty-three Auburnians to the stand in his effort to prove that Freeman was hopelessly insane. Ira Curtis, a merchant who had known the Negro for many years, concluded that he was "a part of the time an idiot; both idiotic and insane." When he had learned that he was to be called as a witness for the defense, he had visited Freeman in jail. "Did it never occur to you," Sherwood asked him, "that he was trying to impose on you, to get up the plea of insanity?" Yes, the thought had crossed his mind, but it had "vanished in a moment" when he had seen the defendant's condition.

In 1840, Freeman had been given a five-year sentence at Auburn for stealing Mrs. Martha Godfrey's horse. Two of

---

* In front of the present structure is a cast-iron tablet whose raised letters read: "In 1846, William H. Seward in Cayuga County Court House defended a man accused of murder and based his plea on Insanity. Although scorned and humiliated by many for his stand, at that time, History has since vindicated him as a man of principle, courage and foresight."

the prison guards agreed that he was "a being of very low degraded intellect, hardly above a brute." Although Theron Green, his keeper, stated that he was not capable of judging whether the Negro was insane or not, he "didn't think him a man that would realize the consequences of killing a person. He comes as near a brute as a human being can." Green, who had tried to teach him to read and write, had been unable to get him past the first three letters of the alphabet.

Warren T. Worden had, at the suggestion of a local physician, tried to talk to Freeman in jail several months before the trial. According to him, the prisoner had stated that he had struck Van Nest when the latter said, "If you are going to eat my liver, I will eat yours." Worden was convinced that Freeman was insane. "I came to the conclusion," he said, "that he was incapable of judging between right and wrong. His whole appearance and conversation was different than that of a sane man."

On the Saturday before the murders, the defendant had asked Magistrate Lyman Paine to issue a warrant "for the man who put him in state prison." When the young Negro had been unable to give him any details about the nature of his grievance, Paine had refused to grant the writ. "He left the office in a passion," the witness recalled, "slammed the door very hard, but came back in the afternoon. He then said he wanted a warrant for the man and woman that sent him to prison, one of which was Mrs. Godfrey. He acted strange, but I attributed it to deafness and ignorance."

Freeman's mother insisted that her son had changed radically in prison. "He was a different boy from what he was when he went there," she insisted. His sister testified that he had lost his hearing when a prison guard "hit him on his head with a board." Although he had been a very normal boy when he was sentenced, five years at Auburn had changed him completely. "I don't think he is in his right mind now," she told Seward. Robert Freeman, who had worked with him in 1838 at the American Hotel, thought that "he did not appear like the same boy when he came out of prison."

Two doctors who had known the defendant for many years had examined him in the county jail. Dr. Lansingh Briggs, the physician at Auburn Prison, had formed no opinion as to his intellect, but "I came away with the impression . . . that the boy had become demented." Dr. Charles Van Epps shared his colleague's opinion. "My opinion of the condition of his mind," he stated, "is that it was dementia, or idiotic derangement." The cause? "Brutal treatment."

On March 26, Reverend John M. Austin, the pastor of the Universalist Church and an outspoken abolitionist, had spent an hour in Freeman's cell. His conversation with the suspected murderer had convinced him that he was hopelessly insane. "I should not consider him of sound mind," he told Seward. On cross-examination, the young minister admitted that he had written articles about the case for the Auburn *Daily Advertiser* and other papers. Yes, he had said that the real cause of the crime might be the village's indifference to Negroes.

"Then you think the community responsible for the crime of Freeman?" Sherwood snapped. Austin's answer was a hundred years ahead of his time. "My opinion is that one of the legitimate causes that lead to this tragical event is the utter neglect shown to the moral, intellectual and religious instruction of the colored people," he replied.

With the testimony of Amariah Brigham, the superintendent of the State Lunatic Asylum, that Freeman had "a very weak mind . . . a trifling intelligence," the defense rested. Sherwood, breathing confidence, assured the jurors that he would prove to their complete satisfaction that the defendant was as sane as the next man. "If we can show him competent to distinguish between right and wrong," he urged, "we shall insist that he is legally sane and answerable to the law for the horrid crime of murder." As he turned to call Nathaniel

Lynch, his first witness, he looked triumphantly at Seward, who was sitting quietly at the counsel table. The lawyer did not return his glance.

Lynch, who had lived in nearby Sennett, had met Freeman sixteen or seventeen years ago when the latter's mother had asked him to raise the boy. At Sherwood's request, he had visited the suspect shortly after his arrest. Freeman had described to him, in some detail, how the murders had occurred. After killing Van Nest, he had stabbed his victim's wife as she entered the house from the backyard. He had then plunged his knife into "a person" who had been lying on a bed in the living room. He had "sliced up" another man who had hit him with a candlestick when they grappled at the head of the stairs. Lastly, he had cut down a woman who had tried to follow him out of the house. "My opinion is," said Lynch, "that he is sane but of weak intellect."

Israel G. Wood, the warden of the county jail, remembered that Freeman had broken out of the prison while he was awaiting trial on the horse-stealing charge in 1840. He had also seen the defendant on several occasions after he was released from Auburn five years later. "I discovered no difference from what he was before in jail, except his deafness. I never thought him insane, till this affair."

Police Officer Thomas F. Munroe, who had known Freeman since his childhood, "never heard that he was crazy till since the murders. My opinion is I never saw any insanity in him. I think if he is insane, most of the Negroes in Auburn are." The witness was quick to admit to Seward that, shortly after the Negro had been spirited away from the crowd at the Van Nest house, he had said, "if they had hung him, it would have saved the county a great deal of expense."

Q. Have you not said that counsel ought to be tarred and feathered for defending him?

A. I might have said they deserved it for the course they have taken in his defense.

"I am opposed to the course pursued," he explained, "because I supposed all the testimony about his derangement was manufactured."

Constable Abraham A. Vanderheyden, who had picked up Freeman for the theft of Mrs. Godfrey's horse, had questioned him after his arrest for the Van Nest murders. "I asked him how he came to commit the murder. He said, 'You know there is no law for me.' I asked what he meant by that. He said, 'They ought to pay me.' I asked him how he come to kill the child. He said he didn't know it was a child. I then asked him how he left. He said he took a horse. I then asked him where he rode the horse. He said he rode to New Guinea. I asked him what he did with him. He said the horse fell, and he left him there." Despite the strange answers to some of his questions, he didn't think that Freeman was crazy.

During the defendant's term in prison, he had often worked in the harness shop. Because he had proved to be a slow worker, James E. Tyler, one of the keepers, had started to flog him. When Freeman had tried to defend himself, by attacking the guard with a knife, Tyler had beaten him over the head with a basswood board. "It was . . . two feet long, fourteen inches wide, and half an inch thick," he recalled. But he didn't think that the blow had hurt his prisoner. "He worked well after that," he concluded.

After four more guards had sworn that they didn't consider Freeman insane, Sherwood called Dr. David Dimon, an Auburn physician. Based on six examinations of the defendant, he had come to the conclusion that he was not deranged. No, he told Seward, he had never treated an insane patient.

Q. Do maniacs smile?
A. They do. The smile of a maniac is very peculiar and unmeaning.

Seward glanced at Freeman, who had worn a perpetual grin since the hearing began. "Is not the smile of the prisoner peculiar?" he asked the physician. Dimon nodded. "It is somewhat so," he agreed.

Before Sherwood and Van Buren called it a day, they called a number of witnesses to testify to Freeman's preparations for the murders and his activities on the night of the crime. Smith Morris, who had refused to make the knife for him, "thought him keener than many men about making a bargain." George Hyatt identified the state's Exhibit 1 as the knife he had forged for the Negro on Monday, March 9. Carpenter Simpson recollected that Freeman had come to his shop several days before the murders and after sharpening "a large butcher knife," fitted something into a hole he had bored "in the end of his hickory club."

After Peter Williamson had described the carnage at Van Nest's, Cornelius Van Arsdale said that it had been the defendant who had stabbed him in the chest with Exhibit 1. "It struck on the breast bone," he said, "and glanced off to the left side." The hired man had pushed his assailant down the stairs and then driven him from the house with a broomstick. Helen Holmes, the Van Nest's maid, who had been in bed, had heard her mistress scream, "Some one is here and going to kill us all!" Miss Holmes identified Freeman as the man she had seen peering in the living room window just before she ran to the Brooks' farm for help.

For his rebuttal, Seward called three physicians, all of whom agreed that Freeman was insane. Dr. John McCall, the President of the New York Medical Society, had been in the courtroom during most of the earlier testimony. Based on what he had heard and his own examination of the prisoner he had "no doubt of his insanity, that his mind is impaired." Despite a vigorous cross-examination by Van Buren, McCall stuck to his original diagnosis that Freeman was suffering from some form of dementia.

He was followed by Dr. Charles B. Coventry, Professor of Medical Jurisprudence at Geneva College. "I visited the prisoner in the jail, yesterday," he said. "His appears to be a mixed case of dementia and partial mania." It was not unusual, he said, for an insane man to "design and plan homicides with deliberation." They often do this, he explained, when they are "laboring under a delusion." "Have you any doubt that the prisoner is insane?" Seward asked. "I cannot say that I have," the physician replied. "I have not seen anything to raise a doubt of it in my mind."

Superintendent Brigham of the State Lunatic Asylum was recalled. During his first stint on the stand, he had insisted on hearing all the testimony before giving his opinion as to Freeman's mental condition. Now, he was prepared to state that "the prisoner at the bar is insane." First of all, Freeman's aunt and uncle were insane. Secondly, the change that occurred in his personality during his prison term was "a characteristic of insanity." Lastly, his actions before the murders, and the stabbings themselves indicate "an unnatural, if not irrational, condition of mind."

Independence Day was devoted to the summations and Judge Whiting's charge. It was five minutes short of midnight when the jury retired with his Honor's admonition that, even though the next day was Sunday, "in case they should agree upon a verdict, the court would convene . . . to receive it." The next morning, Foreman Stone announced that only one juror, Cyrus H. Davis, had voted to find the defendant insane because "although he was proved to have memory and knowledge of events, he had not been proved to have made an induction of reason."

But Davis soon came around when Whiting explained to him that "the main question for the jury to decide is whether the prisoner knows right from wrong." At eight P.M., a verdict was handed to the clerk. "We find," it read, "the prisoner sufficiently sane in mind and memory to distinguish between right and wrong." Although Seward pleaded with him to disregard the jury's verdict, as inconclusive, Whiting ordered it entered. "It is equivalent to a verdict of sanity," he remarked.

Freeman's long delayed trial for murder began the next morning. After reading the indictment aloud, Sherwood turned to the defendant. "Do you desire a trial of the charges?" he shouted. Freeman looked bewildered. "No," he answered. "Do you have counsel?" the district attorney demanded. The Negro shook his head. "I don't know," he stammered. "Are you able to employ counsel?" asked Sherwood. The answer was no. Whiting had had enough. "Enter a plea of not guilty," he directed the clerk.

The judge looked directly at Seward who was sitting toward the rear of the courtroom. "Will any one defend this man?" he asked in a subdued voice. With all eyes upon him, the ex-Governor pulled himself to his feet. "May it please the court," he said slowly and deliberately, "I shall remain counsel for the prisoner until his death." As Seward made his way to the counsel table, Whiting looked as if the weight of the world had suddenly slipped from his shoulders.

Before selecting a jury, Seward had three motions to make. In the first place, he wanted a postponement. Public feeling was running so strongly against his client "that any trial . . . however fairly conducted by the court, would be but a hollow form, unless by accident some cool, dispassionate persons might find their way into the jury box." In addition, the Wyatt case and Freeman's sanity trial had caused him to neglect his own practice "in behalf of prisoners who needed the highest professional effort without being able to render any reward." Whiting was not impressed by either argument. "Motion denied," he ruled.

Mr. Seward then moved that the indictment be quashed. It seemed that John O'Hara, one of the grand jurors who voted for it, was John Van Nest's brother-in-law. "What difference does that make," growled Whiting. "The jury was unanimous. Your motion is denied." Seward turned to more immediate matters. He challenged the entire panel of prospective jurors who filled ten of the courtroom's thirty aisles of seats. The reason: Richard Searing, whose name had been included in the list compiled by the county clerk, had been suddenly and mysteriously discharged from jury service. Sherwood owned that this had been done because Mr. Searing was a Quaker with scruples against inflicting the death penalty. That was good enough reason for Whiting. "Empanel the jury," he ordered the bailiff.

It took sixty-eight residents of Cayuga County before the bailiff succeeded in obeying his Honor's directive. Some, like Charles Eldred, did not believe in capital punishment. Cyrus Davis, the reluctant juror in the sanity trial, still believed that Freeman was "irresponsible, and would under no circumstances find him guilty." Others, like Joel Hoff, were convinced that "it is a case of wicked, deliberate murder, done when he was in his senses, and he is morally responsible." Of the twelve who were finally selected, Obidiah A. Cooper was typical. "The heart is deceitful," he told Seward, "but I think I can weigh the evidence fairly."

The state's first witness was Dr. Joseph T. Pitney, a physician who had arrived at the Van Nest's shortly after midnight of March 12. Mr. Van Nest had been killed instantly by a stab wound of the heart. His wife, who was several months pregnant, had suffered "a severe wound in the left side and of the lower part of the abdomen." Mr. Van Arsdale had been "bleeding profusely from a knife which had cut the cartilages of the ribs, and entered a left lobe of the lungs, just above the heart." Mrs. Wyckoff, whom he had examined at the Brooks farm, had "a severe wound in . . . the lower part of the abdomen." She had died two days later from what Pitney called "a violent inflammation."

The two blacksmiths and the carpenter repeated the testimony they had given at the sanity hearing as to Freeman's purchase of a knife just before the murders. Joseph W. Quincy, a barber who "didn't shave colored people," remembered that Freeman often wore a Webster coat and cap. Young Williamson, with a highly developed sense of the dramatic, retold his story of what had happened after he started home from the Van Nest's at 9:30 P.M. on March 12. Harrison Masten, who had found Mrs. Wyckoff's horse lying on its side near New Guinea, had taken the exhausted animal back to its stable. William B. Patten had seen Freeman south of the Van Nest house just before the murders. "He had something under his coat, and on his arm, which I supposed was a gun. He had on a Webster coat of a mixed color, as I took it."

About a week before the murders, Freeman had shown Nathaniel Hersey "a couple of old knives." The defendant had told him that "he had found the folks that put him in prison, and he meant to kill them, because they put him in prison."

Q. Did he tell you who they were?
A. He said they were Van Nests.

Twenty-year-old Helen Holmes recalled that, early in March, Freeman had come to the house looking for work. When her employer said that he already had a hired man, the Negro had left the house. She didn't think that any member of the family had been involved in the 1840 horse-stealing charge against the defendant.

Frederick Bennett was the first witness to testify that Freeman had known Van Nest long before the murders. He remembered that a man named De Puy had worked for the dead man in 1838 "and a boy was living there with him, and that the boy's name was William Freeman." However, Van Nest's aged mother had "never heard of . . . this Negro." Some time between eight and nine P.M. on March 12, she had noticed "a black man in the yard of our house." He had lingered near her fence for a few minutes and "he then turned around and went toward my son's as fast as he could walk."

Shortly after Freeman's arrest at Greggs' Tavern on suspicion of horse-stealing, one of his captors had ridden to Phoenix to obtain a warrant. When George B. Parker, a Phoenix attorney, heard of the application, he suspected that the Negro might be the man who had killed Van Nest. He had arrived at the tavern shortly after Constable Taylor. He had started to question Freeman but the latter, after answering a few queries, had shouted "I shan't answer any more; if they can prove anything against me, let them prove it!"

"I couldn't get him to admit he'd killed anybody," Parker said. "I boxed his ears, and he called the constable. My feelings got the better of my judgment, and I pulled his hair a little." When Taylor had entered the room, Freeman asked him to protect him against his infuriated inquisitor. "I was highly excited against him," Parker confessed. "I attributed it to his playing possum, and was wrought up pretty high, and he abruptly declined answering. It didn't occur to me that he was insane."

The defendant had been more communicative with Dr. Leander B. Bigelow, the Auburn Prison surgeon who had begun visiting him in the county jail in June. Freeman had admitted to the physician that, after he had killed "five" people at the Van Nest house, he had stolen a horse from George Burrington's barn. He had gone to Schroeppel because "my hand was cut, and I thought I'd go down there till I'd cured it up." When Bigelow asked him why he had murdered the Van Nest family, he had answered, "Well, to see if I couldn't get revenge, or get some pay for being in State Prison about a horse; and I didn't do it."

As to Freeman's sanity, Bigelow had no doubt. "I find him a man that I consider of low, degraded intellect, and of very limited knowledge. I suppose he was put into prison at fourteen or fifteen years of age, and had little chance there. From my examination I have made of Freeman, I am satisfied that he is deaf in one ear, and partially so in the other, and can hear but few words that are addressed to him. But I saw nothing to satisfy me that the prisoner was insane; not enough to satisfy me."

"Thank you, Doctor," purred Van Buren. "The people rest, your Honor."

Wright was pressed into service again to make the defense's opening statement. The lawyer walked slowly over to the jury box. "I very well know, gentlemen," he said softly, "that we have been censured, and in no measured terms, by those who wish to be considered as good citizens, and worthy, and honest, and law-abiding men, for appearing at all in defending the prisoner at the bar." He paused for a moment to let his words sink in. "But not so have we learned our duty," he continued. "I do most conscientiously believe, gentlemen, that the conviction of this man, if man he can yet be called, by reason of public clamor . . . would be a greater calamity to our common country than the death of those who have fallen by his insane hand."

As Seward proceeded to present his defense, the town's hatred of its only state-wide celebrity reached a new degree of intensity. He couldn't walk the few hundred yards from his South Street house to his office in the Exchange Building without being insulted by a score of people who had once been his friends and clients. Every morning found a spate of threatening or vilifying letters tacked to his front door. As Charles Francis Adams later observed, "At this juncture, had William H. Seward been found anywhere at night alone and unprotected . . . his body would probably have been discovered in the morning hanging from the nearest tree."

The defense's strategy was the same as it had been during the sanity hearing. It was to call as many people as possible who had known the defendant before he went to jail in 1840 for stealing Mrs. Godfrey's mare. If Seward was to convince Foreman Preston and his eleven colleagues that Freeman had been insane at the time of the murders, he would have to prove to them that five years in Auburn had changed his client from "a bright, active boy" to a strange, withdrawn man who was "idiotic and crazy." Accordingly, he and Wright had scoured the village to find an even dozen Auburnians who were willing to stand up and be counted.

John De Puy, who had married Freeman's sister, told the jury that Jane Brown and Sidney Freeman, the prisoner's aunt and uncle, "were both crazy." He thought that Bill, who had been "an active, smart boy," before going to prison, "didn't appear to be in his right mind" after his release.

Q. Why did you think he wasn't in his right mind?
A. He appeared stupid and took no notice of any thing. He acted so very strange that we talked about it at the house.

Sally Freeman, the defendant's mother, was in tears as she attempted to explain the changes she had noticed in her son. "When he came to see me," she sobbed, "he would ask how I did, and then sit down and laugh; what he laughed at was more than I could tell. He laughed as he does now. There was no reason why he should laugh. He was laughing to himself."

David Winner, a tall, lanky Negro who conceded that he could not read nor write because "my master didn't give me no learning," had known Freeman for sixteen years. "When this boy was twelve or thirteen years old," he said, "he was a pretty sprightly lad, sensible and very lively." He had seen him a week after his release from prison, and he had hardly recognized him.

Q. How did he look to you then?
A. He then appeared to be a foolish man. He was sitting down in a chair, sniveling, snickering and laughing, and having a kind of simple look.

During Wyatt's trial, Winner had shared a room with Freeman at Mrs. Willard's boardinghouse. "I stayed there three nights and slept with William in the same bed. At night, he got up and talked to himself. I couldn't understand what he said. He appeared to be foolish." One day, he had given his roommate a dollar and asked him to pick up a pound of tea, some sugar and a steak at the corner grocery store. Freeman had returned with a dollar's worth of beef steak. "When I asked him what he did that for," Winner said, "he said nothing, but laughed at me."

In 1832, the defendant had lived at the home of Ethan A. Warden, the president of the Village of Auburn. "We considered him a bright, active boy," he recalled. Warden had not seen him again until he visited him in state prison shortly before his release.

Q. How did he look to you at that time?
A. He appeared changed, the difference was so peculiar I don't know as I can describe it.

When he had interviewed Freeman in the county jail after the murders, he had become convinced that he was insane. "I don't think he is of sound mind," he concluded. "I am of the opinion he is deranged."

Ira Curtis, who was a member of Reverend Austin's church, had once employed the defendant as a kitchen helper. He remembered that Freeman had been "a dull, morose, stubborn boy . . . a singular boy." He had been such a poor worker that Curtis had fired him a week later. In June, at Austin's request, he had accompanied the minister to the county jail where both men had attempted to interview the prisoner.

Q. Are you certain that he was not feigning insanity?
A. I don't believe it is in the power of all in this room to teach him to carry on a piece of deception for fifteen minutes. He is incapable of understanding. He is part fool, bordering on idiocy.

Most of Auburn had, it seemed, visited Freeman's cell

after his capture. Warren T. Worden, a local attorney, had dropped in "for the purpose of satisfying myself whether he had mind enough to be held legally responsible for his acts." What he had seen had convinced him that the Negro was not "a responsible being."

Q. What led you to believe that he was insane?
A. His whole appearance and behaviour.

John R. Hopkins had stopped by because "I had understood that he was a man of very weak intellect, and was anxious to ascertain how that was from personal inspection." He had come away with the feeling that Freeman was "little above the brute." Reverend Austin considered him "incapable of discriminating between right and wrong."

In trying to defend herself, Mrs. Wyckoff had slashed her attacker's right wrist with a butcher knife. On March 16, Dr. Blanchard Fosgate was called to the county jail to dress the wound. The cut had been a deep one, severing the tendons "down to the radial artery." From his visits to Freeman's cell, the physician had noticed that "there were persons continually coming to the grating and calling him names." In fact, the crowd often became so huge that it blocked off most of the outside light, making it difficult for him to change the bandages on his patient's wrist. Despite the severity of his wound and the heavy shackles on his feet, Freeman had never complained to him of pain or discomfort.

"I look upon him as a person who is sinking into idiocy," the witness told Seward. "I think he does not comprehend the idea of right and wrong—that he has no moral sense of accountability." Such a man, he continued, would be unable to see any difference between killing a human being and wringing a chicken's neck.

Q. On what do you base your opinion?
A. My reasons for this opinion are his insensibility to pain, his never inquiring relative to the prospect of his hand

recovering, his irresistible propensity to laugh, his indifference to remorse or fear, and his indifference to sympathy.

Fosgate was the first of seven medical men called by the
defense to support Seward's insanity theory. Dr. Lansingh
Briggs adhered to his earlier testimony that, at the time of
the murders, Freeman was suffering from "an insane delusion." Dr. Charles Van Epps shared this opinion. "I think
that he thinks that he has a right to kill people in satisfaction
of his claim that he ought to have pay for the time that he
was in prison, and that is a delusion," he said. Dr. Bingham
was back to elaborate on his conclusion that the defendant
was incurably insane. "At any stage of this remarkable case,
had it been submitted to me, I should have admitted him
into the asylum as a patient, and should have assured those
who brought him that his case was incurable."

As Dr. John McCall saw it, Freeman "undoubtedly acted
under an irresistible influence, or delusion, when he committed the offense, for which he ought not to be held responsible." Prof. Coventry of Geneva Medical College had no
doubt of the defendant's dementia. "I cannot conceive it possible," he emphasized, "that a sane man would go forth and
commit such a butchery without any reason whatever."

Dr. Thomas Hun of Albany Medical College, who had not
testified at the first trial, had made the long trip from the
state capital at Seward's insistence. When he announced that
he had not examined Freeman until July 15, Van Buren
leaped to his feet with an objection. Since one jury had
already found the defendant sane as of July 6, he couldn't
see what purpose Dr. Hun's testimony would serve. Whiting
didn't quite agree. "The witness may give his opinion as to
the sanity or insanity of the prisoner," he ruled, "upon facts
within his knowledge, before the sixth of July, instant, or
from the personal appearance of the prisoner; but not from

his conversation with him since the sixth of July, nor from the testimony in the cause."

Hun, who spoke in slow, deliberate terms, stated that, from Freeman's appearance, he would "suspect him to be insane." He based his conclusion on "the idiotic expression" on the Negro's face. "If on the twelfth day of March, he appeared as he does now," he said gravely, "I would suspect him of being insane then." Dr. James McNaughton, one of Hun's colleagues at the Albany Medical College and New York's Surgeon General, agreed with his predecessor that Freeman was insane. "If he looked as he does now on the twelfth of March, I should have given the same opinion of him then that I do now."

Q. Does he not now look as if he were sane?
A. If I were to judge from his looks alone, I would say he never was particularly sane. Nature has written that pretty clearly on his countenance.

McNaughton's full-throated Scottish burr was still reverberating around the courtroom when Seward turned to the bench. "The defense rests, your Honor," he said in a tired voice.

Van Buren had a bevy of rebuttal witnesses. Nathaniel Lynch, who claimed that Freeman had lived with him "some sixteen years ago," thought that he had not changed greatly since his release from prison. "When I saw him in jail," he testified, "I discovered no change in him." On cross-examination, Seward succeeded in damaging his credibility by drawing from him the admission that the farmer had been forced to resign from the First Presbyterian Church for "having had unlawful intercourse with one Catherine Ramsay."

Aaron Deman, Freeman's uncle by marriage, also had noticed no significant change in him. As he recalled it, his nephew "always had that smile and that down look." David Mills, an Auburn guard, shared Deman's opinion. "I have noticed his appearance in court here," he told Van Buren. "That was always the same. There was always a smile on his countenance. He would smile when there was no occasion for it." Israel Ward, a former employer, had a "distinct recollection" of the defendant before he was sentenced to prison. "I cannot see any difference in him now," he assured the Attorney General.

Van Buren had a seemingly inexhaustible supply of witnesses who were ready to swear that the man on trial had not changed in prison. Attorney Daniel Andrus had represented Freeman when the latter had been accused of stealing Mrs. Godfrey's horse.

Q. Is he in any manner changed from what he was then?
A. I can see no difference in him, only in his growth and deafness.

Walter J. Simpson, who had known the prisoner since boyhood, thought that "he always had very much the same appearance that he has now." Lewis Markham, an acquaintance of some twenty years' standing, had "a very distinct recollection of the smile, which was the same as I see now."

After a dozen more Auburnians had divested themselves of similar observations, Van Buren began to call on his medical reserves. Dr. Dimon reappeared to repeat his testimony at the preliminary hearing that, although he considered Freeman "ignorant and depraved," he had found "nothing about him indicating insanity." He was followed by Dr. Sylvester Willard, who, on the basis of "six or eight" examinations of the defendant, stated unequivocally that "I did not find evidence sufficient to make me think him insane." Dr. Bigelow returned briefly to assert to the now thoroughly confused jury that "I am satisfied that the prisoner is an ignorant, dull, stupid, morose and degraded Negro, but not insane."

Dr. Thomas Spencer of Geneva Medical College was Van Buren's trump card. After twelve interviews with Freeman,

Spencer had "no reasonable doubt" of his sanity. With the assistance of a chart listing thirty-six self-styled "Faculties of the Mind," the fast-talking physician took more than six hours to elaborate the reasons for his conclusion. All of the faculties of the Negro's mind, he asserted, were "healthful" and the murders were based, not on an insane delusion, but on the "absurd conclusion of a sound mind."

Q. Is there anything in the personal appearance of this prisoner indicating insanity?

A. His smile at first induced me to believe him insane. But I have seen other people who were addicted to that singular habit. I have investigated the matter thoroughly and have come to the conclusion that there is nothing in his personal appearance that necessarily indicates insanity.

Van Buren fairly glowed as he turned to the defense table. "You may examine," he said triumphantly.

Seward found Dr. Spencer an agile witness. Not only did the physician refuse to hedge on his opinion that Freeman was not insane, but he insisted that, with the exception of his hearing, the defendant's senses were "natural."

Q. Did you ever know a maniac or demented person who manifested less imagination?

A. I cannot call up any particular case.

Q. Is not his surprisingly low and feeble?

A. It is not below that of many sane men. Like many of his other faculties, it is dull, as it is apt to be in uneducated men.

Spencer was certain that, if the jurors understood his chart, they would come to the same conclusion.

In his direct examination, the witness stated proudly that he had examined "the asylums in London and Paris." Seward, who had given up any hopes of a major breakthrough in Spencer's testimony, decided to attack these vaunted trips to European hospitals.

Q. What hospital of the insane did you visit in London, and who had charge of it?

A. I visited the large hospital near Charing Cross. I don't recollect the superintendent's name.

Q. How long were you there?

A. I don't recollect of being there more than one day.

As for those in the French capital, he couldn't remember the names of the institutions he had visited or even on which side of the Seine they had been located.

Seward began his summation on the morning of July 22. For more than seven hours, he urged his fellow villagers not to hang an insane man. "I speak with all sincerity and earnestness," he said in his low, somewhat harsh voice. "Not because I expect my opinion to have weight, but I would disarm the injurious impression that I am speaking merely as a lawyer for a client. I am not the prisoner's lawyer. I am indeed a volunteer in his behalf; but society and mankind have the deepest interests at stake. I am the lawyer for society, for mankind; shocked, beyond the power of expression at the scene I have witnessed here of trying a maniac as a malefactor."

As the long day wore on, he treated his listeners to a biting condemnation of the "contemptible compromise verdict" returned by the first jury, an eloquent plea for racial tolerance, a learned discourse on the causes and effects of insanity, and a comprehensive analysis of the testimony. After disposing of most of Van Buren's witnesses, he turned his fire on Dr. Spencer. "The doctor pronounces the prisoner sane," he said in his low monotone, "because he has the chief intellectual faculties, sensation, conception, attention, imagination and association." He walked over to the counsel table and picked up a hand-carved pine spoon. "Now here is a delicate piece of wooden cutlery, fabricated by an inmate of the lunatic asylum at Utica, who was acquitted of murder on the ground of insanity. He who fabricated it evinced in the manufacture,

conception, perception, memory, comparison, attention, adap
tion, co-ordination, kindness, gratitude, mechanical skill,
invention and pride. It is well for him that Dr. Spencer did
not testify on his trial."

The harvest moon was well up in the sky when an
exhausted Seward drew to a close. He looked over at John
Van Nest's elderly parents who, with the dead man's two
surviving children, were sitting behind the rail. "Although
we may send this maniac to the scaffold," he said slowly, "it
will not recall to life the manly form of Van Nest, nor restore
to life and grace and beauty the murdered mother, nor call
back the infant boy from the arms of his Saviour. Such a verdict can do no good to the living and carry no joy to the dead."
He paused a moment to wipe his glasses with a large pocket
handkerchief. "If your judgment shall be swayed at all by
sympathies so wrong, although so natural, you will find the
saddest hour of your life to be that in which you will look
down upon the grave of your victim, and 'mourn with com-
punctious sorrow' that you should have done great injustice to
the 'poor handful of earth that will lie mouldering before
you.' "

Van Buren took over the next morning. Impeccably dressed
in a dark blue suit, he spent the first part of his closing
remarks flattering his adversary. "The learned gentleman
who has just addressed you," he told the jury, "has not only
brought to the task his usually great ability, but throughout
the trial . . . has seemed to believe, and I fear has impressed
the jury with the belief that his own character and position,
rather than those of the prisoner, are involved in your decision." But William Freeman and not William Seward was
the man on trial. There was only one issue to be decided—
the defendant's sanity on March 12, 1846—and he hoped that
Foreman Preston and his eleven disciples would keep that
clearly in mind.

As far as he was concerned, the law was quite explicit.

Unless the evidence showed that Freeman couldn't tell the difference between right and wrong or that he was suffering from some mental illness that made it impossible for him to resist killing the Van Nests, the jury would have to bring in a verdict of guilty of murder in the first degree. There wasn't a shadow of doubt in his own mind that the Negro "knew he was doing wrong, and had full control over his actions." The latter, a convicted thief with a past history of drunkenness and a vicious temper, had simply decided to revenge himself on the Van Nests because, for some strange reason, he believed that they had been responsible for putting him in prison.

None of the doctors whom Seward had put on the stand had examined Freeman until long after the murders. Dr. Brigham, for example, had not seen him until almost three months after his arrest. But even if the diagnoses of Brigham and the other medical experts who shared his opinion were accepted at face value, they only added up to the fact that Freeman was a born criminal, but not a lunatic. However, in the last analysis, it was up to the twelve men in the jury box, not to "a squadron of doctors," to decide this case. "Criminal responsibility," Van Buren reminded the panel, "is a question of law, not of medicine."

It was four P.M. on July 23 when the Attorney General finished. Judge Whiting's charge was mercifully short. "To establish the plea of insanity," he stated, "it must be clearly proved that the party is laboring under such of defect of reason, from disease of the mind, as not to know the nature of the act he was doing, or, if he did know it, that he did not know he was doing what was wrong."

The courtroom clock read a few minutes shy of five P.M. when Sheriff Pettibone escorted the jury to the little room where it was to conduct its deliberations. Less than an hour later, Foreman Preston led his colleagues back to the jury box. "Mr. Foreman, have you reached a verdict?" Whiting asked. "We have, your Honor," Preston replied. "We find the prisoner at the bar guilty of the crime wherewith he stands charged in the indictment."

Court reconvened the next morning at 6:30 A.M. Despite the earliness of the hour, the courtroom was jammed with villagers who had been waiting since dawn for the formalities to begin. Those who had not been able to crowd into the building pressed against every available door and window in the hopes of hearing what went on inside. When Seward strolled up the courthouse's front walk, he was greeted by the same stony silence that had characterized his public appearances since the beginning of the trial. A handful of boos followed him into the building.

Before imposing sentence, Whiting asked the defendant whether he had anything to say. Freeman did not appear to hear the question. When the judge repeated it, the Negro, in a nervous, high-pitched voice, replied, "No, sir." Whiting adjusted his glasses and began to read from a sheaf of papers on the bench in front of him. "The judgment of the law is," he recited in a sonorous tone, "that the prisoner at the bar, William Freeman, be taken from this place to the place from whence he came, there to remain until Friday, the eighteenth day of September next, and, that on that day, between the hours of one and four in the afternoon, he be taken from thence to the place of execution appointed by law, and there be hung by the neck until he shall be dead."

The trial was over. That evening, Seward sat down in his study and wrote his old friend, Thurlow Weed. "For the first time in two months," he said, "I lay aside the papers in my murder trials, and look out upon the world, behind, around and before me. I rise from these fruitless labors, exhausted in mind and in body, covered with public reproach, stunned with protests. It remains to be seen whether I shall be able to retrieve any of these losses. If I know the line of personal, or that of professional duty, I have adhered to it faithfully and unflinchingly."

But there was more to come. Two days after Freeman's sentence, Seward applied to the Governor and the Supreme Court for a stay of execution so that he would have time to prepare an appeal. When the stay was granted, he submitted a writ of error containing twenty-seven errors committed by the trial court, the most important of which was that the verdict of the first jury on the question of Freeman's sanity was "not express and certain . . . and did not cover the whole issue." After the Whigs had gone down to defeat in the November elections, a defeat which was largely attributed to Seward's defense of Freeman, the ex-Governor and Van Buren argued the appeal before a three-judge bench of the Supreme Court in Rochester.

As the long Auburn winter passed slowly, Seward became increasingly despondent. "All our work has been in vain," he repeatedly told his patient partners. However, on February 11, 1847, Justice Beardsley of the Supreme Court announced that the conviction had been set aside and a new trial ordered. He and his two colleagues decided that the verdict of the preliminary jury that Freeman was "sufficiently sane in mind and memory to distinguish between right and wrong" was defective. "They should have been required to pass directly on the question of insanity," he said, "and should not have been allowed to evade it by an argumentative verdict of any sort."

There was never to be a second trial. Early on the morning of August 21, the warden of the Cayuga County Jail was informed that Freeman had died of tuberculosis during the night. A few hours later, Dr. Dimon removed the dead man's brain and packed it in ice. Later that evening, Doctors Brigham and McCall returned to Auburn to make a thorough examination of the brain. In the presence of McCall and five other physicians, Brigham dissected the organ.

As soon as each doctor had examined its various portions, they signed a unanimous report in which they agreed that "this organ presented the appearance of chronic disease." Three weeks later, Brigham wrote to an Auburn attorney that he had "very rarely found so extensive disease of the brain in those who have died after long continued insanity, as we found in this instance; and I believe there are few cases of chronic insanity recorded in books, in which were noticed more evident marks of disease."

The physicians' report ended the furor against Seward. In early 1847, he was able to write that "less than a year has passed since no execrations were too severe for the people who now judge favorably of my conduct, without any regard to the question whether my client deserved death or not." However, it remained for Dr. Fosgate to write the most appropriate epitaph to the tragic episode. In the April, 1848, issue of the *American Quarterly Retrospect of American and Foreign Practical Medicine and Surgery,* he stated: "How much the cause of justice and philosophy is indebted to the unwearied perseverance of the eminent advocate who withstood the tide of popular indignation in conducting the prisoner's defense, is left for other hands to register; but true it is, that over prejudice and error, science has gloriously triumphed."

The Whigs, who had been so vociferous in their condemnation of Seward for his defense of Freeman, did a complete about-face after they unexpectedly carried New York in the election of 1848. On February sixth of the following year, the ex-Governor was named as the state's junior United States Senator. The years that followed were full ones for the energetic redhead.

In 1855, he left the rapidly disintegrating Whigs and followed Thurlow Weed into the new Republican Party. Despite the opposition of the latter's Know-Nothing wing, he was promptly re-elected to the Senate, where he served until

March 5, 1861, when he accepted the newly inaugurated Lincoln's invitation to join the Cabinet as Secretary of State. When he resigned at the end of Johnson's administration, he embarked on a series of trips that took him to most of the countries of the world. He died in Auburn on October 10, 1872, while dictating one of his travel journals to his adopted daughter.

In the fall of 1848, Seward met Lincoln for the first time in Boston, where both men were campaigning for Taylor's election to the Presidency. After listening to a biting anti-slavery speech by the ex-Governor, Lincoln said to him, "I reckon you're right. We have got to deal with this slavery question, and got to give much more attention to it hereafter than we have been doing." Seward took his advice seriously. In the years that followed, he constantly reminded his fellow citizens that there was a "higher law" than the Constitution, under which all men were entitled to freedom. But he never expressed himself better than he did toward the end of his summation in the Freeman case when, tired and hoarse, he had urged his twelve jurors to remember that the white man had a solemn obligation to "lift up the Negro race from the debasement into which he had plunged it."

This thought might have been very much in his mind on New Year's Day of 1863 as he trudged through the mud of Pennsylvania Avenue to bring the Emancipation Proclamation to the White House for the President's signature. "I do order and declare," the historic document read, "that all persons held as slaves . . . are and henceforth shall be free." Seward had already decided this for himself when, seventeen years earlier, he had put his career on the line for a demented Negro whose civil rights were in grave danger of being violated by a bitter and frightened community.

# Reverdy Johnson

Some measure of the feeling against those responsible for the Good Friday assassination of Abraham Lincoln and the near-fatal stabbing of Secretary of State Seward is indicated by the fact that rewards of more than two hundred thousand dollars were immediately offered for the capture of John Wilkes Booth and two of his suspected confederates. Three days after the President's death, the *New York Herald*, one of the staunchest supporters of his mild reconstruction program, proclaimed that "the lives of the wretched assassin or assassins in this horrid business will not meet the requirements of justice, and that justice should now take its course against treason and traitors wherever found." In Chicago, Cleveland and San Francisco, to name a few, the police were hard pressed to prevent the lynching of indiscreet souls who had expressed some degree of satisfaction over the bloody events of April 14.

The Easter Sunday sermons were scarcely less restrained than that day's edition of the *Herald* which placed the responsibility for Lincoln's death squarely on "the fiendish and malignant spirit developed and fostered by the rebel press . . ." Boston's Reverend Edwin B. Webb castigated the "indecent leniency" shown to the Confederate leaders whose "hell-born spirit . . . dastardly takes the life of our beloved President." Reverend John E. Todd recommended that Jefferson Davis and his colleagues "be hunted down like wild beasts, and sent to prison and the gallows." Calling for the public hanging of all traitors, Reverend W. S. Studley urged the new President to "chastise them with scorpions."

On April 21, after lying in state in the White House's East Room for three days, Lincoln's body was placed on a train for the start of a sorrowful journey that would take it to most of the larger cities of the North before it reached its final destination, Springfield's Oak Ridge Cemetery. As the funeral cortège wended its way westward, preparations were underway to try seven men and one woman accused of conspiring to murder the President. As Secretary of War Edwin M. Stanton put it, in one of his reward circulars, the defendants were "subject to trial before a Military Commission and the punishment of DEATH."

With the country crying for swift and terrible vengeance, there were few lawyers in Washington, or anywhere else for that matter, who were willing to stand up for Stanton's captives. In fact, it was not until the trial's third day that each defendant, with some sharing, was represented by counsel. Mrs. John H. Surratt, the sole female prisoner, was fortunate in that she was able to interest three attorneys in her cause. Two of them were young men who had comparatively little to lose by defending her. But the third—Reverdy Johnson— was one of the country's finest lawyers and a United States Senator from Maryland, to boot.

Johnson had volunteered his services because, as he explained, Mrs. Surratt was an ex-Marylander who had urgent need of an experienced legal hand. But he was far too intelligent a man to imagine that this was his only reason for injecting himself into a case which could hardly increase his popularity. With Sumner, Stevens and the other radical Republicans in Congress closing ranks in anticipation of their ability to convince the new President that a harsh peace was what the beaten South deserved, the Senator from Maryland was not only willing to risk his professional future but prepared as well to sacrifice any chance he might have had to convince his colleagues that Lincoln's moderate reconstruction plans should be adopted. For such stakes, there had to be more than one woman's need.

There was. Although Johnson would have been the last to put it in these terms, his real client was the Constitution itself. "There is a responsibility," he later was to tell the Military Commission, "that every gentleman, be he soldier or citizen, will constantly hold before him, and make him ponder—responsibility to the Constitution and laws of his country . . ." And if the President could, at his discretion, deprive Americans of their right to a public trial by jury, then the Constitution was nothing but "a dead letter." Convinced that the rights and liberties won at Concord, Lexington, Saratoga and Yorktown were intended to survive all the crises of government, he refused, at any cost to himself, to sit silently by as his countrymen proceeded to scrap them.

"All history tells us," he liked to say, "that war, at times, maddens the people, frenzies government and makes both regardless of constitutional limitations of power. Individual safety, at such periods, is more in peril than at any other. The safety which liberty needs, and without which it sickens and dies, is that which law, and not mere unlicensed human will, affords. Nature, without law, would be chaos; government, without law, anarchy or despotism. Against both these last, in war and in peace, the Constitution happily protects us." For such a principle, he was more than willing to chance his political future, his prestige, his legal career and, if necessary, his life itself.

## Reverdy Johnson and the trial of Mary
## Eugenia Surratt, May 10 to June 30, 1865

SHORTLY AFTER eight o'clock on the morning of Palm Sunday, April 9, 1865, Robert E. Lee sat down at a field table
and wrote a brief note to General Grant, requesting an interview "with reference to the surrender of this army." That
afternoon, at the McLean farmhouse on the edge of Appomattox village, the fifty-eight-year-old Lee turned over the
Army of Northern Virginia to its self-conscious conqueror.
The brief surrender document was written out in pencil by
Grant at a table in the McLean living room and corrected
by Lee who, resplendent in dress uniform, sat across the room
from the somewhat disheveled Union commander. At 3:45
P.M., the Confederate general signed his acceptance of Grant's
terms and went out to explain to his incredulous troops what
he had done.

Even though Joe Johnston and Kirby Smith were still at
large in the deep South, the Civil War was all but over. Two
days after Appomattox, Grant and his wife arrived in Washington where the general was promptly lionized by a city
gone wild after more than four nerve-wracking years of being
a front line capital. In honor of the couple, Mrs. Lincoln
had done her part by inviting them to a theatre party at
Ford's Opera House on the evening of Good Friday, April
14. *Our American Cousin,* a new comedy with Laura Keene,
had been playing to enthusiastic audiences throughout the
North and, although the President wasn't particularly over-
joyed at the prospect of sitting through a late evening play,
he knew better than to obstruct his wife's plans. However, at

the last moment, the Grants begged off, primarily because the general had little stomach for what he disdainfully termed "show business."

At nine o'clock on Good Friday evening, coachman Francis Burns stopped the White House carriage in front of Ford's, between E and F on Tenth Street. Outside of the Lincolns, his only other passengers were Major Henry Reed Rathbone and Clara Harris, an engaged couple, who were filling in for the Grants. When the quartet entered the Presidential box, Major Rathbone and Miss Harris took the two seats nearest the stage with their hosts sitting behind them. Lincoln sprawled in a haircloth rocking chair directly in front of a door that opened on a narrow hallway. Sometime during the afternoon, a small hole had been bored in the door, through which it was possible to observe the box's occupants from the corridor.

Shortly after the Lincoln party had entered the box, John F. Parker, a perennially thirsty patrolman who had been assigned by the Metropolitan Police to guard the President, decided to leave his post in the hallway and look for a nearby bar. At 10:15, just as Harry Hawk, the play's leading man, was referring to Mrs. Mountchessington as "you sockdologizing old mantrap," actor John Wilkes Booth opened the now unguarded door and put a bullet into the head of the dozing man in the rocker. The rest was for the chroniclers—the leap to the stage, the broken shinbone, the mad dash across the Navy Yard Bridge, the frenzied manhunt through the woods and swamps of Northern Virginia, the end of the trail in a burning barn on Garrett's farm, just south of Port Royal.

The self-styled avenger, who believed that "God . . . made me the instrument of his punishment," was destined to die just before sunrise on April 26 on the front porch of a Virginia tobacco farm. The cause of death—a bullet wound in the neck. Whether Booth shot himself, as Colonel Everton Conger, the leader of the cavalry patrol which had run him to earth, believed, or was killed by fanatical Sergeant Boston Corbett, who claimed that God had been looking over his shoulder when he squeezed the trigger, didn't change the essential fact that the assassin was as dead as he was ever going to be. The troopers who searched his body found a small diary and the daguerreotypes of five women in his pockets.

A few minutes after Booth's one-shot derringer had earned him a sizable place in the history books, a wild-eyed young man on a bay horse pulled up in front of Secretary of State William H. Seward's mansion on Lafayette Square. Pretending to be a messenger sent by Seward's physician, he broke into the Secretary's bedroom, where he stabbed him three times. Only a steel frame which the victim had been wearing to support a fractured jaw suffered in a carriage accident nine days earlier saved him from death. The intruder then fought his way out of the house, seriously wounding four other people in the process, and rode pell-mell toward the east.

Meanwhile, four Pennsylvania artillerymen carried the President's unconscious form across Tenth Street to William Peterson's house. There he was placed on a walnut cot in the first-floor bedroom of William Clark, one of Peterson's boarders. He lingered during the night, but it was soon obvious to the six physicians in the room, who could do little more than remove the pressure-causing blood clots that continuously formed at the entrance to the wound, that their patient would never see another day. By dawn, his breath had become stertorous and labored and, at 7:22 A.M., Surgeon General Joseph K. Barnes recorded the last heartbeat. "Now," Secretary of War Stanton was supposed to have said as he closed the dead man's eyes, "he belongs to the ages."

Some four hours earlier, a Metropolitan Police squad, headed by a detective named John Clarvoe, had arrived at a small boardinghouse at 541 H. Street, which was owned by forty-eight-year-old Mary Eugenia Surratt, a widow who had come to Washington from Surrattsville, Maryland, in the fall of 1864. They were looking for Mrs. Surratt's son, John, who, one of Clarvoe's men told her, had just murdered Secretary Seward. When Mrs. Surratt informed them that John had left for Canada when Richmond fell on April 3, the squad searched the eight-room brick building from cellar to attic. After ordering Louis J. Weichmann, one of Mrs. Surratt's boarders, to report to headquarters the next morning, the policemen left the house.

As soon as Lincoln died, Stanton, to whom one cause was as good as another, so long as he remained in command, announced that he would not rest until he had found and prosecuted everybody who had anything to do with what his reward circulars referred to as "the stain of innocent blood." Booth and David E. Herold, a slow-witted youth, whose only redeeming feature was his devotion to the actor, had been identified as soon as they fled across the Navy Yard Bridge, minutes after the murder. Herold had been captured by Colonel Conger's cavalry patrol, just before it set fire to the barn in which the two men had been hiding.

By that time, Stanton had rounded up seven other persons whom he accused of conspiring to kill the President. There was Lewis Payne,* a Confederate deserter and the son of a Florida minister, who had created the havoc at the Seward house. Payne and George A. Atzerodt, a carriagemaker from Port Tobacco, had both boarded at Mrs. Surratt's prior to the assassination. Atzerodt, who, with Herold's help, was supposed to kill Vice-President Andrew Johnson at the Kirkwood House, had lost his nerve and spent the night of April 14 wandering aimlessly around the streets of Washington. He was finally captured on April 20 at his cousin's farm in nearby Germantown. Payne was picked up when he showed up at the H Street boardinghouse at midnight on April 17,

* His real name was Lewis Thornton Powell; he had adopted the alias after his desertion.

with his head wrapped in a bloody shirtsleeve, just as Major H. W. Smith was in the process of arresting Mrs. Surratt.

Edward Spangler, the cantankerous stage carpenter at Ford's, had held Booth's horse while the actor was about his murderous business in the President's box. Samuel Arnold and Michael O'Laughlin, both of whom had known Booth since childhood, had been persuaded by him to help out in an 1864 scheme to abduct Lincoln and hold him a hostage until the North came to terms with the Confederacy. After almost a year of fruitless discussions with Booth about ways and means, both men had withdrawn from the project. On the night of the President's murder, O'Laughlin had been on a drinking bout in Washington with three friends while Arnold was working for a sutler at Fortress Monroe near Baltimore. Lastly, there was Dr. Samuel A. Mudd, the Maryland physician who had set the murderer's broken leg the morning after the shooting.

With his eight captives held incommunicado in the brigs of some gunboats moored near the Navy Yard, Stanton had everybody he wanted. All that remained was the selection of a court. The Secretary of War was determined not to let his prizes enjoy the benefits of a civil trial, and urged the new President to appoint a military commission to try them. Johnson agreed and, on May 1, named a commission composed of seven generals and two colonels "for the trial of David E. Herold, George A. Atzerodt, Lewis Payne, Michael O'Laughlin, Edward Spangler, Samuel Arnold, Mary E. Surratt, Samuel A. Mudd . . . implicated in the murder of the late President, Abraham Lincoln, and the attempted assassination of William H. Seward, Secretary of State, and in an alleged conspiracy to assassinate other officers of the Federal Government at Washington City." The main charge—"maliciously, unlawfully, and traitorously murdering the said Abraham Lincoln, then President of the United States and Commander-in-Chief of the Army and Navy of the United States."

As far as Mrs. Surratt was concerned, Brigadier General Joseph Holt, the Judge Advocate General, didn't bother to mince words. She did, he said, "receive, entertain, harbor and conceal, aid and assist, the said John Wilkes Booth, David E. Herold, Lewis Payne, John H. Surratt, Michael O'Laughlin, George A. Atzerodt, Samuel Arnold and their confederates, with the knowledge of the murderous and traitorous conspiracy . . . with intent to aid, abet and assist them in the execution thereof, and in escaping from justice after the murder of the said Abraham Lincoln, as aforesaid." On Wednesday, May 10, Mrs. Surratt and her seven co-defendants pleaded, "Not Guilty."

Their trial, which began officially at ten A.M. that day, was held in a large room on the third floor of the Old Penitentiary. Several days earlier, the defendants had been transferred from their nautical prisons to cells in the same building where they were kept in solitary confinement. Even their guards were forbidden by Stanton to utter a word to them. Shortly after their arrival at the Penitentiary, the male prisoners' heads were encased in heavy canvas sacks which were split in the vicinity of their mouths. Payne's attempted suicide by butting his head against his cell's stone wall had alerted the Secretary of War to the possibility that some of his captives might succeed in beating their brains out before he could properly hang them. When Major General J. F. Hartranft, the Special Provost Marshal assigned to the commission, suggested the hoods, Stanton was quick to order them.

The courtroom itself was a dimly lit rectangular room with only three small windows to illuminate its more than twelve hundred square feet. The prisoners' dock consisted of a railed-off raised platform at the far end of the room. There were two small tables directly in front of the makeshift dock, which had been provided for the defense attorneys. In the middle of the chamber were two long tables, one of which was to be occupied by the members of the commission, with the other reserved for the official reporters. The witness stand was located in dead center between two of the three pillars that supported the room's eleven-foot ceiling. The walls had been freshly whitewashed, and coconut matting had been spread over the stone floor.

As the prisoners filed in, at precisely ten o'clock on the trial's first day, Benn Pitman, the chief court stenographer, and his fellow reporters noticed that all except Mrs. Surratt and Dr. Mudd were wearing ten-inch manacle bars, which prevented them from bringing their hands together. Mudd sported ordinary handcuffs, while the feet of all the male defendants were shackled together with chains. With Atzerodt and the half-mad Payne, Stanton had taken the additional precaution of welding heavy weights to their steel anklets which made it impossible for them to walk without the help of their guards.

Mrs. Surratt looked frightened as she sank into her chair at the far right-hand side of the prisoners' dock. The team of reporters from the *Philadelphia Daily Inquirer,* which must have included a Shakespearian scholar, described her as "a stout buxom widow fitting Falstaff's ideal, fair, fat and forty." Neatly dressed all in black, with her dark hair parted severely in the middle, she seemed out of place seated next to the unkempt, dull-eyed Herold. "We failed to notice," one of the Philadelphia scribes wired to his editor that night, "that cold, cruel gleam in her gray eyes which some of the gentlemen of the press have attributed to her."

Since all the defendants asked for time in which to find lawyers who had enough gumption to represent them, General David Hunter, the luxuriantly mustached president of the commission, gave them twenty-four hours in which to do so. The nine officers spent the rest of the day in thrashing out a stringent set of rules of procedure. With the exception of Sundays, the commission would be in session from ten A.M. to one P.M., recess for a one-hour lunch break, and then continue into the evening. No newspapermen were to be admitted, but the Judge Advocate General was authorized to furnish daily reports of the proceedings to the Associated Press.* The prisoners' attorneys would be required to furnish proof of having taken the loyalty oath, of 1862, which required them to swear that they had never voluntarily borne arms against the United States, or been associated with any hostile "person . . . pretended government, authority, power or constitution."

The next morning, Mrs. Surratt applied for permission, as Pitman recorded it, "to introduce Frederick Aiken, Esq. and John W. Clampitt, Esq. as her counsel, which applications were granted." Dr. Mudd was the only other defendant to have drummed up a lawyer, and Hunter adjourned the commission to the next day "to allow further time for the accused to secure the attendance of counsel." By Friday, Herold, Arnold, Atzerodt, O'Laughlin, Payne and Spangler had managed to find attorneys.

Aiken and Clampitt were two young lawyers who had volunteered their services in Mary Eugenia's behalf. Neither had had much experience in criminal trials, and they were only too happy to welcome Reverdy Johnson, the United States Senator from Maryland, who felt that the least he could do for an old constituent was to help her defend her life. A worthy successor to Daniel Webster as the country's leading constitutional lawyer, the seventy-year-old Johnson was nearing the end of a long and distinguished career. First elected to the Senate in 1845, he had resigned four years later to become Zachary Taylor's Attorney General. He had

* Opposition by the press was so great, however, that, on May 13, Hunter announced that a limited number of reporters would be admitted to all future sessions.

been returned to the upper house in 1862, but did not take his seat for more than a year because Lincoln had sent him to New Orleans to check on complaints against General Benjamin Butler.

Although he had represented the bondsman in the Dred Scott case, he firmly believed that slavery, which he regarded as a local issue, was morally wrong. As hopes for peace began to fade rapidly in the waning months of Buchanan's administration, Johnson had maintained that secession was treason and urged both sides to reach some sort of an amicable solution. When war broke out, he was instrumental in persuading his fellow Marylanders to remain in the Union. However, he had bitterly resented Lincoln's interference in some of his state's local elections and had supported McClellan in the 1864 campaign. But his rancor did not prevent him from representing the Senate as one of the dead President's pall bearers.

A rotund man of medium height, he was, at the time of the conspiracy trial, almost blind. In 1842, he had accidentally shot himself in the left eye and what little sight remained to him had gradually failed over the years. To compensate for his inability to distinguish faces, he had become an expert at recognizing voices and had little difficulty in maneuvering around the many courtrooms in which his portly frame had become a familiar sight. He had a healthy respect for Stanton, with whom he had tangled horns in successfully defending the validity of Cyrus McCormick's reaper patent in 1846.

On Friday, May 12, his youthful co-counsel introduced him to the commission, only to find that one member—Brigadier General T. M. Harris—objected to him because he had publicly questioned the loyalty oath of 1862. On October 7, 1864, Johnson had circulated a letter to his constituents, who were about to vote on a new constitution for the state. It was his opinion that the Maryland Constitutional Convention had exceeded its power by making the oath a condition of voting on the new constitution. "Because the Convention has transcended its power," he had written, "that is no reason why the people should submit. The taking of the oath under such circumstances, argues no willingness to surrender their rights."

The sentiments expressed in this letter, argued Harris, made Johnson unfit to defend Mrs. Surratt because it was obvious that "he did not recognize the moral obligation of an oath designed as a test of loyalty." The Senator was flabbergasted by Harris' objection. First of all, he had not been alone in his opposition to the taking of the loyalty oath. Every lawyer in Maryland had supported his position. Secondly, he had not urged his fellow citizens not to take the oath. "All that the opinion was, was that to take the oath voluntarily was not a craven submission to usurped authority, but was necessary in order to enable the citizen to protect his rights under the then Constitution, and that there was no moral harm in taking an oath which the Convention had no authority to impose."

As far as Mrs. Surratt was concerned, guilty or innocent, she deserved the best defense she could get. "I am here at the instance of that lady," he boomed in his deep oratorical voice, "whom I never saw until yesterday and never heard of, she being a Maryland lady and thinking that I could be of service to her." * He moved closer to the commission's table, rested his hands on its oaken surface, and peered at the blur of blue uniforms in front of him. "I deemed it right, I deemed it due to the character of the profession to which I belong, and which is not inferior to the profession of which you are members, that she should not go undefended. I knew I was to do it voluntarily, without compensation. The

* Mrs. Surratt's request that Johnson represent her was interpreted by the *New York Times* as evidence of her evil character. "That female fiend incarnate who figures as the 'mater familias' of these criminals," it wrote, "evinces her boldness in sending for Hon. Reverdy Johnson, Senator from Maryland, too well known to need any explanation."

law prohibits me from receiving compensation; but if it did not, understanding her condition, I should never have dreamed of refusing upon the ground of her inability to make compensation."

Johnson, whose temper index had been steadily rising as he argued for his admission, was livid as he concluded his remarks. "I have taken the oath in the Senate of the United States; I have taken it in the Circuit Court of the United States; I have taken it in the Supreme Court of the United States . . . and it would be a little singular if one who has a right to appear before the supreme judicial tribunal of the land, and who has a right to appear before one of the legislative departments of the Government . . . whose law creates armies and creates judges and courts-martial, should not have a right to appear before a courts-martial." He paused for a moment to catch his breath. "I have said all that I propose to say," he finished wearily.

By the time Johnson had finished, the shade of Hunter's complexion matched the lawyer's. "Mr. Johnson has made an intimation in regard to holding members of this court personally responsible for their actions," he blurted. The Maryland Senator shook his head emphatically. "I made no such intimation," he protested. "I had no idea of it. I said I was too old to feel such things, even if I would."

"I hoped the day had passed," Hunter replied bitingly, "when freemen of the North care to be bullied and insulted by the bumbling chivalry of the South."

Although the commission voted to permit Johnson to stand up for Mrs. Surratt, it was hardly gracious in doing so. After Harris had grudgingly withdrawn his objection, Hunter announced that the Marylander could appear for the defendant if he still had a mind to. But he wanted it clearly understood that neither he nor his eight associates approved of the Senator's stand on the loyalty oath. Johnson stepped back until he was standing between Clampitt and Aiken.

"I appear, then, as counsel for Mrs. Surratt," he said quietly.

As soon as all the defendants were represented by counsel, they were given permission to withdraw their "Not Guilty" pleas, and attack the commission's jurisdiction. Each prisoner took the position that, since they were all civilians and there were appropriate Washington civil courts available to try them, the military commission did not have any power over them. The Judge Advocate answered this by claiming unequivocally that "this Commission has jurisdiction in the premises." Hunter, who was very much Stanton's man, went through the formality of clearing the courtroom, and then announced that the prisoners' pleas were overruled. After a motion for separate trials had suffered the same fate, all of the defendants then reaffirmed their innocence.

As it put in its case against the eight defendants, the prosecution digressed for hours attempting to prove that Jefferson Davis, who had been captured on the trial's first day, and the other Confederate leaders had been responsible for Lincoln's murder. In fact, Holt and his aides were determined to show that the assassination plot had been tied up with Southern guerrilla warfare in New York and Vermont as well as with the maltreatment of Union prisoners at Andersonville and other rebel prisons. Although the evidence hardly supported their grandiose thesis, they succeeded in creating an illusion that the prisoners in the dock were part of a gigantic plot in which the President's death was only one of many factors.

Late on the afternoon of Saturday, May 13, the provost marshal escorted Lou Weichmann to the witness stand, a raised platform, surrounded on three sides by waist-high rails, that faced the commission's table. The War Department clerk stated that he had first met John Surratt in the fall of 1859 at St. Charles College in Maryland. Because of this friendship, he had moved to the H Street boardinghouse on November 1, 1864. He remembered that his landlady had requested him to visit John Wilkes Booth at the National Hotel twelve days before the President's murder "and say that she wished to see him on 'private business.'" Later that same evening, Booth had come to the house and closeted himself with Mrs. Surratt for more than an hour.

On April 11, Mrs. Surratt had asked her boarder to see whether the actor would lend her his buggy for a trip to Surrattsville, which was some ten miles southeast of the capital. Booth informed Weichmann that he had just sold his vehicle, but gave him ten dollars "that I might hire one." Weichmann had rented a surrey at Howard's Stables and then driven Mrs. Surratt to Surrattsville "for the purpose of seeing Mr. Nothey, who owed her some money." The couple had returned to Washington late that afternoon.

After lunch on Good Friday, Mrs. Surratt had again asked Weichmann to drive her into the country because, she told him, she had received a letter "in regard to that money Mr. Nothey owed her." She had given him a ten-dollar bill with which to hire another rig. The two had reached Lloyd's tavern in Surrattsville at 4:30. "We took with us only two packages; one was a package of papers about her property at Surrattsville; and another package done up in paper, about six inches, I should think, in diameter. It looked to me like perhaps two or three saucers wrapped up. This package was deposited in the bottom of the buggy and taken out by Mrs. Surratt when we arrived at Surrattsville." Lou had headed for the taproom while his passenger went into the parlor of the two-story frame structure. When he had called for her at six o'clock, he noticed that Booth was with her and that the two were deep in conversation.

Before John Surratt left Washington early in April, Booth had been a frequent visitor at 541 H Street. When the actor called, he had always asked for young Surratt or his mother. "Sometimes, when engaged in general conversations, Booth would say, 'John, can you go upstairs and spare me a word?'

They would then go upstairs and engage in private conversation which would sometimes last two or three hours. The same thing would sometimes occur with Mrs. Surratt."

He had first seen Lewis Payne at the boardinghouse early in March. The defendant, who had been introduced to Weichmann as Wood, had arrived with no luggage and remained overnight. The next morning, Payne had taken the early train to Baltimore. He had returned three weeks later, this time dressed as a Baptist preacher, and said that he had just finished a seven-day term in a Baltimore prison but that the experience had taught him a lesson. "He had taken the oath of allegiance, and was now going to become a good and loyal citizen."

From the first time he saw Payne, he was convinced that the latter was up to no good. One day, he had found a black false mustache "of medium size" on the table in his room. "When I found it, I thought it rather queer that a Baptist preacher should use a mustache. I took it and locked it up because I did not care to have a false mustache lying round on my table." Later, he had entertained his fellow clerks in the office of the Commissary General of Prisoners with "a pair of spectacles and the mustache."

One evening, he had returned to the house to find Payne and Johnny Surratt "playing with bowie knives" in his room. He had also noticed two Navy revolvers and four sets of new spurs on the bed. Just after the assassination, the Metropolitan Police had found one of these spurs in Atzerodt's room at the Kirkwood House. Weichmann had seen Atzerodt, whom the ladies at Mrs. Surratt's called Port Tobacco, "at the house, ten or fifteen times." Like Booth, the carriagemaker had always asked for John Surratt or his mother.

Although Weichmann had never seen Arnold or McLaughlin before, he had met Dr. Mudd walking with Booth on Seventh Street on January 15, 1865. The actor had invited him to join them for a glass of wine in his room at the National. There, Booth and Mudd had had a private conversation in the hallway, a discussion which Weichmann was told had to do with the contemplated purchase of the physician's farm by Booth. "Dr. Mudd apologized to me for his private conversation and stated . . . that Booth wished to purchase his farm, but that he did not care about selling it, as Booth was not willing to give him enough." It was after this meeting that Booth had begun to show up frequently at the boardinghouse.

Herold had been at H Street once. But Weichmann had also seen him at Surrattsville in the summer of 1863. The only other time that he had met him was in March of 1865, when Booth, who was then playing the part of Pescara in *The Apostate*, had given Surratt and Weichmann two complimentary tickets. On the way to the theatre, the two young men had met Atzerodt and Herold, who were also going to the play. After the final curtain, he had seen Atzerodt and Herold in the restaurant adjoining the theatre, "talking very confidentially to Booth." When the Judge Advocate asked him to identify Herold, Weichmann pointed at the defendant. Benn Pitman, using his brother's new shorthand system, noted that Herold "smiled and nodded in recognition."

Senator Johnson took over the brunt of the cross-examination. Weichmann admitted that Mrs. Surratt, whom he had met through her son, was a "member of the Catholic Church and a regular attendant upon its services." In fact, he had usually accompanied her to church on Sunday mornings. Yes, he was on friendly terms with her son, John, who had "never intimated to me . . . that there was a purpose to assassinate the President." The only thing Surratt had told him about Booth was that he hoped to go on the stage with him in Richmond, after the war.

No, there was nothing suspicious about Mrs. Surratt's April 11 visit to Surrattsville. A John Nothey had owed her 479 dollars for more than thirteen years, and she had decided to see him personally about it. She had met Nothey early that afternoon in the parlor of a tavern she had leased to a retired Washington policeman by the name of John M. Lloyd, for fifty dollars a month, just before she had moved to the H Street house in the fall of 1864. Her second visit, three days later, was motivated by a letter she had received from George H. Calvert, Jr., "urging the settlement of the claim of my late father's estate." When her husband had died in 1862, he still owed Calvert Senior part of the purchase price of the Maryland property.

When Johnson sat down, young Clampitt took over. He wanted to know whether Weichmann had heard Booth or Mudd discuss anything subversive when he saw them at the National Hotel in January. The witness had not. As for the ten dollars which Booth had given him to hire a buggy for Mrs. Surratt, "I thought at the time that it was nothing more than an act of friendship. I said to Booth, 'I am come with an order for that buggy that Mrs. Surratt asked you for last evening.' He said, 'I have sold my buggy, but here are ten dollars, and you go and hire one.' " No, he had never told Mary Eugenia about that. A few minutes later, he informed Aiken that he had written a letter for his landlady to Mr. Nothey, threatening him with a law suit if he did not pay what he owed her at once. He remembered that he had once helped her to calculate the interest on "the sum of 479 dollars for thirteen years."

When Weichmann stepped down late in the afternoon, Hunter adjourned for the day. Since the next day,—May fourteenth—was a Sunday, the commission did not reconvene until the fifteenth. The first witness called on Monday was Mrs. Surratt's tenant, John M. Lloyd. He recalled that Herold, Atzerodt and John Surratt had come to his house some five or six weeks before the assassination. They had brought with them "two carbines with ammunition . . . a rope from sixteen to twenty feet in length, and a monkey wrench." Surratt asked him to hide these articles and even showed him a secret hiding place "underneath the joists of the second floor of the main building."

On April 11, he had met Mrs. Surratt on the road at Union-town. "When she first broached the subject to me about the articles at my place, I did not know what she had reference to. Then she came out plainer, and asked me about the 'shooting irons.' . . . Her language was indistinct, as if she wanted to draw my attention to something, so no one else would understand. Finally, she came out bolder with it, and said that they would be wanted soon."

Three days later, when he returned from watching a trial in Marlboro, he had found Mrs. Surratt in his backyard. "She met me by the wood pile as I drove in with some fish and oysters in my buggy. She told me to have those shooting irons ready that night, there would be some parties who would call for them. She gave me something wrapped in a piece of paper which I took upstairs, and found to be a field glass. She told me to get two bottles of whiskey ready, and that these things were to be called for that night."

At midnight, Herold had awakened him and said, "Lloyd, for God's sake, make haste and get those things." The tavern owner immediately went to the place where he had hidden the carbines and gave them to Herold. For some reason, he had not turned over the rope and the monkey wrench. Herold had taken the bottle of whiskey which Lloyd gave him and offered it to a man who was sitting on a light-colored horse in front of the tavern. In the bright moonlight, the tavern keeper had watched this man, who "was a stranger to me," put the bottle to his lips and drink deeply.

The two men had stayed for only five minutes before riding off in the direction of Tee Bee, a hamlet a few miles to the south. Just as they were leaving, the man who was with Herold had said, "I will tell you some news, if you want to hear it. I am pretty certain that we have assassinated the

President and Secretary Seward." As they had ridden off, only Herold had taken a carbine with him. The other man "said he could not take his because his leg was broken."

Whether it was the unseasonably hot weather or a monumental case of stage fright, Lloyd had wilted fast as the long morning wore on. By the time the prosecution let him go, he was on the verge of collapse. As Colonel John A. Bingham, Holt's chief assistant, took him through his paces, the ex-policeman's back country drawl frequently became so low that even the members of the commission, who were sitting directly in front of him, had difficulty in hearing him. Both Aiken and Clampitt, who could barely hear the witness from where they were sitting, were constantly imploring Hunter to instruct him to raise his voice, requests that the president consistently ignored.

On cross-examination, Aiken couldn't shake Lloyd's story. But he did get him to admit that there might have been a witness present at the April 14 conversation with Mrs. Surratt about the "shooting irons."

> Q. Are you positive again that Mrs. Surratt told you at that
>    time that the shooting irons would be called for that
>    night?
> A. I am very positive.
> Q. Was there any other person present during the interview?
> A. Mrs. Offutt, my sister-in-law, was, I believe, in the yard;
>    but whether she heard the conversation or not I do not
>    know.

No, he couldn't remember whether or not he had told "these circumstances" to Mrs. Offutt.

As for the package which Mrs. Surratt had brought to the tavern with her on Tuesday, the eleventh, he had taken it upstairs at once.

> Q. Did you undo it immediately when you got upstairs?
> A. As soon as I got upstairs, I saw what it was.

Q. Did you lay the package down and leave it anywhere before you went upstairs?
A. No, sir.

He was sure that he had told Mrs. Offutt, shortly after Mrs.
Surratt had started back to Washington, "that it was a field
glass she had brought."

He had gone to bed early on Good Friday because "I was
right smart in liquor that afternoon and after night I got
more so." He had been sleeping soundly when Booth and
Herold arrived. As soon as they had ridden off, Lloyd went
back to bed. When he awoke the next morning, his yard was
being picked over by Union soldiers who had traced Booth
and Herold there. He was asked whether he "had seen two
men pass that way in the morning." He told the troopers
that he had not. "That is the only thing I blame myself," he
said remorsefully. "If I had given the information they asked
of me, I should have been perfectly easy regarding it. That
is the only thing I am sorry I did not do." In fact, it was not
until the middle of the next week that he had decided to tell
Captain George Cottingham, who had locked him in Roby's
Post Office in Surrattsville for safekeeping, that Booth and
Herold had been at the tavern at midnight on April fourteenth.

As Lloyd rushed out of the hearing room, obviously destined for the first bar he could find, Holt recalled Weichmann. Outside of some elaboration of his previous testimony
about the strange goings-on at the Surratt boardinghouse, he
contributed nothing further to the case against Mary Eugenia. He conceded that he had not heard the conversation
between his landlady and Lloyd at Uniontown. It seemed
that Mrs. Surratt "leaned sideways in the buggy and whispered, as it were, in Mr. Lloyd's ear." When Aiken asked
him why he hadn't told somebody about the mysterious circumstances at the house on H Street, he insisted that "my

suspicions were not of a fixed or definite character." Besides, when he had tried to tell Captain Gleason of the War Department about some peculiar remarks he had heard Booth utter about kidnaping the President, the officer had "laughed and hooted at the idea."

After Lloyd was brought back briefly to explain that he now wasn't sure where he had taken the package which Mrs. Surratt had brought to the tavern on Friday, April 14, Emma Offutt took the stand. The plump, middle-aged woman had been in the carriage with Lloyd when they had met Mrs. Surratt near Uniontown, three days before the assassination. She had not heard the conversation because her brother-in-law had left the carriage to talk to Mrs. Surratt and "I was some distance off." As far as Good Friday was concerned, she hadn't heard a word that was said between Lloyd and Mary Eugenia in the tavern's backyard. Mrs. Offutt had spoken to Mrs. Surratt shortly after the latter's arrival that afternoon, but she "gave me no charge in reference to her business, only concerning her farm, and she gave me no packages."

Major H. W. Smith had been in charge of the troops who had arrested Mrs. Surratt on the night of April 17. "While we were there, Payne came to the house. I questioned him in regard to his occupation, and what business he had at the house that time of night. He stated that he was a laborer, and had come there to dig a gutter at the request of Mrs. Surratt." Major Smith had asked Mrs. Surratt, who was sitting in the parlor, whether she had hired Payne. She had stepped out into the vestibule and, from a distance of three feet, taken a long look at the man. "Before God, sir," she had told Smith, "I do not know this man, and have never seen him, and I did not hire him to dig a gutter for me."

When Holt showed the witness a brown and white coat he promptly identified it as the coat that Payne had been wearing that April night. Ten minutes later, when William E. Doster, Payne's attorney, asked him whether he was sure that the brown and white coat had been worn by the defendant, he repeated that "I am certain that this is the coat." Seconds after the words had left his mouth, Major Smith was busy eating them. Doster shoved a drab-gray coat under his nose and asked him whether he didn't want to change his testimony. He did. "The coat now shown me is the one worn by Payne on the night of his arrest." It had been very difficult, in the poor light of Mrs. Surratt's vestibule, he said, to tell one coat from another. But now he was certain that "the coat just shown me is the one."

Both Smith and R. C. Morgan, who had been sent to H Street to superintend "the seizing of papers," had found photographs of such Confederate leaders as Beauregard, Jefferson Davis, and Alexander H. Stephens. Lieutenant John W. Dempsey, the officer in charge of the search party, had turned up a rotogravure of John Wilkes Booth hidden behind a small framed lithograph entitled *Morning, Noon and Night* which had been hanging on the wall of Mrs. Surratt's first-floor bedroom. But Captain W. M. Wermerskirch, Smith's executive officer, swore that he had also seen a photograph of Union General George McClellan in the parlor.*

Weichmann had testified that the H Street boardinghouse had been a beehive of activity during March and early April of 1865. On May 22, Holt called Honora Fitzpatrick, one of Mrs. Surratt's more attractive boarders. Miss Fitzpatrick was a very definite young lady. "During the month of March last," she said, "I saw John Wilkes Booth and John H. Surratt there." Payne and Atzerodt had also dropped in, but only once or twice. Early in March, Payne and Surratt had taken her to a performance at Ford's Theatre. "I do not know what box we occupied, but I think it was an upper box. John

* Later, Mrs. Surratt's sixteen-year-old daughter, Anna, testified that the photographs of the Southerners had been given to her by her father. She had purchased the Booth portrait at a Washington store because she was "acquainted with him."

Wilkes Booth came into the box while we were there."

On May 23, the trial's thirteenth day, the Judge Advocate ended his direct case, and Messrs. Johnson, Aiken and Clampitt began their labors on behalf of Mrs. Surratt. Their first witness was George Cottingham, the special officer who had arrested John Lloyd on April 15. For two days, he had urged his prisoner to tell him what he knew about Booth and Herold. Finally, Lloyd had broken down and sobbed, "O, my God, if I was to make a confession, they would murder me!" When Cottingham had asked him who had designs on his life, he was informed that it was "these parties that are in this conspiracy."

Then the dam had burst. The conscience-stricken Lloyd had told Cottingham everything. "He stated to me that Mrs. Surratt had come down to his place on Friday between 4 and 5 o'clock; that she told him to have the firearms ready; that two men would call for them at 12 o'clock . . ." The two men had turned out to be Booth and Herold, who had arrived at midnight and picked up a carbine and some whiskey. As Lloyd unburdened himself to Cottingham, he had cried out, "O, Mrs. Surratt, that vile woman, she has ruined me! I am to be shot! I am to be shot!"

Cottingham had obviously caught the defense by surprise. Aiken had interviewed him in the bar of the Metropolitan Hotel on May 20, and, at that time, Cottingham had told the lawyer that Lloyd had not mentioned Mrs. Surratt. But, he insisted, "I had an object in that answer. He wanted to pick facts out of me in the case, but that is not my business; I am an officer, and I did not want to let him know anything either way. I wanted to come here to the Court and state everything that I knew."

> Q. Did I ask you if Mr. Lloyd, in his confession, said anything at all in reference to Mrs. Surratt?
> A. That question you put to me, and I answered; I said, "no."

Q. That Mr. Lloyd did not say so?

A. I did say so. I do not deny that.

Q. Then you gave me to understand, and you are ready now to swear to it, that you told me a lie?

A. Undoubtedly, I told you a lie there; for I thought you had no business to ask me.

Q. No business! As my witness, had I not a right to have the truth from you?

A. I told you you might call me into court; and I state here that I did lie to you; but when put on my oath, I will tell the truth.

The fact that the Commissioners of Prince George's County had offered a two-thousand-dollar reward for information leading to the arrest of "anybody connected with the assassination" had had nothing to do with this fine distinction.

At this juncture, the defense introduced two letters which it claimed would satisfactorily explain Mrs. Surratt's April 14 trip to Surrattsville. The first was signed by George H. Calvert, Jr., and was dated April 12. When Mr. Calvert took the stand, he identified his letter which insisted that Mary Eugenia "pay the balance remaining due on the land purchased by your late husband." The second communication, which had been written by the defendant to John Nothey from Surrattsville on April 14, demanded that he pay off his debt to her "within the next ten days" or she would "settle with Mr. Calvert and bring suit against you immediately." B. F. Gwynn, who had read this note to the illiterate Mr. Nothey, said that he had received it from Mrs. Surratt at the tavern on the afternoon of the fourteenth.

Lloyd had previously testified that he had been "right smart in liquor" on that fateful Good Friday. The defense team saw nothing to be lost by exploiting this admission to the fullest. Gwynn had seen him on the Marlboro road at 4:30 that afternoon and "he had been drinking right smartly." Joe Nott, the bartender at Lloyd's tavern, claimed that his employer "had been drinking a good deal; nearly every day and night, too, he was pretty tight. At times, he had the appearance of an insane man from drink." As far as the fourteenth was concerned, "he was pretty tight that evening."

Zad Jenkins, Mrs. Surratt's brother, thought that Lloyd "was very much intoxicated at that time." Richard Sweeny, who had also run into the tavern owner on the Marlboro road, remembered that "he was considerably under the influence of liquor and he drank on the road." James Lusby had ridden back to Surrattsville with him and said he was "very drunk on that occasion." Mrs. Offutt thought that her brother-in-law was "very much in liquor, more so that I have ever seen him in my life." So much so, in fact, that he had become deathly ill shortly after returning from Marlboro and had to lie down. But Lloyd was evidently a man of great recuperative powers, because she had seen him heading back to the taproom a few minutes later.

As the trial dragged on, it was obvious that the Judge Advocate was relying heavily on Mrs. Surratt's refusal (as he called it) to recognize Payne in the vestibule of her house on the night of April 17. But Zad Jenkins swore that her "eyesight is defective," while her daughter Anna testified that "my mother's eyesight is very bad, and she has often failed to recognize her friends." It was only her vanity, Anna said, that kept her from wearing glasses. Honora Fitzpatrick, who shared Mrs. Surratt's room, said that her landlady had "complained that she could not read or sew at night, on account of her sight. I have known of her passing her friend, Mrs. Kirby, on the same side of the street, and not seeing her at all." Honora had also been unable to identify Payne that night until "the skull-cap was taken off his head." Mrs. Eliza Holahan, another boarder, knew that "Mrs. Surratt's eyesight was defective." Anna Ward, an old friend, stated that the defendant "has failed to recognize me on the street."

On the trial's sixteenth day, Augustus S. Howell, a former Confederate artilleryman and a suspected blockade runner, took the stand. He had first met Mrs. Surratt at Surrattsville in 1863 and had often stayed at her boardinghouse when he had business in Washington "because it was cheaper than a hotel." He, too, recalled that the defendant's eyesight was very bad. "I was present one evening," he said, "when she handed me a newspaper to read for her; and I called one evening at her house . . . and although the gas was lit in the hall, she failed at first to recognize me."

During one of his visits to H Street, he had met Weichmann, whom he taught to make a cipher table similar to one that had been found among Booth's effects. The War Department clerk had informed Howell that he was anxious to get a job in Richmond. "He told me that his sympathies were with the South, and that he thought it would ultimately succeed. He said he had done all he could for the South; he expressed himself as a friend of the South, as a Southern man or a secesh sympathizer would."

The rest of the case for Mrs. Surratt consisted of evidence of her good character and loyalty to the Union. Anna Ward knew her as "a perfect lady and a Christian," while four Catholic priests attested to her religious devotion. Her brother recalled that she frequently gave "milk, tea and such refreshments as she had in her house to Union troops when they were passing." Rachel Semus, who, Pitman noted, was "colored," had been the Surratt cook for six years. She remembered that her employer had "fed Union soldiers at her house, sometimes a good many of them; and I know that she always tried to do the best for them that she could, because I always cooked for them." Rev. E. F. Wiget, the president of Gonzaga College, had "always heard everyone speak very highly of her character." John and Bill Hoxton, two Surrattsville neighbors, had "never heard her utter a disloyal word."

On June 13, the defense suddenly recalled Mrs. Offutt. As

she took the stand, Aiken told the commission "that at the time Mrs. Offutt gave her testimony before, she came here very unwell. If I have been correctly informed, she had been suffering severely from sickness, and had taken considerable laudanum." Her mind had been considerably confused at the time, and she now wished to correct her testimony in an important particular. Colonel Bingham was on his feet in a flash.

> Q. Is it something you swore to here in court?
> A. Of course, I took the oath when I appeared here.
> Q. Do you want to correct anything you have sworn to here in court?
> A. Yes, sir, I should like to do so.

There wasn't much Bingham could do with an obviously determined lady, and he sat down as abruptly as he had gotten up.

Mrs. Offutt reminded Hunter and his colleagues that when she had testified on May 17, the Judge Advocate had asked her whether Mrs. Surratt had handed her a package at Lloyd's tavern on April 14, and her answer had been "No." Now, she remembered that "she did hand me a package and said she requested to leave it there." Later on, she had seen it "lying on the sofa in the parlor." After Mrs. Surratt had left for Washington, the witness noticed that Lloyd went into the parlor and "had a package in his hand." She thought that "after the package was handed to me, it might have been taken by Mrs. Surratt and handed to Lloyd, but I did not see her give it to him."

As Clampitt reminded the commission, "Mr. Lloyd, under oath, swore that he received a package from Mrs. Surratt. We wish to show that a package was received of Mrs. Surratt by Mrs. Offutt. We wish to show in this connection that it was the same package that Mr. Lloyd swore to. If we can show that this was the identical package that Mr. Lloyd swore to receiving, we can show that his testimony is not worth the snap of a finger." But Mrs. Offutt did not know what was in the package; all she remembered was that Mrs. Surratt had given it to her around 5:30 that afternoon and she had "laid it down" on the parlor sofa. She had no idea of what had happened to it after that, except that she had seen a package in her brother-in-law's hands when he entered the house a few minutes later.

When the defense rested on June 13, the Government trotted out John Ryan, Frank Smith, James P. Young and P. T. Ransford, all of whom swore that Lou Weichmann, its witness-in-chief, was a very trustworthy fellow indeed. But only one—Young—had known him for any length of time. John T. Holohan, who had occupied a second-floor room at Mrs. Surratt's in early 1865, was sure that he had never heard anyone mention his landlady's bad eyesight. With the testimony of six Prince George's County neighbors that Zad Jenkins was, among other things, "one of the most disloyal men in the county," the prosecution had closed its case as far as Mrs. Surratt was concerned.

The closing arguments began on June 16, and continued for twelve days. While they droned on, John Clampitt tried to introduce the joint affidavit of Louis Carland and John P. Brophy, two friends of Weichmann, who swore that he had told them that he had perjured himself during the trial. He, and not Mrs. Surratt, had suggested that he try to borrow Booth's buggy for the April 11 trip to Surrattsville. He had also informed Carland and Brophy that he had told a fellow clerk in the War Department all about the kidnap plot as early as February, and that Stanton had forced him to testify against Mrs. Surratt, despite the fact that Lou thought she was innocent. But he had played along with the Secretary of War because "I didn't want to hang."

But Holt wasn't going to let a piece of notarized paper spring Mary Eugenia. He rejected it as hearsay and, when

Clampitt offered to produce Brophy in person, the Judge Advocate thumbed down his request on the ground that it was too late to call another witness. But on June 27, eleven days after the prosecution had closed its case, Holt called Printer John Contlin to testify to an anonymous advertisement printed in the Selma, Alabama, *Dispatch* on December 1, 1864, offering to kill Lincoln, Seward and Johnson, for one million dollars. Brophy felt so strongly about the rejection of his affidavit that he tried to see Andrew Johnson about it, but the President was incommunicado as far as the trial was concerned.

In his closing argument, which was read by Clampitt, Reverdy Johnson pointed out that the Military Commission lacked the power to try Mrs. Surratt. "As counsel for one of the parties," he told the commission, "I should esteem myself dishonored if I attempted to rescue my client from a proper trial for the offense charged against her, by denying the jurisdiction of the Commission, upon grounds that I did not conscientiously believe to be sound. And, in what I have done, I have not more had in view the defense of Mrs. Surratt, than of the Constitution and the laws. In my view, in this respect, her cause is the cause of every citizen. And let it not be supposed that I am seeking to secure impunity to any one who may have been guilty of the horrid crimes of the night of the fourteenth of April. Over these, the civil courts of the District have ample jurisdiction, and will faithfully exercise it if the cases are remitted to them, and guilt is legally established, and will surely award the punishment known to the laws."

Johnson left it to his associates to discuss the case against Mrs. Surratt, and young Aiken did his best. What had "two months of patient and unwearying investigation, and the most thorough search for evidence that was probably ever made" developed insofar as his client was concerned? Only that she knew the gregarious Booth (and who in Washington didn't?) and that she had taken a message to Lloyd (so had many others), and that she had failed to recognize Payne (bad eyes in a dim light). The chief witnesses against her—the unreliable Weichmann and the drunken Lloyd—were both trying to save their own skins. He ended in a blaze of rhetoric, asking the commission's members to disregard "suspicion fastened and fed upon the facts of acquaintance and mere fortuitous intercourse with that man in whose name so many miseries gather, the assassinator of the President."

Colonel Bingham, who summed up for the prosecution, ended his two-day presentation with the observation that Mrs. Surratt was "as surely in the conspiracy to murder the President as was John Wilkes Booth himself." After all, wasn't her house the headquarters of the conspirators? And didn't she deliver a field glass to Lloyd and instruct him to have the carbines ready? Would an innocent woman fail to recognize a man who had been her boarder? If she wasn't involved in the plot against the President, why did Booth always ask for her when he visited H Street? As far as the Special Judge Advocate was concerned, the questions answered themselves.

When he sat down late in the afternoon of June 28, the court was cleared for the last time and the commission began its deliberation. It took only minutes for it to decide that Payne, Herold and Atzerodt should be hanged. Dr. Mudd, Mike O'Laughlin and Sam Arnold were sentenced to "hard labor for life," while Ed Spangler drew six years. But the commission couldn't make up its collective mind about Mrs. Surratt. On its first ballot, only four of its members voted to execute her. The other five could not be convinced that the evidence had disclosed that she was guilty of anything more than running a boardinghouse that catered to a mighty strange lot of roomers.

But two days of Washington's heat did what all of the Judge Advocate's arguments had failed to accomplish. At noon, on June 30, the five recalcitrants voted that "the said Mary E. Surratt be hanged by the neck until she be dead, at such time and place as the President of the United States shall direct." However, they insisted on appending a petition for commutation of the "sentence of death . . . to imprisonment for life" to the record of the case, which Holt was to submit to Johnson. On July 5, the President formally approved the commission's sentences and ordered that Herold, Atzerodt, Payne and Mrs. Surratt be executed "on the seventh day of July, 1865, between the hours of ten A.M. and two P.M. of that day." Whether he ever saw the recommendation for mercy or not, no one could say.

President Johnson's decision was not made public until late the next afternoon. The news that their client would die in less than twenty-four hours caught the defense attorneys by surprise. "So sudden was the shock," Clampitt later wrote, "so unexpected the result, annoyed beyond expression at the celerity of the order of execution, we hardly knew how to proceed." When he and Aiken were unsuccessful in seeing the President, they telegraphed their senior counsel, who had returned to Baltimore. "Attempt to obtain a writ of habeas corpus," Reverdy Johnson wired back.

At two o'clock in the morning of July 7, the two young men awakened Andrew Wylie, one of the justices of the Supreme Court of the District of Columbia. They waited nervously as the judge pored over their hastily prepared petition. "Inasmuch as your petitioner was a private citizen . . . and not subject to military jurisdiction," it read, "and that all crimes committed . . . are under the Constitution and laws of the United States, to be tried only before its criminal tribunals, with the right of public trial by jury, she prays your Honor to grant unto her the United States' most gracious writ of habeas corpus." After what seemed an eternity, Wylie agreed to order Major General W. S. Hancock, the commander of the Middle Military Division, to bring Mrs. Surratt into his court the next morning at ten o'clock.

But Stanton had an ace up his sleeve. When Hancock, accompanied by Attorney General James Speed, walked into Judge Wylie's courtroom, almost two hours after the time specified in the writ, he did not have Mrs. Surratt with him. What he did have was a message from the President, declaring that "I do hereby especially suspend this writ, and direct that you proceed to execute the order heretofore given upon the judgment of the Military Commission." Judge Wylie had no choice—he yielded to the suspension of the writ. "We have failed," Clampitt and Aiken informed Johnson.

The scaffold had been built in the courtyard of the Old Penitentiary Building. Just as General Hancock was presenting Johnson's suspension order to Judge Wylie, Captain Christian Rath, the officer in charge of the execution, approved the drop. Four graves had been dug to the left of the gallows near the prison wall. At the side of each one was a pine box containing glass bottles in which the name of each defendant had been placed. Shortly before two o'clock, Mrs. Surratt, despite Payne's last minute statement that she "was innocent of the murder of the President," was led from her cell. Accompanied by two priests, she climbed the fifteen steps to the gallows' platform, where she sat in an armchair while an officer read the sentences aloud. Five minutes later, with her hands tied behind her back and her face covered by a white hood, she dropped into eternity.

On July 15, the four surviving defendants, who had begun serving their terms in the Albany Penitentiary, were re-sentenced to "hard labor in the military prison at Dry Tortugas, Florida." In 1867, O'Laughlin died of yellow fever, but Mudd was pardoned in 1868, and Spangler and Arnold one year later. In 1867, John Harrison Surratt, who had been captured in Egypt, was tried by a civil court for his part in the conspiracy. The jury voted eight to four for acquittal, and the Government decided to call it a day and dropped the charges against him. By this time, everyone knew that Stanton had suppressed Booth's captured diary which contained an entry for April 14, clearly indicating that it had not been until that very day that the actor had decided to kill rather than kidnap the President. Mary Eugenia had never had even a fighting chance.

On the day that Mrs. Surratt's trial began, a young man, who had been sentenced to death by a military commission for subversive activities in Indiana, petitioned the Circuit Court in that state for a writ of habeas corpus. Lambdin P. Milligan, a key figure in Harrison H. Dodd's Order of American Knights, had been found guilty of a multitude of crimes, the least serious of which was giving aid to the Confederacy. By all rights, he should have been hanged on May 19, 1865, but, three days earlier, President Johnson granted him a two-week reprieve.

Milligan's petition had stressed the fact that, because he was not a member of the armed forces, the military commission had no right to try him. He asked the Circuit Court to be "turned over to the proper civil tribune, to be proceeded against according to the law of the land, or discharged from custody altogether." When the two circuit judges could not reach a decision, the case was certified to the United States Supreme Court. Faced with a long delay before Milligan's fate could be decided, President Johnson overrode Stanton's strenuous objections and commuted the defendant's sentence to life imprisonment in the Ohio State Penitentiary.

In March of 1866, the nine justices listened to several days of arguments in what was now officially known as *ex parte Milligan*. Although Reverdy Johnson had been unable to convince Mrs. Surratt's military judges that they had no constitutional right to try her, Milligan's triumvirate of attorneys, which included future President James N. Garfield, trotted out the same arguments that the Marylander had advanced in the Old Penitentiary eight months earlier. A military commission, they urged, had no power to sit in judgment on a civilian unless there were no regular courts available.

This time, Johnson's rationale was more persuasive. On April 3, the court announced that it had decided to free Milligan. "The Constitution of the United States," wrote Justice David Davis for himself and five of his colleagues, "is a law for rulers and people, equally in war and peace, and covers with the shield of its protection all classes of men, at all times and under all circumstances. No doctrine involving more pernicious consequences was ever invented by the writ of man than that any of its provisions can be suspended during any of the great exigencies of Government. Martial law can never exist where the courts are open, and in the proper and unobstructed exercise of their jurisdiction."

"A great triumph," Johnson told a friend, "but ten months too late for Mrs. Surratt."

With military commissions a thing of the past, Johnson next leveled his sights on the loyalty oath. In July of 1865, A. H. Garland, an attorney who had been a member of the Confederate Congress, had been granted "a full pardon and amnesty" by the President, provided he would swear to "faithfully support and protect the Constitution of the United States and the union of States thereunder." He promply took the required oath and asked to be allowed to practice again before the United States Supreme Court.

Six months earlier, Congress had ruled that no person could practice law in the Federal courts unless he were willing to take the omnibus loyalty oath of 1862. Garland's application was opposed by Attorney General Speed, because of the lawyer's refusal to take the second oath. Johnson, remembering his own reservations about the constitutionality of such oaths, was quick to spring—free of charge—to Garland's aid. Congress' refusal to allow his client to practice law unless he bent his knee to the conqueror, he maintained, was tantamount to "depriving him of his property without due process of law."

An outspoken opponent of a harsh peace for the defeated Confederacy, Johnson couldn't resist an opportunity to do a little proselytizing when Garland's petition for reinstatement reached the top of the Supreme Court docket. The day may soon come, he reminded the justices, "when all the states shall be again within the protecting shelter of the Union." What better way to prepare for that eventuality than "by the bringing within those courts of the United States, a class of men, now excluded, who, by education, character and profession are especially qualified by their example to influence the public sentiment of their states, and to bring those states to the complete conviction which, it is believed, they must largely entertain—that to support and defend the Constitution of the United States . . . is not only essential to their peoples' happiness and freedom, but it is a duty to their country and their God."

Johnson may have eschewed short sentences, but the court followed him all the way. Garland was admitted to practice without having to take the oath of 1862. "It is not within the constitutional power of Congress," echoed Mr. Justice Field, "to effect punishment beyond the reach of executive clemency. From the petitioner, therefore, the oath required by the act of July 24, 1862, could not be exacted."

The last ten years of Johnson's life were as active as the first seventy. After helping engineer the acquittal of his namesake in the White House on impeachment charges, he succeeded Charles Francis Adams as Ambassador to Great Britain. He returned to Baltimore after Grant's election, where he began to practice law again. A major portion of his practice consisted of the defense of Southerners accused of disloyalty to the Union during the Civil War.

On February 11, 1876, he was scheduled to argue an appeal before the Supreme Court of Maryland at Annapolis.

He arrived in the capital the night before, where he was the guest of Governor John Lee Carroll. After a hearty dinner at the Executive Mansion, he decided to take a stroll around the grounds. As he was returning to the Executive Mansion, he tripped on a piece of coal and fell against a sharp corner of the building, fracturing his skull in two places. He died instantly.

Eight days later, a memorial service was held for him by the Bar of the United States Supreme Court. There were many things said about him that day with which all of his friends and most of his foes could agree. But for those who had watched him stand up for Mary Surratt, the words that meant the most were spoken by Frederick T. Frelinghuysen, one of his bitterest opponents in the Senate, who was to become Chester Arthur's Secretary of State. "He had faced the storm of popular prejudice, and had calmly and resolutely waited until public opinion came to do him homage. He had the courage to stand and wait."

# John Peter Altgeld

With the hanging of four of the Haymarket bombing defendants on the morning of November 11, 1887, "the acute paranoia from which Chicago had been suffering," as one writer described it, began to subside. No sooner had the executed men been buried in Waldheim Cemetery than Governor Richard J. Oglesby began to receive requests for the commutation of the sentences of Samuel Fielden, Michael Schwab and Oscar Neebe, the three surviving defendants who had begun serving long jail terms. During the administration of Joseph W. Fifer, Oglesby's successor, it was a rare week when at least one petition for executive clemency was not received in Springfield.

The campaign to obtain the release of the three prisoners was accelerated by the dismissal for bribery in 1889 of several of the policemen who had testified at the trial, including Inspector John Bonfield who, many thought, had been responsible for the Haymarket tragedy. In 1890, an Amnesty Association was formed which was as respectable as it was active. Sparked by William Penn Nixon, the editor of the arch-Republican *Chicago Inter-Ocean,* the new organization managed to attract such men as William Dean Howells, Lyman J. Gage, Henry Lloyd and Robert G. Ingersoll, and, by 1893, was able to persuade most of Chicago's business and professional leaders to join with sixty thousand other signers in petitioning John P. Altgeld, the newly elected Democratic governor, to pardon the Haymarket survivors.

With so much public support for the prisoners' release, Altgeld could have freed them as an act of executive mercy without seriously compromising his political future. However, it was his earnest belief that no man should be pardoned merely as an act of official benevolence. If Fielden, Schwab and Neebe were guilty of murder, he had told his friend, Judge Samuel P. McConnell, shortly after his inauguration, he wouldn't lift a finger to help them. But if they were not, they would be released. When McConnell had pointed out that this approach would be extremely unpopular, Altgeld had flown into a rage. "If I decide they are innocent," he had roared, "I will pardon them if I never hold office another day!"

On Monday, June 26, 1893, after many months of painstaking investigation, the Governor signed the three pardons. That same day, his reasons for doing so were released to the press. They were everything McConnell had feared. Instead of taking the tack that, after seven years of imprisonment, the defendants were entitled to mercy for mercy's sake, Altgeld based his decision on the jury's prejudice, the prisoners' innocence and the trial judge's "malicious ferocity." He concluded: "I am convinced that it is clearly my duty to act in this case for the reasons already given, and I, therefore, grant an absolute pardon to Samuel Fielden, Oscar Neebe and Michael Schwab."

With almost no exceptions, the country's newspapers and periodicals bitterly condemned Altgeld for the manner in which he had acted. Leading the pack, the *Chicago Tribune* blared that he had been motivated by his un-American attitudes. "Poorly concealed for years," it raged, "they broke forth at last in the hysterical denunciation of American principles, law, judges, executive and judicial officers, and of people who deliberately and conscientiously approved of them." According to the *Washington Post,* he was "a mysterious fragment of jetsam from the Lord knows where [who had] aspersed a Judge the latchet of whose shoe he is unfit to unloose." Murat Halstead, a widely syndicated columnist, thundered that "the greater offense is not in the act of clemency . . . but the disgrace and the danger is the most unseemly, scandalous and incendiary reasons given by the Governor for his action." The *Brooklyn Union* editorialized that "the Governor cheapened human life in his state by his free pardon of the anarchists and the abuse of the stern and just judge who tried them."

Altgeld never had any illusions about the effect of his pardon message. His closest friends and political advisors had repeatedly warned him that it would destroy himself and his party. He always had a ready answer. "Our party," he said, "must stand or fall by its principles and its policy. As for myself, no man has the right to allow his ambition to stand in the way of the performance of a simple act of justice." His old friend, Clarence Darrow, put it somewhat more eloquently. "He fearlessly and knowingly bared his devoted head to the fiercest, most vindictive criticism ever heaped upon a public man, because he loved justice and dared to do the right."

John Altgeld was never the same man again. Three years later, he was soundly defeated in his bid for re-election and, in 1899, ran a poor third for Mayor of Chicago. In the latter year, his favorite project, a sixteen-story building on North Dearborn Street, was taken over by the banks, leaving him nothing of his once considerable holdings but a heavily mortgaged home on Malden Street. His health, which had never been particularly robust, began to fail rapidly as the abuse against him continued throughout the remainder of his term as Governor.

But he never regretted pardoning Fielden, Schwab and Neebe. "I found that I either had to take the step I did, or shirk a duty," he later told the *New York World*'s Nelly Bly, "and while I have been badly whipped at different times in my life for holding my ground, I never ran away from anything, and I could see no reason for running away from my duty in this case."

*"No man has the right to allow his ambition to stand in the way of the performance of a simple act of justice."*

# Governor John Peter Altgeld and the pardoning of the Haymarket defendants, June 26, 1893

ON APRIL 26, 1886, the *Chicago Mail* carried an article by John Peter Altgeld, a German-born attorney who was one of the city's largest property owners. Entitled "Protection of Non-Combatants: or, Arbitration of Strikes," Altgeld's piece was in direct opposition to President Cleveland's dismissal of compulsory arbitration of labor disputes as "unworkable and undemocratic." "The consciousness that arbitration can be forced upon them," Altgeld wrote, "would induce both employer and employee to get together and to try to adjust their own differences, and this nearly always results in a settlement." To many Chicagoans, who lived in daily fear of a general strike in support of the clamorous eight-hour-day movement, his plan came as a welcome alternative to the administration's policy of *laissez faire* and the class warfare urged by the labor extremists.

Six days after the appearance of Altgeld's article, a bloody clash occurred at Cyrus McCormick's Black Road reaper works between "eight-hour-day" union men and the plant's employees. When the police finally restored order, two of the rioters were found shot to death. The next evening, a group of radical labor sympathizers met in the basement of Greif's Hall on Lake Street to plan a mass meeting in the West Side's Old Haymarket Square "to denounce the latest atrocious act of the police, the shooting of our fellow workmen yesterday afternoon." Before the meeting ended at eleven P.M., a circular calling on all workingmen to "appear in full force" at Haymarket the following night had been prepared in English and German. Early the next morning, the copy was delivered to a printer, and, before noon, the bilingual circulars had been distributed to every union hall and saloon in Chicago.

That evening, a disappointing crowd of some fourteen hundred unionists showed up at the square. Because of the slim turn-out, the meeting place was shifted at the last moment to Desplaines Street at the entrance to Crane's Alley, a little less than a block south of Haymarket proper. By ten P.M., the mild quality of the speeches and the threat of a spring rainstorm had combined to reduce the audience to a few hundred diehards. Mayor Carter Harrison, a bearded ex-Kentuckian with a liberal bent, who had expected trouble to develop, left shortly before ten after ordering Inspector John Bonfield of the Desplaines Street station house to dismiss the large force of patrolmen which had been waiting there. Nothing had occurred yet or looked likely to occur, he told the police officer, to require interference.

Instead of obeying Harrison's directive, Bonfield, who was an exponent of "vigorous measures" as far as union men were concerned, led his 186 men toward Crane's Alley as soon as the Mayor had gone home. As they approached the wagon from which Samuel Fielden, an erstwhile Methodist lay preacher who was the last speaker of the evening, was decrying the lack of communication that existed between

Chicago officialdom and the city's laborers, Captain William Ward cut him off abruptly. "I command you," he shouted, "to immediately and peacefully disperse." Fielden looked stunned. "But we are peaceable," he stammered.

Seconds later, a tremendous explosion shattered the air. When the smoke cleared, a number of wounded policemen were found lying on the cobblestones in front of Crane's Alley. Bonfield, who had had his flowing mustache singed by the blast, immediately ordered those of his men who were still on their feet to fire into the confused crowd around Fielden. According to next morning's *Tribune,* "an incessant fire was kept up for nearly two minutes, and at least 250 shots were fired." It was only when the policemen had emptied their magazines that the shooting stopped.

Desplaines Street was filled with bleeding men. Those who could still maneuver under their own power staggered or crawled into nearby saloons and drugstores, pleading for help. Cries of "Oh, God, I'm shot!" and "Please take me home!" were heard everywhere. Of the sixty-seven injured policemen, Officer Mathias J. Degan and six of his colleagues had been fatally wounded. As those men who had been able to find shelter in the doorways that lined Crane's Alley streamed back into the street, the big bell in the tower of the police station began to toll out a riot alarm.

The next afternoon, a hastily summoned coroner's jury came to the conclusion that Degan had been killed by "a piece of bomb thrown by an unknown person aided and abetted and encouraged by August Spies, Michael Schwab, A. R. Parsons, Samuel Fielden and other unknown persons." On May 21, the Cook County Grand Jury, in a sixty-nine-count indictment, accused ten men of killing the hapless Degan with "a certain deadly and destructive instrument . . . charged with divers dangerous and explosive substances, a certain pistol, commonly called revolver, and with certain means, instruments and weapons, a more particular description of which is to the said jurors unknown." The ten—Albert R. Parsons, Michael Schwab, Adolph Fischer, Louis Lingg, Samuel Fielden, August Spies, George Engel, Oscar Neebe, Rudolph Schnaubelt and William Seliger—were undoubtedly Chicago's most vocal labor agitators. Each defendant was charged both with committing Degan's murder and, in the alternative, with "aiding, advising, abetting and encouraging" the real killer.

Only Spies and Fielden had been present when the bomb exploded. Parsons, who had been one of the first speakers of the evening, had departed early in order to take his Negro wife and two young children home. Neebe and Engel had not left their houses that night, while Fischer had gone home shortly after the meeting had begun. Twenty-one-year-old Louis Lingg had been on the North Side, several miles away from Crane's Alley, and the remaining three defendants had all been attending meetings in other parts of the city.

The trial of eight of the accused men (Schnaubelt and Seliger were never prosecuted) began in the Cook County Criminal Court on the first day of summer. Parsons, who had fled to Wisconsin after the bombing, had arranged with his lawyers to surrender voluntarily on the trial's first day. As the bailiff called out the names of the defendants, the missing man walked into the courtroom. However, before he could inform the bench of his intentions, he was recognized by a member of the prosecutor's staff who leaped to his feet and called for his "immediate arrest." The labor agitator was promptly seized by two deputies and escorted to the prisoners' box behind the defense table, where he joined his seven co-defendants.

The chief counsel for the defendants, who had advised Parsons to take this step, was William Perkins Black, a corporation lawyer who had agreed to defend Spies and the others after every other experienced attorney in northern Illinois had refused to take the case. A tall, dark-haired man with what one of his associates called "a sense of the dramatic," Black was to lose most of his corporate retainers before the trial was over. But he apparently considered his new clients worth the risk. "I loved these men," he later said. "I knew them not until I came to know them in the time of their sore travail and anguish. As months went by and I found in the lives of those with whom I talked the witness of their love for the people, of their patience and courage, my heart was taken captive in their cause."

After some motions by the defense for a postponement and separate trials had been denied, the tedious business of selecting a jury began. But it was to be almost a month before one could be seated. Black and the three young lawyers * who were assisting him found it next to impossible to isolate twelve residents of Cook County who had not formed an opinion about the Haymarket bombing. By the time that Harry T. Sanford, the twelfth juror, was being questioned, 757 talesmen had been rejected for cause, and the defense had exhausted its 160 peremptory challenges.

Judge Joseph Easton Gary, who had replaced John G. Rogers as trial judge when the defense objected to the latter as "hopelessly prejudiced," had very definite ideas about the qualifications of jurors. As he saw it, even though "a person called as a juryman may have formed an opinion based upon rumor or upon newspaper statements, but has expressed no opinion as to the truth of the newspaper statement, he is still qualified as a juror if he states that he can fairly and impartially render a verdict thereon in accordance with the law and the evidence, and the Court shall be satisfied of the truth of such statement." Despite this standard, however, he overruled Black's objections to Theodore Denker, who frankly admitted that he had formed an opinion as to the defendant's guilt and that it would prevent him "from rendering an impartial verdict in the case."

* Moses Salomon, Sigismund Zeisler and William A. Foster.

Sanford was the last of 982 men who had been rounded up by Special Bailiff Henry L. Ryce as prospective jurors. Like Denker, he, too, had a definite opinion as to whether the eight men at the defense table had been responsible for the Haymarket tragedy. But he did not regard newspaper accounts "as being in the nature of sworn testimony." He was certain that, despite his "decided prejudice," he could "listen to the legitimate testimony introduced in court and, upon that, and that alone, render and return a fair and impartial, unprejudiced, and unbiased verdict." Gary overruled Black's challenge for cause and the jury was, at long last, complete. At two P.M. on Thursday, July 15, four salesmen, two shipping clerks, a bookkeeper, a public-school principal, a music dealer, the owner of a hardware store, and two freight clerks swore that they would "harken unto the evidence and render a just and fair verdict."

With the jury finally sworn, State Attorney Julius S. Grinnell, a large, flamboyant man who had been on the Democratic ticket with Altgeld when the latter ran unsuccessfully for Congress in 1884, proceeded to harangue it for more than two hours. He was going to prove, he asserted, that long before the explosion the defendants, who were "endeavoring to make anarchy the rule," had made up their minds to attack the police. Where they cried "murder," "bloodshed," "anarchy," and "dynamite," he thundered, they have meant what they said and proposed to do what they threatened. Even if he were unable to show which one of the men in the dock had actually killed Degan, the jury, he was sure, could still convict them all. "A conspiracy to murder," he concluded, "is the same as murder itself."

Grinnell's first witness on Friday morning was architect Felix C. Busehek. As Busehek pushed his way through the packed courtroom to the witness stand, Judge Gary decided to give the jury the benefit of his interpretation of the phrase "conspiracy to murder."

"If there was a general combination and agreement among a great number of individuals to kill policemen if they come into conflict with parties with whom they were friendly," he explained, "and if violence was used and resulted in the death of the police, then those who were a party to the conspiracy are guilty of murder." Busehek was then sworn in and, with the help of some hand-drawn maps, proceeded to describe the physical layouts of Greif's Hall, Haymarket Square, and Zeff's Hall.

Inspector Bonfield was next. On the night of May 4, he had ordered some 160 men to break up the meeting in Crane's Alley. The policemen had been given strict instructions not to fire unless told to do so by their superior officers. After Ward had ordered the crowd which had been listening to Fielden to disperse, its ranks had parted "in a peculiar manner." Then he had heard a "hissing noise" which had been followed by an explosion.

As soon as the bomb went off, the crowd had fired at the police "for a minute."

Q. How many shots do you estimate were fired on you before you ordered the fire returned?
A. It would be hard to make an accurate statement, but I should say at least one hundred.
Q. What officer was killed on the spot?
A. Officer Degan.

It was then that he had ordered "our men to fire." He was certain that Fielden had not been on the wagon when the latter had assured Captain Ward that "we are peaceable." "He was standing so close to me," he recalled, "I could touch him."

In the afternoon, Gottfried Waller, a Swiss cabinet maker who was a former member of the *Lehr und Wehr Verein,* a "Socialist society for exercising arms and instructions," testified that he had been the chairman of the protest meeting at

Greif's Hall the night before the explosion. There had been some eighty men present in the room when he called the meeting to order at 8:30. After some discussion about the incident at McCormick's reaper works, the rostrum had been turned over to George Engel who had introduced a resolution calling for the Haymarket conclave. The word *Ruhe* (silence) in next morning's *Arbeiter Zeitung* was decided upon as the signal for the meeting.

If riots should occur, Engel had said, "we should storm the police stations and cut the telegraph wires. Then we should down everything that came against us. If one police station was stormed, they should do the same with the others, mowing down all that came. Engel said the easiest way would be to throw a bomb in the station."

Only a small reconnaissance committee was to be sent to Haymarket. "If they should report that something had happened, then the others should come down upon the police, then the militias—whatever should come against them. We should simply strike them down however we best could, with bombs, whatever should be at our disposal." Most of the people present at Greif's already had bombs because Adolph Fischer had distributed some several years ago when it had been feared that the police were going to break up a Thanksgiving Day rally.

Engel had voiced similar sentiments at Bohemian Hall on May 2. He had told Waller then that he had worked out an attack plan which called for the bombing of Chicago police stations. After the bombs had been thrown, *Lehr und Wehr* riflemen were to shoot any policemen who tried to escape from the demolished buildings. We were to kill everybody who opposed us, Engel had instructed him.

Bernhard Schrader, a carpenter who spoke with a heavy Russian accent, had also attended the Greif's Hall meeting. As he remembered it, only thirty or forty men had been present that night. Although it had been agreed to "destroy the officers" if the police tried to break up any of the protest meetings, nothing whatsoever had been said about bombs. Assistant State's Attorney George C. Ingham, who had been questioning Schrader, looked thunderstruck. "Was anything said about dynamite?" he demanded. The witness shook his head. "In the meeting, did you hear any reference to the word *Ruhe?*" "No, sir," was Schrader's answer.

The defense, which had been unable to shake Waller's damaging testimony, was jubilant. When Ingham, who, according to the *New York Times* correspondent, looked as if he were about to have an apoplectic fit, finally growled, "Your witness," Black immediately exploited his unexpected advantage. Had Schrader also attended the May 2 meeting at Bohemian Hall? He had. Had there been any discussion about bombs? There had not.

> Q. Then in those two meetings, no agreement was made to throw bombs at the Haymarket?
> A. Not while I was there.
> Q. Then it was not agreed to use dynamite to destroy the police at the Haymarket?
> A. Not that I am aware.

On re-direct, a frantic Ingham waved a sheaf of papers under the carpenter's nose and screamed, "Did you not make a written statement to Police Captain Schaak?" When Black objected to the question, Ingham was beside himself with rage. "We wish to show," he roared at Gary, "that time and time again, the witness has said he heard the word *Ruhe* used." While the judge pounded the bench in a fruitless attempt to silence the furious assistant prosecutor, the latter shouted, "It is evident from the action of the witness and from the action of counsel that Schrader is their witness and not our witness."

The packed courtroom was still buzzing when Lieutenant Quinn, who had commanded one of Bonfield's police companies, took the stand. As he and his men had marched toward Crane's Alley, he had heard Fielden shout, "Here come the bloodhounds! You do your duty, and I'll do mine!" Seconds later, Fielden, who had been standing on the speakers' wagon, "pulled a revolver from his hip and point-blank fired at Ward, Bonfield and the officers behind them. The bomb exploded almost the same instant." As he described the Haymarket carnage, Quinn became so agitated that he rose to his feet and barked his answers to Grinnell's last questions from a standing position.

When court resumed on Monday morning, Lieutenant James Stanton, who had been wounded at Haymarket, swore that he had seen the bomb before it went off. Just as Captain Ward had ordered the streets cleared, Stanton had heard a hissing noise above his head. When he looked up, he had seen an object, which he estimated to be about the size of "two fists put together," falling through the air. It had struck the ground near him and he had just had time to notice that it had a two-inch fuse before it exploded.

Stanton was followed by Officer H. F. Krueger of Lieutenant Steele's company. He, too, had heard Fielden cry out, "Here come the bloodhounds!" Grinnell asked the bearded Fielden to stand up. "Was this the man who made that remark?" he asked. Krueger nodded. "That's the man," he said. "I saw him draw a revolver, and I am sure he fired two shots."

Q. What then?
A. He took cover behind the wagon. I returned his fire. Then he started into the crowd and I shot at him again. I saw him limp off. That's the last I saw of him.

Officer John Wessler, another member of Steele's company, had also seen Fielden, whom he described as "a man with big bushy whiskers," shooting at the police from behind a wagon. The policeman had fired at the defendant, and he was certain that he had wounded him.

Grinnell's next witness was Luther V. Moulton, a Knight of Labor from Grand Rapids, Michigan. Moulton had first met August Spies at a meeting at which the latter had been the principal speaker. Spies had told him that he was dedicated to "reorganizing society so that the laboring man would have a more equitable share in the fruit of his product." When the witness had expressed the opinion that this could be accomplished by better labor legislation, Spies had insisted that "force was the only agency to be depended on." James K. Magie had been present at Turner's Hall on October 11, 1885, when Spies had introduced a resolution "recommending the use of force and arms instead of the ballot box to redress the wrongs of the laboring man."

There was an audible gasp in the courtroom when the bailiff called out the name of John E. Doyle. The tall police officer, who had been grievously wounded at the Old Haymarket, hobbled up to the witness stand on crutches. Ingham's voice was gentle as he led him through his paces.

Q. You were facing the mob when the bomb was thrown?
A. Yes.
Q. And were wounded in thirteen different places?
A. Yes.
Q. The wounds are both shell and bullet?
A. Yes.

Doyle was "positive" that Fielden had shouted, "Now's your time!" as the police had marched toward Crane's Alley.

On Tuesday morning, Grinnell led off with Henry Heinemann who, like Magie, had heard Spies talk in Turner Hall in the fall of 1885. Spies had urged his listeners to join with him in creating a new labor movement which was to come into being on May Day, 1886. "Death to the enemies of the human race, our despoilers!" he had concluded. His audience had been so inflamed by his remarks that they had unanimously voted to use force, if necessary, to bring about "the age of the workingman."

Officer J. A. West of the Hinman Street Station had been sent to McCormick's on the day of the Black Road riot. After Spies had delivered a speech, the mob had opened fire on the police. James T. Frazer, who worked around the corner from the reaper works, confirmed the patrolman's story. The defendant's words had been so incendiary that when he had finished, one of the men in the crowd had pointed at Mc-Cormick's and shouted, "Let's go and kill the damned scabs!" As the angry men had rushed off toward the reaper works, Spies had boarded a downtown streetcar.

Theodore Fricke, business manager of Spies' *Arbeiter Zeitung,* was next. He identified the original copies of a circular which had been distributed in Chicago on the night of the McCormick riot as being in the handwriting of Spies and Schwab. The circular, which was captioned "Revenge! Workingmen to Arms!!" exhorted its readers to "rise and destroy the hideous monster that seeks to destroy you." Fricke also thought that the word *Ruhe,* which had appeared in the newspaper's early editions on May 4, had been inserted by Spies.

Grinnell warmed to his task. Had Mr. Fricke ever noticed any copies of Johann Most's anarchist pamphlet, *Science of Revolutionary War,* around the *Arbeiter Zeitung* office? Yes, he had. He had also seen them sold by Spies, Parsons and Fielden at labor meetings throughout Chicago. When Black protested that Grinnell was probing a period of time that antedated the bombing, Gary overruled him abruptly. "If a man is teaching the overthrow of civil order by force," he observed, "and is engaged in a conspiracy to further that end, then the possession of a book or books illustrating the methods of such destruction or advocating their use is competent evidence against him."

Eugene Seegar replaced Fricke in the witness chair. Seegar, a linguist, had translated Spies' *Arbeiter Zeitung* articles into English. As the witness identified a score of fire-eating editorials as having been authored by Spies and Schwab, Grinnell read them aloud to the jury. As he droned on, the reporter for the *New York Times* watched the faces of the eight defendants. "Spies," he wrote the next day, "laughed and sneered by turns. Schwab assumed a philosophical aspect. Parsons was merry in the extreme. Fielden listened intently but maintained a stolid countenance."

The reason for William Seliger's absence from the prisoners' dock became clear on Wednesday morning when Ingham called him as his first—and only—witness of the day. The squat carpenter, who had been granted immunity for turning state's evidence, looked drawn and pale as he waited nervously for the assistant prosecutor's first question. Young Louis Lingg had boarded with him and his wife at 442 Sedgewick Street. On the morning of the Haymarket explosion, he had ordered Lingg to get rid of some bombs which the latter had stored under his bed. "I want those bombs removed from my dwelling," he had told his boarder.

Lingg had promised to do so that very evening if Seliger would "work diligently at them." The witness had repaired some defective shells until one P.M. when Lingg had returned from a meeting on the West Side. Even though Seliger "had no pleasure in the work," he and Lingg had worked all afternoon filling the shell casings with dynamite.

Q. How many bombs were made that afternoon?
A. I can't tell.
Q. A dozen?
A. Oh, more. Perhaps forty or fifty. I can't say exactly.

Lingg had driven him unmercifully because the bombs "were to be used that night."

Later that evening, he had helped Lingg carry a trunkload of bombs to Neff's Hall at 58 Clyborne Avenue, where they had been stored in a hallway. Shortly after they arrived, his companion had begun to distribute bombs to people in the hall. The witness had put two of the makeshift grenades in his own pocket.

Q. Tell what you were going to do that night.
A. A distribution was to be made on the North Side. That was arranged previously. Other distributions were to be made on the West Side to prevent the police from massing at any one point.

When news of the Haymarket bombing began to trickle into Neff's Hall, several men had accused Lingg of playing a part in the tragedy. "Lingg said nothing," Seliger testified. "On the way home he said that even now he was scolded and gibed at for the work he had done; that his brothers in the cause did not appreciate him." Before the two men returned to Sedgewick Street at midnight, they had hidden the undistributed bombs in a crevice under a sidewalk.

He had often heard Engel recommend that workingmen ought to have plenty of bombs. Ingham walked over to the counsel table and picked up a piece of gaspipe. "Is this the way a bomb looks when it is ready to go off?" he asked. Gary sat bolt upright. "Is that loaded?" he demanded. Ingham nodded. "Yes, your Honor," he replied. The judge looked frightened. "This is no place for it!" he barked. When Ingham suggested that the detonator cap could be easily removed by the police in the next room, Gary ordered him to take it to the lakefront. "That's the right place for it," he observed testily.

Thursday's lead-off witness was M. P. Williamson, a former reporter for the *Daily News*. He had covered the dedication of the new Board of Trade Building the previous winter. After the ceremonies, Williamson had followed a parade of socialists through the downtown streets. When the procession had broken up in front of the *Arbeiter Zeitung* office at 107 Seventh Avenue, Parsons and Fielden had urged the crowd to follow them and attack nearby department stores, including Marshall Field's, and help themselves to "the necessities of life."

Q. What was said about the new Board of Trade?
A. Both speakers said the building was put up out of money stolen from them, that everyone who did business there was a robber and a thief.

When the meeting ended, Williamson had gone upstairs to the *Arbeiter Zeitung* office where he had interviewed Parsons. The latter had told him that he and his followers would have blown up the new building if there hadn't been so many police in the vicinity. Besides, the time wasn't ripe for such violent action. "The time hasn't come yet," Parsons had said. "When the time does come, we will meet the police with dynamite and bombs."

Q. When did he say the time would come?
A. Some time during the year.

Parsons had shown the reporter some shells, caps and sticks of dynamite. On *der Tag,* the bombs were to be hurled from the roof tops. "In that way," he had told Williamson, "they could assassinate any force of police or militias that could be assembled."

On May 5, Bonfield had sent a squad of policemen to search the *Arbeiter Zeitung* office. Lieutenant Shea, who had led the search party, had found some fuses, percussion caps and dynamite in Spies's roll-top desk. He and his men had seized the newspaper's files and type settings and taken them to police headquarters. He identified a galley proof as a copy of the "Revenge" circular which had been distributed all over Chicago after the riot at McCormick's. Several thousand copies of this circular had been discovered in the composing room.

Grinnell's last two witnesses of the day were John Ryan, a retired naval officer, and reporter Henry Wilkinson. On

Sunday, May 2, Ryan had heard Spies, Parsons, Schwab and Neebe speak at various lakefront meetings. The former had referred to the police and other officials as "the natural enemies of the workingman." He had urged his listeners to buy rifles or pistols. If they couldn't afford either weapon, they could buy enough dynamite for a quarter to blow up the Pullman Building.

The defense could do little with Ryan, and, after a spate of desultory questions, Black excused him. As the ex-commander started to leave the stand, Parsons hurriedly whispered something in his attorney's ear. The latter immediately requested the witness, who had almost reached the spectators' benches, to return for one more question. "Mr. Ryan," he asked, "was not one of the speakers at these meetings an Irishman?" Yes, that was true. And did Mr. Ryan know this man's name? He did not. "No further questions," said Mr. Black.

Henry Wilkinson had interviewed Spies in January. The editor had explained to him that, on the day of the expected putsch, bombs were to be thrown from the roofs of buildings and infernal machines detonated under sewer manholes. Maps of strategic downtown street corners, showing means of access to adjoining housetops, had been prepared and distributed to socialist shock troops in order to facilitate the dropping of bombs when the signal was given.

The trial's twenty-seventh day opened with Franz Hein, the owner of a saloon at 354 South Clark Street, facing Grinnell. Neebe had stopped at the bar on the evening of May 3, and left copies of the "Revenge" circular. He had informed Hein and several of his patrons that six or seven workingmen had been killed at McCormick's that afternoon. "There will come a time perhaps," he had said hopefully, "when everything will go the other way."

An hour before Neebe had entered Hein's saloon, Gustav Lehman had been attending a carpenters' meeting at Zeph's

Hall. When a man sitting near him had shown him that morning's *Arbeiter Zeitung* which contained a notice of the McCormick protest meeting at Greif's Hall, he had hurried over there. As he entered the hall, he saw that guards had been posted at its entrance.

    Q. What did you hear?
    A. I only heard a large man with a blonde mustache say he
       would take it upon himself to distribute handbills.
    Q. Who is this man?
    A. I was told afterward his name is Fischer.

Lehman belonged to the North Side Socialistic Group which drilled with guns at Neff's saloon every Monday night. He remembered that Engel had once instructed his unit on how to fill sections of gaspipe with dynamite.

When the Board of Trade Building had been dedicated, officers Friporn and Sullivan had been assigned to watch out for any suspicious characters who might show up at the ceremonies. Dressed in civilian clothes, they had mingled with the crowd, which had listened to Parsons' speech in front of the *Arbeiter Zeitung* office. The latter had exhorted his listeners to assassinate members of the Board of Trade with rifles and bombs. When he had finished, an impromptu procession, led by Mrs. Parsons, who was carrying a red flag, had started toward the new building. On the way, its members had thrown a brick at a passing carriage, severely injuring its woman occupant.

The day drew to a close with the testimony of Maurice Neff, the proprietor of the Clyborne Street saloon that bore his name. A dwarf with piercing dark eyes, he recalled that Seliger and Lingg had brought in fifty dynamite-filled shells on May 4 for distribution. He had also been tending bar the night Engel had made a plea for funds with which to start a new paper to be called *The Anarchist*. According to Engel, the *Arbeiter Zeitung* had not been outspoken enough in advocating the use of dynamite to settle labor-management disputes. "The nobility of France had yielded only to the guillotine, the slaveholders of the South to bayonets, and the wage slaves of the present would never gain an inch without the use of dynamite."

When court opened on Saturday morning, Judge Gary, who had permitted several lady friends * to sit beside him during the early part of the trial, was sharing the bench with ex-Governor Bross. After a city fireman said that he had found three bombs under the sidewalk in front of his house where, Seliger had testified, he and Lingg had cached them on the night of the Haymarket explosion, reporter William M. Knox took the stand. He had interviewed Spies at police head-quarters on May 5. The defendant had asked him what the coroner's jury had decided. When Knox had informed him that he was to be held without bail on a charge of murder, Spies had looked surprised. He had said that he hadn't wanted to go to the Haymarket in the first place but Schwab had asked him to come and make a "quieting speech."

In the afternoon, as the telegraph wires from the east were humming with the news that Steve Brodie had jumped off the New York end of the Brooklyn Bridge, Andrew C. Jansen, a Pinkerton operative, swore "to tell the truth, the whole truth and nothing but the truth." In February of 1885, he had been ordered by his employer to join the American branch of the International Workingmen's Union. He had attended all of its meetings through January of 1886, reporting on them to W. A. Pinkerton himself. On one occasion, he had heard Fielden ask the membership for a resolution con-demning the acquittal of a man named Wight which, he had assured his audience, was the result of "his high standing in society." Spies had opposed the resolution. What's the use of

* One of these women, the daughter of Judge John G. Rogers, later said that Gary had been working on a puzzle while the attorneys were arguing a motion before him.

passing resolutions? the editor had asked. "Now is an opportunity for some of our young men to go and shoot Wight." In
April, Spies had expressed the same sentiments about a police
sergeant who had been cleared of bribery by a departmental
board of inquiry.

The week before the opening of the Board of Trade Building, Fielden had indicated some interest in its destruction.
"What a splendid opportunity there would be," he had
exclaimed, "for some bold fellow next Tuesday evening to
make the capitalists tremble by blowing up the building and
all there is in it." Parsons had been the leader of the union's
armed section, to which the witness had been assigned. At
one of the unit's drill sessions, the defendant had said, "Look
here, boys, why can't we make a raid on the First Regiment
Armory. Only two or three men are on guard." The foray,
however, had never taken place.

Jansen was still on the stand when Gary adjourned for the
week end. On Monday, July 26, he told the packed courtroom
about a conversation between Spies and an unidentified
"aged gentleman" on Decoration Day of 1885. Spies had
said that he thought that no more than six bombs would be
required to scatter the state militia which was then parading
through downtown Chicago. The next day, Fielden had
addressed the Internationalists and predicted that the government would be forcibly overthrown on May 1, 1886.
He had repeated this forecast during the August strike of the
street car operators, adding that the social revolution would
be inaugurated by the assassination of Inspector Bonfield.

After a physician had identified a small mountain of nuts,
bolts and bullets as having been removed by him from the
bodies of Haymarket victims, Grinnell called Paul C. Hall,
a reporter for the *Daily News*. Hall, who had been listening
to Fielden's speech on the night of the blast, had heard Ward
order the crowd to disperse. Seconds later, he had seen a
"spark of fire" rise from the audience and fall among the

approaching police. The explosion had followed immediately.

> Q. What was the effect of the explosion?
> A. It seemed to level to the ground the first and third ranks of the police.

On cross-examination, William A. Foster, a trial lawyer who had been imported from Iowa to assist Black, wanted to know if Hall had heard any of the speakers refer to Jay Gould. "Not that I can remember."

> Q. You think that Mr. Gould was not present?
> A. I don't know.
> Q. You think that Mr. Gould may not have been present?
> A. Do you mean Mr. Jay Gould?
> Q. Yes.
> A. No, Mr. Jay Gould was not present.

The laughter that swept the courtroom infuriated Gary. "When you are so tickled that you cannot restrain yourselves," he lectured the amused spectators, "you can go out the door." Grinnell spent the rest of the day reading a number of Socialist newspapers aloud to the jury.

That night, two thousand of the defendants' sympathizers met at Turner's Hall. The meeting was a quiet one despite the fact that Mayor Harrison, who was taking no chances, had assigned a small army of policemen and detectives to attend the rally. Most of the speakers criticized the press for what they termed its "prejudicial coverage" of the trial. Before adjourning, the enthusiastic audience, by a voice vote, adopted a resolution "recommending to the organized workers of Chicago to follow in the footsteps of the Central Labor Council of New York which is entering the arena of political action for the purpose of counteracting the repressive legislation that the capitalistic class will no doubt attempt to railroad through our legislative bodies."

As the defendants filed back into the courtroom on Tuesday morning, a stout matron in a white dress gave each one of them a bouquet of summer flowers. Grinnell started to say something to Judge Gary but thought better of it, and contented himself with calling his first witness, a reporter named Whitin Allen who had covered the Haymarket meeting. Allen had heard Parsons say, "What good are these strikes going to do? You will have to go back to work for less wages than you formerly received." When he had mentioned Jay Gould's name, someone in the crowd shouted, "Hang him! Throw him in the lake!" Parsons had shaken his head. "No, no, that won't do," he had answered. "If Jay Gould was put out of the way today, another Jay Gould or a hundred Jay Goulds would rise up. It is not the man, but the system that ought to be destroyed."

H. O. Heineman, a German newspaperman, had arrived at Haymarket at 7.30 P.M. According to him, the bomb had been thrown by somebody standing in Crane's Alley. He had seen Spies, Schwab, Fielden and a man named Rudolph Schnaubelt standing on the speaker's wagon just before the explosion. He remembered that Spies's account of the McCormick riot had been extremely inflammatory. But, when Black took over, he forced the witness to admit that, by ten o'clock, the crowd had quieted down and the threat of rain had considerably reduced its numbers.

From the look on Grinnell's face when the bailiff called out the name of M. M. Thompson, it was obvious that this was no ordinary witness. Thompson, who worked for Marshall Field & Company, had been on his way home from a business trip to the West Side when he had seen the crowd assembling in the Haymarket. When Spies had climbed onto the speaker's wagon, he had asked for Parsons. Then he and Schwab had descended and walked toward Halsted Street. Thompson had followed them.

Q. Did you hear any words spoken by either of the men?
A. I heard the words "pistols" and "police." Then one of the men asked the other, "Would one be enough?"

Near Halsted Street, Spies and Schwab had been joined by a third man.

> Q. What happened then?
> A. The three men started toward the Haymarket. I went along and once, when I got close to them, I saw Spies hand the third man something which he put in his right-hand coat pocket.

A moment later, he had heard Schwab say, "Now, if they come, give it to them!" Spies had replied, "I don't think we can, for they won't give us a chance tonight."

Harry L. Gilmer, a Chicago house painter, was Wednesday's star witness for the prosecution. He had arrived at the Haymarket fifteen minutes before the explosion. He had been listening to Fielden when he had noticed that one of the speakers on the wagon had jumped down and walked quickly towards the mouth of Crane's Alley, where four or five men were standing, deep in conversation.

> Q. You say a man came from the wagon and joined this group. Can you recognize any of the defendants as that man?
> A. Yes.

The witness pointed at Spies. "It was that one," he said.

A few minutes later, Gilmer had heard someone shout, "Here comes the police!" He had then seen the man who had left the wagon strike a match and ignite something which another member of the small group was holding in his hand. This was followed by what he termed "a sizzling noise." The second man had immediately thrown the lighted object at the advancing police line. When Grinnell showed him a photograph of Rudolph Schnaubelt,* Gilmer immediately identified him as the man who had hurled the grenade.

---

* Shortly after the explosion, Schnaubelt had left Chicago on an Anchor Line Steamer. On July 29, his badly decomposed body was found in the bay at Erie, Pennsylvania.

On cross-examination, Foster wanted to know if the witness had told this story to anyone but Grinnell. No, sir. The State's Attorney was the only one to whom he had spoken about the incident.

> Q. Mr. Grinnell, you say, is the first man you ever told that you knew the man or could identify him as the man who had lighted the fuse or threw the bomb?
> A. I think I had some conversation with Lieutenant Kipley and others in authority at the Central Station.
> Q. When did you tell Mr. Grinnell about this?
> A. I think he was at the Central Station on one of my visits there.

Foster looked perplexed. If Mr. Grinnell knew all about this, why then, he asked, weren't you called before the Coroner's Jury or the Grand Jury? Gilmer's face was a study in blankness. "I don't know," he answered, "what Mr. Grinnell knew or what he understood."

> Q. Well, you told him you thought that you could identify the man who threw the bomb?
> A. I think so.

Foster returned to the counsel table. "No further questions," he said resignedly.

Officer Martin Quinn had searched Engel's home three or four days after the explosion. In the basement, he had found a heavy metal crucible. Engel had explained that a man had brought it to him several weeks before the Haymarket meeting. The defendant told Quinn that the crucible's owner had informed him that it was used for melting metals in order to make bombs.

Grinnell promptly offered the device in evidence. According to one reporter, "it stood three feet high and rested on three strap-iron legs." Inspector Bonfield, a machinist before joining the force, returned briefly to explain that the exhibit was "a small blast furnace used for smelting metal." He was followed by tinsmith Lewis Mullendorf, who remembered that he had built the crucible for Engel and that the latter had carried it home from his shop.

Louis Lingg had been arrested in his room at Seliger's house by officers Schuttler and Lowenstein. Schuttler had the packed courtroom hanging onto every word as he described Lingg's capture. "When Lingg discovered that I was after him," he said, "he drew a big Navy revolver. I grasped the weapon and we clinched and fell to the floor together. We struggled together till another officer came to my assistance and we finally got him handcuffed."

> Q. Did Lingg say something to you when you had secured him?
> A. Yes, he was very violent and said, "Shoot me, kill me, or I'll shoot myself!"

After Lingg had been subdued, the two policemen found another pistol, a ladle and some iron implements in his trunk.

Grinnell caused a sensation the next morning when he asked Gary's permission to let the jury inspect the bloodstained garments of the injured policemen. Black leaped to his feet. If his Honor pleased, the prosecution was trying to inflame the minds of the jurors with "sensational but irrelevant" exhibits. Grinnell pooh-poohed the idea. "If I wanted to be sensational," he said, "I would bring in the blast survivors and let them expose their wounds." The judge shared his opinion and the sanguinary clothing was circulated among the jurors.

Captain Louis Schaak had talked to Lingg at the Chicago Avenue station house on May 14. According to him, Lingg had admitted that the bombs that he and Seliger had made had been intended for use at the Haymarket. It had been decided to employ dynamite and not guns "because the militia had guns and the Socialists had to use dynamite." The defendant, who had learned how to manufacture bombs from a text book, had used clay molds to fabricate three types of explosives. He hated the police for what they had done to the strikers at McCormick's reaper works.

Foster spent the rest of the day trying to overcome the effect of the officer's testimony. Wasn't it true that Lingg had told him, in effect, that "there was to be a conflict between the police and the gatling guns on one side and the laboring men on the other, and that he was making those bombs to use when that time came?" "That's about it," Schaak replied, "only he said the time had actually come."

Q. Do you know of the two detectives at your station who went to Lingg's cell late at night and exhibited a rope, saying they were going to hang him?

A. I do not, and I do not believe anything of the kind was done.

Foster looked almost grateful when Gary finally broke in to announce that it was time to adjourn.

Friday was so cloudy that his Honor ordered the lights turned on as soon as court opened at 9:30 A.M. Grinnell only had a few more witnesses to complete the State's case. Charles B. Prouty, a gun dealer, identified Engel and Parsons as prospective customers who had visited his shop and priced some "large guns." The county physician, a Dr. Bluthardt, who had performed the autopsy on Degan's body, said that death had been caused by a piece of lead which had severed the femoral artery in the patrolman's left thigh. Lastly, Officer John Smith testified that he had found "a revolver, a breech-loading rifle, a sword and a red flag" in Neebe's house when he had searched it on May 7.

As Smith left the stand, Grinnell informed Gary that he had no further witnesses. But he did have some more articles from the *Arbeiter Zeitung* which he wanted to read to the jury before calling it a day. Unfortunately, they were still in the process of being translated and, if Mr. Black wanted to start his case, he could read them into the record tomorrow. The defense attorney was perfectly willing to follow Grinnell's suggestion if he would agree to call no further witnesses. When the State's Attorney refused to make such a bargain, Gary gave the jurors the rest of the day off, recommending that they take a carriage ride and get some fresh air. "By all means," echoed Black, "let the jury take a ride."

The next morning, Grinnell read a dozen or so *Arbeiter Zeitung* editorials to the jury. The only persons in the courtroom seemingly interested in his sonorous recitation were the defendants who listened intently to the familiar exhortations to resistance, riot and rebellion. One article outlined the violence that would follow the inauguration of the eight-hour-day movement. Another called for rifle drills to prepare for the May First revolution. A third urged workingmen not to assemble on D-Day unless they were adequately armed.

Grinnell's last witness was a detective who identified some red flags and banners which had been found in the *Arbeiter Zeitung* office. "Boys, stick together!" read one. Another proclaimed that "Every Government is a Conspiracy Against the People." When they had all been marked in evidence, a weary prosecutor walked back to his table. "Here the State rests," he announced.

After *pro forma* motions to dismiss the indictments against all the defendants except Spies and Fielden had been denied by Gary, Moses Salomon, one of Black's young assistants, made the opening statement for the defense. "We expect fully to prove," he told the jury, "that none of these men have done murder or have conspired to do murder. We expect to prove that these men assembled at the Haymarket on the night of the fourth of May to exercise the right of free speech, to hold a peaceable meeting for the purpose of discussing the rights of laboring men. We expect to show you that Mr. Fielden fired no shot at that meeting, and that he had not then and never had a revolver. We expect to show you that the witness

Gilmer is a constitutional and professional liar. We expect to prove that on the night of the Haymarket meeting, Mr. Schwab did not speak to Spies, but that he left the meeting some time before the explosion occurred."

At this point, Salomon was interrupted by a fit of violent coughing. He drank deeply from a glass of water before continuing. "We expect to show," he resumed, "that Parsons and Fielden left the meeting early and were seated in Zeph's Hall, perhaps drinking a glass of beer, when the bomb exploded. We shall prove that Neebe was at home and expect to show that he had no knowledge of the meeting. You are familiar with the movements of Lingg. We expect to show that none of these defendants fired shots at the Haymarket meeting and that the first shots were fired by the police." When Salomon sat down after his two-hour stint, his eight clients, all of whom, with the exception of Spies, sported red boutonnieres, were smiling broadly.

The courtroom was buzzing on Monday morning when Black called Mayor Harrison as his first witness. The Mayor had gone to the Haymarket because he had been alarmed by the riot at McCormick's and the "Revenge" circular which had followed it. Several hours before the explosion, he had called his police captains together and told them to disperse the crowd at the Haymarket if things looked ominous. When Spies had spotted him in the audience, the tone of his voice had softened, and Harrison had told Bonfield that he thought "there would be no trouble." Accordingly, he had directed the inspector to dismiss the reserves who had been standing by at the Desplaines Street station.

Martin Simonson, a traveling salesman, had been standing near the speakers' wagon when the police arrived. He had not heard anyone shout, "Here come the bloodhounds!" The bomb had exploded several seconds after Ward had ordered the crowd to disperse. Simonson was certain that the man who had thrown it was standing behind some boxes about twenty feet south of Crane's Alley. It had been the police and not the spectators who had commenced firing after the blast.

The salesman's version of the shooting was confirmed by John Ferguson, a janitor, who had also been listening to the Haymarket orators. He had seen Bonfield's men "rush out" of a side street and "whirl down" on Fielden's audience. Just as he had heard one officer shout "Hurry up!" there had been a loud "report." This had been followed by "pistol flashes."

Q. Where were the flashes?
A. They were all in the middle of the street south of Randolph.
Q. Did you see any flashes on either side of the street where the crowd stood?
A. No, sir.

The defendants' lawyers were late on Tuesday morning. Mrs. Black took advantage of their absence to distribute newspapers and magazines to the prisoners. When her husband finally put in an appearance, he called James D. Taylor as his first witness of the day. Taylor, who was extremely deaf, claimed that he had heard every word at the Haymarket meeting but could remember only that Fielden had shouted, "Damn the law, throttle it!" He had kept his eyes on the latter after the explosion, and he had not seen him use a revolver. Like Simonson, he was sure that the bomb had been thrown by a man standing behind some boxes twenty feet south of the alley. Although the police had been shooting constantly, no one in the crowd had returned their fire.

Joseph Katscher and William Urban told much the same stories. The former had watched the police open fire as they neared the speakers' wagon.

Q. Did you see anyone else firing?
A. No, sir.
Q. The police did all the firing?
A. Yes, sir.

No, he had not heard any one say, "Here come the blood-hounds."

Urban had noticed the "glint" on the officers' pistols as soon as the crowd had been ordered to disperse. He was positive that no one in the audience had drawn a gun. On cross-examination Grinnell forced him to admit that most of the crowd had been standing between him and the police.

Q. How was it then that you could see that the police had revolvers in their hands?
A. I saw them.
Q. And you saw no shining revolvers in the hands of anyone else?
A. No, sir.

William D. Gleason, a special agent of the State Trade and Labor Board, also blamed the police for firing the first shots.

On Wednesday, Black called woodworker August Krumm to the stand. The witness and a friend had been listening to the Haymarket speakers shortly before the explosion. Because of the strong wind that had sprung up during Fielden's stint on the wagon, they had gone into the more sheltered Crane's Alley in order to light their pipes. The defense's strategy was obvious. Krumm was, with the exception of his red hair, a dead ringer for Spies. What Gilmer had depicted as the ignition of a bomb fuse by the *Arbeiter Zeitung* editor, might have been nothing more sinister than the lighting of a pipe by an innocent bystander.

Rebuttals were very much the order of the day. During the trial, several prosecution witnesses had sworn that, in April, Engel had prescribed revolvers to the Carpenters' Union as an antidote to the workingman's woes. Fred C. Groh had attended the same meeting and he had heard no talk about arms. As he recalled it, Engel had confined himself to urging his listeners to organize if they expected to better their lot. August Krause, the former president of the union, who had invited the defendant to speak that night, stated emphatically that the word "revolver" had never been uttered.

M. M. Thompson had testified that he had seen Schwab at the Old Haymarket and that he had been discussing "pistols" with Spies. However, Wilhelm Radke, a saloonkeeper, had heard the latter address four thousand people near McCormick's reaper works that same night. After the meeting, Schwab had gone to Radke's saloon, where Frederick Behrens had seen him drinking beer between ten and eleven o'clock.

On Thursday and Friday, Black called a number of witnesses to prove that many of the defendants had not been at the Haymarket when the bomb went off. M. T. Malkoff, a correspondent for a Moscow newspaper, had seen Parsons at Zepf's Hall five minutes before the explosion. According to slow-speaking Thomas Brown, who was also under indictment for his alleged part in the Haymarket riot, Parsons and Fischer had been in a saloon near Zepf's Hall at the time of the blast. Edward Preusser swore that Schwab had arrived at the Deering Harvester Company, several miles outside of Chicago, at 9:30 P.M. on May 4. He had spoken for "fifteen or twenty minutes" and then gone to a nearby saloon for a drink. The witness had seen him board a city-bound street-car shortly after ten o'clock.

Samuel Fielden was the first of the defendants to testify. Speaking in a clear but, according to the *New York Times,* "a trembling voice," he claimed that he had walked over to the Haymarket from the *Arbeiter Zeitung* office with Parsons. After being introduced to the crowd, he had spoken extemporaneously for some twenty minutes. He conceded that he had said something about "throttling the law," but he had meant the remark only in a figurative sense. It had been his purpose to suggest that certain antilabor legislation had to be repealed before the workingman could progress.

The spectators in the courtroom hung on to his every word as he described the scene in the Haymarket. "As I was concluding my remarks," he said, "I noticed the police coming toward me. When they were quite close, Captain Ward said in an angry tone of voice, 'I command you in the name of the State of Illinois to disperse.' I then stepped down from the wagon and said in a conciliatory tone of voice, 'Why, Captain, this is a peaceable meeting.' He made an angry retort, and I started for the sidewalk. As I walked along, I saw a flash across my shoulder and heard the explosion of the bomb. Then I heard the police pouring shots into the crowd from their revolvers and many groans of agony. About this time, I felt a sharp pain in my knee and did not know I was shot until I reached Desplaines Street and mounted a Van Buren street car."

Before Fielden stepped down on Saturday morning, he denied that he had any knowledge about violence or bombs. A peaceful solution had always been his objective, he maintained. He was followed by John Burnet, a young German candymaker, who had been standing some forty feet south of Crane's Alley when the explosion had taken place. Like Gilmer, he had seen the man who had thrown the bomb. Black showed him a picture of Schnaubelt. "Is that the man you saw throw the bomb?" the lawyer asked. "I don't think it is," Burnet replied. The most that Grinnell could get out of the witness was that he had run away after the explosion "because I did not wish to be killed."

In anticipation of the appearance of Spies on the witness stand, the largest crowd of the trial thronged into Judge Gary's courtroom on Monday morning. It was not disappointed. After Schwab had denied that he had been at the Haymarket on May 4 or had had anything to do with the explosion, the bailiff called out the name of the thirty-one-year-old newspaperman. Spies, who had come to the United States from Germany in 1872, had been the editor of the *Arbeiter Zeitung* for the past six years at a weekly salary of eighteen dollars. On the day of the McCormick riot, he had been addressing a meeting of the Lumber Shovers' Union on Black Road. "My speech was commonplace," he said. "I told the men to stand by the union. While speaking, someone cried out in an unknown language and three hundred or four hundred men detached themselves from the meeting and made an attack on McCormick's."

He readily admitted that he had authored the now famous "Revenge" circular. But he insisted that he "did not write the word 'revenge.'"

    Q. Can you tell how it happened to be in there?
    A. I cannot.

When he had first seen the copy for the Haymarket meeting notice, he had insisted that the phrase, "Workingmen, Come Armed!" be deleted. In fact, he had sent Fielden to the printer's to make sure that this was done.

His speech at the Haymarket had been "an ordinary one." He had merely pointed out, as he had many times in the past, that the masses were being exploited and degraded by the capitalistic system. He had remained on the wagon during all the speeches. Toward the end of Fielden's talk, he had heard Ward's order to disperse. "When I reached the sidewalk," he told Black, "I heard a detonation and I thought that the people were firing a cannon to frighten the police." He had gone to Zepf's Hall as soon as the firing began.

    Q. Did you light the bomb?
    A. I never did.

The word *Ruhe*, which had appeared in the *Arbeiter Zeitung* on May 4, had resulted from an anonymous letter which he had received the previous evening. It had read: "Mr. Editor, please insert in today's letter box the word *Ruhe* in prominent letters." The next day, he had been told by Balthaser Rau that the word was a signal to the armed sections of the various unions "to keep their powder dry for use against the police." He had warned Rau that this was foolish, and he had asked Fielden to tell the armed sections that a mistake had been made.

As for the "two small packages of dynamite" which the police had found in his office, he had purchased them because "I had read a great deal about dynamite; I thought I would like to investigate further." The four iron percussion bombs which he had kept in a drawer of his roll-top desk had been given to the paper's bookkeeper three years ago by a man "who said he was from Cleveland." When Grinnell showed him a letter from Johann Most, offering to sell him dynamite "of genuine quality," he admitted that he had received the communication but insisted that he had never ordered any explosives from the revolutionist.

Parsons, whose brother, a general officer assigned to the Treasury Department, had come to Chicago to assist him, was the only native-born defendant. In his Haymarket speech, he had asked the crowd if it was "going to submit tamely to being trampled down like dogs or will you take up arms against your aggressors and save yourselves from hunger and desperation, and your children from infamy?" At that moment, a man in the audience had shouted, "We are ready to do it now!" But he had assured his enthusiastic listener that "now was not the time."

Grinnell concentrated on another portion of Parsons' address. Hadn't he also said that the *Chicago Times* advocated putting strychnine in the workers' bread, and that the newspaper was "the first dynamiter in the country?" Yes, sir, he had said that.

Q. Did you advocate retaliation by the same means?
A. No, sir. I simply told them to defend themselves.

That's all he had ever urged the workers to do.

The closing arguments, which dragged through nine of the summer's hottest days, were a welter of rhetoric. Black, who compared his clients' social philosophies to those preached by "Jesus, the great Socialist of Judea," asked the jury to spare their lives. "I say to you in closing," he concluded, "only the words of that Divine Socialist: 'As ye would that others should do to you, you do even so to them.'"

Grinnell was more down-to-earth. The defendants, whom he characterized as "organized assassins," had preached murder for years. "Personally, I have not a word to say against these men. But the law demands that they be punished. They have violated the law, and you, gentlemen of the jury, stand between the living and the dead. Do your duty. If you think that some of them do not deserve the death penalty, give them a life sentence, but do your duty. Gentlemen, this is no pleasant task for me, but it is my duty. Do yours."

At 2:50 P.M., Thursday, August 19, the jury filed out of the courtroom. Two bailiffs escorted its members to the Grand Jury room on the top floor. At 7:20 P.M., they left the Criminal Court Building for the Revere House, where they had all retired by ten o'clock. On Friday morning, court resumed at 9:56 A.M. "Gentlemen of the jury, have you reached your verdicts?" asked Gary. "We have, your Honor," replied the foreman. Clerk Doyle read them aloud. "We, the jury, find the defendants, August Spies, Michael Schwab, Samuel Fielden, Albert Parsons, Adolph Fischer, George Engel and Louis Lingg guilty of murder in manner and form charged in the indictment and fix the penalty at death." Tinsmith Oscar Neebe was given fifteen years in the penitentiary. As the verdicts were announced, Mrs. Schwab fainted and had to be carried out of the courtroom.

On September 14, 1887, the Supreme Court of Illinois affirmed the convictions. Several weeks later, the United States Supreme Court refused to intervene because, as Chief Justice Waite put it, "there is no Federal question involved." The executions were set for November 11, 1887. However, twenty-four hours earlier, Governor Richard J. Oglesby, in response to an avalanche of pleas for mercy from all over the world, commuted the sentences of Fielden and Schwab to life imprisonment because, as he explained it, the two men had said they were sorry for their part in the Haymarket tragedy. Several hours before the Governor's action, Louis Lingg killed himself in his cell by biting on a percussion cap which had been smuggled into the Cook County Jail by a friend.

At 11:30 A.M. on November 11, Spies, Fischer, Engel and Parsons, wearing white robes, were hanged from a gallows which had been erected in their cell block. Just before the trap was sprung, Spies shouted, "There will come a time when our silence will be more powerful than the voices you strangle today!" A few days later, Fielden and Schwab joined Neebe in the Illinois State Penitentiary at Joliet.

Two months after the Illinois Supreme Court had refused to disturb Gary's sentences, John P. Altgeld, who had not uttered a public word about the Haymarket bombing or the trial, was elected to the Superior Court bench. Four years later, with the help of labor, the liberals, and a national Democratic trend, he became the first foreign-born Governor in the history of Illinois. On January 10, 1893, still suffering from a nervous breakdown that had afflicted him shortly after the campaign, he was inaugurated in Springfield. He was still so weak that his inaugural address had to be read for him by the clerk of the House of Representatives.

Shortly after his inauguration, Altgeld began poring over the records of the anarchists' trial. While he was studying the transcript, Judge Gary published a remarkable article in the April, 1893, issue of the *Century Magazine,* in which he maintained that "the anarchists were rightly punished, not for opinions, but for horrible deeds." Gary's article was all the catalyst that Altgeld needed. He determined to pardon Fielden, Schwab and Neebe and, by the end of May, had completed an eighteen-thousand-word statement explaining his reasons for extending executive clemency.

On Monday, June 26, 1893, several days after the unveiling
of a monument to the five dead defendants in Chicago's Waldheim Cemetery, Altgeld signed the pardon papers and asked
E. S. Dreyer, a banker who had been the foreman of the grand
jury that had returned a true bill against the defendants on
May 21, 1886, to deliver them personally to the three prisoners. Dreyer, who had been urging for years that the men
should be released, took the next train to Joliet and, by nightfall, the surprised but delighted anarchists were back in
Chicago, where they promptly disappeared into obscurity.

Altgeld's *Reasons for Pardoning* were immediately published in pamphlet form. The sixty-three-page document condemned Special Bailiff Henry L. Ryce for "summoning only
prejudiced men" as prospective jurors, and Judge Gary for
his "adroit manipulation" of the talesmen so as to insure a
hostile jury. As far as the proof of the defendants' guilt was
concerned, even Gary had written to Governor Oglesby on
November 8, 1887, that there was no evidence that Fielden
"knew of any preparation to do the specific act of throwing
the bomb that killed Degan." Grinnell had not only shared
his Honor's opinion as to Fielden but had gratuitously added
that "I believe that Schwab was the pliant weak tool of a
stronger will and more designing person." On March 21,
1889, ex-Mayor Harrison had stated publicly that the State's
Attorney had told him at the end of the prosecution's case
that "he did not think there was sufficient testimony to convict Neebe."

Lastly, Altgeld shared the prisoners' claim that Gary had
conducted the trial "with malicious ferocity." Not only had
he forced the eight defendants to be tried together, but he
had constantly favored the prosecution throughout the trial,
made "insinuating remarks" in the presence of the jury, and
unjustly restricted Black and his associates in their cross-
examination of the state's witnesses. The extent of Gary's
"venom," Altgeld wrote, could best be judged by the fact

that, in his *Century Magazine* article, he had not only castigated the defendants anew but also attacked Black and his
wife. "It is urged that such ferocity . . . is without a parallel
in all history; that even Jeffries in England contented himself
with hanging his victims, and did not stoop to berate them
after they were dead."

On September 15, 1894, Altgeld, in discussing the pardons,
said that "I knew that in every civilized land, and especially
in the United States, the press would ring out loud and bitter
against me for what I did." He was hardly inaccurate. Led by
Joseph Medill's *Chicago Tribune,* most of the country's
newspapers were vituperative to the extreme in their coverage of the prisoners' release. Altgeld was an "anarchist," an
"apologist for murder," "a slimy demagogue" and a man
"without a drop of true American blood in his veins."

For those who could not bring themselves to believe that
one of Chicago's wealthiest landowners could be an anarchist
or a socialist, Medill offered an alternative explanation. The
Governor had pardoned Schwab, Fielden and Neebe in order
to revenge himself on Gary for an 1889 decision reversing a
$26,494.60 judgment in favor of Altgeld for damage caused
by the City of Chicago to a building he owned on Market
Street. "He blamed Judge Gary for the decision which prevented his getting the $26,494," blared the *Tribune.* "Alt-
geld has sought to get even with him ever since." *

The years ahead were hectic ones for the harassed Governor. The depression of 1893, the Pullman strike, the free
silver crusade, the candidacy of William Jennings Bryan—
these and many other issues of local and national importance
taxed the strength of a constitution which had never completely shaken off an attack of swamp fever contracted during
Altgeld's brief tenure as a private in the Ohio National

* Medill did not bother to explain that Gary was only one of three judges
on the Appellate Court and that its decision to send the case back for a new
trial was written by Judge Garnett.

Guard during the closing days of the Civil War. But Medill would never let him forget that, as far as the *Tribune* was concerned, he was nothing more than a "vindictive foreigner" with "anarchistic tendencies."

In the fall of 1896, despite the fact that he had been told by his physician that he was suffering from locomotor ataxia, he consented to stand for a second term. During the campaign, he spent most of his failing strength on behalf of his friend Bryan who was running for the Presidency against Ohio's William McKinley on a platform which was largely the result of Altgeld's efforts at the Democratic National Convention which had nominated the Nebraskan after the latter's electrifying "Cross of Gold" speech.

Mark Hanna, who was managing McKinley's campaign, kept his candidate on his Canton, Ohio, front porch, while Republican orators concentrated their fire on Altgeld, whom they characterized as "the brain and inspiration of the movement for which Mr. Bryan stands." As former President Benjamin Harrison put it, "Whenever our people elect a President who believes that he must ask of Governor Altgeld permission to enforce the laws of the United States, we have surrendered the victory the boys won in 1861." In editorials, cartoons and speeches, the Illinois Governor was depicted as an "ambitious and unscrupulous Communist" who was looking forward to the day when he could fly the red flag of anarchy over the White House.

Hanna's strategy was eminently successful. On Election Day, both Bryan and Altgeld went down to defeat. The next morning's edition of the *Chicago Tribune* was exultant. John Pardon Altgeld, it pointed out gleefully, had been beaten by a larger plurality than he had won by in 1892. "His cynical misconduct, his criminal sympathies, his anarchistic tendencies, his fostering of evil, his industrious, sedulous efforts to breed social discord," wrote Medill, had made him unfit to hold public office. On inauguration day, two months

later, his successor, *Tribune*-backed John R. Tanner, at
Medill's urging, refused to allow him the customary courtesy
of making a farewell speech. "Illinois has had enough of that
anarchist," the new Governor told the inauguration committee.

Altgeld was only forty-nine years old when he left Springfield. But his health had been permanently impaired by his
four years in the Governor's mansion, and it was obvious to
his friends that his days were numbered. In 1899, he took a
last fling at politics when he ran unsuccessfully for Mayor of
Chicago as an independent candidate, polling less than one-
sixth of the vote. Following the loss of all his real estate holdings, except a heavily mortgaged home on Malden Street, he
became a partner in Clarence Darrow's burgeoning law firm.
On March 12, 1902, after he had addressed a meeting in a
Joliet theater, on behalf of the embattled Boers, he collapsed
on the stage. He died in his hotel room six hours later of
what was subsequently diagnosed as a cerebral hemorrhage.
Even the repentant *Tribune* admitted that "a great man" had
passed away.

"If I pardon the Haymarket anarchists," Altgeld had once
told Darrow, "from that day on, I will be a dead man." The
lawyer must have remembered those prophetic words as he
made the forty-mile trip to Joliet the next day to bring his
friend's body back to Chicago where it lay in state in the Public Library Building until the funeral two days later. Because
the two clergymen who were asked to officiate at the services
refused to do so, Darrow gave a moving extemporaneous address.

"In the days now past," he told his graveside audience,
"John P. Altgeld, our loving chief, in scorn and derision was
called John Pardon Altgeld by those who would destroy his
power. We who stand today around his bier and mourn the
brave and loving friend are glad to adopt this name. If, in
the infinite economy of nature, there shall be another land

where crooked paths shall be made straight, where heaven's justice shall review the judgments of the earth—if there shall be a great, wise, humane judge, before whom the sons of men shall come, we can hope for nothing better for ourselves than to pass into the infinite presence as the comrades and friends of John Pardon Altgeld, who opened the prison doors and set the captive free."

# Clarence Seward Darrow

Clarence Darrow had been the general attorney for the Chicago & Northwestern Railroad for a little more than two years when the Pullman Strike of 1894 began. Despite his official position, his sympathies were wholly with the strikers. "I really wanted the men to win," he wrote in *The Story of My Life*, "and believed that they should. I had no feeling that the members of labor unions were better than employers; I knew that, like all other men, they were often selfish and unreasonable, but I believed that the distribution of wealth was grossly unjust, and I sympathized with almost all efforts to get higher wages and to improve general conditions for the masses."

Several days after the trains had stopped running, Darrow was notified that he had been placed on one of the railroads' joint antistrike committees. Because of his leanings toward Eugene V. Debs and his American Railway Union, he offered his resignation to Marvin Hewitt the president of the Chicago & Northwestern. "I felt . . . that the road had the right to men who were in full accord with their policy; but they urged me to stay, and, of course, their confidence and fairness made a strong appeal to me. So I told them that I would remain, and that if it ever came to a point where either they or I should feel any embarrassment, we would take up the question again."

The point came sooner than either man had anticipated. On July 4, 1894, eight days after Debs had ordered a boycott against all trains hauling Pullman cars, President Cleveland, at the request of the roads, ordered Federal troops into Chicago. Three days later, Debs and most of the union's officers were arrested for criminal conspiracy, and lodged in the Cook County Jail. In the interim, Cleveland's Attorney General, a former railroad executive, had appointed the general counsel of the Chicago, Milwaukee & St. Paul as the government's special attorney to secure an injunction against the strikers. "I did not regard this as fair," Darrow wrote in 1932. "The government might, with as good graces, have appointed the attorney for the American Railway Union to represent the United States."

This time, Darrow could not be talked out of his determination to leave the Chicago & Northwestern, and to accept an invitation to defend the union. "It hurts me too much," he confided to Governor John P. Altgeld, "to see Debs and men like him faced with the possibility of spending years in prison." Accordingly, he again submitted his resignation to Hewitt, and took up the cudgels for the beleaguered union. His life was never to be quite the same again.

Until the Pullman strike, Darrow had been quite content at the Chicago & Northwestern. The sizable salary checks which were delivered to his desk twice a month had enabled him to repay his brother, Everett, for the money he had borrowed to move to Chicago six years earlier, and to buy a comfortable house in one of the city's better residential sections. He was well-liked at the railroad and could look forward to an interesting and lucrative career as its legal representative. The news that he had voluntarily left the fold astounded his associates. As one of his biographers put it, "A young man at the height of his career, counsel to a powerful railroad, a man being sought after by large corporations; for this man to renounce all this and to defend a poverty-stricken labor leader, a madman, the enemy of his country—this was unthinkable."

Despite the speed with which he made his decision, Darrow knew what he was throwing away when he became Debs' attorney. It would not be easy for a thirty-seven-year-old man, with a wife and son to support, to start over again with an impoverished, out-of-favor union as his only client. "I did not want to take the position, and felt that I should not, but I had not been able to justify my strong convictions with a refusal to aid them in their contest." He could no more help taking the plunge than he could control the unruly lock of hair that so often tumbled over the right side of his prominent forehead.

Was Darrow's resignation an act of courage? Edgar Lee Masters, his future partner, never thought so. "He posed as an altruist and a friend of the oppressed," he wrote in 1936. To a large degree, Darrow himself shared Masters' cold appraisal. As he once told Altgeld, "If it were easier for me to go on being counsel for the Northwestern, I'd do so. But, Governor, you understand, the price is too high. Like the man who drops a dime in a blind man's cup to buy ten-cents-worth of relief from social pain, I am buying relief, too. It isn't idealism at all, it's just plain, downright selfishness."

Perhaps it was just a matter of semantics, after all.

## Clarence Darrow and the conspiracy trial of Eugene Victor Debs, January 25 to February 12, 1895

IN 1892, two men, who were destined to have a profound effect on each other's lives, started new careers. In Terre Haute, Indiana, thirty-seven-year-old Eugene Victor Debs, the secretary-treasurer of the Brotherhood of Locomotive Firemen, resigned to devote his energies to his "life's desire to unify railroad employees and to eliminate the aristocracy of labor." Some two hundred miles to the south, Clarence Seward Darrow, who, at thirty-five, was Chicago's Corporation Counsel, had just left public life to become the general attorney of the Chicago & Northwestern Railroad. Two short years later, the dapper labor leader and the perenially unkempt lawyer were to stand side by side in a Chicago courtroom as a Federal judge wrote finis to what a hostile press had somewhat fancifully labelled, "The Debs Rebellion."

By the spring of 1893, Debs' thinking on industrial unionization had crystallized. As he explained to Professor John R. Commons of Indiana University, he intended to create an "American Railway Union, modeled after the Constitution of the United States, which would include subordinate organizations of all railway employees as 'states' in the union." He had wasted no time in implementing his plan. On June 20, despite the opposition of the old-line craft unions, the American Railway Union was born in Chicago, with membership open to all white, non-managerial railroad employees. Debs was named president, with George W. Howard, the leader of the Brotherhood of Conductors, Sylvester Keliher, the secretary-treasurer of the Carmen's Union, and L. W. Rogers, who had published the *Railroad Trainman,* filling the posts of vice-president, secretary and editor respectively.

The first ARU lodge came into being on August 17 and, as the depression of 1893 deepened, worried railroaders flocked to join the new union. At the end of the year, Debs could boast of more than a hundred lodges, affecting every railroad operating west of Chicago. On New Year's Day, 1894, Rogers issued his first edition of the *Railway Times,* and his persuasive prose helped to push ARU membership beyond the 150,000 mark. By early spring, Debs proudly proclaimed the organization of some twenty-four roads as well as the fact that even the workers at the Pullman Palace Car Company, whose autocratic president regarded unionism and hard liquor as twin evils, were carrying ARU membership cards.

On April 13, 1894, Debs ordered a strike on James J. Hill's Great Northern where wages had been reduced three times since August of 1893. Eighteen days after the strike began, it ended with an arbitrated settlement under which the strikers received, as their president stated, "97½ per cent of what they claimed as their rights." With the prestige of the ARU at the highest point it was ever to achieve, a jubilant Debs proclaimed that "the one grand achievement of this strike is to prove to organized labor that there is nothing in violence. I do not think that there will be more strikes for a long time."

But, even as the ARU president rode home to Terre Haute for a much-needed rest, trouble was brewing in Pullman, Illinois, George M. Pullman's company town, whose underpaid and overworked inhabitants were smarting under wage-cuts that ranged between 33⅓ to 50 per cent. On May 7, a forty-man grievance committee called on Pullman vice-president Thomas H. Wickes and asked him to do something about raising their wages and/or lowering their rents. When Wickes temporized for three days, the committee called an emergency meeting of the work force at Turner Hall in neighboring Kensington. Although Howard and Keliher, who had been sent to Kensington by Debs, urged caution, the Pullmanites voted, after three ballots, to strike.

At noon on May 11, three thousand Pullman workers walked out of their shops. "We do not expect the company to concede our demands," their leaders pessimistically declared, "but we do know that we are working for less wages than will maintain ourselves and families in the necessaries of life and on that proposition we absolutely refuse to work any longer." Three days later, Debs arrived in town to investigate conditions for himself. On May 18, he returned to Terre Haute after agreeing with the strikers that "the paternalism of Pullman is the same as the self-interest of a slaveholder in his human chattels. You are striking to avert slavery and degradation."

On June 12, with the Pullman strike one month old, the first annual ARU convention was called to order at Uhlich's Hall in Chicago. Three days after it had opened, it was addressed by Thomas Heathcote, the chairman of the Pullman strike committee. "We joined the American Railway Union," he told the more than four hundred delegates, "because it gave us a glimmer of hope. We will make you proud of us, brothers, if you will give us the help we need." He was followed on the rostrum by Jennie Curtis, a Pullman seamstress, who brought the delegates out of their seats with a moving commentary about working conditions in the country's only feudal barony.

Although the convention was ready to vote a boycott of every train hauling Pullman cars, Debs persuaded its members to hold their fire until a twelve-man committee could explore the possibility of arbitration. The next day, the committee reported back that George Pullman would not meet with any ARU men. With the delegates chafing at the bit, Debs made one more attempt to avoid a strike. He appointed another committee, this time composed only of Pullman employees, and ordered it to try again. But it fared no better than its predecessor. With Pullman's "There is nothing to arbitrate!" ringing in their ears, the committee members reported back to the convention, which promptly voted to send the strikers two thousand dollars as a contribution to their war chest.

On June 22, a special ARU strategy board, which had been appointed six days earlier, recommended to the convention that, unless Pullman agreed to arbitrate by noon on June 26, it should order a union-wide boycott of all trains with parlor or sleeping cars. The delegates roared their approval and voted unanimously to accept the board's recommendation. When the deadline passed without any word from Pullman, Debs bowed to the inevitable and dispatched telegrams to every division point, ordering ARU members to refuse to haul Pullman cars. Within three days, more than 100,000 railroad workers were enforcing the boycott which all but halted traffic on twenty roads operating into Chicago. The carriers immediately retaliated by reactivating their General Managers' Association, which had been so successful a year earlier in breaking a wildcat switchmen's strike in Buffalo.

Despite the fact that Debs had warned his members to avoid violence, it wasn't long before trains were being stoned, freight cars overturned and engines sabotaged. The situation became so tense at Cairo, Illinois, that its mayor, at the request of the Illinois Central, sent a telegram to Governor John P. Altgeld, urging him to call out the state militia. Altgeld responded by rushing three infantry companies to the beleaguered city. However, despite the fact that strikebreakers hired by the General Managers were pouring into Chicago, the violence that did occur was sporadic and did not cause a great deal of property damage. But this did not deter United States Attorney Thomas E. Milchrist from sending a frantic wire to Attorney General Richard Olney, asking for permission to hire special deputies to protect mail trains.

On July 2, Olney, at the instigation of the railroads, obtained an omnibus injunction from two Federal judges—Peter S. Grosscup and William A. Woods—which, among other things, restrained Debs and his chief officers "from in any manner interfering with, hindering or stopping any trains carrying the mails . . . or inducing any of the employees of any of the said railroads to refuse or fail to perform any of their duties as employees." Even the staid *New York Times,* which had not been overly sympathetic toward the strikers, called the judges' order "one of those peculiar instruments that punishes an individual for doing a certain thing, and is equally merciless if he does not do it." The next morning, copies of the injunction were served on Debs and his co-defendants at strike headquarters in Uhlich's Hall.

That afternoon, in response to an urgent (and quite misleading) telegram from Grosscup and Milchrist, Olney persuaded President Grover Cleveland to order Federal troops into Chicago. The next day, as the city prepared to celebrate the Fourth, ten thousand soldiers from nearby Fort Sheridan poured into town and took up positions in all the railroad yards and terminals. Governor Altgeld was aghast at the President's action and, in two long telegrams to him, pointed out that the situation was not as serious as the "pure fabrications and wild exaggerations" of the newspapers had suggested, and that the State of Illinois was perfectly capable of preserving order. Cleveland replied curtly that "the presence of Federal troops in the city of Chicago was deemed not only proper but necessary . . . to restore obedience to law and to protect life and property."

But there was more to come from Washington than marching orders. Six days after the arrival of the troops, Debs, Howard, Keliher and Rogers were indicted for criminal conspiracy by a Federal grand jury which had heard only one witness—a

Western Union official—and read a few incriminating telegrams which had been carefully culled by Milchrist from the
thousands which had emanated from strike headquarters.
The four men were quickly released on bail of ten thousand
dollars each but the respite was only temporary.

A week later, Federal marshals reappeared at Uhlich's
Hall and arrested the ARU officers (as well as four of its directors) for violating the Woods-Grosscup injunction of July
2. This time, the union men refused to post bail and were
sent to the Cook County Jail, a forbidding granite structure
that stood on the corner of Austin Avenue and Dearborn
Street. There, Debs later wrote in his *Walls and Bars*, "I was
given a cell occupied by five other men. It was infested with
vermin, and sewer rats scurried back and forth over the
floors of that human cesspool in such numbers that it was
almost impossible for me to place my feet on the stone floor."
The rats were so large and ferocious that even a fox terrier
which the prisoner borrowed from a guard to exterminate
them had to be precipitously rescued from its intended prey.

As soon as the injunction orders had been served, Debs had
sought legal help in the most unlikely of places, the plush
corporate offices of the Chicago & Northwestern Railroad.
Through friends, he had asked Clarence S. Darrow, the road's
general attorney, to help him fight the restraining order.
Darrow, who had come to Chicago from Ashtabula, Ohio, in
the fall of 1887, had so impressed John P. Altgeld with his
refutation of Henry George's single tax theory that the future
Governor, then a Superior Court judge, had persuaded Mayor
Creiger to give his new protégé a job in the city's law department. Within a year, the ungainly, shaggy-haired lawyer had
worked himself up to corporation counsel. In 1892, he had
suddenly resigned his public office to become chief counsel
to the Chicago & Northwestern.

It took Darrow only one day to make up his mind about
Debs' request. Cleveland's use of troops and the appointment

of Edwin Walker, general counsel for both the Chicago, Milwaukee & St. Paul Railway Company and the General Managers' Association, as special attorney for the government in
the injunction proceeding, had so affronted his sense of fair
play that he decided to throw in his lot with the strikers. "I
did not want to take it up," he later wrote, "knowing what
would be involved. I knew it would take all my time for a
long period, with no compensation; but I was on their side,
and when I saw poor men giving up their jobs for a cause,
I could find no sufficient excuse, except my selfish interest, for
refusing."

With Debs languishing in jail, the troops bringing the
trains through, and the crippling Federal injunction in effect, the strike rapidly petered out. The ARU had been all
but destroyed and its members were finding it almost impossible to obtain work on any western railroad. Even Debs
seemed to have lost heart and, despite his original intention
to remain in jail until his trials for conspiracy and contempt
of court were concluded, he reluctantly accepted bail after
the preliminary hearing on the latter charge. He addressed
the union's last strike meeting at Uhlich's Hall and then
returned to Terre Haute where, ill and despondent, he spent
the next two weeks in bed. He was prepared, he said resignedly, to "accept with philosophic composure any penalties,
however severe, the courts may see fit to impose."

In August, Cleveland named Carroll D. Wright, the director of his Labor Bureau, as the head of a three-man commission to investigate the boycott on the Illinois Central and
the Rock Island. Hearings began in Chicago on August 15.
Wright, who was determined to be fair to all sides, called
scores of witnesses—union men, railroad executives, and public officials—whose testimony filled almost a thousand pages
of the printed record. Darrow, who attended every session,
was convinced that the strikers had made a more than satis-
factory showing.

Even the Pullman officials who testified had to admit that their striking employees had done their best to protect the company's shops and that, "from May 11 to July 3, there was not the slightest disorder or destruction of property." A battery of Chicago policemen swore that any violence that had occurred in the city's yards had been caused by hoodlums who were not ARU members. Debs took the stand and explained that, out of the almost ten thousand telegrams dispatched by the union during the strike, only one contained any reference to force. The exception, a wire dated July 2, 1894, which had been sent to an ARU organizer at South Butte, Montana, ended with the admonition to "save your money and buy a gun." Although his name appeared at the bottom of the telegram, Debs insisted that the last sentence had been added by a young, overzealous office worker.

Before the ARU president stepped down, he told Wright and his fellow commissioners that Federal ownership of the railroads was the only way to avoid future strikes. "Government ownership of railroads," he declared fervently, "is decidedly better than railroad ownership of government." As far as the strike itself was concerned, he felt that it had been more than justified. "It seems to me," he observed, "that if it were not for resistance to degrading conditions, the tendency of our whole civilization would be downward; after a while, we would reach the point where there would be no resistance, and slavery would come."

Debs was followed by George Pullman who revealed that, at the very time he was slashing his employees' wages, his company had a cash reserve of twenty-eight million dollars and had just paid dividends of almost three million dollars to its stockholders. When Wright asked him why he hadn't used some of this surplus money to maintain his wage levels, Pullman retorted that "my duty is to my stockholders and my company. There was no reason to give those workingmen a gift of money."

Although Wright's report to President Cleveland "seriously questioned whether courts have jurisdiction to enjoin citizens from 'persuading' each other in industrial or other matters of common interest," the Government had no intention of dropping the contempt charges against the union officials. Early in September, the latter appeared before Judge Woods to show cause why they should not be punished for violating the Woods-Grosscup injunction. According to United States Attorney Milchrist, Debs and his co-defendants were guilty of "wilful and repeated violations of said injunction." That, said Woods, was the only issue in the case, and he warned both sides to eschew "the irrelevant and the extraneous."

The Government's case was presented by Milchrist and Walker. In the main, it consisted of parading before Woods the many telegrams sent by the ARU to its organizers and shop stewards after the issuance of the injunction. On Wednesday, September 5, Edwin W. Mulford of the Western Union Company walked to the stand with a bulky manila envelope under each arm. They contained, he informed Woods, duplicates of every wire filed by the ARU after July 2, but he was unwilling to disclose their contents unless the judge ordered him to do so. His Honor promptly did so, and the telegrams were read into the record. Only two, it seemed, had been signed by Debs.

After Mulford had testified, Milchrist called scores of witnesses to attest to the fact that railroad employees had been "assaulted and intimidated by the strikers and driven from their post of duty, either by physical violence or threats of personal injury." William Mackey and Charles E. Mills, an engineer and foreman respectively for the Chicago, Milwaukee & St. Paul, said that they had been forced to leave their train by ARU members. H. F. Sembower, a Baltimore & Ohio engineer, had been stopped by strikers as his train entered Chicago. A mob had halted a Michigan Central freight at Kensington and "persuaded" engineer J. F. Murphy to leave his cab. These were just a few of the more than fifty railroaders summoned by Milchrist and Walker to buttress their claim that violence had been an integral element of the boycott. On cross-examination, most of them admitted that the tabs for their expenses in coming to Chicago to testify were being picked up by their employers.

The prosecution was determined to overwhelm Woods with evidence that his injunction had been openly flaunted by the union. Frank Andrews, a Chicago reporter, swore that Debs had told him on July 4 that "he was not afraid of any court or injunction, as he had committed no wrong, that his union would continue to fight on the same lines as before the Woods-Grosscup injunction was issued." Another newspaperman, who had interviewed most of the defendants after they had been served with copies of the two-judge order, had heard one of them say that "the American Railway Union would simply laugh at this injunction."

Henry Swan, a Rock Island fireman, had been present at Blue Island when United States Marshal John W. Arnold had read the injunction aloud to the strikers. "The men heard the injunction read," he recalled, "but jeered all the time and hooted Marshal Arnold and Deputy Allen who read it." When Arnold tacked the order on a yard bulletin board, ARU men had immediately "pulled it down and ripped it into pieces."

Before Milchrist rested, he called James Hogan, one of the defendants, and L. P. Benedict, Debs' private secretary. Both men refused to answer any questions, and the prosecutor asked Woods to order them to testify. "I expect to prove through these witnesses," Milchrist explained, "that Debs and the other defendants knew and approved the contents of the telegrams that the union filed with Western Union." When Woods refused to grant the prosecutor's request, the latter produced the messenger boys who had picked up the telegrams at strike headquarters. But they were of little help.

Only on three or four occasions did any of them remember receiving outgoing wires directly from any of the defendants.

Outside of trying to convince Woods that the injunction itself was illegal, the defense concentrated on proving that the strike had been peacefully conducted. Almost every ARU telegram had contained the admonition, "Commit no violence." Early in July, Debs had warned the strikers to be "orderly and law-abiding. Keep away from railroad yards, or right of way, or other places where large crowds congregate. A safe plan is to remain away entirely from places where there is any likelihood of an outbreak. Respect the law, conduct yourselves as becomes men, and our cause will be crowned with success." In a speech at Uhlich's Hall on July 7, he had emphasized that "we must triumph as law-abiding citizens or not at all. Those who engage in force and violence are our real enemies."

It was the union's contention that the extensive violence that had occurred just before the Federal troops had moved into Chicago had been caused by the 3600 deputies who had been appointed by Marshal Arnold. According to the report of the Wright Commission, they had been "selected by and appointed at the request of the General Managers' Association, and of its railroads. They were armed and paid by the railroads, and acted in the double capacity of railroad employees and United States officers." Debs put it more bluntly. "An army of detectives, thugs and murderers were equipped with badge and beer and bludgeon, and turned loose," he told Woods.

The summations began on September 27. Darrow, who believed that the impending conspiracy trial was more important than the contempt proceedings, had taken a back seat while S. S. Gregory, the former City Solicitor of Chicago, and W. W. Erwin, the ARU's regular attorney, had conducted the defense. Gregory led off. "If the injunction was issued without jurisdiction of the court," he thundered, "my clients had a right to violate it." Woods owned that this was so. In any event, the lawyer argued, the defendants should have been tried by a jury. "If their decision be unjust, they are responsible and the victims are not inclined to look upon their convictions as the arbitrary act of some high and un-limited power." Woods shook his head. "This is not a crim-inal action, Mr. Gregory, and you know as well as I do that your clients have no right to a jury trial in this type of pro-ceeding."

Gregory was followed by John S. Miller, the general coun-sel of the Santa Fe. A portly, red-faced man, he insisted that "when these men said in their telegrams, 'Commit no vio-lence,' they meant it as much as Marc Antony did when he advised peace over the dead body of Caesar." With the court's permission, he read Antony's famous eulogy aloud to the amused spectators. When he had finished, he turned to look at the ARU president. "That man over there," he urged, "is Chicago's Marc Antony." Even Debs had to smile at the com-parison.

The next morning, Erwin wound up for the defense. "I hold," he told Woods, "that if a man has the right to strike, he has the right to advise others to strike." The judge was willing to concede the point if the strike was "for a legal purpose." Erwin, who appeared annoyed by Woods' inter-ruption, ended in a blaze of rhetoric. "Isn't it a deplorable state of affairs," he asked, "that while the press rang out, while the pulpits roared against the iniquities at Pullman, no power in the law of the country stepped forward to stop them. These people were starving, yet not a flag was raised, not a drum was beaten, not an officer of the government stepped forth to raise his hand in behalf of them. If you should deem it wise to decide against these men, it would be more like a crucifixion of the cause of labor than a punish-ment of these defendants."

Walker, closing for the prosecution, was less colorful but

just as adamant. As far as he was concerned, the ARU was nothing less than "the worst trust that has ever been organized," falling squarely under the prohibition of Senator John Sherman's brand-new Anti-Trust Act. When Gregory broke in to ask whether the President approved of the contempt action, the special prosecutor nodded curtly. "The administration," he assured the union lawyer, "fully approved of all the proceedings now being taken at Chicago, to make the defendants obey the law."

Turning back to the bench, he finished his argument. "I understand," he said, "that it is the effort of the defense to take away all the jurisdiction from the United States courts in cases of this kind. If the courts of equity have no jurisdiction, what recourse have the people in cases of this character? Under what law does the American Railway Union claim powers not given to any other association or individual—the power of obstructing the passage of trains and the business of railroads?"

It took Judge Woods almost three months to reach his decision. On December 14, he announced that he had found all the defendants "guilty of contempt in disobeying the mandates of an injunction issued herein on the second day of July, A.D., 1894." There was no doubt in his mind that the union hierarchy had deliberately flaunted the restraining order that he and his brother Grosscup had issued. "The defendants," he wrote, "conducted and controlled the strike with persistent consistency of purpose and unvarying methods of action, and no essential modification in their course of action either followed or was caused by the injunction." He was also quite sure why they had done it. "The fact it was the purpose of Debs, Phelan and their associates to paralyze the interstate commerce of this country is shown conclusively in this case and is known to all men." Walker's closing words had evidently found their mark.

The following day, the *New York Times* was hardly kinder.

"It is not a matter of great moment," it pontificated, "that Mr. Debs should be punished . . . for contempt of court, except as a means of impressing the significance of this decision upon the public and especially upon those who must follow this example hereafter. It is a matter of great moment that it should be established that there is adequate authority to protect the public from lawless combinations to interrupt the railroad life of the country as a means of forcing the redress of alleged private grievances and that such authority will be fully sustained." With rare exception, the country's press shared the *Times'* opinion.

Debs was given the maximum sentence the court had the power to impose—six months in the Cook County Jail—while his seven co-defendants received three-month terms. On December 24, Darrow, who was convinced that "there was not one word of evidence connecting any of them with any violence," asked Woods to let his eight clients spend the Christmas holidays with their families. His Honor agreed that "jail was no place in which to celebrate the birth of the Prince of Peace," and postponed the defendants' commitments to January 7, 1895.

Over Christmas, the Cook County Jail had become so crowded with holiday drunks that Debs and company were transferred to the McHenry County Jail at Woodstock, Illinois, instead. Although his associates surrendered to United States Marshal John W. Arnold promptly on January 7, Debs did not deign to show up until the following day. Just before he was driven the fifty-two miles to Woodstock, he held an impromptu press conference from the back seat of a deputy's car. "In going to jail for participation in the late strike," he told the waiting reporters, "we have no apologies to make nor regrets to express. There is not a scrap of testimony to show that one of us violated any law whatsoever. I would a thousand times rather be accountable for the strike than for Judge Woods' decision."

The McHenry County Jail consisted of a handful of cells in Sheriff George Eckert's home. Eckert, who was a man of some sensibilities, assured his new charges that he considered them as boarders rather than convicts, and he gave them the run of his preserve. In less than a week, his eight guests had converted the corridor outside their cells into a makeshift library where they spent their two daily self-imposed "quiet periods" reading everything from Robert Ingersoll to the Bible. On January 21, Darrow informed them that he had applied to the United States Supreme Court for a writ of habeas corpus and that they would be free on $2,000.00 bail each until their petition had been decided.

On Friday, January 25, their trial for criminal conspiracy opened before Judge Grosscup who, six months earlier, had declared that "the growth of labor organizations must be checked by law." Specifically, the eight men were accused of conspiring to obstruct a mail train on the Rock Island Railroad. As the defendants followed Darrow and Gregory into the crowded courtroom, the spectators craned their necks to get a look at the infamous ARU president whom the *Chicago Tribune* had labelled "Dictator Debs." If they expected to see a bearded, unkempt anarchist, they were doomed to disappointment. The nearly bald, clean-shaven union leader was dressed in a smartly tailored gray tweed suit and sported a boutonniere. With his mild blue eyes that peered out at the world from behind gold-rimmed eyeglasses, he looked more like a botany professor than the leader of what the *Chicago Evening Post* had depicted as a "frenzied mob . . . bent on death and destruction."

There were many in Judge Grosscup's courtroom who, influenced by the imaginative Loop rewrite men, mistook Darrow for his chief client. In his wrinkled blue serge suit with his unruly brown hair falling over his left eye, he slouched in his chair, sitting, as one writer put it, "on the back of his neck," and looking anything but the cosmopolitan lawyer.

As far as outward appearances were concerned, the fifth of
Amirus Darrow's eight children was still the country barrister
who had brought his wife and son to the south side of Chicago in the fall of 1887.

During his long career, Darrow preferred to try his cases
in front of juries whom he regarded as more independent
than judges. "With them," he wrote in 1922, "the common
man, the accused, has a better chance." In later years, he
prided himself on his meticulous selection of jurors, but
today he was almost diffident in his interrogation of the prospective members of the panel. In a matter of hours, a jury
of eight farmers, an insurance agent, a real estate broker, an
interior decorator and a dealer in farm implements had been
sworn, and Grosscup ordered the government to open its case.

But before Tom Milchrist, who, although he had resigned
as United States Attorney, was still paired with Edwin
Walker as co-prosecutor, could open his mouth, Gregory was
on his feet to object to Walker's participation in the trial.
"We strongly feel," he told Grosscup, "that it is not fair to
these defendants to have the government represented by the
former general counsel for the Chicago, Milwaukee & St.
Paul Railroad, and move for his disqualification." The judge
didn't quite see it that way. "So long as Mr. Walker is not
in the railroad's employ today," he ruled, "I see nothing ir-
regular or unusual in his prosecuting this case. Motion denied. Proceed, Mr. Milchrist."

Milchrist, who had been champing at the bit, needed no
second urging. After reiterating that the railroads had nothing to do with the trial, he concentrated his fire on Debs.
The ARU leader was guilty of everything from urging his
men to strike to murdering the seven men who had been
shot by the Federal troops. In between, he had headed a conspiracy which was determined to starve the country, to choke
its economic life, to shut down its factories, and, as the indictment charged, to stop the mails. "Men have a right to

strike," he conceded, "but they have no right to obstruct the United States mails."

As the prosecutor finished, Darrow, who had been slouched in his chair at the defense table, slowly heaved himself to his feet. His low, almost melodious voice contrasted strongly with Milchrist's gruff tones. "Mr. Milchrist has told you," he began, "that the railroads have no finger in this prosecution and that the government alone is pressing the case. But I will venture the assertion that he is only a puppet in the hands of the great railroad corporations." That was why his clients had been indicted for conspiracy rather than under a statute that makes the stopping of a mail car a misdemeanor, punishable by a fine of one hundred dollars.

He warmed to his task. "In order to make felons of honest men who never had a criminal thought, they passed by that statute to seize on one that makes conspiracy to obstruct the mails a crime punishable by imprisonment in the penitentiary. To hound these men into the penitentiary is their purpose, yet they call this respect for the law. Conspiracy, from the days of tyranny in England down to the day of the General Managers' Association, has always been the favorite weapon of every tyrant. It is an effort to punish the crime of thought."

He paused for a moment to glance at a paper in his hand. "If the government does not, we shall try to get the General Managers here to tell what they know about it. The evidence will show that all these defendants did was in behalf of the employees of the man whose name is odious wherever men have a drop of human blood—Mr. Pullman—except the General Managers' Association. These defendants published to all the world what they were doing, and in the midst of a widespread strike they were never so busy that they couldn't find time to counsel against violence. For this, they are brought to court by an organization which used the government as a cloak to conceal its infamous purposes."

On Monday, January 28, a bitterly cold day in Chicago, the government called its first witness, a reporter named Wallace Rice, who was also a member of the Pullman local of the ARU. He had attended the ARU convention from June 12 to 23, 1894, when the subject of the conditions at Pullman had first been discussed. He had been present when the union's board of directors had recommended to the delegates that, if the sleeping car company did not agree to arbitrate in five days, all trains hauling its cars should be boycotted. After their suggestion had been unanimously approved by the convention, Debs had said that if any road attempted to enjoin the ARU, its entire line would be tied up.

On June 26, Rice had been present at a general meeting at Chicago's Empire Theater when the strike had been voted. As he recalled it, Debs had stampeded the delegates by making a fiery speech in which he had referred to the Pullman Company as a "monumental octopus." Darrow, who had protested unsuccessfully that Rice's testimony was irrelevant, was nettled by the witness' constant repetition of the word "octopus." "That's the third time you have said that!" he roared at the newspaperman. "And that is not as often as you said the same thing in your opening speech Saturday," retorted Walker, who was conducting the direct examination.

Grosscup promptly called a halt to the heated exchange and ordered Walker to finish up with Rice. The reporter recalled that Debs had also told the strike meeting that the coming struggle was to be a death battle with either the General Managers' Association or the ARU destroyed. But when the prosecutor started to read the June and July editorials of the union's *Railway Times* into the record, the judge stopped him in midsentence. "These editorials are hearsay," he ruled, "and inadmissible against the defendants on trial."

Nothing daunted, Milchrist called O. W. Myron, an Illinois Central switchman, who had been an ARU organizer of the road's yardmen. Myron said that, on June 26, he had received an order signed by Debs, instructing him to call out the IC workers. As he started to describe how he had gone to the suburban yards to implement Debs's directive, Darrow lumbered to his feet. Whatever Myron did, he protested, was his own responsibility and not that of the defendants. Besides, the switchman's interpretation of the order he had received was completely foreign to this case. Grosscup decided to think about it overnight and adjourned for the day.

The next morning, the judge ruled that the government was entitled to show, not only what orders were given by the ARU, but also what each witness thought he had to do about them. "If it could be proved that, in pursuance of the order of the directors of the American Railway Union, trains bearing mail had been stopped or violence committed, the conspiracy could be practically established," he ruled. A jubilant Milchrist recalled Myron. The switchman said that when he had received telegrams signed by Debs and other ARU officials, he had tried to persuade IC employees to refuse to haul any trains containing Pullman cars. In his effort to obey the union's directives, he had visited every IC yard in the Chicago area.

As the week wore on, Milchrist did his best to convince the jury that the defendants had urged their members to use force wherever necessary. George Beatty, an engineer for the Grand Trunk road, remembered that Jim Hannahan, the Vice-Grand Master of the Brotherhood of Locomotive Firemen, had threatened to throw him out of his cab unless he abandoned his train which was carrying mail. J. C. Fraill, his brakeman, confirmed his story. However, both men admitted, under Darrow's probing, that they had received orders from their dispatcher not to leave the yard until the next morning.

Wednesday was devoted to the testimony of E. W. Mulford, the Western Union manager, who repeated much of what he had said in the contempt proceeding. For the first time since the trial began, the courtroom was almost empty as the witness read aloud hundreds of telegrams sent by the ARU to local executives in Illinois, Montana, Colorado and Ohio. Between June 26 and July 17, the union had spent approximately six thousand dollars in toll charges despite the fact that Debs had a "half-rate" card. Mulford was followed by a host of messenger boys who said that they had delivered the telegrams read by their boss.

The next morning, as the Pullman Memorial Church—a gift from the sleeping car king in honor of his parents—was being dedicated in Albion, New York, Harry Swan, a Rock Island employee, said that his train had been attacked by a crowd at Blue Island on July 2. He had seen one of the defendants throw a stone through the cab window and hit engineer Fitzgibbons on the head. He was sure that John Merwin, another ARU official, had clambered aboard the train and pulled the brake cord. James Jack, an IC brakeman, had heard a union organizer tell a strike meeting on June 27 that "Dynamite is a good thing to stop traffic!"

When court opened on Friday, "General" Jacob S. Coxey shared the bench with Grosscup. The forty-one-year-old leader of the famous march of unemployed men on Washington in the spring of 1894 listened intently as Elias Perkins, an engineer on the Illinois Central, swore that two of the defendants had tried to persuade him to leave his mail train. After asking a few perfunctory questions, Darrow turned the witness over to Gregory, who represented some of the local leaders who had been indicted along with the ARU officials. "Just a minute," snapped Grosscup, "I will permit only one attorney for the defense to cross-examine any witness." Gregory was dumb-struck. "Then I move," he said, "that all of the evidence in this court against my clients be stricken out on the ground that this court refuses them representation by counsel!"

While the judge mulled this one over, there was a hurried

consultation at the prosecution table. Finally, Walker stood up. "The prosecution does not object to the cross-examination by the counsel," he informed the bench. But Grosscup was adamant. "The interests of the defendants are common," he announced, "and they should elect one of their counsel to ask the questions. Mr. Darrow can ask the questions for all."

Darrow, who had been sprawled in his chair, staring up at the ceiling, rose when he heard his name. "If your Honor please," he said, "we who represent the officers of the union have no more interest in the other defendants than we have in a Hottentot. For all that we care, these men may have done the things charged against them. Our duty is to discover the relation the acts of the men may have to the commanding generals of the strike." Grosscup ended the argument by reversing himself and permitting Gregory to question Perkins.

F. L. Krieger, a switch tender for the Chicago, Milwaukee & St. Paul and the president of the Switch Tenders' Association, was Monday's first witness. When the strike had been voted, he had been working in the Milwaukee yards. Walker put him through his paces.

> Q. Mr. Krieger, were you ever approached by anyone who endeavored to have you call out your organization on a strike?
> A. I was. On the Fourth of July, in the afternoon, I was called on by Con McAuliffe, the vice-president of the Milwaukee branch of the American Railway Union and he showed me a dispatch from President Debs. McAuliffe told me I was to get our union on a strike.

The telegram from Debs had ordered McAuliffe to "get switchmen, firemen and others on Milwaukee out immediately." About twelve switchmen had gone on strike.

After Krieger had testified that he had seen a Chicago-bound mail train stopped by strikers as it left the Milwaukee yards, Walker turned the witness over to the defense. Darrow had only a few questions. "Mr. Krieger," he asked, "were you subpoenaed to appear in this case as a witness?" The switchman shook his head. "No, sir, I was not," he replied. "Then how did you happen to come?" the lawyer demanded. Walker uncoiled. "Oh, we will admit," he said, "that we requested several witnesses to come." According to Krieger, he had been asked to attend the trial by one of the railroad's attorneys who had accompanied him to Chicago. No, he didn't know who had paid for the trip.

Krieger was followed by Charles E. Mills, the fireman of the mail train which the former said he had seen stopped in the Milwaukee yards. "On July 5," Mills said, "several American Railway Union men came to the engine on which I was working just about as we were leaving for Chicago and intimidated me into getting off the engine and going with them." The ARU men had warned him that "if you go on this engine, you'll never leave Chicago alive."

Q. Did you fear personal violence?
A. Yes, sir, I did.
Q. Did you leave your engine on that account?
A. Well, I was afraid to go out.
Q. On account of what was said to you?
A. Yes, partially.

He had joined the ARU "about one hour after I left my engine."

When Walker recalled engineer Perkins to ask him a few more questions about the stopping of his train, Grosscup had had enough. "You don't have to bring in any more witnesses to testify to obstruction of trains," he told Walker, "unless they can state that these defendants actively participated." There was a brief huddle at the prosecution table. When it broke up, Walker approached the bench. "The Government rests," he announced in a confident voice.

The sudden end of the prosecution's case caught Darrow

by surprise. There was a long silence in the courtroom until Grosscup, with an impatient edge to his voice, asked, "Well, Mr. Darrow?" The lawyer, who had been whispering to Debs, got to his feet. "We move for a dismissal of the indictment," he said slowly, "on the ground that the evidence for the government only proves some discord and disturbance existing at the time of the strike, but in no way tends to show that the defendants entered into a conspiracy to obstruct the mails." Grosscup reserved decision on the motion and adjourned for the day.

Tuesday was the coldest day of the year in Chicago. When Grosscup gavelled the trial's tenth day into being at 9:30 A.M., the mercury stood at fifteen degrees below zero. Darrow, who had subpoenaed every member of the General Managers' Association within the reach of a Federal marshal's ingenuity, informed his Honor that he would prove that they, and not the defendants, were guilty of a mammoth conspiracy to depress wages and that they were using the machinery of the Federal government to achieve their end. To prove his point, he called President Thomas of the Chicago & Western Indiana, who doubled in brass as the chairman of the General Managers' Association. But Thomas was more than a match for his interrogator and, despite Darrow's best efforts, would not admit that there had been any collusion between the railroads to reduce wages.

Nothing daunted, Darrow picked up a sheaf of papers from the counsel table and asked Thomas to identify them. The railroad executive conceded that they were the minutes of the General Managers' Association. Taking a leaf from the prosecution's book, the defense attorney began to read the minutes aloud to the jury. In August of 1893, for example, the association had stated that its prime objective was "to provide a central organization of all rail carriers in the United States." A month later, its five-man executive committee had decided that a general reduction of railway wages had become necessary.

As far as he was concerned, Darrow told the jury, the general managers had only one objective—to keep their employees at a uniform minimum wage. If this wasn't a conspiracy, then he didn't know the meaning of the word. "If the managers can organize to keep wages down," he roared, "I can't understand why their workers can't band together to fight to raise their standard of living." Grosscup, who, like everyone else in the courtroom, had been carried away by Darrow's rhetoric, suddenly looked up at the clock on the wall behind him and called it a day.

As Darrow fought his way through the crowd of reporters who waited for him in the corridor, he announced that a subpoena had been issued for George M. Pullman and that he expected the magnate to be his first witness on Wednesday morning. But when court reconvened on the sixth, a Federal marshal informed Grosscup that he had not been able to serve Pullman and that he had heard a rumor that the latter was on his way to Florida in his private railroad car. The news was enough to provoke a five-minute recess out of Grosscup. When he returned to the bench, he looked over at the defense counsel table. "Have you got any more witnesses, Mr. Darrow?" he barked. After a short conference with Gregory, the lawyer called out, "Mr. Debs, will you please take the stand?"

For the rest of the day, Darrow steered his chief client from the time when, as a fourteen-year-old boy, he had gone to work as a paint scraper for the Terre Haute & Indianapolis Railroad until he was arrested for leading the Pullman strike. In between, he had spent seventeen years as the unpaid secretary of the Brotherhood of Locomotive Firemen, been elected Terre Haute's city clerk, served one term in the Indiana Legislature, directed the affairs of the Occidental Literary Club, and organized the American Railway Union. He had not been in favor of the strike at Pullman, and he had done everything in his power to prevent it. When it began, he had supported it wholeheartedly, but he had constantly urged his followers to avoid all violence and, above all, to let the mail trains go through.

Under Darrow's deft questioning, he described why he had resigned from the Brotherhood of Locomotive Firemen to form the ARU. He had envisioned a great industrial union, encompassing all railroad workers. When the General Managers' Association had been launched in the spring of 1893, he realized that its main purpose would be to control wages throughout the roads. That had been all the catalyst he needed. On June 20, 1893, the American Railway Union had been born.

The dapper ARU president was an exhausted man when the day drew to a close. But as he walked slowly down the courtroom's central aisle, he burst into a broad grin as scores of spectators rushed to shake his hand. Flanked by Darrow and Gregory, he fought his way through the enthusiastic crowd and headed for the stairs. "Let's see if George Pullman has as much courage," Darrow shouted to a persistent reporter as the three men left the courthouse.

The next morning, William R. Johnson, a slight, light-skinned Negro, who worked as a porter in Pullman's private office, perched nervously on the edge of the witness chair. Grosscup asked him what had happened on February fifth when Deputy Marshal Jones had tried to serve his employer with Darrow's subpoena. According to Johnson, Pullman had arrived at the office at 10:30 that morning. An hour later, Jones had entered the executive suite and given his card to C. S. Sweet, Mr. Pullman's private secretary. Without leaving the room, Sweet had told Jones that Pullman was not in the office.

His Honor, who had previously not appeared to be over-sympathetic to Debs & Company, turned purple with rage. "Even after this case is finished," he sputtered, "when Mr.

Pullman gets back from Florida, he can be punished for contempt of court if it shall be proved that he evaded the subpoena." But next morning's *Tribune* was more understanding. "It is not strange," it editorialized, "that Mr. Pullman should be unwilling to go on the stand to be questioned by Mr. Darrow. It is not pleasant for a person who is at the head of a great corporation . . . to be interrogated by persons who are unfriendly to him and who may put disagreeable inquiries which he has to reply to civilly."

Jennie Curtis, who had stampeded the ARU convention in June with her story of working conditions at Pullman, testified for the defense. There wasn't a sound in the packed courtroom as the thin, emaciated-looking seamstress described how she had been forced to repay the sixty dollars in back rent that her father had owed the company when he died. When Darrow, with a satisfied look on his face, murmured, "Your witness," Milchrist shook his head. "The government has no questions," he said resignedly.

Debs was recalled. For the rest of the morning, he read portions of his proclamations to the strikers in which he urged all members of the ARU to avoid violence. After lunch, Walker took over and forced the ARU president to repeat much of the testimony he had given on direct examination. According to the *New York Times,* "he stood his cross-examination well."

The trial ground to a sudden halt on Friday morning when the bailiff informed Grosscup that sixty-nine-year-old J. C. Coe, one of the jurors, was home ill with the grippe. On Monday, Coe's condition had worsened and his physician said that it would be at least two weeks before he could return to court. "I think it will be necessary," the judge said, "to adjourn the further taking of testimony in this case." Although both sides indicated that they were willing to proceed with eleven jurors, Grosscup thought that this would invalidate the entire trial.

Darrow, who had become increasingly confident of victory, was furious. "The defense is willing to select a new twelfth juror," he shouted, "and to have the transcript of the testimony read to him." But the judge turned down the suggestion and, on Lincoln's Birthday, discharged the jury with the thanks of the court. As the reporters rushed to file their stories, they noticed that Pullman and his attorney, Robert T. Lincoln, the sixteenth President's son, were waiting in the corridor. Both men refused to be interviewed when they heard the news that the trial was over.

As soon as Grosscup had left the courtroom, several jurors thronged around the counsel table to congratulate Debs and his co-defendants. One of them told Darrow that, prior to Coe's illness, they had stood eleven to one for acquittal. Although the judge had indicated that a new trial would begin on the first Monday in May, the government had lost its stomach for further litigation. Despite all of Darrow's sarcastic taunts during the next few months, Milchrist and Walker refused to move the case for trial, and it was ultimately dismissed for lack of prosecution.

On March 25, the scene shifted to Washington, D.C., where Darrow, Gregory and Lyman Trumbull, one of Lincoln's closest friends and a former United States Senator, attempted to persuade the Supreme Court to issue a writ of habeas corpus in the contempt action. The original petition, which had been addressed to Justice John Marshall Harlan, asked that the defendants "be relieved from said unlawful imprisonment and detention . . . so that your petitioners may at once be brought before your Honor, there to do, submit to, and receive what the law may require and your Honor shall adjudge." After two days of argument, the nine justices reserved decision on whether to issue the writ.

Darrow's rationale was a simple one. If it were legal for workingmen to organize into unions and to strike for their own grievances, "they have the right to strike for all their fellow workmen. No doubt it is difficult for some people to understand a motive sufficiently high to cause men to lay down their employment not to serve themselves but to help some one else. But until this is understood, the teachings of the religionists and moralists will have been in vain."

As far as the violence that had occurred, this had been the result of "brute instincts" that had been unleashed by the strike. "Mankind in his progress from the lower order," he told the court, "still retains many instincts of the brute, and at times of great public excitement, or in the presence of great emergencies, these brute instincts are ever liable to control. While, in the light of history, if it were conceded that violence generally followed strikes, it would by no means follow that a great body of men would not have the right to lay down the tools and implements of their trade to better the conditions of themselves and their fellowmen, although growing out of this violence, bloodshed and crime would surely come."

Attorney General Richard Olney, replete in morning coat, striped trousers and spats, represented the Government. As far as he was concerned, the United States had every right to enjoin a strike that was wrecking its economy. "What was done by the government and its courts at Chicago in the summer of 1894," he argued, "was done on a conspicuous theater and dealt with events striking in themselves and in the scale on which they were conducted and strongly appealing to the imaginations as well as the passions of men." If the defendants violated the injunction, as Judge Woods had already decided, then the Supreme Court should not interfere. Otherwise, the Government would be powerless to end future crippling strikes.

On May 27, a unanimous court refused to free the ARU officials. "A most earnest and eloquent appeal was made to us," wrote Mr. Justice Brewer, "in a eulogy of the heroic spirit of those who threw up their employment and gave up their means of earning a livelihood, not in defense of their own rights, but in sympathy for and to assist others whom they believed to be wronged. We yield to none in our admiration of any act of heroism or self-sacrifice, but we may be permitted to add that it is a lesson which cannot be learned too soon or too thoroughly that under this government of and by the people, the means of redress of all wrong are through the courts and at the ballot box, and that no wrong, real or fancied, carries with it legal warrant to invite as a means of redress the co-operation of a mob, with its accompanying acts of violence."

It was back to the McHenry County Jail at Woodstock for the ARU leaders to finish the sentences imposed by Judge Woods. On August 22, all of the prisoners except Debs completed their terms and were released by Sheriff Eckert. The ARU president, who had been sentenced to six months, spent the long days receiving visitors, reading socialistic literature and answering his voluminous correspondence. Within two weeks after his return to Woodstock, his mail had become so heavy that he was forced to hire a secretary who took his dictation in Eckert's spacious living room.

On the evening of November 22, Debs, sporting a jail-grown beard, left snow-bound Woodstock on a special train. Several hours later, he arrived in Chicago, where more than one hundred thousand of his supporters were waiting to greet him. He was scheduled to speak at the Battery D Armory on Michigan Avenue, but, for a time, it looked as if he would not get there. It took the efforts of a small army of policemen to open a path in the crowd that filled the station and the adjacent streets, so that the union leader could get to the packed armory.

Disheveled and breathless, Debs stood at last on the impromptu stage that had been hastily constructed at one end of the building. In a clear, ringing voice, he railed against the indecisive end of his conspiracy trial. "I know," he said, "that I have been denied a trial, and here and now, I demand a hearing of my case. I am charged with conspiracy to commit a crime, and, if guilty, I should go to the penitentiary. All I ask is a fair trial and no favor. Simple justice is the demand. I am not disposed to shrink from the fullest responsibility of my acts. I have had time for meditation and reflection, and I have no hesitancy in declaring that under the same circumstances, I would pursue precisely the same policy. So far as my acts are concerned, I have neither apology nor regrets."

He had nothing but scorn for Judge Woods' injunction. "I challenge the world," he thundered, "to assign a reason why a judge, under the solemn obligation of an oath to obey the Constitution, would, in a temple dedicated to justice, stab the Magna Carta of American liberty to death in the interest of corporations, that labor might be disrobed of its inalienable rights and those who advocated its claim to justice imprisoned as if they were felons." If the courts had not unlawfully interfered in the struggle between the ARU and the General Managers, "victory would have perched upon the standards of labor." In closing, he called on his listeners to set in operation "forces to rescue their constitutional liberties from the grasp of monopoly and its mercenary hirelings."

As Debs left Chicago to begin an unsuccessful two-year crusade to revive the ARU, Darrow, whose defense of the union leader had cut him off from corporate or municipal employment, opened an office in Chicago's Rookery Building. Despite his fears that the Debs case had ruined his chances of earning a living, he soon found that his anteroom was filled with people who wanted to retain the man who had defended the ARU president. "Neither then nor for any considerable time thereafter," he later wrote, "did I need to worry over business prospects. Naturally, the Debs trial attracted a great deal of attention throughout the country, and, as it resulted in victory for the accused, I was asked to enter other labor cases, and criminal cases as well."

In the years that followed, although they differed on politics, he and Debs remained good friends.* Their paths were to cross in public once more. On Sunday, June 16, 1918, Debs addressed the Ohio convention of the Socialist Party in Canton's Nimisilla Park. As a Government stenographer took down every word, he told the more than a thousand Socialists who crowded around the park's bandstand that World War I had been caused by the capitalists who profited by death and destruction. "The feudal barons of the Middle Ages, the economic predecessors of the capitalists of our day, declared all wars. And their miserable serfs fought all the battles. And that is war in a nut shell. The master class has always declared the wars; the subject class has always fought the wars. The master class has had all to gain and nothing to lose, while the subject class has had nothing to gain and all to lose—especially their lives."

Two weeks later, he was arrested in Cleveland for violating the Sedition Act by "uttering profane, scurrilous and abusive language about the Government of the United States." Darrow volunteered at once to defend him, but Debs ignored the offer because the lawyer had publicly supported the United States' entry into the European war. As Darrow later put it, "I felt that we should join with the allies, but Mr. Debs, who hated war in any form and for any cause, thought that we should stay out." After a three-day trial in Cleveland's Federal court, Debs was convicted and sentenced by Judge D. C. Westenhaver to ten years in jail.

Two years later, Darrow, who had become the chairman of the Debs Amnesty Committee, visited Attorney General Mitchell Palmer in an attempt to obtain a pardon for his old client. Palmer refused to discuss the matter with him unless he had been authorized to represent the prisoner. Darrow made the long trip to the Federal penitentiary at Atlanta,

---

* "Mr. Debs at once became the head of the Socialist party of America," Darrow later wrote. "I never followed him politically. I never could believe that man was constructed as to make Socialism possible; but I watched him and his cause with great interest."

where he asked Debs, who was running his fifth campaign for the Presidency on the Socialist line from his cell, for permission to apply for a pardon. "In answer to my question, Mr. Debs said that he could not ask for anything from the administration, and could make no promises, but if I wanted to help him out, he fully appreciated all that I was doing for him."

On January 31, 1921, Palmer, at Darrow's urging, recommended to President Wilson that, in view of Debs' age and his failing health, the Socialist leader's sentence be commuted. Wilson bluntly refused. "This man was a traitor to his country," he reputedly told Joseph P. Tumulty, his private secretary, "and he never will be pardoned during my administration."

However, on December 23, 1921, the newly elected Warren G. Harding ordered the release of Debs and a score of other political prisoners. "I had always admired Woodrow Wilson and distrusted Harding," Darrow said many years later. "Doubtless my opinions about both in relation to affairs of government were measureably correct; still, Mr. Wilson, a scholar and an idealist, kept Debs in prison; and Mr. Harding . . . unlocked the door." But there was little time left. Less than five years after Warden Fred G. Zerbst had escorted him out of Atlanta Penitentiary, former convict #9653 died of a heart attack at the Lindlahr Sanitarium in Elmhurst, Illinois.

In 1932, six years before his own death, Darrow put into words what Debs had meant to him. "There may have lived at some time, some where, a kindlier, gentler, more generous man than Eugene V. Debs, but I have never known him," he wrote in his autobiography. "Nor have I ever read or heard of another. He was not only all that I have said, but he was the bravest man I ever knew. He never felt fear. He had the courage of the babe who has no conception of the word or its meaning."

It is more than a little possible that Debs would have said the same thing about the lawyer who had stood by his side in a Chicago courtroom in the winter of 1895.

# William Goodrich Thompson

By the summer of 1924, Frederick H. Moore, the California labor lawyer who had been in charge of the Sacco-Vanzetti legal staff for almost four years, was on his way out. A competent, often brilliant, attorney, wholly dedicated to the interests of his clients, he had the unfortunate knack of alienating his friends and supporters. As Eugene Lyons put it, "Always he quarreled with the defense committees or the clients or got himself in some private emotional scrape and lost the laurels of victory." Sacco was no exception. On August 18, 1924, he wrote to Moore, "Many times you have been deluder and abuse on weakness of my comrades good faith, but I want you to stop now and if you please get out of my case . . ."

On March 8, 1923, William G. Thompson, who had been recommended to Vanzetti as "perhaps the most able lawyer of Boston to present a case to the Supreme Court," officially joined the defense team. Thompson, who had, at Mrs. Sacco's insistence, appeared briefly at the beginning of the trial, had retired in Moore's favor after the jury had been selected. As dissatisfaction with the latter grew, Thompson had been persuaded to come back into the case to prepare and argue some of the supplementary motions for a new trial that were eventually overruled by Judge Webster Thayer on October 1, 1924.

Two months after Thayer's decision, he was named as chief counsel for both defendants. "He had not wished to represent Sacco and Vanzetti," one of his associates commented in 1938. "When asked to be their lawyer after the trial was over, he named a retainer large enough, as he thought, to remove the case from his office. To his surprise, these terms were accepted, and Thompson was launched into the most desperate struggle of his career, which he was destined to carry on long after funds, hope, and physical vitality were alike exhausted." His fee: $25,000, which, as Prof. G. Louis Joughin of The New School for Social Research observed, "in effect, bought most of the rest of his life."

Descended from Anthony Thompson, who had migrated to Boston from the south of England in 1637, the new chief counsel was once described as "a passionate American of the best tradition [whose] deepest allegiance was ultimately to what he called 'the invisible republic of the spirit.'" Unlike his predecessor, he was not concerned with causes or creeds. "Had Thompson been radical-minded, the impact of the Sacco-Vanzetti case would have required no great emotional adjustment," wrote one of his co-counsel after his death. "But he was, and remained to the end, a genuine conservative, believing that mankind is better served through progress in the existing order than by sudden change or drastic experimentation."

In the beginning, Thompson was certain he could save his new clients. The hostile atmosphere of the trial, the judge's prejudice against Italians and radicals, the probability that several key witnesses had perjured themselves, the suppression of vital evidence—these were so clear to him that he never doubted that they would be equally clear to everyone else. Herbert B. Ehrmann, one of his associates, later said, "He was sure that the code he believed to exist would never permit men so convicted to be sent to their death. His first shock came when some of his acquaintances not only failed to share his view, but actually evinced a coolness toward him for defending the men."

He did not lose his confidence in ultimate victory until close to the end. In late January of 1927, he argued the final appeal before the five judges of the Supreme Judicial Court of Massachusetts. When he returned to his office after two days of argument, he walked into the room of George E. Mears, one of his partners, and sank wearily into a chair. "There is no hope, Mr. Mears, no hope," he said sadly.

"Mr. Thompson has fought and is fighting bravely and splendidly in our defense," Vanzetti wrote to a friend in March of 1927. Neither he nor Sacco could have asked for a more devoted aide. Whereas Moore had seen in the case a magnificent opportunity to advance the rights of workingmen everywhere, Thompson regarded it as a private struggle for two souls being systematically destroyed by a system he loved and revered. He was, in Prof. Joughin's words, "the only major figure in the whole affair to reject philosophic or scientific premises and to hold steadfastly to the classic tradition of private morality." Toward that end, no sacrifice was too great.

*". . . in his pursuit of justice he could not be diverted by fear of any consequence to himself or to his career."*

# William G. Thompson and the appeals of Sacco and Vanzetti, November 5, 1921 to August 22, 1927.

ON NOVEMBER 23, 1919, Dr. Francis J. Murphy of Natick, Massachusetts, reported the theft of his dark-blue seven-passenger Buick sedan. A month later, a stocky, swarthy man with "a closely cropped mustache," attempted to buy a set of license plates from George Hassam, the owner of the Needham Garage. The stranger, who spoke broken English, told Hassam that "he bought a car in the next town without plates." When the garageman refused to sell any plates unless he saw the car or a bill of sale, the man turned angrily on his heels and left the premises. The following week, Hassam discovered that a set of Massachusetts plates bearing number 01173C were missing from his garage.

At 7:30 A.M. on the day before Christmas, Alfred E. Cox, the paymaster of Bridgewater's L. Q. White Shoe Company, picked up a $33,000 payroll from a local bank. Cox took the money, which had been packed in three metal boxes, to a Ford pick-up truck chauffeured by John E. Graves, which then turned right onto Broad Street. When it reached the Hale Street intersection, a dark touring car, "like a Hudson," spun around the corner into Broad Street and screeched to a stop in front of the oncoming Ford. Three men piled out of the sedan—one armed with a shotgun and the other two with revolvers—and began firing at the truck.

Graves managed to steer the truck around a streetcar in the middle of Broad Street so that the latter was between the Ford and the three bandits. In his excitement, Benjamin J. Bowles, a policeman assigned to guard the payroll, seized the steering wheel causing the truck to run off the road and collide with a telegraph pole. After Bowles fired several shots at them, the three armed men jumped back into their car and drove away. As Broad Street began to fill with curious spectators, a Dr. John Murphy found the cartridge shell lying in the gutter. The physician immediately turned it over to the Bridgewater police.

At 9:18 A.M. on Thursday, April 20, 1920, Shelley A. Neal, the South Braintree agent of the American Railway Express Company, met the early train from Boston. He receipted for a canvas bag containing $15,776.61, the weekly payroll for the

Slater & Morrill Shoe Company. After counting it in his first floor office in Hampton House, the same building that housed the shoe company's executive offices, he turned the money over to Margaret Mahoney, Slater & Morrill's paymistress, who immediately sorted it into pay envelopes which were then placed in two metal carrying boxes.

Shortly before three that afternoon, Frederick A. Parmenter, the shoe company's acting paymaster, called for the boxes. Accompanied by Alessandro Berardelli, a guard, Parmenter left Hampton House and started up the north side of Pearl Street toward the company's main factory building, some five hundred feet to the east. The two men crossed the railroad tracks and had just reached an excavation opposite the Rice & Hutchins shoe factory, several hundred feet away from their destination, when a black touring car drove slowly down Pearl Street in their direction. Two men jumped out of the sedan and opened fire on the paymaster and the guard. As Parmenter and Berardelli fell to the ground, fatally wounded, one of the men picked up the metal boxes and threw them into the waiting car. Then both gunmen leaped aboard as the automobile picked up speed and raced across the railroad tracks. It turned left at the intersection of Pearl and Hancock and roared out of town on the latter street.

Forty-eight hours later, Charles L. Fuller and Max E. Wine, two Brockton equestrians who were riding near the Manley Woods in West Bridgewater, some fifteen miles to the south, found an abandoned Buick sedan, without license plates, hidden among the trees. A few feet away, the horsemen noticed the tire tracks of a smaller car. They telephoned the Brockton police, who promptly sent two officers to the scene. The car, which was soon identified as Dr. Francis J. Murphy's stolen sedan, was driven to police headquarters in Brockton.

On April 19, Mike Boda, an Italian immigrant who lived in a shack on the outskirts of West Bridgewater, with a radical named Coacci, asked Simon E. Johnson, the owner of a garage on Elm Square, to tow his disabled 1914 two-passenger Overland in for repairs. Johnson did so that same day. But it was not until the night of May 5 that Boda, accompanied by three friends—Ricardo Orciani, Bartolomeo Vanzetti and Nicola Sacco—called for his car. Finding the garage closed, the four men walked to Johnson's house on North Elm Street.

Because some of the eyewitnesses to the South Braintree hold-up had indicated that the men who murdered Parmenter and Berardelli were swarthy and dark-haired, Michael E. Stewart, Bridgewater's chief of police, theorized that the crime might have been committed by resident Italians who had access to a car. Accordingly, he asked Johnson to let him know if anyone called for Boda's automobile. While the garage owner was informing Boda that he could not drive the Overland because it lacked 1920 plates, Mrs. Johnson went to a neighbor's house and called the police. A few minutes later, Boda and Orciani drove off on the latter's motorcycle, while Sacco and Vanzetti boarded a Brockton trolley car.

Shortly before ten P.M., when the streetcar reached Brockton's Campello section, it was boarded by policemen who arrested the two men. They were taken to headquarters, where it was discovered that Vanzetti, a thirty-three-year-old Plymouth fish peddler, possessed a .38 Harrington & Richardson revolver and Sacco, an employee of a Stoughton shoe factory, who had just turned thirty, had a .32 Colt pistol. In addition, Vanzetti's pockets contained a number of 12-gauge shotgun shells. Both men were promptly booked on charges of carrying concealed weapons. Orciani, who was apprehended the next morning, was immediately released when the records of the factory at which he was employed indicated that he had worked all day on April 15. Boda was never arrested, and returned to Italy later that month, one step ahead of a deportation order.

Stewart, who had arrived at police headquarters shortly after the arrest of Sacco and Vanzetti, questioned both men until midnight. The next morning, Frederick G. Katzmann, who doubled in brass as the district attorney of both Plymouth and Suffolk Counties, continued the interrogation. On May 11, the police chief filed a complaint against Vanzetti, charging him with armed assault against Alfred E. Cox, the paymaster of the White Shoe Company "with intent to rob him." A week later, at a preliminary hearing in Brockton, four witnesses of the attempted robbery at Bridgewater identified Vanzetti as the man who had fired the shotgun at the payroll truck.

On June 11, the fish peddler was indicted on three counts of assault with intent to rob and kill. Sacco, who had been working on December 24, was not accused of the crime. Vanzetti's trial began in Plymouth on June 22, before sixty-four-year-old Judge Webster Thayer of Worcester, and a jury which included the foreman of a local cordage company from which, four years earlier, the defendant had been fired for leading a strike.

In all, five witnesses* identified Vanzetti as the would-be bandit who had fired two rounds from his shotgun at the Ford. Bowles, the payroll guard, who had testified at the preliminary hearing that the man with the shotgun had a "short croppy mustache," was positive that the defendant was the man he had seen. "I meant trimmed instead of cropped," he explained. He was also certain that the hold-up car had been a Buick and that Dr. Murphy's automobile looked exactly like it.

Paymaster Cox described the shotgun wielder as being "of medium complexion, with prominent cheekbones, rather high; he had a short, well-trimmed mustache . . . not what you would term an awful small mustache, but short." As for Van-

---

* John E. Graves, the driver of the payroll truck, had died before Vanzetti's arrest. However, he had told a Pinkerton operative retained by the shoe company that the hatless man with shotgun had been about thirty-five years old, of medium height and weight, and had worn a black mustache. "He must have been a Greek," he had informed the detective.

zetti, "he looks enough like the man to be the man." He, too, had previously described the bandit's mustache as "croppy," but now claimed that he had omitted the adjective from his trial testimony "because I don't know at this moment just what it means."

Frank W. Harding, a Bridgewater garage mechanic, had been on his way to work when the attempted hold-up took place. He was certain that the "dark complected" man who had run by him to open fire on the shoe company truck was Vanzetti. Harding had then watched him climb into a dark, seven-passenger Buick, whose curtains were drawn. As the car drove off, he had written its license number—01173C—on a piece of paper which he had turned over to the police. Later, George H. Hassam identified the plates as those that had been stolen from his garage the previous winter.

Mrs. Georgina F. Brooks, a Bridgewater housewife, and her five-year-old son had been walking toward the railroad station minutes before the shooting took place. As she crossed Broad Street, she had noticed an automobile containing four men parked at the curb. She recalled that the driver had been a "dark complexioned foreigner," but she was unable to describe the three other passengers. Just as she arrived at the depot, she had heard the shots. There was little doubt in her mind that Vanzetti was the man she had seen at the wheel of the bandits' car.

The last eyewitness was Maynard Freeman Shaw, a fourteen-year-old newsboy, who had been delivering his papers on Broad Street on the morning of the crime. He thought that the holdup car had been "a Hudson or a Buick." Vanzetti was the man he had seen running toward the automobile after the shooting. "I could tell he was a foreigner," he said. "I could tell by the way he ran." He remembered that the fleeing man had very little hair and a dark, well-groomed mustache. On cross-examination, he insisted that he had always been able to tell whether a person was a foreigner by the way he ran, but admitted that the man he saw could have been anything but an oriental, a Negro or an American.

When the prosecution rested, John P. Vahey and J. M. Graham, Vanzetti's lawyers, called eleven Italian witnesses to buttress their client's alibi that he had been selling fish in Plymouth all day on December 24. Mary Fortini, his landlady, said that he had prepared his fish in her kitchen until midnight on the twenty-third. The next morning, at the request of an early customer, she had awakened him at 6:15. He had left the house with a carload of eels at about nine o'clock, accompanied by thirteen-year-old Beltrando Brini, a neighborhood boy who often helped him deliver his orders.

Young Brini, who admitted that he had memorized his testimony "like a piece at school," said that Vanzetti had come to his house on the night of December 23 and asked him to help deliver eels the next day. While the fish peddler was talking to him, Matthew Sassi and Edward Manter had brought in half a pig which his father had purchased from Manter for the family's Christmas dinner. The boy had arrived at Mrs. Fortini's boardinghouse at eight A.M. on December 24, and worked all day filling Vanzetti's orders. Esther Christophori and Adeladi Bonjionnani said that they had received eels from the Brini boy in the middle of the morning. Mrs. Bonjionnani recalled that she had left her house to pay Vanzetti directly because Beltrando could not change a five-dollar bill for her.

Mrs. Alfonsina Brini, the delivery boy's mother, told the court that Sassi and Manter had brought her husband's share of the pig to her house on the night of the twenty-third. She was certain that Vanzetti had been present at the time. When her son had read of the defendant's arrest, he had said, "Don't you remember, Mother, that the night before he came down and called me to go out and sell fish?" When Katzmann took over, she admitted that Vanzetti was a very good friend of her family and that he always put two fifty-cent pieces in her children's stockings on Christmas Eve.

After several other witnesses swore that the fish peddler had sold eels to them on the morning of the Bridgewater assault, John Vernazano, a barber who had frequently cut the accused's hair, took the stand. In the six years he had known Vanzetti, he had never cut or trimmed his long, flowing mustache. In fact, he had never seen the defendant with a trimmed mustache. "Always he had a long mustache," he said in broken English. Mr. Vernazano's testimony on this score was confirmed by Andrew Christophori, who had lived across the street from Vanzetti for more than five years, as well as by many of the latter's customers.

Upon the advice of his lawyers, Vanzetti did not testify. On July 1, after deliberating for a little more than five hours, the jury found him guilty as charged. As the verdicts were announced, the defendant turned to his friends in the courtroom and cried out, "Corragio!" Six weeks later, Thayer sentenced him to from twelve to fifteen years in the state penitentiary, despite Vahey's earnest plea that, because it was a first offense and no one had been injured, his client was entitled to leniency.

Katzmann's investigation of the South Braintree robbery had early convinced him that both Sacco and Vanzetti had been involved in the crime. Shortly after Vanzetti's conviction in Plymouth, the district attorney appeared before the Norfolk County Grand Jury and asked it to indict both men for the murders of Parmenter and Berardelli. On September 11, an indictment was returned, charging that "Nicola Sacco . . . and Bartolomeo Vanzetti did assault and beat Alexander Berardelli with intent to murder him by shooting him in the body with a loaded pistol, and by such assault, beating and shooting, did murder Alexander Berardelli, against the peace of said Commonwealth and contrary to the form of the statute in such case made and provided." In identical language, the two Italian immigrants were also accused of murdering Parmenter.

While the defendants languished in jail, their friends had not been inactive. Sparked by Aldino Feliciani, the editor of the Italian-language newspaper *La Notizia,* a Sacco-Vanzetti Defense Committee had been organized two days after their arrest. As soon as Vanzetti had been sentenced for the Bridgewater assault, Feliciani retained Frederick H. Moore, a California attorney who enjoyed a considerable reputation in Massachusetts for his successful defense of two men indicted for a murder that occurred during a bitter I.W.W. strike in Lawrence, as Sacco's attorney.* Moore was assisted by William J. Callahan, who had been one of the shoe worker's lawyers at a preliminary hearing on the murder charge in Quincy. Vanzetti was represented by two brothers—Jeremiah J. and Thomas F. McAnarney—who were well-known Norfolk County lawyers.

On September 28, both men were arraigned and pleaded not guilty. Early in February of the following year, the case was scheduled for trial on March 7. However, Moore and his associates applied for an adjournment in order to complete their preparations and the trial was postponed until Tuesday, May 31. On that day, it began in the heavily guarded courthouse in Dedham, a well-to-do Boston suburb which was the Norfolk County seat. Several days earlier, the two prisoners had been brought to the county jail under heavy guard, Vanzetti from Charlestown State Prison, where he had begun serving his sentence for the Bridgewater assault, and Sacco from the Dedham House of Correction.

Again Judge Thayer was on the bench. Before the selection of the jury began, Thayer and the lawyers retired to his chambers where Moore tried to convince him that the indictments against both defendants were so vague that they ought

* In reality, Moore was chief counsel for both defendants, but trial strategy dictated that he appear for Sacco only.

to be dismissed. Furthermore, in view of Vanzetti's prior conviction, the Californian felt that the jury might be prejudiced against Sacco if he were tried with the fish peddler. Accordingly, he asked Thayer to order separate trials. His Honor denied all of the defense motions, except one for an additional bill of particulars, and ordered counsel to get on with the selection of the jury.

The sheriff had rounded up five hundred men as prospective jurors. When the panel was exhausted on June 3, only seven had been accepted by both sides. Over the violent objections of the defense attorneys, Thayer promptly ordered the sheriff to scour the county and come up with two hundred additional veniremen by the time court opened the next morning. Before the week-end recess, Thayer had his jury. Walter R. Ripley, a former Quincy police chief, was named foreman of a panel which, in addition to himself, was composed of two machinists, two real estate brokers, a grocer, a mason, a salesman, a mill operator, a shoe worker, a photographer and a farmer.

On Monday morning, the newly sworn jury was taken on an all-day trip to South Braintree, the Manley Woods where Dr. Murphy's car had been found, the Coacci shack in Cochesett and Simon Johnson's house and garage in West Bridgewater. The next day, after Assistant District Attorney Harold P. Williams had made the opening statement for the prosecution, the trial began in earnest with the testimony of the physicians who had conducted the autopsies on the two murdered men. They were unanimous in their opinion that Berardelli had been shot four times and Parmenter twice, and that both men had died of their wounds. Dr. George B. Magrath, who had removed the bullets from Berardelli's body, said that, using a surgical needle, he had marked each one with a Roman numeral on its base. He identified a .32-caliber shell, which bore the numeral III, as the one he had extracted from the fourth wound in the guard's body.

Shelley A. Neal, the Railway Express agent, had not witnessed the actual shooting. But he had seen Dr. Murphy's automobile in South Braintree before and after the murders. He had first noticed the car parked near the railroad tracks when he was returning to his office after picking up the Slater & Morrill payroll from the Boston train on the morning of the crime. As he recalled it, a tall, emaciated man with blond hair had been leaning against the freshly varnished automobile. Neal had run out of his office after the shooting just in time to see a sedan racing over the railroad crossing. He was positive that it had been the same vehicle he had seen earlier that day.

Katzmann had three witnesses who were prepared to say that Sacco had been in South Braintree prior to the shooting. Shortly after eleven A.M., Mrs. Lola R. Andrews, an unemployed practical nurse, had seen the defendant and another man standing next to a car which was parked near the Slater & Morrill factory building where she had gone to apply for a job. Thirty minutes later, real estate broker William S. Tracy had noticed two smooth-shaven, dark-haired men leaning against the window of a Square drugstore. He was fairly sure that Sacco had been one of these men. "While I wouldn't be positive," he said, "I would say to the best of my recollection that was the man." William J. Heron, a railroad detective, was "pretty sure" that the shoeworker had been one of two "nervous" loiterers he had noticed in the station waiting room between 12:30 and 1:00 o'clock.

Of the eight people who had witnessed the shooting of the guard and the paymaster, only one—Louis Pelser—thought that Sacco was the man who had fired a shot into Berardelli's body. Pelser, who was employed by Rice & Hutchins, said that he had watched the tragedy from an open window on the factory's first floor. When Katzmann asked him whether the man who had killed Berardelli was in the courtroom, the young shoeworker pointed to Sacco, who was sitting with Vanzetti in a special iron cage that had been constructed to house the defendants during the trial. "Well, I wouldn't say it was him," he stammered, "but he is a dead image of him." As the car drove down Pearl Street, he had written down its license number, 49783.*

When Moore took over, Pelser admitted that, two months before the trial, he had told one of the defense's investigators that he had not seen the shooting because he had been hiding under a work bench. He had lied, he said, "because I didn't want to tell my story, because I didn't like to go to court." Besides, he hadn't known his questioner well enough to tell him the truth. In fact, until he took the stand, he hadn't revealed to anyone, even to the district attorney, what he had seen that day on Pearl Street. But he was telling the truth now.

Louis L. Wade, a Slater & Morrill shoemaker who had been helping Hans Behrsin, Mr. Slater's chauffeur, fill his gas tank at the company pump, had identified Sacco as one of the murderers at the Brockton police station in May of 1920. Several weeks later, at the preliminary hearing in Quincy, he said he "had a little doubt . . . but he looks like the man." Now he wasn't so sure because he had recently seen a man in a South Braintree barber shop who looked like the man who had shot Berardelli. "I have seen a man that resembled him, the man that I saw that day, and that is the reason why I have a little doubt. If I have a doubt, I don't think he is the man."

Four persons, with varying degrees of certainty, testified that they had seen Sacco in the bandits' car after the shooting. Louis DeBeradinis who operated a cobbler's shop near Hampton House, told Williams that the man who had fired at him from the automobile "looked like the defendant Sacco." As he recalled it, the gun wielder had been "a light-haired, thin man." "You don't mean that Sacco has light hair,

* These plates had been stolen from a Needham automobile on January 6, 1920.

do you?" asked Jeremiah McAnarney on cross-examination. "No," DeBeradinis replied. "Sacco is dark."

Mary E. Splaine, a Slater & Morrill bookkeeper, did not share the shoemaker's doubts. She was absolutely certain that the man with "a good-sized hand" whom she had observed leaning out of the escape car as it crossed the railroad tracks was Sacco. Miss Splaine, who had run to a second-story window of Hampton House when she first heard the shots, portrayed the man she had seen as "a muscular . . . active-looking man [who] weighed possibly from 140 to 145 pounds." During the few seconds he was in view, she noticed that he had a high forehead, a clean-cut face, dark eyebrows, hair that was brushed back and from two to two-and-a-half inches in length, and a complexion which she described as "white, peculiar white that looked greenish." The press corps agreed unanimously that her description fit Sacco to a T.

However, at the Quincy hearing, she had stated, when asked by Katzmann to identify Sacco, that "I don't think my opportunity afforded me the right to say he is the man." She also admitted that, shortly after the shooting, she had told the Brockton police that one of the photographs in their rogues' gallery bore "a striking resemblance in some features" to the man she had seen in the Buick. Later, she had been informed that the man whose picture she had selected was serving time in New York's Sing Sing prison for another offense. But she insisted that time had erased any uncertainties she might have had about Sacco. "From the observation I had of him in the Quincy court and the comparison of the man I saw in the machine, on reflection I was sure that he was the same man."

Frances J. Devlin, another Slater & Morrill bookkeeper, who worked in the same office as Miss Splaine, had also watched the fleeing sedan as it raced over the railroad crossing. According to her, one of the bandits had been leaning out of the car in order to fire into the crowd which had collected around the bodies of Berardelli and Parmenter. "He was a dark man," she recalled, "and the hair seemed to be grown away from the temples, and it was brown-black, and he had clear features, rather clear features and rather good-looking, and he had a white complexion and a fairly thick-set man, I should say." Although she had testified at Quincy that she couldn't say "positively" whether Sacco was the man she had seen, she now was "sure" that he was.

When the shooting started, Carlos E. Goodridge, a phonograph salesman who was whiling away a slow afternoon in Magazu's poolroom, a hundred feet west of DeBeradinis' shop, had run into Pearl Street. As he looked in the direction of the shots, he saw an automobile coming toward him. "I stepped down on the sidewalk," he said, "and it was coming towards me possibly at a rate of speed of ten or twelve miles an hour. Just as I stepped out halfway on the sidewalk, there was a fellow poked a gun over towards me, and I was probably within twenty feet of it, or twenty-five. I went back into the poolroom." The man with the gun "was a dark complexioned fellow with dark hair, and he had his face—kind of peculiar face, that came down pointed." Sacco was that man.

The first time that Goodridge had seen Sacco after the hold-up was in September of 1920 when the salesman had appeared in the Quincy courtroom on a matter of his own. When the defense tried to get him to admit that he himself was presently under indictment in Massachusetts, Thayer immediately shut off this line of inquiry. "You can't attack any witness' credibility," he ruled, "except by showing a record of conviction, and a record of conviction means a sentence, a judgment pronounced by the court." Moore had to content himself with Goodridge's admission that, as late as February, 1921, he had made no attempt to tell the authorities that he had recognized Sacco as the gunman who had almost frightened him out of his wits that fatal afternoon in South Braintree.

Katzmann had no witnesses who claimed to have seen Vanzetti during the shooting itself. However, he did have four who swore that the fish peddler had been in the vicinity of South Braintree on April 15. John W. Faulkner, a Cohasset patternmaker, was positive that a man who had sat behind him on the morning train to Boston and who kept inquiring for East Braintree was Vanzetti. The stranger, who was dressed in old clothes, "looked like a foreigner, with a black mustache, and cheek bones." When Vanzetti's picture had been published in the newspapers after his arrest, Faulkner had recognized him at once as his inquisitive fellow passenger. Yet, he had never mentioned the incident to anyone until more than three months after April 15.

Piano tuner Harry E. Dolbeare was one of the prospective jurymen who had been summoned for the trial. While he was waiting to be interrogated, he recognized Vanzetti as a man he had seen sitting in the back seat of an automobile in South Braintree Square on the morning of the murders. There had been five passengers in the car who "appeared to be foreigners . . . a tough looking bunch." The defendant was the only one of the quintet that he could remember because he had "a very heavy mustache" and was "leaning forward as though he was talking to either the driver or the other person in front of the car." Although he had only gotten a profile view of the man on the rear seat, there wasn't a "particle" of doubt in his mind that it had been the fish peddler.

Michael Levangie, the crossing tender at the South Braintree Station, had just lowered his gates for an expected train when the bandits' car approached the intersection. "It came right up the hill as far as the gate," he told Katzmann. "Of course, I had my gates down, and the first thing I knew, there was a revolver pointed like that at my head. I looked back at the train to see if I had a chance enough to let them go. I saw there was chance to let them go, and I let them, and I put my gates back again where they belonged." Despite the fact that he had admitted, barely two weeks before the trial, that he had not been able to see anyone in the car because all its curtains were drawn, he was now "sure" that Vanzetti was the "dark complected man" who had been driving the vehicle.*

At 4:15 P.M., Austin T. Reed, the youthful gate tender at the Matfield crossing near West Bridgewater, had just lowered his gates when he noticed a car coming toward him "at a pretty fast rate of speed." The automobile screeched to a stop some forty feet away from the crossing and one of its occupants shouted at him in clear English, "What to hell I was holding him up for?" As soon as the train had passed, the car raced over the tracks, only to return a few minutes later and head back toward West Bridgewater. As it passed Reed's shanty, the same man who had spoken to him earlier yelled, "What to hell did you hold us up for?" He was convinced that his questioner ("A dark complected man, with high cheek bones, a stubbed mustache") had been Vanzetti.

When Sacco and Vanzetti were arrested, they were riding on a streetcar being operated by Austin C. Cole. Mr. Cole testified that both men had also been passengers on his car on either the fourteenth or fifteenth of April. He wasn't sure on which of the two dates he had seen them, but those were the only two days in April that he had been on the Bridgewater-Brockton run. He thought that they had boarded his Brockton-bound trolley at Sunset Avenue, which was approximately a mile and a half from the center of West Bridgewater. When Vanzetti entered the car, Cole had first thought that he was a friend of his named Tony, but soon realized his mistake.

On the trial's eighteenth day, the Commonwealth called

* Most eyewitnesses described the driver as a pale, sickly-looking man with light hair, and Katzmann conceded throughout the trial that Vanzetti had not been at the Buick's wheel.

Captain William H. Proctor, a veteran member of the Massachusetts State Police. Proctor stated that his tests of the six bullets recovered from the bodies of Parmenter and Berardelli had revealed that all but No. III has been fired through a Savage automatic pistol. He thought that No. III could have been fired from Sacco's Colt. "My opinion is that it is consistent with being fired by that pistol," he explained. As for the other shells, it was his conclusion that "all five were fired from the same pistol." Charles Van Amburgh, an assistant in the ballistics department of the Remington Arms Company, was "inclined to believe that it was fired, No. III bullet was fired, from this Colt automatic pistol."

In general, the remainder of the Commonwealth's case consisted of trying to prove that the Smith & Richardson revolver found on Vanzetti at the time of his arrest was Berardelli's missing gun, that a cap picked up near the guard's body belonged to Sacco, and that the conduct of both defendants just before and after apprehension indicated a "consciousness of guilt." As far as Berardelli's gun was concerned, his widow thought that Vanzetti's looked "just like" the one her husband usually carried. On March 20, 1920, she and her husband had taken the gun to a sporting goods shop to have a broken spring repaired. Although the shop's records did not indicate that the weapon had ever been called for by Berardelli, the manager of its firearms department "thought" that it had been redelivered, since it had not been included in a sale of abandoned revolvers held in February of 1921.

Shortly after the shooting, Fred L. Loring, a Slater & Morrill employee, had found a cap lying near Berardelli's body. George T. Kelley, Sacco's superintendent at the 3-K Shoe Company in Stoughton, testified that the defendant had sometimes worn "a dark cap" to work. Although he felt that the cap which Loring had picked up was of the same general appearance as the one he had often seen hanging on a nail near Sacco's workbench, he was not prepared to identify it further. "I never saw that cap so close in my life as I do now," he said. "I don't know right down in my heart that that is the cap."

Katzmann's "consciousness of guilt" theory rested on four main foundations. Firstly, Simon Johnson's wife said that when she walked to a neighbor's house to call Chief Stewart, Sacco and Vanzetti had followed her in a suspicious manner. Secondly, Michael J. Connolly, the Brockton policeman who had arrested the defendants on Cole's streetcar, testified that both men had attempted to reach for the guns they were carrying in their pockets. Thirdly, there was the matter of the weapons themselves. Lastly, and perhaps most importantly, the suspects had lied to Stewart and Katzmann after their arrest. Both had insisted that they had no knowledge of Boda or his car, and that they had gone to West Bridgewater to see one Vittoria Papa, a friend of Vanzetti's.

When the Commonwealth rested, Moore called twenty-eight witnesses who had been present in South Braintree on the day of the murders. Mrs. Julia Campbell, who had accompanied Lola Andrews to the Slater & Morrill factory, was certain that Sacco "don't look like the man I saw there." Later in the trial, three Quincy residents stated that Mrs. Andrews had told them that she had not seen the faces of the men who had been working on the car in front of the shoe plant. One of them, a tailor named Kurlansky, swore that she had complained, after being taken to see Sacco in jail, that "the Government took me down and want me to recognize those men, and I don't know a thing about them. I have never seen them, and I can't recognize them."

Five laborers, who had been working at the excavation across the street from Rice & Hutchins, could not recognize either defendant as the men they had seen shooting Parmenter and Berardelli. Barbara Liscomb, a Rice & Hutchins employee who had been working on the building's second floor, had looked out of a window when she heard someone shout that a man had been shot. "I saw two men lying on the ground," she recalled, "and one man, a short dark man, standing on the ground facing me, with his head up, holding a revolver in his hands." Mrs. Liscomb was "positively sure that neither of the men in the dock is the man I saw with the gun."

Some ten minutes before the shooting, Nurse Jennie Novelli saw a large sedan driving slowly up Pearl Street in the direction of the Slater & Morrill factory. She had taken a long look at the two men in its front seat, particularly at the one sitting alongside the driver, whom she first thought was an acquaintance named Mooney. Although a detective later testified that Mrs. Novelli had told him that one of the car's occupants "greatly resembled" Sacco, she insisted that the defendants were not the men she had seen. A few minutes later, Albert Frantello had noticed two English-speaking strangers leaning against a fence outside the factory. He was sure that "neither of them" was Sacco or Vanzetti.

Frank J. Burke, a glass blower who had come to town to lecture on his art at one of the local schools, watched the two men who had shot Berardelli and Parmenter clamber aboard the waiting Buick. As the car approached the railroad crossing, one of its passengers had pointed a revolver at Burke and shouted, "Get out of the way, you son of a b!" Moore asked him if "those men were either of the two defendants in the dock?" "I would say they were not," the glass blower replied. Six construction laborers who were working near the railroad crossing were confident that neither Sacco nor Vanzetti had been in the fleeing car as it plummeted over the tracks.

The remainder of Moore's eyewitnesses added little to his defense. Winfred H. Pierce and Lawrence Ferguson, two Slater & Morrill shoeworkers who had been watching the car from a Hampton House window, would go no further than state that they didn't "think" that the men they saw resembled the defendants. Daniel J. O'Neil, a college student, swore that neither of the defendants had been the one whom he had seen open the rear door of the moving car and walk along the running board to the vehicle's front seat. However, his testimony was later partially nullified when it was pointed out to the jury that the Buick's rear door opened outward toward the front of the car so that a man crawling along the running board would have had to climb over it.

When the last of the defense's army of eyewitnesses—William Gibson, a chauffeur for the contractor who was in charge of the excavation across the street from Rice & Hutchins—had finished testifying that he had not seen either Sacco or Vanzetti in the Buick as it drove slowly by him, Moore put the defendants on the stand. Both men denied that they had been in South Braintree on April 15. Vanzetti swore that he had been in Plymouth all that day, while Sacco stated that he had spent that Thursday in Boston, trying unsuccessfully to validate his passport for a trip back to Italy. Although Katzmann managed to wring from the defendants the fact that they were anarchists and had fled to Mexico in 1917 to evade the draft, he did not succeed in materially shaking their alibis.

Eight residents of Plymouth supported Vanzetti's story. Antonio Carbone remembered selling fish to him one or two days before the fifteenth. A peddler said that the defendant had bought a piece of cloth from him on the morning of the murders and that they had gone to the nearby home of Mrs. Alfonsina Brini to get her opinion as to its value. Mrs. Brini and her daughter verified the peddler's version of the incident. Angel Guidobone was certain that Vanzetti had delivered some codfish to him shortly after noon that day; he was sure of the date because he had had his appendix out four days later. Lastly, Melvin Corl, a fisherman whose testimony was supported by that of his wife and Frank Jesse, a local boat builder, said that Vanzetti had spent part of the afternoon of April 15 watching him paint his skiff on the shore near Ocean Street.

Dominick Ricci, a Needham carpenter, had talked to Sacco on the Stoughton railroad platform at 7:15 on the morning of the murders. Four hours later, the shoemaker had been seen on East Boston's Hanover Street by Angelo Monello. At noon, he had had lunch at Boni's Restaurant with Felice Guadagni, a Hub journalist. The two men were later joined by John D. Williams, an advertising representative for several foreign language newspapers, and Albert Vosco, an editor of *La Notizia*.

At two that afternoon, according to the deposition of Giuseppe Andrower, a former attaché of the Royal Italian Consulate in Boston, Sacco had dropped in "for information how to get a passport for Italy." Unfortunately, the photographs he had brought with him were much too large, and Andrower advised him to return the following week with smaller snapshots. Forty-five minutes later, Antonio Dentamore, a Boston banker, was introduced to the defendant in Giordani's coffee shop by Guadagni. Before returning home, Sacco had paid an outstanding bill at a North End grocery store owned by one Carlos M. Affe. Mrs. Sacco, who testified through an interpreter, recalled that her husband had gone to a Stoughton photographer to have smaller pictures taken shortly after his return from Boston.

Both Sacco and Vanzetti readily admitted that they had lied to the police and the district attorney after their apprehension on May 5. The latter insisted that he thought that he had been arrested for distributing radical literature and that he had not told the truth to protect his associates. "I intend not to mention the name and the house of my friends," he explained to Katzmann. Sacco took the same tack, claiming that "if I say I know Boda, you will ask me a lot of questions, 'if he was a radical or anything, if he was a very good friend of yours.' " *

To counteract the testimony of Proctor and Van Amburgh as to the origin of the fatal bullet, Moore called two ballistics experts of his own. James E. Burns, who had worked for the United States Cartridge Company for thirty years, was convinced that the No. III shell had not been fired from Sacco's Colt. He based his opinion on his comparison of eleven test bullets that had been fired from the defendant's gun with the No. III shell. "It doesn't compare with it at all," he said. J. Henry Fitzgerald, an employee of the Colt Patent Firearms Company, stated emphatically that "my opinion is that No. III bullet was not fired from the pistol given to me as Exhibit 28."

Before the defense rested, Moore and the McAnarney brothers summoned a dozen or so witnesses to contradict the testimony given by Faulkner, Levangie, Mrs. Andrews, Pelser and Goodridge. But it was all in vain. At one o'clock on the afternoon of July 14, after listening to more than three days of summations by the lawyers and Thayer's exhaustive charge, the jury retired. Six hours later, it filed back into the packed courtroom. Foreman Ripley solemnly informed the judge that he and his colleagues had found both defendants guilty of murder in the first degree. The silence that followed Ripley's pronouncements was broken suddenly by Sacco's shrill voice. "They kill an innocent man!" he shouted. "They kill two innocent men!"

As soon as the verdicts had been recorded, Moore moved for a new trial on the ground that they were against the weight of the evidence. This motion was denied by Judge

---

* At the time of his arrest, Vanzetti testified, he was afraid "for I know that my friend there in New York have jumped down from the jail in the street and killed himself. The papers say that he jump down but we don't know." He had reference to the mysterious death on May 3 of Andrea Salsedo, a radical whose body was found on the sidewalk of a building in which he had been held incommunicado by the FBI for several weeks.

Thayer on Christmas Eve. In his long written opinion, the jurist concluded that the trial had been a fair one and that there was ample evidence to support the jury's decision. "I cannot—as I must if I disturb these verdicts—announce to the world that these twelve jurors violated the sanctity of their oaths, threw to the four winds of bias and prejudice their honor, judgment, reason and conscience, and thereby abused the solemn trust reposed in them by the law as well as by the court."

Shortly before Thayer's denial of the motion for a new trial, William Goodrich Thompson, a highly respected member of the Boston legal fraternity, had entered the case to assist Moore. At the very beginning of the trial, Mrs. Sacco, who disliked Moore intensely, had tried to persuade him to withdraw in Thompson's favor, and, when the Californian refused, the latter had refused to participate further. However, after the convictions, he was persuaded to return and soon became the prime mover in the extensive post-trial legal maneuvers that were to make the defendants' names household words throughout the world.

Fifty-seven years old in 1921, Thompson had had a distinguished professional career. After amassing a brilliant record at Harvard College and Law School, he had spent three years as an assistant United States Attorney in Boston. When he resigned to go into private practice in 1895, he became a lecturer in the preparation of briefs at the Harvard Law School. His reputation as a careful, conscientious lawyer soon grew to such proportions that he became senior vice-president of the staid Boston Bar Association and, for seventeen years, was a member (and ultimately the chairman) of its powerful Grievance Committee.

He was perhaps the last attorney in Boston who could be expected to come to the aid of two admitted anarchists. A highly conservative man who believed wholeheartedly in the status quo, he entered the Sacco-Vanzetti case because he felt that it was his duty as a lawyer to do so. As one of his associates put it, he believed that "those who reached the top in such an order, whether through the acquisition of education, wealth, or power, had a corresponding obligation to use these advantages like gentlemen. It mortified him that persons, enjoying all the advantages our civilization could offer, should accept the idea that it was better for Sacco and Vanzetti to die, even if innocent, than for the Commonwealth to admit a mistake under fire."

On November 5, 1921, just three days after the oral arguments on the application for a new trial had been heard by Thayer, Moore, with Thompson's assistance, filed the first of five supplementary motions. The defense had learned that Foreman Ripley, who had died three months after the trial, had exhibited some .38 calibre cartridges to several members of the jury during its deliberations. The dead man's widow had given these shells to the defense team, and Albert H. Hamilton, a ballistics expert, submitted an affidavit in which he said that they contained markings which indicated that Ripley had tried to force them into the muzzle of Vanzetti's Smith & Richardson revolver. In addition, one William H. Daly, a lifelong friend of the Ripley's, swore that the latter, in discussing the defendants before the trial, had said, "Damn them, they ought to hang them anyway."

Some six months later, a second supplementary motion was submitted. It had two purposes—to prove that Sacco had not been in the Buick on the day of the crime, and to discredit Louis Pelser. It was accompanied by the affidavit of one Roy E. Gould, a razor-paste salesman, who had been walking along Pearl Street just after the murders. According to Gould, the man who had climbed from the back to the front seat of the getaway car had fired at him and put a bullet through his overcoat. Although he had told the police what he had seen, he was never called as a witness by Katzmann. Moore had taken him to see Sacco in the Norfolk County Jail on November 9, 1921, and the peddler swore that the defendant was not "the man that he saw at South Braintree on April 15, 1920."

The Gould motion was accompanied by a signed statement which Louis Pelser had given to Mr. Moore seven months after the trial. In it, the Rice & Hutchins employee who had testified at Dedham that Sacco was the "dead image" of the man whom he had seen shoot Berardelli, completely repudiated his testimony. "The fellow I saw on the street," he had told Moore, "I could not identify." He reaffirmed what he had told the defense when he was interviewed before the trial, namely that he had been so frightened by the first shots that he had dived under his workbench while Berardelli and Parmenter were being killed. However, barely two days after giving this statement to Moore, he wrote a letter to Katzmann in which he claimed that he had been induced to retract his testimony by a combination of heavy drinking and the Californian's powers of persuasion.

A third supplementary motion was filed on July 22, 1922. By that time, the defense's investigators had learned a great deal more about Carlos Goodridge, whose positive identification of Sacco had done much to convict him. Moore and Thompson pointed out in their papers that the phonograph salesman's real name was Erastus Corning Whitney, and that he had been convicted twice in New York of larceny. In addition, he was regarded in most of the communities in which he had lived as a liar, a cheat and a philanderer. An affidavit from his divorced wife, to whom he had been married under an assumed name, stated that he had once told her that "he hated all persons that were of Italian nativity." If he could have his way, he had often said, he would torpedo every immigrant ship sailing out of Genoa for the United States.

Less than two months after the Goodridge motion, the defendants' attorneys submitted a retraction which they had obtained from Lola Andrews. She now claimed that, when she told the police that she couldn't be sure that Sacco was the man whom she had seen in South Braintree on April 15, Assistant District Attorney Williams had shouted at her, "You can put it stronger than that! I know you can!" The night before she had taken the stand at Dedham, she had been ordered by Katzmann and Williams to mislead the defense if any of its attorneys attempted to question her. Accordingly, when Jeremiah McAnarney interviewed her later that night, she had told him that "she could not and would not identify either of the defendants."

Shortly after Katzmann received a copy of Mrs. Andrews' retraction, he interviewed her in the Dedham courthouse. She now denied that she had intended to cast any doubt on the testimony she had given at the trial. According to her, Moore had threatened to expose her past life and to bring her nineteen-year-old son into the case unless she recanted. "If I refused," she informed the district attorney, "they would use the evidence against me and that things would be made very disagreeable for both me and the son." She claimed that she hadn't even known what was in the paper she had signed. "I remember hearing the name of Sacco and Vanzetti being called, and I heard them saying something about that I had lied."

By the fall of 1923, Thompson had, for all practical purposes, supplanted Moore as attorney-in-chief for both defendants.* His growing importance in the post-trial maneuvering was reflected by a letter which Vanzetti sent to him on October 4. "I cannot help but write these few words," the fish peddler wrote, "to express you my gratitude and admiration for the your masterly battle in behalf of my life and my liberty (which I love more than life itself). I feel positive that if we have knew you from the beginning of this shame, at this time we would have been freed. I beg you, Mr. Thomp-

---

* He did not officially become chief counsel until November 10, 1924, when he was paid $25,000 by the Defense Committee.

son, to excuse my poor English, and accept my gratitude."

The lawyer's assumption of what Vanzetti was later to call "the defense of two poor Christs" was to cost him dearly. In 1927, he told a reporter that "this trial has been something of a catastrophe to this firm. We've lost friends, clients and a great deal of money. My income last year was less than for more than twenty years before." That Vanzetti at least understood the nature of Thompson's financial sacrifice is indicated by a letter to a friend in the spring of 1927 in which he states that "Mr. Thompson need to do other works to face life's necessities."

Thompson's first act in his own name was to file an affidavit by Albert H. Hamilton, a gun expert who had made microscopic examinations of all the ballistics exhibits which had been introduced at the trial. Hamilton was positive that none of the bullets that had been removed from the bodies of the dead men had been fired from Sacco's Colt. Supported by the findings of Prof. Augustus H. Gill of the Massachusetts Institute of Technology, he also ventured the opinion that none of the fatal shells had been fired from a Savage automatic as Captain Proctor had intimated. He concluded that all of the recovered bullets had come from a Harrington & Richardson automatic pistol.

The five supplementary motions were argued before Judge Thayer on October 1,2,3 and November 1,2 and 8, 1923. On the next to the last day of the oral arguments, Thompson asked the court's permission to submit an addition to the Hamilton motion. He handed Thayer an affidavit sworn to by Captain William H. Proctor who had told the Sacco-Vanzetti jury that the No. III bullet was "consistent with being fired by that [Sacco's] pistol." "That is still my opinion," he stated, "for the reason that bullet number III, in my judgment, passed through some Colt automatic pistol, but I do not intend by that answer to imply that I had found any evidence that the so-called mortal bullet had passed through this particular Colt automatic pistol and the District Attorney well knew that I did not so intend and framed his question accordingly. Had I been asked the direct question: whether I had found any affirmative evidence whatever that this so-called mortal bullet had passed through this particular Sacco's pistol, I should have answered then, as I do now without hesitation, in the negative."

Thayer took almost a year to deny the five motions. On October 1, 1924, in a detailed opinion, he disposed of almost every point the defense had raised. Although he did not refer to Daly's affidavit, he refused to concede that Ripley's conduct in the jury room had prejudiced the defendants. "I find," he decided, "that the mere production of the Ripley cartridges . . . did not create such disturbing or prejudicial influence that might in any way affect the verdict." He did not feel that Gould's story was credible. The razor-paste salesman "must have carried a correct mental photograph in his mind of Sacco for practically eighteen months, when he only had a glance in which to take this photograph on the day of the murder."

As for Mrs. Andrews' retraction, the judge felt that it had been induced by "coercion, fraud, intimidation and duress." While he did not believe that Pelser had been subjected to the same treatment, he concluded that the latter had been under the influence of liquor when he had recanted his trial testimony. He disposed of the information about Goodridge's reputation and criminal record by scolding Moore and his associates for attempting to blacken the witness' name. Lastly, he had not been overly impressed by Mr. Hamilton's findings or Captain Proctor's explanation of his testimony.

After Thayer's denial of the supplementary motions, Moore and the McAnarney brothers withdrew entirely from the case and Thompson became chief counsel for both convicted men, a development that delighted Vanzetti. "Mr. Thompson is a quick and penetrating intelligence, a tongue wonderful," he wrote to the Brini family. "Would we have had Mr. Thompson at the first trial, we would have been in the open long ago."

It was not until January of 1926 that Thompson's appeal from Thayer's refusal to order a new trial for Sacco and Vanzetti was argued in Boston before the five-judge Supreme Judicial Court. Two months earlier, a startling development had taken place in Dedham Jail. On November 18, 1925, Celestino F. Madeiros, a twenty-three-year-old Portuguese, who had been convicted of murdering a bank cashier during a hold-up, gave trusty Edward J. Miller a note to deliver to Sacco's cell. "I hear by confess" wrote Madeiros, "to being in the shoe company crime at south Braintree on April 15, 1920 and that Sacco and Vanzetti was not there."

Thompson immediately rushed to Dedham to interview Madeiros. The latter told the lawyer that the robbery had been committed by a band of Italians who had specialized in hijacking freight cars in the Providence area. However, true to the unwritten code of the underworld, he refused to reveal the names of his confederates. From what Madeiros told him, Thompson was convinced that the crime had been committed by the Morelli brothers, who had been convicted in Providence in May, 1920, of robbing rail shipments, some of which belonged to Slater & Morrill. Since the gang had been at large at the time of the murders of Parmenter and Berardelli, it was entirely possible, he reasoned, that it could have been involved.

Because Madeiros was awaiting a decision on the appeal from his own conviction, Thompson did not present his confession to Judge Thayer until the Portuguese's second trial had terminated in another conviction on May 20, 1926, a week after the Supreme Judicial Court had affirmed the denial of the five supplementary motions. Six days later, the attorney filed a motion for a new trial based on the confession. After mulling over the papers during the summer,

Thayer decided, on October 23, that Madeiros was not to be believed. "Madeiros is, without doubt," he wrote, "a crook, a thief, a robber, a liar, a rum runner, a 'bouncer' in a house of ill fame, a smuggler, and a man who has been convicted and sentenced to death for the murder of one Carpenter." Besides, he was incapable of describing "what the place and the immediate vicinity looked like where the murders were committed."

Coupled with Madeiros' motion were affidavits which Thompson had obtained from Fred J. Weyand and Lawrence Leatherman, two former FBI agents who, at the time of the trial, had been investigating radical activities in the Boston area. The two ex-agents asserted that there had been extensive cooperation between Katzmann and the Department of Justice and that an examination of the latter's files would reveal the extent of this liaison. Weyand was "thoroughly convinced . . . that these men had nothing whatever to do with the South Braintree murders, and that their conviction was the result of cooperation between the Boston agents of the Department of Justice and the District Attorney."

According to Leatherman, former Attorney General A. Mitchell Palmer, who had been stymied in his efforts to deport the defendants, had seized on the murder prosecution as a means of getting rid of them. "It was the opinion of the Department agents here that a conviction of Sacco and Vanzetti for murder would be one way of disposing of these two men." He agreed with Weyand that "Sacco and Vanzetti, although anarchists and agitators, were not highway robbers and had nothing to do with the South Braintree crime." All of the agents who had studied the case thought that the Slater & Morrill payroll had been heisted by "a gang of professional highwaymen."

During the summer of 1926, Thompson tried, without success, to inspect the FBI files. On July 3, he wrote to Attorney General John G. Sargent, asking for permission to examine all "documents and correspondence" in the Boston office pertaining to the Sacco-Vanzetti case. Ten days later, Thompson received a telephone call from a Mr. Dowd, the agent in charge of the Boston Branch of the Department of Justice. Dowd informed the lawyer that "he had no authority to permit Mr. West [the local FBI chief] either to give me the information desired, or to show me any papers whatever." * Thayer was unimpressed with Thompson's charge that the FBI files had been "suppressed." He refused "to find . . . a collusion between these two great governments—that of the United States and the Commonwealth of Massachusetts."

The defendants appealed at once to the Supreme Judicial Court. Late in January, Thompson appeared before the appellate tribunal and urged it to reverse Thayer. According to Vanzetti, the lawyer's argument had been masterful. "I am sorry that you were unable to hear the whole argumentation of Mr. Thompson," he wrote to Alice Stone Blackwell. "He has really been magnificent. A denial of a new trial after the work of Mr. Thompson would solely, most clearly and irrefutably mean: we care, we look, we consider, we want nothing except to doom the defendants. A dangerous answer to the conscience of the world."

However, on April 28, the court unanimously affirmed Thayer's decision. In the words of Justice William Cushing Wait, it found that "an impartial, intelligent and honest judge would be justified in finding that the confession gains no persuasive force from the credibility of Madeiros; that

* On August 22, 1927, the day of the defendants' executions, a summary of the contents of these files was released to a Boston newspaper. It indicated that neither man had been under suspicion by the Department prior to their arrest and that the stationing of an FBI informer in the cell next to Sacco's at Dedham had been only for the purpose of ascertaining what the latter knew about a mysterious explosion that had taken place in Wall Street in the fall of 1920.

the facts relied upon by the defendants in confirmation, if true, go no further than to furnish basis for a contention that he and some members of the Morelli gang . . . took part in the murders at South Braintree, but fall far short of furnishing adequate proof of their guilt or of establishing reasonable doubt of the guilt of the defendants." In disposing of the affidavits of Weyand and Leatherman, the court stated that "the belief of investigators in the defendants' innocence is not evidence which can be submitted to a jury."

With the last appeal out of the way, Thayer got down to the long-delayed business of sentencing the defendants. On April 9, they were brought into his courtroom for the last time. After Winfield M. Wilbar, Katzmann's successor, had moved that sentences be imposed, the clerk asked both men if they had "anything to say why sentence of death should not be passed." Sacco spoke for only a few minutes, affirming that he had "never been guilty, never; not yesterday nor today nor forever." Vanzetti, on the other hand, held the floor for almost an hour, attributing his conviction to his Italian origin and his anarchistic beliefs. "I am suffering because I am a radical," he concluded, "and indeed I am a radical; I have suffered because I was an Italian and indeed I am an Italian . . . but I am so convinced to be right that if you could execute me two times, and if I could be reborn two other times, I would again do what I have done already."

Thayer sentenced both men to die in the electric chair on July 10, 1927. While his clients waited in Dedham Jail for their transfer to Charlestown's death row, Thompson worked with Vanzetti on the preparation of a clemency petition to Governor Alvan T. Fuller. Because Sacco refused to sign the lengthy document, it was presented to Fuller with Vanzetti's signature alone. "It is to me," Vanzetti wrote to Mary Donovan, the recording secretary of the Defense Committee, "legally splendid and passable as to principles." In it, he reiterated what the two men had stressed since their convictions—"that we are innocent and that our trial was unfair."

The Governor responded by appointing an advisory committee composed of President Abbott Lawrence Lowell of Harvard University, President Samuel W. Stratton of MIT, and former Suffolk County Probate Judge Robert Grant. Since Lowell and Stratton could not, because of their academic responsibilities, begin work until July 1, Fuller postponed the condemned men's executions until August 10. The advisory committee concluded its investigation on July 22 and, five days later, submitted a report to the Governor in which its members unanimously agreed that both defendants were "guilty beyond a reasonable doubt of the murder at South Braintree."

On the day the committee closed its hearings, Fuller interviewed Vanzetti, who was in the middle of a hunger strike, in the latter's cell. The Governor returned five nights later, and the two men conversed in the warden's office until after eleven o'clock. "He gives me the impression," Vanzetti wrote to Mrs. Blackwell, "of being an honest man, as I understand it, a sincere, courageous, stubborn man, but well-intentioned at the bottom of it, and in a way, clever. And I would like to tell you that he gave me a good heartfelt handshake before he left. I may be wrong, but I don't believe that a man like that is going to burn us on a case like ours."

Vanzetti was wrong. On August 3, Fuller found "no sufficient justification for executive intervention." Minutes after the announcement of the Governor's decision, Sacco, Vanzetti and Madeiros, who was scheduled to die with them, were moved to the three holding cells adjacent to the electric chair at Charlestown. Thompson, who felt that he could do nothing further to save his "poor Christs," stepped down as their attorney and the last legal moves on their behalf were conducted by Arthur D. Hill, a former Suffolk County District Attorney.

Hill, who had told the advisory committee that he felt

that Thayer had "a strong feeling of prejudice both against the men themselves, their opinion and their counsel, Mr. Moore," hurriedly moved for a revocation of sentence and a new trial on that ground. On August 8, after Chief Justice Walter P. Hall of the Superior Court had refused to disqualify him, Thayer denied the motion, claiming that Massachusetts law prohibited him from granting a new trial subsequent to the imposition of sentence. The following day, he refused to revoke the sentences, a ruling that was promptly sustained by one justice of the Supreme Judicial Court.

"Being still alive, I renew to you my best regards and good wishes," wrote Vanzetti to one of his supporters on August 12. Two days earlier, Fuller had granted the now thoroughly resigned defendants an eleventh-hour reprieve to enable them to appeal Thayer's latest denial to the full bench of the higher court. Meanwhile, Hill was busy filing petitions for writs of habeas corpus with Supreme Court Justice Oliver Wendell Holmes and every subordinate Federal judge he could find in Massachusetts. They were all denied. "In my opinion," said Holmes, "nothing short of a want of legal power to decide the case authorizes me to interfere . . . with the proceedings of the state court."

On August 19, three days before the scheduled executions, the Supreme Judicial Court affirmed Thayer's decision that he had no power either to revoke sentence or to grant a new trial. The next day, Hill and the trio of volunteer attorneys who were assisting him * attempted to persuade Justices Stone, Brandeis and Holmes to stay the executions until October so that a petition for review could be submitted to the Supreme Court. All three refused to intervene. "I cannot say I have a doubt, and therefore I must deny the stay," wrote Holmes.

Sacco, Vanzetti and Madeiros were scheduled to be electro-

* Herbert B. Ehrmann, Elias Field and Michael A. Musmanno.

cuted at midnight on August 22. Earlier that day, Thompson, who was vacationing in New Hampshire, received a message that Vanzetti wanted to see him. The lawyer arrived at the prison in the late afternoon and was taken to the hallway outside the three holding cells. The guards permitted him to sit in a chair in front of Vanzetti's cell and talk to the prisoner through a barred window.

"I told Vanzetti," Thompson later wrote, "that although my belief in his innocence had all the time been strengthened, both by my study of the evidence and by my increasing knowledge of his personality, yet there was a chance, however remote, that I might be mistaken; and that I thought he ought, for my sake, in this closing hour of his life, when nothing could save him, to give me his most solemn assurances, both with respect to himself and with respect to Sacco. Vanzetti then told me quietly and calmly and with a sincerity which I could not doubt . . . that both he and Sacco were absolutely innocent of the South Braintree crime, and that he [Vanzetti] was equally innocent of the Bridgewater crime." After saying farewell to Vanzetti, Thompson stopped in front of Sacco's cell. "He rose from his cot . . . thanked me for what I had done for him, showed no sign of fear, shook hands with me firmly, and bade me goodbye."

At midnight, two guards awakened Madeiros and accompanied him the dozen or so steps to the little white-painted room across the hall from the holding cells. He was quickly strapped into the grotesque wooden chair that stood in the center of the room. As soon as the guards had finished adjusting the electrodes, Warden William A. Hendry signalled to the unseen executioner. The prison lights dimmed as the dynamo pumped two lethal charges into the Portuguese's body. Three minutes later, he was pronounced dead, and his corpse placed on one of the three green mortuary slabs that were hidden from view by a screen.

Sacco was next. While the guards were strapping him in

the chair, he shouted, in Italian, "Long live anarchy!" Then his voice softened as he said, this time in English, "Farewell my wife and child and all my friends." He had just time to add, "Farewell, Mother," when the switch was thrown. At 12:19 A.M., the official physician indicated that the slumping man in the chair was dead.

When Vanzetti entered the execution chamber, he insisted on shaking hands with the warden and several of the guards. As he waited for the latter to finish strapping him in, he said to the witnesses, in a strangely conversational tone, "I am innocent of all crime, not only of this one, but all. I am an innocent man." His voice quickened as he noticed that the warden had raised his arm. "I wish to forgive some people for what they are now doing to me," he whispered. The hum of the current punctuated the sentence. The wall clock read 12:24.

Thompson survived his most famous clients by eight years. On March 19, 1938, the Boston Bar Association issued a glowing tribute in his memory. "It made no difference to William G. Thompson," it said, "whether the cause in which he was enlisted was popular or unpopular with the multitude. His great moral courage was an outstanding characteristic and in his pursuit of justice he could not be diverted by fear of any consequence to himself or to his career. In this respect, he carried out the finest tradition of the Bar, and he earned the right to stand beside those fearless leaders of the Bar who never forsook principle, as they saw it, for popularity."

But the Bar Association's dignified memorial did not adequately explain the fervor of its subject's efforts on behalf of Sacco and Vanzetti or why, after their execution, he spent the remainder of his life attempting to improve the calibre of government officials, particularly the judiciary. "Economic and social status had ceased to have any meaning for him," explained one of his former associates after his death. "The explosion in his soul had brought to the surface hidden qualities of leadership and he attracted a growing number of persons willing to assist him in his fight to lift the standard of Massachusetts."

In the last analysis, it was Vanzetti, the immigrant, the anarchist, the draft dodger, the agitator, and, according to a jury of his peers, the murderer, who transformed the urbane descendant of fourteen generations of solid New Englanders into a man prepared, at any cost, to devote his life "to the love of man and all living things." That Thompson himself was keenly aware of the cause of his personal metamorphosis was undeniable. On May 15, 1927, he told a reporter for the *New York World:* "I went into this case as a Harvard man, a man of old American tradition, to help two poor aliens who had, I thought, been unjustly treated. I have arrived at a humbler attitude. Not since the martyrdoms of the sixteenth century has such steadfastness to a faith, such self-abnegation as that of these poor Italians been seen on this earth. The Harvard graduate, the man of old American tradition, the established lawyer, is now quite ready to say that nowhere in his soul is there to be found the faith, the splendid gentility, which make the man, Bartolomeo Vanzetti."

# Homer Stillé Cummings

IN the winter of 1924, a well-liked Catholic priest was shot
and killed on the streets of Bridgeport, Connecticut. A week
later, Harold Israel, a young itinerant laborer, was arrested
and charged with the crime. The case against him seemed
insurmountable. Not only was there a small army of eyewitnesses who identified him as the man they had seen fire a
bullet into the decedent's head and run away from the scene
of the shooting, but Israel had given the police a full confession. This evidence, coupled with the fact that the suspect
owned a gun of the same calibre as the fatal shell, and had left
Bridgeport shortly after the murder, would have been more
than enough to convince even the most impartial of juries
that he was the killer.

With all of Bridgeport crying for blood, Homer S. Cummings, the State's Attorney for Fairfield County, began preparing the case for trial. By all odds, *State vs. Israel* was a
prosecutor's dream. A surfeit of witnesses, a confession, the
possible murder weapon and flight—Cummings had everything he needed for a certain conviction. But, for reasons
which he himself couldn't adequately explain, he began to
have nagging doubts as to the defendant's guilt. Despite the
public's impatience for a speedy and spectacular trial, he
decided to delay it until he had satisfied himself that his prisoner had murdered the priest.

For a sensitive man, the decision to prosecute or not to
prosecute is an awesome one indeed. This is particularly so

275

when the crime involved is one that has shocked and outraged his community. "The primary duty of a lawyer engaged
in public prosecution," according to the American Bar Association, "is not to convict but to see that justice is done."
But this admonition is small comfort to an ambitious district
attorney who, notwithstanding his own inner doubts, knows
how easy it is to avoid any career complications by shifting
the responsibility to a jury which, in the last analysis, has
little or nothing to lose.

Most prosecutors would agree with Prof. Edwin M. Bor-
chard of the Yale Law School that "among the most shocking
of . . . injuries and most glaring of injustices are erroneous
criminal convictions of innocent people." Yet only a handful
have, over the years, been willing to stand between the crowd
and its intended victim. It has proved far safer to let the law
take its normal course, and trust to the appellate courts to
rectify any errors committed by passion and prejudice. In the
words of President Hoover's Wickersham Committee, "Between the desire for publicity and the fear of offending those
who control local politics, the temptation is strong to fall
into an ineffective perfunctory routine for everyday cases with
spectacular treatment of sensational cases."

Fortunately, Cummings was not one to place career over
conscience. For three months, he devoted almost every waking
hour to interviewing witnesses, inspecting the murder scene
and the killer's escape route, and checking Israel's alibi.
Impressed by the fact that the defendant had retracted his
confession a week after he had made it, he arranged for a
battery of physicians to examine him at periodic intervals and
report on his mental and physical condition. As his investigation deepened, he became increasingly convinced that Israel
had been the unfortunate victim of mistaken identity, unwarranted inferences and his own unstable personality.

For a man like Cummings, there was only one thing to do.
On May 27, 1924, he appeared in Bridgeport's Superior Court

and asked that the charges against Israel be dismissed. As he meticulously outlined the reasons for his extraordinary request, he was fully conscious that there were few people in Fairfield County who would understand that, as he was to tell the students of the John Marshall School of Law a decade later, "To know justice one must feel it." In 1931, however, he had the satisfaction of knowing that the Wickersham Committee had referred to his action as "a notable illustration of the proper discharge of the prosecutor's duty."

Several years after Cummings' death, Paul W. Williams, the United States Attorney for the Southern District of New York, addressed the County Prosecutors Association of New Jersey. "We have learned through grave blunders and miscarriages of justice," Mr. Williams said, "that when the passions of men prevail, injustice triumphs, and that it is only through an extensive search, sifting and analysis of the facts that logical and reasonable conclusions can be drawn." Cummings, who had lived long enough to see the Israel case become a legend, a motion picture,* and his most enduring tribute, would have been the last to disagree with him.

> "... it is just as important for a state's attorney to use the great powers of his office to protect the innocent as it is to convict the guilty."

# Homer S. Cummings and the dismissal of the murder charge against Harold F. Israel, May 27, 1924

IN THE SUMMER of 1920, a new pastor arrived at St. Joseph's Roman Catholic Church in Bridgeport, Connecticut. Fifty-

---

* *Boomerang*, 1947, produced by Twentieth Century Fox Film Corporation and directed by Elia Kazan.

two-year-old Hubert Dahme, a German-born priest who had been teaching foreign languages at St. Thomas' Seminary in Hartford since 1895, took his new parish seriously. In less than three years, he had built a convent and a parochial school, and laid the cornerstone for a new church. Almost half of the cost of the latter edifice had been donated by Father Dahme from money left to him by the will of a former parishioner.

The tall, gray-haired priest rapidly became a familiar—and extremely popular—figure in Bridgeport. Every evening, as he took his customary after-dinner stroll up Main Street, he would exchange greetings with scores of people who had grown to look forward to his nightly appearances. His normal route was well known. After Mrs. Nellie Hines, his housekeeper, had served him his dinner, he generally walked on the westerly side of Main Street toward the north end of town. When he reached High Street, he would usually turn around and return to the parish house on Catherine Street.

The night of Monday, February 4, 1924, was no exception. By 7:45, he had passed the Stratfield Hotel, Congress and Arch Streets, and reached the southerly side of High Street. He paused for a moment in front of Miss Dennis' millinery shop to look across the street at the crowd flocking into the Lyric Theater to see Ethel Barrymore in her new play, *The Laughing Lady*. Suddenly, as he neared the curb on the south side of High Street, a slender young man approached him from the rear and pointed the muzzle of a revolver at the back of his head. There was a shot, and the clergyman fell to the ground. As the assassin ran up High Street, an excited crowd flocked around the wounded man, who was lying on his face in the gutter. He was taken to St. Vincent's Hospital, where he died several hours later, without ever regaining consciousness.

In general, most of the eyewitnesses were uniform in their basic description of the murderer. He was a young man of medium height, who wore a gray cap and a dark, three-quarter length overcoat with a velvet collar. After the shooting, he had turned left into High Street and raced up the hill toward Washington Avenue. According to three pedestrians who were walking down High Street, the fugitive, who had been running in the center of the roadway, veered off to the right as he passed them. A few minutes later, he was seen running on the north side of Congress Street, where he stumbled as he crossed the Harrison Street intersection.

The next morning, an autopsy was performed in St. Vincent's Hospital. Father Dahme's death was attributed to "a gunshot wound in the brain causing hemorrhage and laceration of the brain." According to the medical examiner's report, the bullet had entered the priest's skull "at a point in the lobe of the left ear, passing in the rear through the cerebellum, upward through the cerebrum, and stopped on the right side of the cerebrum." X-rays taken shortly after death indicated that the gun that had killed the priest had been pointed upward at an angle of approximately forty to forty-five degrees. The major portion of a .32-caliber bullet was removed from the dead man's brain.

At 1:20 A.M. on Tuesday, February 11, John E. Reynolds, a South Norwalk plainclothesman, noticed a young man wandering aimlessly around that city. When the stranger told him that he had no money and was looking for a place to sleep, Reynolds took him to headquarters. There he was searched, and a .32-caliber revolver of Spanish make found in his overcoat pocket. Upon examination, it was discovered that one of the gun's five chambers was empty.

The youth said that his name was Harold F. Israel and that he lived in Bridgeport. He had arrived in South Norwalk earlier that evening en route to his sister's home in Connerton, Pennsylvania. He had run out of money and was looking for a place to spend the night when he had been apprehended by Reynolds. He had heard of Father Dahme's murder because two of his friends had been in the vicinity when it had occurred. Later that morning, he pleaded guilty to carrying a concealed weapon and was sentenced by City Court Judge Vosburgh to thirty days in the Fairfield County Jail at Bridgeport.

After Reynolds had escorted him to the county jail, Israel was taken to police headquarters on Fairfield Avenue, where he was again questioned about the priest's murder. He told his interrogators that, prior to leaving for Connerton, he had been living with two friends, Charles Cihal and Nick Cardullo, in a furnished room on the second floor of Mrs. Whelan's rooming house at 354 Stratford Avenue. The three young men had become acquainted in Panama, where they had served in the army together. Six months after his discharge in June of 1923, Israel had come to Bridgeport to live with Cihal. Later, the pair had been joined by Cardullo.

While the police were interviewing Israel, Nellie Trefton, a garrulous waitress in the Star Restaurant on the northwest corner of Main and Arch Streets, told a diner that she was certain that the suspect had killed the clergyman. She was sure of this, she said, because she had seen him pass the front of the restaurant, which was only a block away from where Dahme had been murdered, a few minutes before the shooting. Besides, when she was working at the Philadelphia Lunch, which was located on the ground floor of Israel's rooming house, he had once shown her a pistol and told her that he was going to kill somebody with it. Her customer immediately telephoned the police, and Miss Trefton was soon brought to headquarters, where she identified Israel as the man she had seen walk by the restaurant at approximately 7:40 P.M. on February fourth.

As soon as the waitress had returned to work, the Bridgeport police began to question Israel in earnest. From noon on February 13 to the early evening of the following day, several teams of officers took turns in interrogating him. Finally, he broke down and admitted that he had killed Father Dahme because "something came to my mind." After the shooting, he had run up the middle of High Street, swerving to avoid a man and two women who were walking down the hill toward Main Street. He had turned left on Washington Avenue and raced toward the center of the city, stumbling as he crossed the trolley tracks at Harrison Street. Later that evening, he was taken in a police car to the scene of the shooting, from which he retraced his escape route for his captors.

After Israel had confessed, he was asked what he had done with the empty shell case of the bullet which had killed Dahme. He stated that he had thrown it under the sink in the second-floor lavatory of his boardinghouse. A discharged cartridge was found where the suspect said he had put it. Charles J. Van Amburgh, a ballistics expert who had testified for the prosecution in the Sacco-Vanzetti case, later tested Israel's revolver and the bullet which had been extracted from the victim's body, and concluded that the fatal shot had been fired from the young man's gun.

The results of the police investigation were turned over to Fairfield County Coroner John G. Phelan, who scheduled a hearing for February 18 to determine whether the evidence warranted submission to the grand jury. Because Israel was penniless, Public Defender Robert G. De Forest was appointed to represent him. Subpoenas were issued to talkative Nellie Trefton and some dozen other witnesses, ordering them to appear at City Hall at 9:30 A.M. on the day of the inquest "to be examined under oath on all matters known to you concerning the death by shooting of Hubert Dahme, late of this city."

At exactly 9:30 A.M. on the eighteenth, Phelan, who was the soul of promptness, called Dr. Edward Fitzgerald, the county's acting medical examiner, to the stand. Dr. Fitzgerald and two colleagues had performed the autopsy on Father Dahme's body on February 5. The physicians had discovered "a gunshot wound in the brain causing hemorrhage and laceration of the brain." The witness had brought the fatal bullet to court with him, and it was marked into evidence as State's Exhibit A. The bullet, which he described as the "exclusive cause of death," had been located "on the upper right side of the base of the cerebrum, on the periphery."

Phelan, who had listened intently to the medical examiner's testimony, had a few questions of his own. "Have you any idea, Doctor, as to the relative positions of the man who shot the bullet and the victim towards each other at the time of the shooting?" Fitzgerald had. "Why, I think," he answered, "that the man that held the gun walked to the victim's left side and, in passing, fired into a part of his ear." In addition, he was convinced that the murderer must have been "stooped down" to inflict the wound revealed by the autopsy.

James H. McKiernan, an assistant ticket agent at the New Haven Railroad station, was next. On his way to work on the night of the murder, he had seen the priest leaving his house on Catherine Street. The two men had had a brief conversation about the progress of the new church. When McKiernan asked him whether the building was almost completed, Dahme had replied, "No, it isn't quite. There is an awful lot to be done on it yet." The clergyman had spoken in such "an absent-minded way," that "I thought he wasn't well or something."

Phelan's first eyewitness to the shooting was a carpenter by the name of Frederick W. Morris. The latter, who was on his way home for supper, had been standing in front of Miss Dennis' millinery shop when he had seen two men approaching the intersection. "The little fellow was on the outside of the old gentleman and, as he stepped down there, I saw his hand go up to his head, and I heard the shot fired, and the man ran up the street, about a hundred feet, and crossed in between two cars."

Q. Your belief was that they had come down High Street?
A. That is how it looked to me, it looked to me as if they
   came down High Street or else they might have been
   standing there and stepped out. They stepped down right
   within six feet of me.

He thought that the two men had "come down together."

Because the man who fired the shot had been a half-step behind the priest, Morris had been able to see "his side face." Phelan pointed to Israel. "Do you recognize this party here," he asked, "as being the party?" The witness looked perplexed. "His side face did look familiar to me the night I was called to identify him," he replied, "but I couldn't swear to the man because it just didn't look just like him at that time. His clothes didn't seem to be the same."

What kind of clothes had the murderer been wearing? Morris thought that "he had a dark overcoat and a gray cap, a sort of light colored cap anyway."

Q. Was the coat dark gray?
A. Whether it was a dark gray or dark brown, I couldn't
   say for sure, but it was a dark overcoat, considerably
   darker than the cap.

He was sure that it had been a "medium, not a real long coat and not a real short coat." When Phelan showed him Israel's coat, he said that "that was about the color of the coat."

"Mr. Morris," asked Phelan, "now that you see the accused before you here, what is your impression as to his identity, do you think it is the same man?" There was a long pause before the carpenter answered. "Why, it is a hard thing to say," he replied slowly. "I can't say I could prove it was the same man, but his side face did look familiar to me. I thought he was about the same build of man, he was a medium-built man, but I thought this man was a little bit taller when I came to look at him the second time, at the line-up."

Q. You mean by familiar that you believe that it is him, that is your general belief?

A. Yes, that would be my mind.

But he couldn't be absolutely sure because the killer had been running up High Street "too fast" for any detailed observation.

He had seen the priest fall into the gutter after the shot. But his vision had been somewhat obscured by some men who had been standing between him and the High Street crosswalk.

Q. Between you and the gutter of High Street?

A. Yes, sir.

Then two boys had run across the street and "raised up the victim." Morris had lost sight of the fleeing man when he had run "between two automobiles." No, he had not seen any pistol. "I saw him raise his hands to the man's head . . . and I heard the shot."

Between 7:40 and 7:50 that evening, an emergency call had been received at St. Vincent's Hospital. Dr. Albert Levenson, a city ambulance surgeon, had been sent to the corner of Main and High where he found a "profusely bleeding man . . . near the gutter, very close." The ambulance driver had informed him that the injured man was Father Dahme. "We immediately took the stretcher out and rushed him right down to the hospital." He had been unable to obtain any statement from the priest because "he evidently never recovered consciousness."

Margaret Morrill, a social worker, had been standing in front of the Lyric Theater at the time of the murder. She had first thought that the shot was the result of a blow-out. "When I looked back," she said, "I saw the man crumpled down on his side right at the gutter." She had noticed another man "running up High Street, on the same side as the man, he ran up to the hill and crossed over." Thinking that she might be of some assistance to the injured priest, she had rushed to his side and stayed with him until the ambulance arrived.

"Could you give any description of the person you saw running away?" demanded Phelan. The most she could say was that "he had what looked to me like a mackinaw, a short coat, and a light cap." She couldn't describe the color of the coat because "it was too far away." But she did remember that the murderer had run with "rather a long stride, and I thought that he was a tall man, looked tall going up the hill."

Sixteen-year-old Ralph S. Esposito, a delivery boy for the Thomas P. Taylor Company, had been walking south on Main Street with two friends, Joe Maturo and Eddie Hoffman, when he had noticed two men standing on the High Street corner. One of the men had raised his arm toward the other, "and the way it looked to me, I thought he shot him through the cheek. I heard the shot, and I hollered and there was nobody around hardly at the time." He had watched the assassin "run up High Street, on the left side, and I watched him until he got to the Jewish church, and then I lost sight of him." He was sure that Dahme's assailant had been wearing "a black coat with a velvet collar and a dark cap."

He had been the first one to reach the priest, who had fallen to his knees in the gutter. "I picked him up and pulled him back. I looked at him, and I saw something like a hole in his eye, the eyes were all puffed out." It was only when he had pulled the fallen man's scarf away from his neck that the boy saw the Roman collar and recognized the pastor of St. Joseph's. At that moment, a woman had rushed up to him and shouted, "You better not hold him up!" Minutes later, the ambulance from St. Vincent's had arrived.

When he was questioned by detectives about the murderer's description, he had told them that "I might know him by his build, but I didn't get a good look at his face." On February 13, he had been taken to headquarters and asked to look at some men in a line-up. He had pointed to Israel and said, "I think that is the man there." But he said that he couldn't be sure unless he could see the suspect run. "They had this man run for me," he explained. "He looked like he run the same that night as he did on the night of the murder."

He had been in front of the millinery shop when he had first seen the priest and his attacker. Dahme had been walking a "little bit ahead" of the other man on the portion of the sidewalk nearest to the curb. "They passed the street," he recalled, "he just let him off the curb, about one foot, when he let the man have the gun."

> Q. You were going to tell me something about you saw him with a pistol, did you?
> A. I saw him raise something to his face. I didn't know it was a pistol because it didn't shine. It must have been one of those black pistols.

The two men had "looked like they were talking to each other, but I ain't sure. I didn't hear no words or anything."

As the killer turned into High Street and "trotted over the hill," Esposito noticed that he was wearing "a dark coat . . . a little below his knees." He was "pretty sure" that he had seen a velvet collar. Although Miss Dennis' store had been dark, "it was a pretty good light there." Lieutenant James Bray interrupted to remind the coroner that there was a street lamp some twenty feet south of the millinery shop.

After Esposito had testified that Israel's cap was not as dark as the one which the assassin had worn, Phelan asked the boy how he had identified Israel. "Well, partly by his cap," the witness replied. "When I seen the man run, he run like a Jewish man." The coroner looked puzzled. "I never heard of that before," he said, "What kind of a run is that?" Esposito thought that one good question deserved another. "Did you ever see a Jewish man walk from one side to the other?" he asked.

Q. A kind of side-wheel movement?
A. Yes.

But he was still far from positive that Israel was the man he had seen. "I didn't see the man clear in the face," he explained.

Alfred Berry, another Bridgeport teen-ager, had been standing in front of Rawley's store on the northwest side of High Street when he had seen Father Dahme near the opposite curb. The man who had killed the priest had been running to overtake him.

Q. Where was he, on the right side of Father Dahme or on the left side?
A. I didn't see him until he got right up to him.
Q. How do you know that he ran if you didn't see him run?
A. Yes, I saw him run.

But he hadn't noticed any pistol. "I just saw him pull his hand out of his pocket."

He had seen the killer run away. When Phelan asked him if the man had been running rapidly, Berry shook his head. "No, sir," he answered, "he didn't run very fast." He had been wearing a "dark brown long overcoat, came about a little past his knees." He thought that it had been "a little longer" than Israel's overcoat. No, he hadn't seen the man's face because his coat collar had obscured it. The murderer had been wearing a cap, but he hadn't taken any notice of its color.

February 4 had been the birthday of Mrs. Jennie Boynton, the supervisor of the high school lunchroom. To celebrate it, she had asked her niece and nephew to go to the movies with her at Poli's Theater. The trio had been walking toward Main Street on the south side of High when they had heard the shot. Her niece had exclaimed, "There, someone shot someone!" But her nephew had disagreed. "That is only a backfire from an automobile," he had said. Then they had heard people shouting and, several seconds later, a man had raced "up the street, in the middle of the street." As he neared them, he had crossed over to the north sidewalk. "This man was running up High Street, his hand in his overcoat pocket and his overcoat seemed to be opened. He was running, not very fast, I would say like a soldier runs in tempo, when they have a big load."

She had gotten a good look at the man because he had passed under a street light on the north side of High Street. He had been wearing a gray cap and what looked to her like "an old-fashioned German overcoat." The garment that Phelan showed her "looks like the overcoat." What had impressed her the most about the man she had seen was "the pallor of his face, he was pale." When she had first seen Israel in the line-up at police headquarters, she had "recognized him as quickly as I stepped inside the door," but she had been reluctant to say so.

"But my conscience bothered me," she explained to Phelan, "and I wasn't able to sleep that night, so I told some friends at school about it. I told them if the outcome would not be different by the end of the day, I would have to tell at police headquarters that I did recognize the man." Later that day, when she heard that Israel had confessed, she had informed the police that he was the man she had seen.

Q. Are you able to recognize him now?
A. Yes, sir.

Although she had only seen the side of his face, she was "pretty sure it is the same person."

Hilda Baer, Mrs. Boynton's niece, was a twenty-six-year-old German immigrant who was unable to speak English. With her aunt acting as interpreter, she testified that the fugitive had been wearing "a dark coat and a light cap." The former garment had been "a stiff-looking coat with a velvet collar set in." Although it had been dark on the street, she was certain that Israel's overcoat was "the same coat."

> Q. If it was dark, how could you see?
> A. I did see the stuff because it was two kinds of goods.

She had no difficulty in picking the suspect out of the line-up. She had identified him "by the height of him, the coat and by his nose."

Edward Flood, a packer with the American Chain Company, had arrived at St. Augustine's Church on Washington Avenue at approximately 7:45 on the night of Dahme's murder. After hurriedly saying his prayers, he had left the church ten minutes later in order to make the last show at Poli's Theater. As he drove toward Main Street, he had seen "a man running on the north side of Congress Street on the sidewalk." He explained, "it struck me rather odd at what the man was running for, and naturally being attracted that way, I kept my eyes on him." As the man crossed Harrison Street, he had stumbled over "the curbing or a depression."

Like Mrs. Boynton, Flood recalled that the man's face had been "very pale and colorless." As the latter had raced by him, the packer had noticed that "he was puffing rather hard as though he had been running some distance." Because of a "very deep frown" on the man's face, he had come to the conclusion that "he was depressed about something."

On February 15, Flood had picked Israel out of some fifteen men in the line-up at police headquarters. Phelan asked the suspect to stand up. "This is the man you saw running that night?" he asked. The witness wasted no time in answering. "Yes," he snapped.

> Q. Any question about it?
> A. No, sir.

No, he had "no hesitation" about his identification.

According to Flood, Israel's overcoat had fallen "a little below his knees" and had a turned-up velvet collar. "That is the type of coat that I saw," he told Phelan when the coroner asked him to identify the overcoat that had been previously shown to the other witnesses. As for the cap which Israel had been wearing, it was "lighter than the coat."

Nellie Trefton had known Israel for "about three or four weeks" before Father Dahme's murder. She had met him when she was working at the Philadelphia Lunch on East Main Street. The Wednesday before the shooting, the suspect had shown her a pistol while she was serving him his dinner. As he left the restaurant that night, he had told her, "I'm going to kill somebody with that revolver."

> Q. Did he tell you who he was going to shoot?
> A. No, sir.

But she hadn't questioned him about his contemplated victim's name because "I thought that he was fooling when he said it."

Miss Trefton had gone to work at the Star Restaurant three days before the priest's death. On the night of the murder, Israel had passed by the lunchroom's front window "between seven thirty and twenty-five minutes of eight." He had been walking toward High Street which was several blocks to the north. She was sure of the time because she had been "taking cash" from a customer, and she always looked at the clock whenever she went to the register.

> Q. There is no mistake as to his identity going north at that time?
> A. No, sir.

In fact, she remembered that Israel had "waved his hand to me" as he walked by.

She had remembered the incident when she had read of Israel's arrest in the newspapers on February 13. "I was ready to call the police that night," she said, "when two of the detective force walked in, and I was carried to police headquarters on Fairfield Avenue." After she had told her story to the authorities, she had been taken to the line-up where she had identified Israel. When Phelan showed her a pistol, she said that it looked "about the same" as the gun she had seen in the Philadelphia Lunch. It was promptly marked as State's Exhibit B.

Early on the morning of February 12, John E. Reynolds, a member of the South Norwalk Police Department, had noticed Israel lurking near the viaduct. He had followed him because he was "acting kind of suspicious." After trailing the young man through most of town, Reynolds had taken him to headquarters. "If you are all right," he had told him, "we will let you stay there, and if you are not, why, you will stay there anyway." Although Israel had denied possessing a gun, a .32-caliber revolver had been found in his overcoat pocket. "It belonged to my buddy," he had explained.

When Reynolds asked him about Dahme's murder, Israel had told him that "I heard about it. My buddy was in the vicinity and heard the shot fired." He had then "turned pale and started to sweat." He told Reynolds that he felt sick because he had eaten no food since noon. The officer had locked him in a cell and brought him an egg sandwich and some coffee. The next morning, Judge Vosburgh had fined him fifty dollars and sentenced him to thirty days in the Fairfield County Jail for carrying concealed weapons.

Reynolds had taken his prisoner to Bridgeport on the noon train and turned him over to the clerk of the county jail. The policeman had then reported to police headquarters and told Detective John H. Regan that it might be worth his while to question Israel about the priest's murder. Regan had driven him back to South Norwalk to pick up the suspect's gun. It had been "a cheap make revolver, nickel-plated, five shot, .32-caliber, five chambers." Yes, Exhibit B was the pistol in question.

Frank McNamara, a salesman for the Karm Terminal, had been walking down Sanford Avenue, some two hundred feet from the corner of High and Main, when he heard the shot. A minute or so later, he had seen a man running up the hill toward him. When the latter had passed under a street light, he had gotten a good look at him. "He was about five feet four, I should judge, clean-shaved, and wearing a cap." Although he hadn't noticed any velvet collar, he was sure that the man's coat had been "dark brown" and that he had been wearing a light cap.

After the lunch recess, Phelan suggested to Mr. De Forest that Israel take the stand. The public defender leaped to his feet. "Now, don't you say anything," he barked at his client, who had started for the witness chair. Harold froze in his tracks. De Forest then informed the coroner that Israel was not prepared to testify at this time. "He is mentally exhausted, if not worse, as a result of the questioning that he has undergone and one thing or another." When the lawyer insisted that he didn't want Israel to make "any statement at this time," Phelan called it a day.

At 9:30 the next morning, Charles Cihal, who was now living with Cardullo at 364 Stratford Avenue, was the coroner's first witness. A molder's helper with the City Lumber Company, he had first met Israel in Panama in May or June of 1920. Cihal had left the Canal Zone in the spring of 1923, and he had next seen the suspect at Fort Hamilton, New York, in June, when both men had been discharged. Just before Christmas, Israel had visited Cihal at the home of the latter's parents in Trumbull. At that time, the witness had asked his friend to come and live with him in Bridgeport.

Israel had been unable to find work, and he had eventually run through the three hundred dollars he had saved during his army hitch. At the time of the murder, he owed Cihal twenty-seven dollars for meal tickets which the latter had bought for him. Cardullo had arrived in Bridgeport on February second on the six P.M. train and had immediately moved into Mrs. Whelan's boarding house with his two Army buddies. The three men had shared the same bed in their second floor room.

Cihal knew that Israel owned a pistol. "I fired it myself," he said, "when I used to go up to the country." In fact, the only time that he had ever seen Harold use it was in Trumbull, when he and his roommate used to shoot at trees in the woods behind his father's house. The last time that they had gone to the country with the gun was a month or so before Dahme's murder. Israel had kept the ammunition loose in a bureau drawer in their room at Mrs. Whelan's. Cihal thought that his friend had had "about a dozen bullets."

He had seen the revolver in the bureau dresser just before he left for his job early on February 4. Because he was only scheduled to work a half-day, he had returned to the rooming house at noon, where Israel told him that Cardullo had found a job that morning shining shoes at the railroad station. After visiting Cardullo, Cihal had gone to see a movie at the Empire Theater. Then he had returned to the station and waited for his friend to finish. The two men, who had a date with a couple of Bridgeport girls that evening, returned to their room "a little after six." At 6:20, when they left to pick up their dates, Harold had been lying on the bed. That was the last time they had seen him before the shooting.

The witness had arrived home at 9:30 P.M. He had found the door to his room locked and had knocked on the door to awaken Harold, whom he described as "a sound sleeper." After pounding on the door for several minutes, he had asked Mrs. Whelan to open it for him with her passkey. The room was empty, and Cihal had played some records on his victrola until ten o'clock, when Israel had returned. "I have been to the moving picture show," he had told his roommate. The two had played cards until they went to bed at eleven. It had been about midnight when Cardullo came home.

Cihal had first heard of Dahme's murder the next day at a luncheonette on Seaview Avenue and Third Street. When he learned where it had occurred, he had told his informant, "I had been on High Street that same night and come down, and I told him I had seen a crowd there, but didn't know what it was about, and I didn't inquire what it was about." He and Cardullo had discussed the incident that evening in their room, but Harold, who was present, had said nothing about it. But he was certain that, when Israel had returned to the boardinghouse the night before, he had not been "excited or scared. He came home just the same as if nothing happened."

Phelan wanted to know if Israel had any enemies in Bridgeport. Cihal was positive that he did not. Did he ever say anything about "getting even" with someone? No, he had never heard anything like that. Hadn't there been some bad blood between Israel and Cardullo? Cihal shook his head. Harold had not been too pleased about Nick's arrival, but he couldn't say that the two men disliked each other. As for himself, he had been rather fond of Israel, but he had frequently criticized him for not getting a job.

The coroner was almost through. Had Israel gone to the bathroom when he came home at ten P.M. on February fourth? Cihal couldn't remember whether he had or not. Had the witness heard the "click" of a suitcase after his friend had entered the room? No, sir, he had not. Wasn't it true that Harold had exchanged overcoats with Cardullo at two P.M. on February eleventh? Yes, that was so.

> Q. What kind of a coat was that one that he gave to Harold?
> A. It was a brown coat with a velvet collar.

Exhibit A was the coat in question.

Nicholas Cardullo, who described himself as an unemployed laborer, had looked "all over the west end" for work on the morning of February 4. Finally, he had found a temporary job as a bootblack at the railroad station. Israel had been in the room when he and Cihal had returned at 6:10 that evening to dress for their dates. He was still there when they had left "between 6:20 and half-past six" to pick up their girl friends. When the witness returned at midnight, his two roommates had been asleep.

He and Charlie had discussed the murder the next day. Israel had not joined in the conversation, and "he didn't even look excited or mad or anything." He had first seen the pistol in Harold's drawer on the night he had arrived in Bridgeport. He had noticed it in the same place when he was dressing on Monday evening for his double date with Cihal. When Phelan asked him to take a look at State's Exhibit B, he identified it as the gun he had seen in Israel's drawer. He recognized it by the "knocks around the trigger."

Captain John H. Regan, the chief of Bridgeport's detective division, had taken Officer Reynolds' suggestion that Israel might be Father Dahme's killer seriously. On February 12, he had sent Lieutenant Bray and Sergeants Garrity and McCullough to interview the county jail's newest resident. Meanwhile, he had driven Reynolds back to South Norwalk to pick up the pistol which the latter had found in Israel's overcoat pocket earlier that day. Yes, sir, he assured Phelan, Exhibit B was the gun he had brought back to Bridgeport on Lincoln's Birthday.

The next day, he had visited the county jail. Israel had maintained that he had never left his room on February 4. If the detective didn't believe him, he could check his story with Charlie and Nick. As for the gun, it had been in his bureau drawer all that night. He was sure of this because he had looked there after his friends had left to call for their dates. When Regan had asked him why he had checked on the pistol, he had replied, "I don't know, I just looked in there."

On February 14, Harold had admitted that he had left his room on the night of the priest's murder. After Nellie Trefton and several other witnesses had identified him in the line-up, he told Regan that he had walked up Main Street that evening, but insisted that "he didn't go on the west side of it." He had looked at the displays in front of two movie theaters—Poli's and the Majestic—and then strolled "up Main Street by High Street."

Regan, who was alone with the suspect, had pointed out to him that, "If you did shoot, why, your conscience must be troubling you, and if you did shoot him and feel as though you wanted to relieve your mind and your conscience, why, go ahead and tell us." The detective's words had fallen on fertile soil. "There ain't no use of my denying it any further or any longer," Israel had responded. "You got the gun, you got the cartridge, you have got one that knows me, that seen me there. What is the use of me denying it any further?"

Regan had gone to the door and asked Sergeant Lyddy, a police stenographer, to come in. Then Israel had dictated a statement in which he admitted the crime. After looking at the movie displays, he had walked up the west side of Main Street until he reached Miss Dennis' millinery store. "Then something came over him," Regan recalled, "that he pulled the revolver out and he shot this man." After the murder, he had run up High Street to "where the Kochiss girl lives . . . turned to the left and ran down the street to the left." "Did you fall or stumble?" the detective had asked him. "Yes, I stumbled," had been the answer. When he reached Main Street again, he had gone to the Empire Theater.

At this point, Regan had gone home for dinner while Israel had been given lunch in his cell. Two hours later, the latter had repeated his statement in front of the witness, Lieutenant Bray, Superintendent Flanagan and another stenographer. As soon as it had been typed, he had signed it voluntarily. Had the prisoner been abused in any way, asked Coroner Phelan. Regan's eyebrows shot up a full inch. Absolutely not, your Honor. Were any promises made to him? None whatsoever.

Then the officers had taken their suddenly loquacious captive to Main Street in a "closed car" and asked him to show them his escape route. After shooting Dahme, he had run up High Street where he had seen "two girls coming down the street when I crossed over." He had turned left on Washington Avenue, stumbled on the trolley tracks at Harrison Street, slowed to a walk when he passed police headquarters on Fairfield Avenue, and then proceeded down the east side of Main Street until he reached the Empire Theater. During the ride, he had also told the officers that he had thrown the empty shell "under the sink in the latrine." Later that afternoon, two officers—Sergeants Daniel Brolley and Frank M. Holbrook—had been sent to Mrs. Whelan's to look for the cartridge case.

When Brolley and Holbrook arrived at the boarding-house, they had first searched the room occupied by Israel, Cihal and Cardullo. In the closet, the two officers had found, among some newspapers, "an empty pasteboard cartridge box of 50 or 100 cartridges . . . and a cloth that has cleaned a gun sometime or another." An exploded shell had been discovered "six to eight inches" under the oilcloth that covered the top of the bathroom sink.

> Q. This shell was found just about the place that you were informed Harold said he placed it?
> A. Yes, sir, underneath the sink. Israel didn't say he put it under the oilcloth, but the oilcloth was loose and it was about six inches under the oilcloth. It had worked in there.

Before the two officers returned to headquarters, Mrs. Whelan had found another shell "near the bathtub as she was sweeping up."

Sergeant Holbrook had also discovered a pile of morning newspapers for February 4 in a small closet in the hall. He had returned to the house after taking the newspapers, the empty cartridge box and the grease-stained rag to headquarters. Suddenly, Brolley, who was searching the bathroom, had shouted, "I have found the shell!" It had been located beneath the oilcloth under a hand washbowl. Exhibit C "resembled" the cartridge case that his partner had uncovered.

Before Phelan adjourned for the day, he asked De Forest whether he was now prepared to let Israel testify. The lawyer was not. "In our judgment," he told the coroner, "the young man has been questioned so much that he is in no condition to be questioned further at this time." Phelan looked disappointed. In that case, he said, he would give him a few days in which to pull himself together. "This hearing will resume on Saturday, February 23, at 9:30 A.M.," he announced.

According to De Forest, his client's condition had not improved by Saturday. "I don't consider that he is in any fit condition to make any statement further in this court," he informed Phelan.

Q. If his physical condition grew any better, would there be any chance that you would permit him then to talk, or is it final?

A. I feel that I should say that it is final.

The hearing room was so crowded with spectators who had expected the prisoner to take the stand that, before calling his first—and only—witness of the day, the coroner decided to conduct the rest of the inquest in the more commodious criminal courtroom of the Common Pleas Court.

The background of Captain Charles J. Van Amburgh, an engineer in the ballistics department of the Remington Arms Company, was impressive. In addition to nine years service at the Springfield Arsenal, he had supervised the manufacture of rifles for the New England Westinghouse Company and machine guns for the Colt Patent Firearms Company, and taught ordnance and marksmanship in the United States Army during World War I. He had testified as a ballistics expert in several other criminal cases, including the Sacco-Vanzetti trial in Dedham, Massachusetts, in 1921.

He classified Israel's pistol as a "tip-up or break type of revolver, five chambers, five grooves, five lands and a right twist." Several days after the murder, both the gun and the bullet found in Dahme's brain had been turned over to him. "After my examination," he told Phelan, "I believe that that bullet was fired from that barrel."

Q. And not from any other gun?
A. And not from any other.

Although he hadn't completed his tests, he was "quite convinced that that bullet was fired from that particular revolver." He couldn't "conceive" of anything further that would change his opinion.

Before closing the hearing, Phelan ordered Israel's contradictory statements of February 13 and 14 to Captain Regan included in the record. In the earlier one, he had insisted that he hadn't left his room after six P.M. on February 4. The next morning, however, he had admitted to the police officer that he had walked downtown shortly after his roommates had gone to call for their dates. When he had reached the corner of High and Main, "something came to my mind, I don't know what it was, it just happened to come to me, so quick I pulled out the gun and shot it. I shot the man. I didn't know the man at all." When he returned home that night, he had put the gun in his suitcase. The next morning, he had thrown the empty shell in the bathroom and cleaned the revolver with "some cotton."

Although De Forest had refused to permit Israel to take the stand, Phelan had access to the stenographic record of the latter's answers to questions put to him by Flanagan, Regan and Bray after he had confessed on February 14. On the night the priest had been killed, the prisoner had told them, he had lent Cardullo his overcoat. After his roommates had gone out for the evening, he had found ten pennies which Cihal had left for him on top of the dresser. He had started downtown at "going on to seven," with his gun, which was fully loaded, in his pocket. "I don't know why I took it," he had said, "but just happened to stick it in my pocket."

He had decided to kill Dahme, whom he did not know, when he had seen him pass Miss Dennis' millinery shop.

Q. Did you realize when you shot this man what you had done?
A. No, sir, I didn't realize it at the time; I did after.

No, he had never wanted to shoot anyone before. But he had suffered from spells "every once in a while." He could only remember two of them. Once he had had an impulse to desert from the army; another time, he had been tempted to steal from a Connerton farmer who owed him some money. But, in both cases, he had managed to control his impulses.

Although he had been born a Lutheran, he had attended Catholic services in Panama. Since coming to Bridgeport, he had occasionally accompanied Charlie Cihal to the Slavic Catholic Church. One of eight children, he had left school in Broad Mountain, Pennsylvania, after struggling through the fourth grade. He could read and write, but "I can't add figures very good." He had contracted gonorrhea in Panama but had been cured of the disease by the army medics. After finishing a three-year enlistment, he had been honorably discharged at Fort Hamilton, New York, on June 15, 1923.

On February 25, Phelan submitted his report. "I find," he wrote, "the deceased came to his death at the time, place and from the cause shown as the result of the criminal act of Harold F. Israel of Bridgeport, Connecticut, formerly a resident at 354 Stratford Avenue." In recommending that Israel be tried for Dahme's murder, the coroner listed a number of reasons for his decision. First of all, he pointed out, Nellie Trefton had noticed the youth a block away from the corner of Main and High Streets, five or ten minutes before the shooting. Secondly, Morris and Esposito had seen a man wearing a gray cap and a dark overcoat shoot the priest and run up High Street. Thirdly, Jennie Boynton, Hilda Baer and Edward Flood had identified Israel as the person who had run away from the scene of the murder. Fourth, the suspect had not only confessed, but had shown the police his escape route and told them where he had hidden the empty shell of the fatal bullet. Lastly, Captain Van Amburgh was certain that Israel's gun had killed the clergyman.

On the strength of Phelan's report, Israel was formally charged with murder in Bridgeport's City Court which found that there was "probable cause" that he had shot Father Dahme. While the defendant ruminated in the county jail, the case was set down for trial in the Criminal Superior Court for May 27, 1924. The results of the police investigation and the coroner's finding were forwarded to Homer Stillé Cummings, the state's attorney for Fairfield County.

The fifty-four-year-old Cummings was one of southern Connecticut's most successful lawyers. After his graduation from Yale Law School in 1893, the Chicago ex-patriate had settled down in Stamford where he had served three terms as mayor around the turn of the century. An exceptionally tall man whose bald head and pince-nez glasses gave him a scholarly appearance, he had been named state's attorney by the county's judiciary in 1914. According to Superior Court Judge William M. Maltbie, "the method of appointment of the states attorneys has made that office one of high honor, and, despite the small salaries provided by law, the very leaders of the bar have been willing to assume its onerous duties; so it has removed the office from the stress of politics and the vagaries of popular feeling and given opportunity for the untrammeled exercise of independence in judgment and action."

The Israel case did not appear to be one to test a prosecutor's skill. As Cummings recalled it, "the case against the accused seemed overwhelming. Upon its face, at least, it seemed like a well-nigh perfect case, affording but little difficulty in the matter of a successful prosecution. In fact, it seemed like an 'annihilating' case. There did not seem a vestige of reason for suspecting for a moment that the accused was innocent. The evidence had been described by those who believed in the guilt of the accused as '100 per cent perfect.' "

But, despite his open-and-shut case, Cummings had his own private doubts about Israel's guilt. Relying more on intuition than logic, he came to the conclusion that the defendant might have been "the victim of a most extraordinary combination of circumstances." He was to later explain: "My own view, was that . . . there were sufficient circumstances of an unusual character involved to make it highly important that every fact should be scrutinized with the utmost care and in the most impartial manner. It goes without saying that it is just as important for a state's attorney to use the great powers of his office to protect the innocent as it is to convict the guilty."

Cummings' first official act was to order E. Earl Garlick, the assistant state's attorney, to have Israel examined by three physicians. Their report, which was dated February 15, made interesting reading. They were unanimous in concluding that the defendant was "in a highly nervous condition, physically and mentally exhausted," and completely incapable on either February 14 or 15 of making a dependable statement. When one of the doctors had asked him whether he had murdered Father Dahme, he had both admitted and denied the crime in the same breath. Three days later, after he had been permitted to rest, he was examined again and found to be "competent to confer with a representative of the state's attorney's office and with his own counsel."

The physicians informed Cummings that it was their opinion that Israel "was a person of low mentality, of the moron type, quiet and docile in demeanor, totally lacking in any characteristics of brutality or viciousness, of very weak will, and peculiarly subject to the influence of suggestion." Any sustained questioning of such a person, the doctors stated, would reduce him to such a mental state that he "would admit practically anything that his interrogators desired." In the light of their examination, they did not believe that his confession would stand up in court.

When Cummings studied Israel's statements of February 14, he discovered that "all of the admissions of an incriminating character were admissions with reference to facts already known to the police prior to the examination of the accused and presumably related to the accused during the period of his examination." This was also true of Harold's trip in a squad car over his supposed escape route during which he had been asked such leading questions as "Where did you cross at High Street?" and "Did you fall or stumble at Harrison Street?" Lastly, Cummings was impressed by the fact that the defendant had retracted his confession on February 18 and, from that day on, had consistently denied any part in the priest's murder.

Phelan had placed great stress on the finding of an empty shell in the second-floor bathroom where Israel said he had disposed of it. Cummings was not overly impressed by this evidence. In the first place, Mrs. Whelan had found another empty cartridge in the same place shortly after Sergeant Brolley's discovery. Israel and Cihal had been in the habit of firing the former's pistol in the woods around the city and, according to their landlady, frequently emptied the gun in the lavatory. "I often found empty shells in the toilet room," she told Cummings.

When the two cartridge cases were examined under a high-power miscroscope, it was discovered that they both had been exploded by a dull firing pin. Several weeks before the murder, Cihal, at Israel's suggestion, had taken the pistol to the carpenter shop where he worked, and sharpened the firing pin. "Harold thought that the gun would shoot better if this were done," he explained. Test shots fired from the Israel revolver after his arrest clearly indicated that "the supposed fatal cartridge, which it was assumed had been the cause of the death of Father Dahme, had actually been exploded long before the crime was committed."

However, Cummings still had to contend with Captain Van Amburgh's opinion that the fatal bullet had been fired through the Israel revolver. To counter it, he enlisted the aid of a metallurgist and three engineers of the Remington Arms Company, the head of the ballistics laboratory of the Winchester Operating Arms Company, and a firearms expert for the New York City Police Department. After examining the defendant's pistol and comparing the fatal bullet with the experimental shots fired by Van Amburgh, Cummings' six experts informed him that "there is no evidence that the mortal bullet came out of the Israel revolver." In fact, they were convinced that it had been fired from "some other unknown weapon."

In reaching his conclusion that Dahme had been killed by a bullet fired from Israel's revolver, Van Amburgh had relied chiefly on photographs of the fatal bullet and several test bullets fired by him. To prove his point to Cummings, he had cut a slit in a photograph of the bullet found in the priest's body and inserted an enlargement of one of the test shells. After manipulating the two pictures for some five minutes, he had finally satisfied himself that they matched perfectly. "All the markings coincide," he had announced.

But Cummings was far from satisfied. "Lift up the flap and look and see what is under it," he had ordered. When Van Amburgh had done so, both men had compared the two photographs. "On the under picture," Cummings was later to tell a Superior Court judge, "we saw a scene totally different from that which we saw in the upper picture. It seemed obvious to me that, instead of demonstrating that the mortal bullet had been fired through the Israel revolver, it demonstrated that the mortal bullet had not been fired through the Israel gun." His six experts agreed with him.

But the state's attorney had more than Van Amburgh's inability to line up a set of photographs to reinforce his now firm belief that the defendant's gun had not killed Dahme. Tests had revealed that a sizable quantity of rust had accumulated in the middle of its barrel. Because of this deposit, the marks made by the initial rifling on a fired bullet were eliminated. "As a matter of fact," Cummings had been told, "the experimental bullets fired through the Israel revolver do not bear any such perceptible marks." But the bullet that had killed the pastor did.

Furthermore, the fatal shell had not shown any sign of a grease groove. Under ordinary circumstances, Cummings' experts had informed him, a bullet fired from a weapon in good condition would, in addition to the rifling marks, retain the impression of its grease groove. All of the experimental shells that had been fired through Israel's pistol "showed the evidence of a grease groove." This was also true of the four cartridges that had been found in the chambers of the defendant's gun when he was arrested by Reynolds.

With the confession and the gun out of the way, Cummings turned to the eyewitnesses. Frederick W. Morris, who had been standing only six feet away from the scene of the murder, was the only spectator who said that the priest and his slayer had stepped around the corner from High Street. Although he had been nearer to the killer than any of the other witnesses, he had been unable to give the coroner any better description of the murderer other than that he had worn an overcoat and a cap. In addition, he had failed to identify Israel when he had seen him in the line-up. "I couldn't swear to the man," he had told Phelan, "because it just didn't look just like him at the time."

Young Ralph Esposito had been standing some twenty or thirty feet away from the corner of Main and High when the shooting had taken place. According to him, the murderer had been wearing "a dark cap," whereas most of the other witnesses had said that it had been a gray cap. When Cummings looked at the cap which Israel was wearing when Reynolds had arrested him, he saw that it was "of a slightly greenish or olive tinge [which] could hardly be called gray and hardly would be called dark."

The state's attorney had also been impressed by the fact that Esposito had told the coroner that the gun he had seen in the killer's hand was "one of those black pistols that did not shine." Since Israel's gun was nickel-plated, Cummings was convinced that, in the glow of the street light near the corner of High and Main, "it is quite likely it would have glittered." He conceded that an excited spectator might not have noticed such a reflection, "but when the witness voluntarily states that it was a black revolver . . . it presents a very interesting situation which would in itself prove quite embarrassing to the state."

Moreover, Esposito's identification of the defendant was hardly what one would call positive. The delivery boy had told the police and the coroner that "I might know him by his build, but I didn't get a good look at his face." But he had been sure that Israel was the man who had shot the priest because he had the same "Jewish run" as the escaping killer. "No comment is necessary," Cummings reasoned, "to justify the assertion that an identification based upon this ground is without value."

He turned next to the testimony of Jennie Boynton and Hilda Baer, her niece. Although Frank Roter, the former's nephew, had not been able to identify Israel as the man who had run up High Street, both women had informed the coroner that they were sure that it had been the defendant. However, Mrs. Boynton had first told the police that she couldn't be sure of her identification. It was only when she had read in the newspapers that he had confessed that her doubts had been dissipated. But even then, she had not given the coroner a definite statement. The most she could say was that she was "pretty sure it is the same person."

Miss Baer had not been able to pick Israel out of the line-up at police headquarters. In fact, it had not been until she appeared before the coroner that she had identified him "by the height of him, the coat and by his nose." The latter, she said, had been a "very long one." The defendant's nose, Cummings noticed, was of average size and, at the time of the coroner's hearing, his picture had appeared frequently in the local press.

To buttress his conclusion that the women had been mistaken, Cummings made several visits to High Street at approximately the same time of night as Father Dahme had been murdered. "I have no doubt that they did see the fleeing assassin, but I am perfectly satisfied that it was utterly impossible for either of these witnesses to identify the assassin under the conditions that existed at that time. I personally was unable to distinguish the features of a person I knew well at such a distance and under the given circumstances. I could not even tell a friend of mine within the distance that these ladies say they identify a stranger whom they saw running." As far as he was concerned, their identification of Israel two weeks later "passes all credulity."

Edward Flood was next. The packer had seen a man running down Congress Street at 7:55 P.M. on February 4. In his first statement to the police, he had failed to mention that the man had been wearing a cap. However, when he testified at Phelan's inquest, he had not only added the cap to his description of the person he had observed, but he swore that he had noticed "a very deep frown" in his colorless face, "as though he was depressed about something."

Again, Cummings had conducted his own on-the-spot tests.

He had gone to the corner of Congress and Harrison and had one of his assistants go "through the motions supposed to have been gone through by the fleeing person." He had been unable to identify the young man's face. Then he had watched bystanders walking down Congress Street "to see whether I could sufficiently fix their features in my mind so as to permit me to identify them subsequently." He had been equally unsuccessful. According to Flood's testimony, he had only seen the running man for three or four seconds in a dim light. "I confess that I am shocked when I think that any person would, in a case of this character, assert a positive identification based upon such circumstances and taking place two weeks thereafter with reference to a person the witness had never seen before."

But Israel had not been a stranger to Nellie Trefton. Although she had not seen the murder, she had noticed the defendant walk by the Star Restaurant ten minutes before it took place. Since he now claimed that he had been in the Empire Theater from seven P.M. until a little after nine that evening, Miss Trefton's testimony could not be disregarded, even by a prosecutor who now seriously doubted the defendant's guilt. Besides, she had also said that Israel had once shown her his gun and stated that he was going to kill somebody with it.

Cummings had been suspicious of the waitress as soon as she had filed a claim for the sizable reward which had been offered for any information leading to the murderer's conviction. He had visited the Star Restaurant one night, much to the consternation of its patrons, and tried to identify people walking along Main Street. His vision had been obscured by a glass partition between the front window and the cashier's booth. "I found," he later said, "that it was very difficult to distinguish any person passing on the sidewalk . . . on account of the distortion caused by the double windows."

When he interviewed Miss Trefton, he discovered that she

was not as certain that she had seen Israel as she had told the police and the coroner. A pretty, flirtatious girl, she readily admitted that she often waved to total strangers who smiled at her as they walked by the restaurant. "This solitary dubious identification," Cummings concluded, "standing by itself, is worthless." As for Israel's statement when he had shown her his gun, not only had she not reported this to the police, but she conceded that she had thought that he was joking.

Any lingering doubts which Cummings may have had about Israel's innocence were dissipated when he checked his alibi. As soon as Harold had retracted his confession, he told the state's attorney that he had spent the early evening of February fourth at the Empire Theater. He had entered the theater shortly after seven P.M. and left at nine. There had been four pictures on the bill—"The Leather Pushers," "The Mystery Girl," "The Fighting Skipper," and "The Ghost of the Canyon." According to Israel, the last half of "The Leather Pushers" had been on the screen when he took his seat. He had not gone home until he had seen the first picture through again.

According to the Empire's manager, "The Leather Pushers" had begun at 6:50 P.M. and terminated twenty minutes later. After "The Ghost of the Canyon" had ended at 8:57, "The Leather Pushers" had not been shown again until 9:17. It was then, Israel told Cummings, that he had left the theater and returned home. "It is obvious that, if he was in the Empire Theater on the evening in question and saw the last half of "The Leather Pushers," when it was first presented and the remaining part of it when it was next presented, he saw the full program and was in the theater at the time the murder was committed."

When Cummings' investigation was through, he tried one more gambit. He asked the sheriff and a member of his staff to look around the courtroom during the February term, when it was crowded with curious spectators who anticipated that the Israel case might be tried that month, and pick out people who resembled the defendant. On one day in particular, fifteen men fitting Israel's general description were selected. Early in March, Cummings happened to notice a spectator, who was dressed in a three-quarter length overcoat with a velvet collar, and a gray cap, sitting in the courtroom. When the man, who looked "strikingly" like the prisoner, was brought to the prosecutor's office, "he nearly fell on the floor and collapsed when asked why he was in the courtroom." Although the man had an iron-clad alibi for the night of February 4, the incident made a strong impression on Cummings. "It shows how easy it is," he noted, "for similarities in appearance, and especially similarity in clothes, to be made the basis for a mistaken identification."

On May 27, 1924, Cummings appeared before Judge L. P. Waldo Marvin in the Criminal Superior Court. After informing the judge of the results of his investigation, he asked his Honor's permission to dismiss the charges against Israel. "In view of what I have said about every element of the case," he said, "I do not think that any doubt of Israel's innocence can remain in the mind of a candid person. Therefore, if your Honor approves, as I trust you will, of my conclusions in this matter, I shall enter a nolle [a refusal to prosecute] in the case of *State vs. Harold Israel*."

Marvin was thoroughly convinced. "I feel," he stated, "that the state attorney's office is entirely justified in the recommendations that have been made, and it is so ordered. It is perfectly evident that a great deal of painstaking care has been expended in this case and that the attitude of the state attorney's office has been what it always should be, one of impartiality and a desire to shield the innocent as well as a determination to prosecute those who are guilty."

Although the Bridgeport police, who were convinced of Israel's guilt, hardly shared Marvin's sentiments, the defend-

ant was released and driven back to Pennsylvania that evening. For the rest of his long life, Cummings, who, in 1933,
became Franklin D. Roosevelt's first Attorney General, sent
periodic gifts of money to the dim-witted youth who had
settled down in Pennsylvania. "I went out on a limb for
him," he once remarked, "and I wanted to be sure that he
never got in trouble again."

Harold more than justified his benefactor's faith. In June
of 1938, Cummings asked the FBI to give him a full report
on Israel. The agent assigned to the investigation found his
subject, who was now married and the father of two children,
living in a neat house in a respectable section of Pottsville.
A miner, he had been regularly employed for more than
twelve years. He had become an active member of the Methodist Church, whose pastor described him as "one of my most
devoted parishioners." The Attorney General couldn't have
asked for a more gratifying report.

# Harold R. Medina

In August of 1942, Harold R. Medina, one of New York's best known trial lawyers, was asked by a Federal judge to defend Anthony Cramer, a former German national charged with high treason. "He told me," Medina later recalled, "that Cramer was wholly without means to hire any lawyer, that it was important to demonstrate to the American people and to the world that, under our system of American justice, the poor man is just as much entitled to the advice of competent counsel as is a man with plenty of money. He explained that he wanted me to defend the accused as a patriotic duty." Without hesitation, the lawyer accepted the unpaid assignment.

The summer of 1942 was hardly the most propitious time in which to represent suspected traitors. After eight months of war, the United States had had an almost unbroken diet of military reverses. In Asia, the Japanese, after all but destroying the American Pacific Fleet, had overrun the Philippines as well as Guam and Wake Islands, and had established a beachhead in the Aleutians. On the other side of the world, the German *Wehrmacht*, which had crushed the rest of the European continent, was deep in Soviet territory. For America and her allies, the future looked anything but bright.

Under such circumstances, defending a man who had been indicted for aiding a group of Nazi soldiers who had been spirited into the United States to sabotage its war effort was a delicate and dangerous task. "I went into it with my eyes open," Medina once acknowledged to Hawthorne Daniel, his biographer. "I knew there would be public feeling. I expected criticism. My friends—many of them—wouldn't like it. Some people would be sure that I must be getting something for it. I was sure to take a beating. But according to my idea of a lawyer's obligations to his profession and the community, he is duty-bound to accept such a call. Nobody could have made me do it, but if I refused, I couldn't have held up my head before my friends or my associates at the bar."

Unlike Reverdy Johnson, with Mary Surratt, Medina did not volunteer to represent Cramer. He accepted the case because a judge asked him to do so. But, as far as the general public was concerned, he was either a Nazi sympathizer or he was receiving a clandestine fee from the Third Reich. During the trial, the wife of one of his associates overheard a courtroom conversation between two spectators seated near her. One pointed to Medina and asked, "Who's that fellow with the black mustache?" The other replied, "Oh, he represents the German Government."

Medina easily could have avoided most of the bitterness that was directed at him by emphasizing the fact that he was a court-appointed attorney. Other lawyers who have accepted similar assignments have not bothered to keep the nature of their retainer a state secret. Medina, on the other hand, took the position that, as far as the jury was concerned, he would be a far more effective battler for his client if it was not generally known that he had not come into the case under his own steam.

It was for this reason that he objected so strenuously when the presiding judge at Cramer's trial informed the jury, just before it retired to consider a verdict, that the defendants' lawyers were serving as assigned counsel without compensation. "What was I to do?" Medina plaintively asked a University of Georgia audience fourteen years after the trial. "I had made up my mind from the beginning that not one word should come from my lips to give the jury the impression that I was anything other than a lawyer retained by Cramer to defend him. He was entitled to the best defense we could give him. He was entitled to the full advantage of everything which went with the fact that I was there standing by his side as his lawyer. Nor did I want the jury to think for even one moment that perhaps I thought Cramer was guilty but was defending him only because I had been assigned by the court to do it."

A year after the trial, Medina received a letter from Cramer who was then Convict No. 35647 at Atlanta Penitentiary. "I still marvel," Cramer wrote, "about your abilities as a lawyer; about your enchanting eloquence, your undaunted courage and your fighting spirit with which you defended a hopeless case against prejudice, calumny and lies." Obviously, Cramer was not the only one to share these sentiments. On May 15, 1947, President Truman nominated Medina as a Federal district judge. Four years later, after presiding over the marathon trial of eleven top-ranking American Communists accused of advocating the violent overthrow of the government, he succeeded the retired Learned Hand on the United States Court of Appeals for the Second Circuit. Courage is not always only its own reward.

*"I worked harder on that case than I did on any other in my whole professional experience."*

# Harold R. Medina and the defense of Anthony Cramer, November 9 to 18, 1942.

IN EARLY MARCH of 1942, a notice was tacked on the bulletin boards of all German army posts. English-speaking soldiers with a knowledge of machinery, who had once lived in the United States, were asked to volunteer for special duty. Those interested were informed that the assignment would be an extremely hazardous one which would require an extended period of foreign service.

Despite this warning, the response was so overwhelming that it took almost a month to winnow down the more than fifteen hundred volunteers to eight enlisted men, ranging in age from twenty-two to thirty-nine, all of whom had spent at least five years in the United States. At the beginning of April, the successful applicants—George John Dasch, Ernest Peter Burger, Richard Quirin, Heinrich Harm Heinck, Edward John Kerling, Herbert Hans Haupt, Werner Thiel and Otto Herman Neubauer—were sent to a confiscated Jewish estate in Brandenburg, some thirty miles west of Berlin, where, for three weeks, they were given an intensive course in factory sabotage. The purpose of their training, they were informed, was to give them a knowledge of "incendiaries and explosives for damaging the American light metal industry." On May first, their course was concluded.

After a two-week furlough in Berlin, the eight volunteers were taken through those German aluminum plants which most nearly resembled their American prototypes, where they were instructed in "vulnerable spots and points." Their inspection tour finished, the men returned to Berlin, where they were split into two groups. The first, with Dasch as its leader, was composed of Burger, Quirin and Heinck. Thiel, Haupt, Neubauer and Kerling made up the second contingent, with the latter named as its *führer*.

Before leaving Berlin, the men were issued marine uniforms and boxes containing "blocks of explosives, time device fuses, detonators and fountain pens which contained sulphuric acid." The explosives were disguised as "lumps of coal." The men were told that they would be landed by submarine at two undisclosed locations on the east coast of the United States, and each group was given two trench shovels which were to be used "to bury the boxes of explosives on the shore immediately after landing." The code name for their venture was Operation Pastorius.*

On May 21, the eight soldiers were taken by train to Paris. After two days of sight-seeing in the occupied French capital, they were driven to the German naval base at Lorient, where they were given their final instructions. They were to be taken by submarine to two isolated beaches on the east coast of the United States—one in Florida and the other on Long Island—from which they were to sally forth and sabotage plants of the Aluminum Company of America located in Alcoa, Tennessee; Massena, New York; East St. Louis, Illinois, and Philadelphia. In addition, they were given an ambitious potpourri of secondary objectives, including New York's Hell's Gate Bridge, the marshalling yards of the Pennsylvania Railroad at Newark, New Jersey, and hydroelectric power plants at Niagara Falls. They would receive help, they were assured, from German sympathizers living in New York and Chicago.

Kerling's group, which was scheduled to make the Florida landing, left Lorient on May 26. Two days later, Dasch led his men aboard a U-boat which submerged as soon as it had

---

* Named after Franz Daniel Pastorius, the leader of the first settlement of Germans in the American colonies in 1683.

left the harbor, and pointed its blunt nose in the general direction of Long Island. On June 12, the four men assembled in the submarine's wardroom where they were each given five thousand dollars in fifty dollar notes, and four hundred dollars in smaller denominations. They were instructed to put the larger bills in the money belts which had been issued to them in Lorient. An additional seventy thousand dollars, which were to be used to enlist supporters, was furnished to Dasch.

Shortly after midnight of the following day, the sub surfaced five hundred yards off Amagansett Beach, a summer resort and fishing village on the eastern end of Long Island, some 125 miles from New York City. As soon as Dasch and his men had been rowed ashore in a rubber boat, they buried the boxes of explosives in the sand along with their marine uniforms. Then they donned civilian clothing which they had brought with them from Berlin, and started walking toward the low dunes that separated the beach from the Montauk Highway.

They had only gone a few feet when twenty-one-year-old John C. Cullen, an apprentice seaman at the Coast Guard station some three hundred yards down the beach, emerged out of the fog which blanketed the area. Suspicious at the sight of four men on the lonely beach at that hour of night, Cullen asked them what they were doing there. Dasch replied that they had been fishing, but offered to pay the sailor $260.00 if he would forget that he had seen them there. Cullen accepted the money and walked off in the direction of Amagansett. As soon as the fog had closed behind him, he ran to his station and informed the duty officer of what had occurred on the beach. An Army patrol, which arrived fifteen minutes later, was unable to find any trace of the men.

At 6:45 the next morning, a swarthy man approached Ira Baker, the Long Island Railroad's station master at Amagansett. He wanted four tickets to Jamaica. "The fishing hasn't been very good out here," he told Baker. "In fact, it's miserable because of the fog and I guess we'll go home." An hour after he had seen the swarthy man and his three companions board the westbound train, Baker found some green bathing trunks, a sport shirt, white tennis shoes and a pair of socks in a hedge near the station. Intending to burn them when he had a chance, the agent put them in a box near the incinerator.

At 10:30 that morning, Reginald Martin and Donald Boges, two shoeshine boys, were plying their trade on 161st Street in Jamaica. When Martin noticed two men with wet shoes coming toward him, he asked them whether they wanted a shine. The men shook their heads and walked on. They returned some twenty-five minutes later, wearing new shoes, and asked the two boys to polish them. As a tip, one of the men gave Martin a package containing some wet shoes and socks.

Three nights later, Kerling's group was landed at an isolated beach near Ponte Vedra, Florida. After burying their lethal cargo, the four men walked to State Highway 78, where they caught a bus to Jacksonville, some thirty miles to the north. Shortly after noon, two men, who gave their names as William Thomas and Herbert Haupt, registered at the Mayflower Hotel. At 12:30, the room clerk at the Seminole Hotel assigned Room 402 to Kerling and Neubauer. Later that afternoon, Kerling approached Fred Speer, the assistant manager of the Mayflower Hotel "and asked me for the room numbers of Herbert Haupt and Thomas."

On Saturday night, June 27, J. Edgar Hoover dramatically announced the capture of all eight men.* Heinck, Quirin and Burger had been arrested in New York on June 20, and

* For security reasons, his press release made no mention of the fact that Dasch, with Burger's moral support, had, on June 19, revealed the sabotage plot to the FBI. Although the German had been immediately placed under protective custody, he had not been formally arrested until June 26.

Dasch six days later. Neubauer and Haupt had left Florida on June 18 and made their way to Chicago where they were both taken into custody on the 27th. The remaining two—Kerling and Thiel—were picked up in New York on June 23 and 27 respectively. With the help of Dasch and Burger, FBI agents found the eight boxes of explosives and incendiaries which had been cached at Amagansett and Ponte Vedra.

The would-be saboteurs were taken to Washington, D.C., where, on July second, President Roosevelt told his press conference that they would be tried as spies by a military commission composed of seven general officers. Their trial began on Wednesday, July 8, in the fifth-floor assembly room of the Department of Justice. Reporters, who were not admitted to the trial, noticed that the glass doors at the entrance to the room had been blacked out and that they had been supplemented by another set of wooden doors. Soldiers, in full dress and carrying bayonetted rifles, patrolled the corridor outside the makeshift courtroom.

Despite Elmer Davis' earnest efforts to keep the public informed as to what was going on on the fifth floor of Justice, Major General Frank R. McCoy, the commission's president, would go no further than to authorize the issuance of terse, noncommittal communiqués at the end of each day's session. The attorneys for the Government and the defense proved equally uncommunicative. Attorney General Francis Biddle, who, with Major General Myron C. Cramer, the Judge Advocate General, headed the prosecution staff, grew hoarse shouting "No comment" to the hordes of reporters who besieged him every time he left the courtroom. Colonels Cassius M. Dowell and Kenneth C. Royall,* who had been named defense counsel, were obviously under strict orders to speak to no one about the case.

* Kenneth Royall was later to become Secretary of War and, after the establishment of the Defense Department, the first Secretary of the Army.

The trial was to last three weeks. On its fifth day, the FBI reported that it had arrested four men and two women in New York who, it charged, had helped the Germans during the week or so they were at large. One of these men was Anthony Cramer, a naturalized American citizen, who worked nights in the boiler room of a Brooklyn licorice factory. Cramer, who had been in the United States since 1925, was arraigned in Manhattan on July 17 before District Judge Bascom S. Deaver. The charge—treason. Bail was set at an impossible fifty thousand dollars and the prisoner was returned to the Federal House of Detention.

The day after Cramer's arraignment, Biddle rested the Government's case against his eight defendants. While Dowell and Royall were presenting the defense's side of the matter—which consisted of trying to prove that the so-called spies had, in fact, come to the United States to escape from Nazi Germany—the two officers found time to file applications for writs of habeas corpus with the United States Supreme Court. On Wednesday, July 20, Chief Justice Harlan Fiske Stone ordered his vacationing colleagues to return to Washington the following day to hear arguments on the defendants' petitions. After listening to more than nine hours of oratory on Thursday and Friday, the nine justices refused to issue the writs. As they saw it, the President had the right to order a military trial of war-time spies, the commission had been legally constituted, and the eight men were lawfully under its jurisdiction.

The saboteurs' trial ended on August first. After two days of deliberation, the commission found all eight men guilty of espionage and recommended that six of them be put to death. Because Burger and Dasch had cooperated with the prosecution, they were given prison terms of life and thirty years respectively. The President promptly approved the sentences and ordered the executions of Quirin, Heinck, Thiel, Kerling, Haupt and Neubauer to be carried out "as soon as is practicable." At noon on August 8, a rainy Saturday, the six men were electrocuted in the District of Columbia Jail. In the interest of national security, the Attorney General was directed to seal the records of the trial until the end of the war.

Three weeks later, a Federal grand jury in New York indicted Cramer for "unlawfully, feloniously, traitorously and treasonably adhering to the enemies of the United States, to wit, to the Government of the German Reich." Specifically, he was accused of "receiving, harboring, relieving, assisting and treating with Werner Thiel and Edward John Kerling, enemies of the United States . . . aiding, abetting, advising and counselling Werner Thiel and Edward John Kerling . . . receiving, possessing, transferring, holding, carrying, safeguarding and concealing property and funds of Werner Thiel . . . carrying out requests and instructions of Werner Thiel and endeavoring to establish contact and communication between Werner Thiel and other persons residing in the United States . . . and giving to officers, agents and employees of the United States false information regarding Werner Thiel and Edward John Kerling with intent to conceal their identities and purpose and their acts in the United States." The grand jurors listed ten overt acts which had influenced them to return a true bill against Cramer.

On September 4, the defendant pleaded not guilty and his case was set down for trial on Monday, November 9, before District Judge Henry W. Goddard. A few weeks earlier, Judge John C. Knox, the senior judge of the United States District Court for the Southern District of New York, had telephoned Harold R. Medina at the latter's summer home in Westhampton, Long Island. Knox wanted Medina, who, two years earlier, had been forced by his burgeoning trial practice to stop teaching at the Columbia Law School, to defend Cramer. "He explained," Medina later said, "that he wanted me to defend the accused as a patriotic duty. Of course, I accepted."

With the help of two associates,* the erstwhile professor began to prepare Cramer's defense. "I can honestly say," he was later to tell a University of Georgia audience, "that I worked harder on that case than I did on any other in my whole professional experience." One reason for his diligence was the fact that, shortly after he had accepted the unpaid assignment, he noticed that "people in general and my friends in particular . . . began to treat me with a certain coolness. It was hardly perceptible at first. But then I heard one or two of these *sotto voce* remarks . . . to the effect that, 'Of course, Harold Medina isn't doing all this for nothing,' and other slurs and little hints. When we actually got on trial, this hostile attitude became more pronounced. The general public which thronged in the courtroom every day of the trial indicated to us very plainly that they thought perhaps we were in some way involved." One spectator expressed his low opinion of Medina and his client by spitting in the lawyer's face as he was walking to the counsel table after a mid-morning recess.

The trial opened the day after the Allied landings in North Africa. Because of Medina's insistence on challenging every prospective woman juror, it took all morning to seat a completely masculine panel. After the luncheon recess, Matthias F. Correa, who, at thirty-two, enjoyed the distinction of being the youngest United States Attorney, opened to the jury. "The indictment in this case," he told them solemnly, "charges what I suppose is the gravest crime known to our law, the crime of treason in time of war." Then he proceeded to outline the steps taken by the German High Command in the spring of 1942 to recruit and train eight volunteers who were to engineer "a sceret armed invasion of the United States."

* John McKim Minton, Jr., and John W. Jordan.

Two days after the Florida group had landed at Ponte Vedra, Kerling, its leader, and Thiel had arrived in New York City. On the morning of June 22, they had slipped a note under the door of Cramer's fifth-floor apartment at 171 East 83rd Street. "Be at the Grand Central Station tonight at 8 o'clock," it had read, "the upper platform near the information booth. Franz from Chicago has come into town and wants to see you; don't fail to be there." Although Cramer later claimed that he didn't know any "Franz from Chicago," he had kept the rendezvous.

Following this meeting, Correa insisted, Cramer had embarked on a deliberate program of doing everything in his power to assist the two saboteurs. But the tall prosecutor, convinced that he had a foolproof case, could afford to be generous. "Do not make up your minds at any stage of the case," he cautioned the jurors, "until all the evidence is in and the case has finally been submitted to you for your verdict. When that time comes, I feel confident you will be convinced of the guilt of this defendant of the crime with which he is charged beyond any reasonable doubt."

Medina, tugging at an out-sized black mustache, was on his feet. First of all, he wanted it clearly understood that the defense conceded that Kerling and Thiel were spies. But that didn't mean that Cramer also fell into that category. "The law requires in a treason case," he said in the low, friendly tones that two decades of Columbia law students had come to know so well, "that no man be convicted of treason without intending a traitorous and treasonable intent. You cannot convict a person for merely doing something that is an unintelligent or negligent thing or something that is a stupid thing. You have to have a traitorous intent." Cramer's intent was "the one hundred percent issue in this case."

As far as his client was concerned, it was true that he had been in the German Army during World War I. But he had just turned eighteen when the war had ended. Seven years later, he had come to the United States as a quota immigrant and gone to Iowa to do farm work. In 1929, he had met Thiel in Detroit and the two men had become good friends. Shortly after the creation of the Third Reich, Thiel had persuaded him to join the Friends of New Germany in Hammond, Indiana, but he had resigned when the society's activities became more bundist than bacchanal. In 1941, Thiel had gone back to Germany, and Cramer hadn't seen him until June 22 of this year. All the defendant wanted now was "justice according to our American standards."

On Tuesday morning, Correa called his first witness, Jean Hurst, the deputy clerk of the district court of Hammond, Indiana, who had brought Cramer's naturalization papers with her. She was followed by Ernest Burger, one of the two saboteurs who had been spared by the military commission. Burger, a slightly plump man with a small jaw and puffy lips, whose dark hair was parted precisely in the middle, was dressed in a gray suit and sported a crimson tie. He answered Correa's questions in a flat, colorless voice which contained only a hint of a German accent.

Burger, who had come to the United States in 1927, had returned to Germany shortly after his naturalization in 1932. Like Kerling, Thiel and the others, he had volunteered for "special duty" in the spring of 1942. As Correa started to lead him slowly through his training as a saboteur, Medina came to sudden life. He objected to "the repetition, the rubbing of it in, and the elaboration of it." It would, he told Goddard, "divert the attention of the jury from the real issues." The judge didn't think that Correa had been guilty of any excess elaboration. "If that takes place," he assured the irate defense attorney, "I will meet it." Burger continued his recitation of the details of Operation Pastorius.

Two FBI men were next. On July 1, Leon O. Prior, of the Miami field office, had found four German marine caps and two trench shovels buried in the sand some four miles south of Ponte Vedra Beach. D. J. Parsons, a technical expert whose job it was to examine "evidence received in criminal cases . . . including explosives, sabotage devices and similar materials," had inspected the contents of the four boxes that Kerling's group had dragged ashore. He had found "blocks of trinitro toluol, or TNT, blocks containing explosives made to simulate lumps of coal, a standard fuse to set off explosions, detonators of several kinds, small incendiary devices, time devices constructed or concealed as pen and pencil sets, and a paper pen containing an abrasive mixture." In all, there had been forty-six blocks of TNT, four coal bombs, and 175 detonators of various types.

When Parsons stepped down, Correa turned the next nine witnesses over to Louis W. Goodkind, one of his three assistants. Immigration Inspector Grover D. Bushman identified an incoming manifest of the *S.S. Ohio* which had arrived in New York on July 27, 1925, with one Anton Cramer, a farmer from Ollendorf, Germany, among its passengers. Cramer, who was bound for Iowa as a permanent resident, had been issued immigration visa No. 12798 at Cologne three months before his arrival. He had spent the summer of 1936 back in Ollendorf with his brother Josef, returning to the United States on September 12 with re-entry permit No. 1099632. That had been his only visit to Germany since his arrival in the United States.

Fifteen-year-old Reginald Martin identified Dasch and Burger as the two men who had given him and Donald Boges, his fellow bootblack, a box of shoes and socks at 161st Street in Jamaica on the morning of Saturday, June 14.

Q. Where did you see the men?
A. On the same street I was shining.
Q. Did you notice anything about their appearance at that time?
A. Yes. Their shoes was wet and we asked for a shine.

Twenty-five minutes later, he had seen the two men again. This time, they were wearing new shoes, and he and Boges had shined them. As a tip, they were given a cardboard box.

Q. What did you find in it?
A. I found shoes and socks. They were wet.

Charles R. MacInnes, a New York FBI agent, was the first witness to connect the defendant with the saboteurs. At 8:30 P.M. on Tuesday, June 23, he had seen Cramer sitting at a table in the Twin Oaks Inn on 44th Street and Lexington Avenue with Kerling and another man. "They were sitting, talking and they were taking occasional drinks; apparently not eating but just had drinks in front of them." When Kerling left at 9:45, MacInnes had followed him to Lexington Avenue and 49th Street where the German had been arrested.

Four days later, MacInnes and his partner, John Willis, were staked out in front of Cramer's apartment house at 171 East 83rd Street. At 10:15 A.M., the defendant had left the building, walked to the Lexington Avenue subway entrance at 86th Street, and taken the downtown express to Grand Central. The two agents watched him look into Thompson's Cafeteria on 42nd Street and then enter the Commodore Hotel. When he did not emerge, MacInnes and Willis returned to 83rd Street.

At 2:30 that afternoon, Cramer, accompanied by a woman, came out of his building and returned to Grand Central. The couple went into Thompson's where they stayed for half an hour, "eating and talking." Then they had taken the subway back to 86th Street. They had parted company at 88th Street and Lexington Avenue, and Cramer had walked back to his house.

A few minutes before nine o'clock that night, the defendant had left his house and walked to the Kolping House, a German Catholic society at 165 East 88th Street. At 10:50 P.M., MacInnes, Willis and another agent entered the building. "We asked for Anthony Cramer," the witness said. "He was sitting at one of the tables in the back room and he came up to us. We told him we would like to see him at the office, would like to have him accompany us to the New York field office, which he did."

Medina, who had not bothered to cross-examine any of the previous witnesses for the prosecution, drew the line at MacInnes. How many FBI men had been watching the three men at the table in the Twin Oaks Inn on Tuesday night? MacInnes tugged at his ear. Until "shortly after nine o'clock," he had been the only agent who had been watching the restaurant. Even after reinforcements had arrived, he had been "the only one inside."

> Q. You were not close enough from where you sat to hear
> what they were saying, I take it?
> A. No, I was not.

In fact, during the two days he had shadowed the defendant, he hadn't heard any conversations between him and anyone else.

Special Agent W. Willis Fisher had arrived at the Twin Oaks "shortly before 9:30 p.m." He had watched the defendant talking to Thiel and Kerling. "Their lips were moving," he recalled, "although I did not hear the voices." When Kerling left, he had followed him up Lexington Avenue until the spy was arrested by agent T. J. Donegan. The two FBI men had taken Kerling downtown to their Foley Square office where he was searched. The prisoner had been wearing a money belt which contained $3,700 in fifty-dollar bills.

An hour later, Fisher was back at the cafe. Shortly after his arrival, Cramer and Thiel had left and walked over to Thompson's Cafeteria where they had a bite to eat. Then Thiel had accompanied the defendant to the subway entrance in Grand Central, where the two men separated. During their stroll, they had been deep in conversation, but, the witness assured Medina, "I could not get close enough to hear it."

Agent Rice elaborated on Fisher's version. According to him, Cramer, Thiel and Kerling had been "talking very earnestly." The bespectacled Medina was on his feet again with an objection. The witness had no right to "characterize" the conversation. Goddard disagreed. "I think that the witness may characterize the conversation, as to whether it was earnest, desultory or anything of that sort," he ruled. The lawyer "respectfully" excepted. "I think I can tell when you are quite earnest," the soft-spoken judge continued. "I am earnest all the time, your Honor," Medina retorted.

After Cramer had been arrested, Agents Carden and Crow had searched his apartment. They had found a money belt in a metal shoe box "under a radio table beside the bed." They had also discovered six post cards, two typewritten sheets of paper, a page of the *New York Times,* and some torn scraps of paper in a wastebasket. Two fifty- and three twenty-dollar bills had been inserted in the pages of a book entitled *Knowledge of Music.*

Mr. Medina wanted to know if the defendant had cooperated with the agents who had searched his room. Carden admitted that Cramer had given him permission to enter the room and had told him exactly where the money belt and the currency were. The room had been "an ordinary type of room, consisting of various pieces of furniture, a bed, a chair, a desk, dresser, table and radio—it was not elaborate in any way." The box in which the money belt had been found had been "just an ordinary shoe box," containing a brush, some cans of polish and a rag. No, nothing had been locked in the room.

John G. Willis had arrested the defendant in Kolping House on the night of June 27. He had interviewed him in the United States Courthouse from 11:20 P.M. until two in the morning. At first, Cramer had told him that the man with whom he had gone to Thompson's Cafeteria on June 23 was a William Thomas, whom he had met in Detroit in 1929. The two men had come to New York the following year, where Thomas had remained until March of 1941 when he had gone to the West Coast to work in a factory. He had not seen him again until four nights ago in the Twin Oaks. He was certain that Thomas had never been out of the United States since 1929.

He had changed his story shortly after the questioning had begun. William Thomas was really Werner Thiel. He had been using an alias because he "was having difficulty with the draft board." As for the money belt which had been found in his room, Thiel had given it to him. "I owe you that much money," Thiel had told him, "and I want to pay my debt to you." The $3,500 in his safe-deposit box had been the result of selling some securities. When Willis asked him why this money hadn't been deposited in his savings account, he answered that he felt "it is more safe in the safe-deposit box rather than being in my bank account."

At this point in the interview, Cramer had asked to speak to Agent Alvin E. Ostholhoff alone. When he returned to the room, he admitted that he had lied because "he wanted to protect Werner Thiel."

Q. Did he state protect him from what?
A. He wanted to protect him because Werner Thiel was his friend.

It had been at the Twin Oaks that Thiel had told him that he was looking for a safe place for his money. When Cramer had suggested that he put it in his safe-deposit box, Thiel had given him the money belt. Two days later, after making a list of the denominations, he had taken the money to his bank. The bills which Carden and Crow had found in *Knowledge of Music* had been put there at Thiel's request, "in the event [he] needed it in a hurry."

Norma Kopp had been Werner Thiel's girl friend from

1937 until he had left New York. At the Twin Oaks meeting, Thiel had asked Cramer to arrange a meeting between Norma and himself. Accordingly, the defendant had written to the girl, who was working as a domestic in Westport, Connecticut, and asked her to come to New York. At 3:45 P.M. on June 27, he had accompanied her to Thompson's Cafeteria where they had waited in vain for Thiel to show up. Then he had taken her back to Kolping House.

When Correa showed Willis a piece of paper containing the entries "71-50$, 5-20$, 10-2$; 8 gold notes," the agent identified it as a list which Cramer had told him he had made after Thiel had given him the money belt. On its reverse side, Cramer had written: "I hereby identify the writing on the back of this page as my own writing. The figures were made by me to indicate the denominations of cash and of each bill given to me by Werner Thiel on June 23, 1942, and the amount of each denomination. The total sum according to these figures amounts to $3,670." The defendant had also admitted that an envelope addressed to "Mr. William Thomas, Hotel Commodore, City," was in his handwriting.

Medina settled down to a long cross-examination. How long had it been, he asked Willis, before Cramer admitted that he had been lying to the FBI men? An hour or so after he had been arrested.

Q. As your experience goes, he was a pretty docile customer, wasn't he?
A. Cramer is phlegmatic.

He had made no "fuss or any trouble." In fact, once he had stopped lying, he had cooperated fully with Willis and his fellow agents.

Medina turned to something else. Wasn't it true that Cramer had explained that Thiel was using the name of Thomas because he was having trouble with his draft board? When the witness started to answer "Well he did elaborate . . ." the

lawyer broke in to observe, "Well, that is what I am trying to
bring out." Correa uncoiled. "Let the witness answer, please,"
he snapped. "He started to say, 'He did elaborate' to you and
you interrupted." Medina was all contriteness. "I did not
mean to interrupt at all," he murmured. Willis seemed
amused at the exchange. "He did elaborate," he continued,
"by saying that the draft board was trying to ascertain the
whereabouts of Werner Thiel."

> Q. And did he not indicate to you that the truth was that
> Thiel had not registered for the draft and that is what
> was making the trouble?
> A. Yes.

Although no stenographer had been present that night,
Cramer had signed a written statement the next morning.
Medina turned to Correa. "I call for the production of that
statement," he demanded. The prosecutor refused. Since his
adversary had indicated that the defendant was going to
testify, he preferred that he "not have the advantage of
refreshing his recollection as to what story he gave the FBI
before he repeats it here on the stand." Medina didn't think
that "it is fair to have the jury sitting here waiting until a
special and appropriate time to be told the rest of the story as
to what he stated. I think that it should come out now." Goddard didn't share his opinion but indicated that he could
renew his motion later.

The disgruntled attorney turned back to the witness. Over
Correa's objection, he forced Willis to repeat everything
Cramer had told him on Friday evening and Saturday morning. The defendant had said that he had met Thiel in Detroit
in 1929. In 1941, Thiel, who, he knew, was a member of the
Nazi Party, had left New York for the West Coast from where
he had returned to Germany via Japan. He had met him
again at Grand Central Terminal on June 22, 1942, where
he had gone "out of curiosity" after receiving a note that

"Franz from Chicago has come into town." At the Twin Oaks that night, Thiel had asked him about Norma and their other mutual friends, as well as inquiring about American morale.

The next day, Thiel had given him the money belt. "Cramer said he asked Thiel if Thiel had come over on a submarine. Thiel smiled and put him off and said, 'I will tell you later.' " When Willis was curious as to just why Cramer had mentioned a submarine to Thiel, the prisoner had told him, "That is a logical question because steamship service has been suspended and there would be no other way for Thiel to come from Germany to the United States except by submarine." But Cramer had confessed that he had "a hunch that is the way he came over when he saw Thiel smile."

Willis remembered that Cramer had told him that he thought Thiel had come "to spread stories and spread rumors to create unrest. He said if that was so, he would never have turned Thiel in because Thiel was his friend, but he said if Thiel were here for a more sinister purpose, such as sabotage and resultant death to American citizens, he would have turned him in, motivated as much by a desire to protect Thiel as to protect the innocent ones who would be harmed and the damage which would be caused by such violent acts."

According to Cramer, Thiel had owed him two hundred dollars for loans over the years. He had shown Willis a little book in which he had listed the money he had advanced to his friend.

> Q. Isn't it a fact that he seemed concerned over the $200 because he did not want it taken away from him?
> A. Yes.

But he had admitted to the agent that he had thought that the money in Thiel's belt had come from the German Government.

Correa evidently had undergone a change of heart during

the lunch recess because, as soon as court opened at two
o'clock, he offered to give Cramer's written statement to
Medina. Without even bothering to glance at the five-page
document, the lawyer immediately offered it in evidence.
Goddard agreed with Correa that it was a "self-serving decla-
ration" and refused to admit it. When Medina, who had
noticed the name of Norma Kopp in the statement, began to
question Willis about her, Correa was on his feet again. This
was going beyond his direct examination, he protested, and
should be excluded. His Honor agreed.

Medina, who was an old hand at skinning cats, handed
Cramer's statement to the witness. He wanted him to look
through it and tell the jury anything he had omitted during
his examination. Willis leafed through the typewritten pages.
Yes, he now remembered that Cramer had told him that
Kerling, who had been present with Thiel at the Twin Oaks,
was a man known to him only as Eddie whom he had met
some years earlier at a chauffeur's ball at Jaeger's Cafe in
Yorkville. The defendant had been surprised to see Kerling
because he knew that the latter had gone back to Germany in
1939.

As he read through the statement, there were two other
items that the agent wanted to clarify. First of all, he had
testified that Cramer had told him that he had gone into the
delicatessen business in Florida with a man named Hubert
Thielmann in 1937. Thiel had also been involved in this venture which had proved to be a failure. In addition, he had forgotten to say that Cramer had admitted receiving a post card
from Thiel which had been mailed from Tokyo as well as a
letter from Berlin in which his friend had asked about
Norma.

Willis was followed by agent Ostholhoff, who confirmed
his partner's version of the interviews with Cramer. When the
defendant had spoken to Ostholhoff alone, he had told him,
"I realize that you men know a great deal and that it is use-

less for me to try to lie any further. So I am going to tell the truth." As he poured out his new story to Ostholhoff, he had owned that "Thiel told me that he is on a mission for the German Government." His own interpretation of Thiel's intentions was that "he is here to stir up unrest among the people and probably spread propaganda."

The last witnesses of the day were anticlimactic. John A. O'Brien, the safe-deposit superintendent of the 86th Street Branch of the Corn Exchange Bank said that Cramer had renewed Box No. 1254 on June 25. Four days later, Philip Muller, the branch's manager, had opened the box for Willis. It had contained $3,500 in fifty-dollar bills. Catherine O'-Meara and Florence E. Smith, mail clerks at the Commodore, identified an envelope addressed to William Thomas as one that had been put in the hotel's uncalled-for-messages box on June 27. On July 17, it had been turned over to the FBI by Robert F. Carney, the Commodore's assistant manager.

Friday the thirteenth started out slowly. Leonard Higdon, a hair and fibre analyst for the FBI, had compared the money belts Burger and Kerling had been wearing with the one found in Cramer's room. "I made a very detailed examination of the three belts," he said, "and compared the detailed information obtained and reach the conclusion that they were similar in construction." A handwriting expert, who had examined all the post cards and letters found in Cramer's apartment, certified that they had all been written by Werner Thiel. He had also compared the signatures "William Thomas" and "Edward J. Kelly," which appeared in the Commodore's registration records, with samples of the handwriting of Thiel and Kerling, and he was positive that they had been written by the two saboteurs.

After the United States had entered the war, Paul Powers, the manager of the Manufacturers Safe and Deposit Company at 85th Street and Third Avenue, had volunteered as a minuteman to sell war bonds. At 6:30 P.M. on June 22, he had attempted to persuade Cramer to buy some bonds or stamps. The defendant had told him that he wasn't "even interested in the purchase of a ten-cent stamp." When Powers had knocked on the door again so that he could talk to some of the other roomers in Cramer's apartment, the latter had "opened . . . and closed the door." Although Medina tried to strike Mr. Powers' testimony as "irrelevant," Goddard decided to "let it stand."

Emma Kopp, who was also known as Norma, was, by all odds, the day's key witness. A tiny brunette in her early thirties who spoke in halting, breathless English, she had come to the United States from Frankfurt-am-Main in 1928. She had met Cramer, whom she knew as Tony, in May or June of 1937, and had been introduced to Thiel by him at "the end of June, 1937." On June 25, 1942, she had received a letter from Cramer in Westport, Connecticut, where she was working as a "laundress and kitchen maid" for Mrs. H. C. Tate, asking her to come to New York. She had arrived in the city early the next evening.

Later that night, she had visited Cramer in his room. When he told her that Werner Thiel was in town, she had replied, "It can't be." Cramer had assured her that he was telling the truth. "Eddie is with him; he is not alone," he had said. "They came about six men with a U-boat, in a rubber boat, and landed in Florida. They live in the Hotel Commodore." When the girl had asked him how Thiel was supporting himself, Tony had informed her that "they brought so much money along from Germany, from the German Government." In fact, some of the money—"three and a half thousand"—was cached in his safe-deposit box.

As he walked her back to Kolping House, he had told her that he would leave a note for Thiel at the Commodore. If she would come back to his room the next afternoon, he promised to take her to Thompson's Cafeteria to meet their mutual friend. On June 27, she had accompanied him to Thompson's but, although they waited for over an hour, Thiel had failed to put in an appearance. That evening, Cramer had been arrested at Kolping House where he had been visiting her.

Medina had never taken his eyes from Miss Kopp's face during her direct examination. When Correa said, "You may inquire," he rose slowly to his feet and, with deliberate steps, walked over to the witness stand. Now, Miss Kopp, you called the defendant Tony, did you not? She did. And your relations with him were pleasant? She nodded. "He always had been a gentleman to me."

> Q. You have no reason to harm him in any way, have you?
> A. (No answer)
> Q. Or have you?
> A. (No answer)
> Q. Why are you silent?
> A. I have no reason to harm him.

When Tony had told her that Thiel was in the United States, what did she think he was here for? "I did not think anything," she replied. "I could not believe it." Medina looked incredulous. "That lets you out, doesn't it?" he snorted. Goddard sustained Correa's objection. But Miss Kopp was a stubborn witness. She insisted that she had gone to Thompson's to see for herself whether Cramer was telling the truth about Thiel.

Medina quickly turned to something else. How long had she been questioned by the FBI? She didn't know; she hadn't looked at the clock. The lawyer thought that the witness was being "flippant" but he found little support from the bench. "I don't think so, Mr. Medina," Goddard said. Miss Kopp reiterated that she didn't know how long she had been interviewed. When Medina observed that "you seem to have a pretty good memory of other things," she changed her tune abruptly. She now remembered that she had been questioned "no longer than two hours."

Suddenly, the witness looked frightened. Would it be possible, she implored, to have an interpreter? Medina didn't cotton to the idea. Correa broke in. "I suggest," he remarked dryly, "if counsel does not want an interpreter that he is using the biggest words he can think of." Mr. Medina smiled. "I do not think they are the biggest I can think of," he murmured.

Miss Kopp had first learned about the saboteurs' capture when she had seen the *New York Times* in a friend's restaurant the day after Cramer's arrest. "Then I began to realize," she told Medina, "why Tony was arrested." But she had not been frightened by the news.

Q. Didn't it occur to you that you might get into trouble?
A. No, sir.
Q. The thought never came into your mind that you would like to keep out of trouble, did it?
A. Yes. I did think so.

But she had made up her mind to "tell the truth" if she were questioned.

No, she hadn't called the authorities when she read that Cramer and Thiel had been apprehended. "I thought it was not necessary," she explained, "because both had been arrested." Besides, she didn't have time and "it made me nervous." Medina wanted to know whether the agents who had picked up Cramer at Kolping House had taken her name. She was sure that they had not.

Q. Did you have any reason to know that the FBI men knew who you were?
A. No, sir.

She had left Mrs. Tate's employ "on my own accord." No, she had not bothered to leave a forwarding address, but, as an enemy alien, she had informed the FBI in Hartford on July 5 that she had moved.

At noon on July 14, some FBI agents had called for her in Greenwich and taken her by car to New York. She had been questioned that evening and the following morning. No, she had not been worried about herself during the two interviews. She couldn't remember whether she had told her interrogators all the facts about her friendship with Thiel and Cramer that first night. But before they were through with her, she had told them everything they wanted to know.

When Thiel and Cramer had come to New York from Detroit in 1937, they had taken an apartment together at 164 East 85th Street. Norma, who had fallen in love with Thiel shortly after meeting him, had often cooked dinner for both men on her evenings off. But her romance with the saboteur had been far from placid. The couple had had many arguments about Werner's drinking and his attentions to other women. In addition, Thiel had accused her of seeing a man "I had been going out with years ago." In fact, whenever her lover had met this man on the street, they had argued over her.

Four days before Thiel had left for Germany, he and Norma had announced their engagement. She had been heartbroken by his departure. "I did not expect him to return during the war," she told Medina

Q. Did you know that this fellow Thiel was a Nazi?
A. I don't know that he was a Nazi.
Q. Are you trying to tell the jury that you don't know what a Nazi is?
A. Thiel had been a Nazi.

She had not intended to follow Thiel back to Germany and marry him there. She had known that "as soon as he would leave the country, everything would be over for me."

Medina took an earlier tack. Didn't it ever cross her mind

that, after Cramer's arrest, she "might be taken off to prison as an enemy alien?" No, it never did. The lawyer handed her a copy of the *New York Times* of June 28, and asked her to turn to Page 30, where the photographs of the eight saboteurs appeared. Had she read the article about their capture? No, she had not. Medina's face mirrored his disbelief.

> Q. You did notice on that page a photograph of the man you were engaged to marry?
> A. Yes, sir.
> Q. And yet you tell this jury that you did not take the trouble to read the printed matter when you saw that paper first on Sunday, June 28?
> A. I did not read the paper.

She had never had the newspaper in her hand. It had been spread on the bar of her friend's restaurant, and she had just glanced at it.

After she had visited Tony on June 26, he had walked her to a room she rented at 248 East 87th Street. "I kept that room for convenience while I worked in the country," she explained. She had kept some clothes and other personal effects there. No, she hadn't dressed specially for her trip to New York after receiving Cramer's letter. "It was my day off," she said, "the only day in one month. I wanted to look nice."

The next evening, when the FBI agents had entered Kolping House, the defendant had been watching a quartet of card players in the recreation room. Because she had thought that her friend had been arrested "on account of the minuteman," she had not been particularly worried about him.

> Q. Did you want to get back at Tony for maybe saying something about you that led to your own arrest?
> A. No, sir.

She was certain that Tony had not given her name to the FBI and that they must have found her address in his room. Medina's voice was heavy with sarcasm. "If anybody found out about you," he asked, "the last man in the world to tell them would be Tony Cramer?" Miss Kopp's answer was an emphatic "That is right."

The long Friday afternoon was almost over. With a glance at the courtroom clock, which read 3:45, Medina raced through his last few questions. Was Miss Kopp a German spy? She most certainly was not. Did she know anything about Nazi spy rings in the United States? She did not. On re-direct, she told Correa that not once during the four hours she had been questioned on July 14 and 15 had any FBI agent threatened her. As she left the stand, Correa turned to the bench. "The Government rests, your Honor," he informed Goddard. After denying the defense's *pro forma* motion to dismiss the indictment on the ground that the prosecution had failed to prove its case, the judge adjourned for the week end.

On Monday morning, Medina called his first—and only —witness. As Anthony Cramer shuffled up to the stand, he seemed anything but an agent of the Third Reich. A dark, nearly bald, middle-aged man with a thin, prim mouth, there was nothing in his appearance that would make even an over-zealous FBI man give him a second glance. After he had settled himself in the hard-backed witness chair, he looked expectantly at his lawyer.

Medina spent the whole morning steering his voluble client from his birth in Ollendorf in 1900 until March of 1941 when his friend Thiel had left New York. One of his farmer-father's seven sons, Cramer had been drafted in the summer of 1918. However, he had been deferred until November "on account of the farm and because I had five brothers in the army." After only three weeks of service, he had been mustered out of the army when the war ended, and returned home to help his father tend his forty-five acres.

In 1920, he went to Hamburg where an uncle had arranged a job for him in a shipyard as a flange turner. After three years in Hamburg, he had returned to Ollendorf to work in a mine on the outskirts of town. It was about this time that he had begun to correspond with Elizabeth Maria Schildmeyer, his older brother's sister-in-law, who lived in Waucome, Iowa. Mrs. Schildmeyer was so enthusiastic about life in the United States that Cramer had decided to emigrate. His sister-in-law persuaded a neighboring farmer to send him his fare and, in July of 1925, he had landed in New York. A week later, he was sowing corn on Frank Kuennen's farm in Waucome.

Two years later, he left Iowa and went to Chicago, where he worked as a day laborer and a blacksmith. In 1928, he had changed his first name from Anton to Anthony because "I like that better," and filed his notice of intention to become an American citizen.

> Q. When you signed the paper containing that statement in it, did you sincerely and honestly mean to renounce any allegiance to the German Reich?
> A. Yes, sir.

In December of that year, he had gone first to South Bend, Indiana, and then to Detroit where he worked, in quick succession, for Studebaker, Dodge, Briggs and Chrysler as a die fitter. "The die-making season is very short, you know," he explained.

He had come to New York in the fall of 1929 when the depression made it impossible for him to find work in the automobile industry. Ten months later, Werner Thiel, with whom he had played chess at Detroit's Kolping House, had looked him up. Cramer, who was then ekeing out a meager living as a painter's helper, managed to rent two rooms for Thiel and himself in an apartment owned by one William Henke on St. Nicholas Avenue.

In July of 1933, a friend who was employed as the maintenance superintendent of St. Margaret's Hospital in Hammond, Indiana, wrote that he had a job for him. For the next three years, Cramer worked as "a mechanic and fireman" in the hospital's boiler room for seventy-five dollars a month plus room and board. He had resigned in June of 1936 in order to visit his parents and take in the Olympics which were being held in Berlin that year.

On his return from Germany, he had received a letter from Hubert Thielmann, a friend who lived in Fort Meyers, Florida, inviting him to invest in a delicatessen in that city. Thiel, who had followed Cramer to Hammond, was also interested in Thielmann's proposition and the two men had bought a half-interest for five hundred dollars, most of which was supplied by the defendant. The venture failed, and, in the early part of 1937, Cramer had returned to New York where he found a job as a maintenance man for the Pepsi-Cola Corporation.

When the company moved its factory, he had gone to work as a door-to-door salesman of Silver Seal pots and pans. This was followed by a year with the Modern Art Craft Company at the World's Fair, during which time he obtained a license from the city as a boiler engineer. In 1941, he was hired as a night man in the boiler room of the National Licorice Company at forty-five dollars a week, the job he had held at the time of his arrest.

He and Thiel had become close friends in Detroit. "He looked a little lost at that time," he told Medina, "and so I took to him." After Hitler had come to power in Germany, Werner had become very interested in "this Nazi business." But Cramer had not wanted any part of it. He had argued with Thiel that "the expansion of a nation was never worth a human life." But his friend had not shared his view. "You know that a couple of hundred thousand men could easily be sacrificed for the expansion or glory of a nation," Thiel had maintained.

In 1939, he and Thiel had moved from Henke's to an

apartment at 164 East 85th Street. A year later, the two men had rented a furnished room at 171 East 83rd Street, where the defendant was still living. In March of 1941, Thiel had gone back to Germany because he was "afraid that this country might come to a war with Germany so that he, as an alien, might be put in a concentration camp." His friend, who was "pretty well up to his ears in this Nazi doctrine," had felt that "his future would be brighter in Germany."

Just before Werner left New York, Cramer had asked him to pay back some two hundred dollars he had borrowed since 1937. Thiel had refused to do so, claiming that, if Cramer hadn't forced him to go to Hammond in 1933, he wouldn't have had to borrow the money. After several bitter arguments, Werner had said that "I may have a chance some other time to repay it." A few days later, Cramer, Norma and "twelve or fourteen people" had seen Thiel off at the Greyhound Bus Terminal on 42nd Street.

After Pearl Harbor, Cramer had had a change of heart about his adopted country's war effort. Before the Japanese attack, he had thought "that America should not join the European war at all, because my fatherland was involved. But since this United States, our country, got attacked, I have changed my opinion because we can't do anything but fight and win. Otherwise, it will be the end of our country."

Q. Going back to the time before the United States was in the war, did you genuinely sympathize with the German people?

A. With the German people; yes, sir, I did. I believe coming from Germany I am entitled to a little love for my fatherland.

After the luncheon recess, Medina picked up again. When had Tony next seen Thiel? Well, on June 22 of this year, just after he had returned home from the licorice factory, someone had rung his neighbor's bell. He had heard a man asking for him. Because it was "a strange voice," he had pretended to be asleep. Ten minutes later, a note had been pushed under his door. It had read: "Be at Grand Central Station tonight at 8 o'clock, the upper platform near information booth. Franz from Chicago has come into town and wants to see you. Don't fail to be there."

Although he didn't recognize the handwriting and didn't know any Franz, he had gone to the terminal that evening because "curiosity got the best of me." At 8:10 P.M., just as he was ready to go home, he had heard someone shout, "Tony!" It had been Werner Thiel. He had been so surprised to see his friend that he had asked him whether he had come to the United States in a submarine. Thiel had answered, "Some other time I am going to tell you all about this. Remember now my name is Bill Thomas and I am anti-Nazi."

At the Twin Oaks that night, the two men had discussed everything from Norma Kopp to Germany's chances of defeating Russia that summer. Thiel had told him that the former's brother, Herbert, had been killed on the eastern front and that another brother had lost an eye in combat. "He seemed very much under the strain of emotion at that time," Cramer recalled. Werner had also said that he had almost four thousand dollars with him and that he was now in a position to pay back his debt. It was at this time that the defendant had told him that he could put the money in his safe-deposit box. Before they parted company, they had arranged to meet the following night at the Twin Oaks. Thiel had refused to come to Cramer's room because "I have too many acquaintances there, and I don't want them to see me."

At the cafe the next night, he had told Thiel about the minuteman who had knocked on his door earlier that day. He had complained that "the man was very provocative and very imposing upon me." When he testified that Thiel replied that he was "going to buy bonds myself," a wave of laughter swept the courtroom. Just before Cramer had gone home, his friend had given him the money belt. Werner had told him to take out the two hundred dollars he was owed, and to put the remainder, with the exception of a few dollars which he was to keep in his room, in his safe-deposit box.

On Wednesday evening, he had written to Norma and urged her to come to New York. "When you do come," he had said, "don't waste any time . . . because I have great news and at the same time a pleasant surprise for you." The next morning, he had taken Thiel's money to his bank. Norma had arrived on Friday night, but they had been unable to contact Thiel. After taking Norma to Kolping House, he had written two notes to Thiel. He had torn up his first effort because "I disliked the writing of the letter" and thrown the scraps in the wastebasket. He had delivered the second note, which asked Thiel to meet Norma and himself at Thompson's Cafeteria at 4:00 P.M. on Saturday, to the Commodore the following morning. But his friend had not shown up, and he had never seen him again.

It took Medina only twenty minutes to conclude his direct examination on Tuesday morning. Had Cramer freely cooperated with the FBI agents? Yes, he had. The lawyer handed him his signed statement. Would he explain those portions on the typewritten sheets that were in this own handwriting? Some of the agents had suggested that he add those. "To their meaning something was left out which might have been of importance," he explained, "and they asked me to put it in there." As for Thiel's proposed activities in the United States, he did not know why his friend had come here or anything about espionage or sabotage.

Q. Did you at any time have any purpose or intent to hurt the United States or to help its enemies in defeating this country?
A. No, sir; never.

Mr. Medina walked back to his chair. "Your witness," he informed Correa.

The prosecutor started with a rush. Did Mr. Witness remember that he had testified on direct that he had left the Friends of New Germany because he "did not like their marching around and their activities?" Yes, he did. Wasn't the real reason for his resignation that there had been a scandal over the misuse of the organization's funds? No, it was not. "I disliked their marchings and activities, and the swindle at the same time," he explained. Why hadn't he told Mr. Willis that he was the Hammond unit's treasurer? "I was never asked the question," he replied, "and never paid any attention to it."

Mr. Correa picked up a newspaper from the counsel table. "Isn't it a fact, sir," he asked the witness, "that at one time, you were particularly interested in the law of treason?" Cramer shook his head vigorously. "No, sir, I have never been interested in that." Medina leaped to his feet. "I object to that question, your Honor," he told Goddard, "and move to strike the answer. I think your Honor realizes that we are approaching now a matter of considerable significance, and I want my record clear." The judge thought so, too, and excused the jury "so that the matter may be discussed."

In view of the witness' answer to his last question, Correa said, he was going to offer in evidence a page of the *New York Times* containing a copy of the Constitution which had been found in the defendant's room. Article III, section 3, the provisions relating to treason, had, as Cramer had admitted to Willis, been underlined by him "on a date which I do not recall." According to Medina, "this paper is dynamite and it has absolutely no judicial value whatsoever." The judge wasn't so sure. "If it is dynamite," he observed dryly, "he created it." Medina's objection was overruled, and the page admitted as Government Exhibit 55.

When the jury had returned to the courtroom, Correa circulated the paper among its members. Medina contented himself with observing that the defendant had marked other

sections of the Constitution having nothing to do with trea-
son. As the jurors were reading the exhibit, Correa asked
Cramer when he had "placed these markings on this paper."
He thought that he had done it "in the early months of 1941."

> Q. That is about the time Werner Thiel went to Germany,
> isn't it?
> A. That is right, yes, sir.

He didn't have "the slightest idea" why he had marked the
paper. "I could not tell you," he told the prosecutor. "I do
not recall the time I marked it, and I do not recall for what
purpose I did it."

Correa turned next to several portions of Cramer's direct
examination which conflicted with his statements to the FBI.
How did he explain the fact that he had told Willis that he
had first counted the money in Thiel's belt on June 24, while
he had admitted in court that this had been done the day
before? "I was a little confused at that time about this,"
Cramer retorted. Yes, Agent Willis had read the statement
to him after it had been typed and he recalled "having read it
myself and with Mr. Willis."

After lunch, Correa roared back to the attack. If Mr. Witness had loved the United States so much, why had he criticized the country in his letters to Germany? Cramer had a
ready answer. "I would say that I have criticized a few persons," he admitted. "I have never criticized the United States
as such." Correa pounced. If that were so, why had his nephew
warned him that his letters home were so vitriolic that he
would be put "on the blacklist"? The witness stood his
ground. "If I have been critical," he protested, "it was only
about certain persons, and my brothers have believed them
hostile because, if you criticize a man in Germany, it is a
crime, and I want to show them that it is not in the United
States."

Cramer insisted that he had not known that Thiel had

come to the United States on a mission for the German Government. "The only hunch I had," he conceded, "was that he had come by submarine."

Q. Did not the thought ever cross your mind, now here is a man who had come here in a hostile submarine in time of war and I ought to call his presence here to the attention of somebody in the authorities?
A. No, sir; that thought never occurred to me.

In fact, he had concluded that his friend had escaped from Germany. Correa looked dumbfounded. "Did you feel that the German government had put a submarine at his disposal for that purpose?" he asked. "No, sir," was the rejoinder. "Somehow by pretending and telling lies, he may have gotten away." But he hadn't mentioned this theory to the FBI because "I believed it rather groundless, ridiculous."

On Wednesday morning, Medina tried to mend a few fences. What had prompted Mr. Cramer to keep the page of the *New York Times* containing the Federal Constitution? "I tore out this page and took it to my room for the purpose of studying the Constitution of the United States." As to just when he had underlined certain portions, it had been suggested to him by Mr. Willis that it might have been "a year or two ago."

Q. Is it a fair statement to say . . . that some time you put those lines there to indicate the parts of the Constitution that you thought were unusual and did not understand?
A. That is correct; yes sir.

It had always been his habit to look up English phrases which he did not understand.

The summations began after Correa had withdrawn all the overt acts of which the defendant was accused except the June 23 meetings with Thiel at the Twin Oaks Inn and Thompson's Cafeteria, and the false statements made to the FBI on the night of his arrest. Medina reiterated, in substance, the main theme of his opening statement that his client had not been guilty of any traitorous intent. "You cannot convict this man," he concluded, "because he was a fool, because he was stupid, because he was negligent, because he did something that if he had any sense he would not have done. You have got to find the traitorous intent." It was his "confident hope" that the jury would return a verdict of not guilty.

As far as Correa was concerned, Cramer had been an integral part of the German High Command's plan to sabotage American installations. "I fear," he said, "that the High Command and the German Government know all too well who are the Cramers among our population. They know who are the disaffected individuals, men like this defendant, who have assumed the cloak of citizenship, availed themselves of all the benefits and privileges and protection which citizenship confers, only to betray their sacred trust at the moment when their adopted country most needs the allegiance they have so solemnly sworn." The defendant was a traitor, and he was sure that the verdict would confirm this.

When Correa sat down, Goddard said that he wanted to thank Medina and his two associates "for having accepted the assignment by the court to represent this defendant." Far from being delighted at this praise from the bench, the defense attorney objected strenuously to his Honor's remark. "I do not think the jury should have been told that," he protested. "I have tried to keep it from them myself, and I have not mentioned it." Goddard, who was patently surprised by Medina's outburst, didn't think that "any harm had been done."

The jury retired at 5:40 P.M. A little more than two hours later, it filed back into the courtroom. Its foreman announced that "we find the defendant guilty as charged." On December 2, 1942, Cramer appeared before Judge Goddard for sentencing. Although Correa had asked for the death penalty, the court thought that "a term of imprisonment of forty-five years" was ample punishment. "Cramer," he reasoned, "had no more guilty knowledge of any subversive purpose on the part of Thiel or Kerling than a vague idea that they came here for the purpose of organizing pro-German propaganda and agitation."

On June 7, 1943, Medina asked the Court of Appeals in New York to reverse Goddard. In his argument, he pointed out that the trial judge should not have permitted Minuteman Powers to testify, Correa to question Cramer about a letter the defendant had received from his nephew, Norbert, and the prosecution to parade photographs of the saboteur's equipment in front of the jury. Two months later, the three-judge appellate court affirmed the conviction.

With Cramer on his way to Atlanta Penitentiary, Medina applied for, and received, permission to appeal to the Supreme Court. "As soon as the Supreme Court took the case," he was to remark in 1956, "I noted a distinctly more favorable attitude of the public generally toward myself and my associates. People were beginning at last to realize that it was absurd to suppose that we were being paid anything to defend Cramer, and it was equally absurd to suppose that we could be in any way associated with what he had done."

That the nine justices were disturbed about the case was apparent when, after the first argument before them, they asked Medina and Correa to come back to Washington to elaborate on the law of treason. Finally, on April 23, 1945, the court made up its collective mind. By a five-to-four vote, it concluded that there was no evidence that Cramer had done anything to give aid and comfort to the Third Reich. "There is no showing," wrote Justice Jackson, "that Cramer gave them [Thiel and Kerling] any information whatever of value to their mission or indeed that he had any to give. No effort at secrecy is shown, for they met in public places. Cramer furnished them no shelter, nothing that can be called sustenance or supplies, and there is no evidence that he gave them encouragement or counsel, or even paid for their drinks."

With Cramer's conviction set aside, the Government prepared to try him again. Since there was a possibility that another jury might convict him of treason for lying to the FBI agents on the night of his arrest, Medina agreed with Correa to have him plead guilty to the lesser charge of violating the Trading with the Enemy Act. On September 28, 1945, he was sentenced by District Judge Alfred Barksdale to serve six years in jail, a term which, with time off for good behavior, he completed in four. The year before his release, President Truman commuted the sentences of Dasch and Burger to the time already served—five years and seven months—and ordered them flown back to West Germany.

As for Medina, he turned back to his active law practice. But he always regarded the Cramer case as one of the high points of his professional career. "It was just wonderful," he said in November of 1961, "to be in there pitching for justice, without any thought of fee and without the prospect of any benefit to myself." But in fact he was doing something more than "pitching for justice." He was living up to the finest traditions of the bar and proving to other lawyers and to the public that every attorney owes it to himself, the other members of his profession and the community at large, when the occasion arises, to step forward and fight to protect with all his might and main the rights of an indigent person charged with crime, no matter how dangerous or how onerous the task may be.

# Joseph Nye Welch

In the early spring of 1954, Wisconsin Senator Joseph Raymond McCarthy was riding high. The Government of the United States, from the President down to the lowliest file clerk in the Bureau of the Census, was lying prostrate at his feet. Generals, Cabinet members, ambassadors and agency heads scrambled over each other in their eagerness to cater to his every whim. His fellow Senators lived in daily terror that he might, if the spirit moved him, invade their hustings and, with a word, imperil their chances for reelection. "The truth is," reporter Richard H. Rovere wrote in 1959, "that everyone in the Senate, or just about everyone, was scared stiff of him."

It was in this atmosphere that the Army-McCarthy hearings opened in Washington on April 22, 1954. Less than thirty per cent of the country's adults, according to a Gallup poll taken three months earlier, disapproved of the Wisconsin Senator's tactics. And, in Massachusetts, whose large Irish-Catholic population had to a great extent flocked to his banners, it is doubtful that the opposition met the national average. John F. Kennedy, the state's junior Senator, so outspoken in other areas, had solved the problem for himself by never referring publicly to the activities of his controversial colleague across the aisle.

Why, then, would a Boston trial lawyer, in his twenty-first

year as a partner in a conservative State Street firm, consent
to do battle in an unfamiliar arena with a man whose knee
had already found the groin of those infinitely more powerful
than himself? Joseph Nye Welch could only explain it in
terms of his ardent Republicanism. When the Army sought
him out as its special counsel a month before the hearings
started, he demurred. "I carefully explained that I had no
political experience whatsoever," he later said, "and I told
them that I would not know how to comport myself in the
presence of television and radio." But the Army, it seems,
wanted him anyway and, out of respect for his beloved GOP,
he dutifully reported to Washington.

There were many moments when he regretted his decision.
As he entered the Senate Caucus Room on the opening day
of the hearings, he was sorely tempted to take the first train
back to Boston. "So many cameras, so much television, those
movies, that bank of lights, all those reporters . . . [I] felt great
fear and paused at the threshold." Whether from timidity or
an excess of caution, he was remarkably subdued during the
first three weeks of the hearings. Except for a few feeble
attempts to relieve the pressure on the embattled Secretary
of the Army, he remained, for the most part, a bemused but
aloof observer of the theatrics taking place about him.

It was not until he realized that the Caucus Room was no
hallowed hall of justice and that his client's adversaries were
operating under a different code of ethics than his own, that
he grudgingly changed his tactics. Cropped photographs,
questionable memoranda and spurious documents were more
than a man accustomed to the ordinary rules of evidence
could long endure. It was then that he had seized the initia-
tive and, with one rapier slash after another, first wounded
and ultimately destroyed the big bad wolf from the land of
lakes and cheeses. The job was done with infinite grace,
charm and wit, but it was every bit as effective as the back-

woods techniques so successfully employed by Indian Charlie's most faithful pupil.

As the hearings drew to a close, a suddenly emboldened
Stuart Symington glared at McCarthy and blurted, "I want
you to know . . . that I am not afraid of anything about you
or anything you've got to say, any time, any place, anywhere."
Although there were still few enough in high places who
were ready to share the Missourian's bravado, it was true
that, mainly because of the efforts of the gentle man from
Boston, the ring of fear had been broken. The bastion that
had withstood scorn, anger, logic and common sense had collapsed at the first breath of ridicule and outraged decency.

As Mr. Welch relaxed on the last of his many train rides
back to Boston, the forces that would complete McCarthy's
rout were very much in evidence. Gallup's pollsters were
already recording a significant increase in the number of
"those opposed to" and a corresponding drain of "those in
favor of" the Senator's *modus operandi*. In a matter of weeks,
Vermont's Ralph Flanders would finish polishing his censure
resolution. Roy Cohn, who felt the ship settling under his
feet, was about to desert it for the safer decks of his lucrative
New York law practice. Private G. David Schine, whose military career had triggered the hearings, was at last free to
finish his unwelcome stint in an Army which could breathe
easily again. Although it was to be three years before hepa-
titis would be given official credit for McCarthy's demise, it
must have been apparent to the perceptive Mr. Welch that
the Senator's political life was all but over.

# Joseph Nye Welch and the Army-McCarthy hearings, April 22 to June 17, 1954

VERY FEW MEMBERS of the Ohio County Women's Republican Club of Wheeling, West Virginia, had ever heard of the speaker its program committee had scheduled for their February 9, 1950, meeting. The flyer that heralded his appearance merely indicated that he was the junior United States Senator from Wisconsin and that his subject would be "Communists in Government." If any of the ladies had bothered to check, they would have discovered that their guest had once run unsuccessfully as a Democrat for District Attorney of Wisconsin's Seventh District, had been elected in 1939—this time on the Republican ticket—as a Circuit Judge, and had overwhelmingly won his Senate seat in November, 1946, after defeating Robert M. La Follette, Jr., in the Republican primary two months earlier. During World War II, he had taken a sabbatical from his judicial duties to serve for two-and-a-half years as an intelligence officer with a Marine Scout Bombing Squadron in the South Pacific.

There was nothing in Senator Joseph Raymond McCarthy's background that would have led his prospective listeners to expect anything more than the usual anti-Democratic tirades so popular in Republican circles around Lincoln's Birthday. Since his election, he had been little more than just another freshman Senator enjoying the heady air of Washington, D.C. Although he made a few isolated headlines by calling for an end to sugar rationing and by accusing the Army of torturing confessions out of the German S.S. troops charged with massacring some 250 American soldiers and Belgian

civilians at Malmédy in 1944, he was scarcely known beyond
the confines of the Senate cloakroom.

What he told his unsuspecting audience on February 9 at
the Hotel McLure was to end forever the anonymity that had
dogged him since he had left Appleton three years before.
Midway through his speech, in a gesture that was soon to
become his trademark, he held up a sheet of paper. "I have
here in my hand," he told the Wheeling ladies, "a list of
205, a list of names that were made known to the Secretary
of State as being members of the Communist Party and who
nevertheless are still working and shaping policy in the State
Department." The next night, in a Salt Lake City radio interview, although the number had dropped to "57 card-carry-
ing members of the Communist Party," the refrain was still
the same—the State Department was honeycombed with
agents of Moscow. But whether he had said 205 or 57 made
very little difference. He had pulled himself up from obscurity by his own brute straps.

Although the Wheeling speech attracted slight attention
in the nation's press, the same could not be said of its reception by Washington officialdom. Undoubtedly prodded by
Secretary of State Dean Acheson, the Democratic majority in
the Senate demanded that McCarthy document his charges
of subversion in high places. He was more than willing to
oblige. Late on the afternoon of February 20, he heaved his
bulk out of his Senate seat and, for the next six hours, proceeded to lecture his fellows on the dangerous situation at
State. With the announcement that he had infiltrated "Truman's iron curtain of secrecy," he began a lengthy discussion
of eighty-one security-risk cases which, he conceded, had been
investigated some years earlier by the State Department Security Office.

"I must say," he began affably, "that I know that some of
these individuals whose cases I am giving the Senate are no
longer in the State Department. A sizable number of them

are not." He was also prepared to admit that some of the individuals concerned were not Communists at all. But he was quick to add that "there is sufficient in the files to show that there is something radically wrong." Since neither Truman nor Acheson was prepared to do anything about the sticky situation at State, "I thought the only thing to do was what I have done, namely, to let the people of the country know what is going on, and then hope that the pressure of public opinion would be great enough to force the President to clean house."

When the tumultuous session broke up at midnight, the wire services were spreading McCarthy's charges from one end of the country to the other. Two days later, Majority Leader Scott Lucas, who had interrupted McCarthy more than sixty times during the latter's marathon harangue, shepherded Senate Resolution 231 through the upper House. The resolution directed the Committee on Foreign Relations "or any duly authorized subcommittee thereof . . . to conduct a full and complete study and investigation as to whether persons who are disloyal to the United States are, or have been, employed by the Department of State."

The Committee on Foreign Relations immediately appointed a special subcommittee under the chairmanship of Maryland's veteran Millard E. Tydings to look into McCarthy's charges. The Tydings Committee, as it soon came to be called, began its hearings on March 8, with the junior Senator from Wisconsin as its first witness. "You are in the position of being the man who occasioned this hearing," Tydings told McCarthy that morning, "and so far as I am concerned . . . you are going to get one of the most complete investigations ever given in the history of the Republic."

Tydings was as good as his word. His committee sat for almost four months, amassing a record that eventually totalled more than 2500 pages of testimony and documentation. It gave witness McCarthy all the time he wanted and the latter was quick to take advantage of its generosity. For four exasperating days, he checked off the names and backgrounds of nine people whose cases, he assured Tydings, would more than justify what he had said at Wheeling and on the Senate floor. "I am not making charges," he prefaced his revelations. "I am giving the committee information of individuals who appear by all the rules of common sense as being very bad security risks."

He led off with Dorothy Kenyon, a former New York City judge, who had never been employed by the State Department. "This lady," he explained, "has been affiliated with at least twenty-eight Communist-front organizations, all of which have been declared subversive by an official Government agency." Haldore Hanson, the chief of State's Technical Cooperation Projects Staff, was next. "Here is a man with a mission," he emphasized, "a mission to communize the world." Hanson was followed by Philip Jessup, Truman's roving ambassador, who had, in the words of his accuser, an "unusual affinity . . . for Communist causes."

Neither one of his next two offerings—Profs. Frederick Schuman and Harlow Shapley—had ever been regularly employed by the State Department. Schuman had once given a series of lectures to Foreign Service trainees while Shapley had served a three-year term on the National Commission for UNESCO. Both men were accused of having been members of a variety of Communist-front organizations. Gustavo Duran, a member of the United Nations Secretariat, who had not worked for State for several years, was suspect because he had supported the Loyalists during the Spanish Civil War.

The cases of Esther Brunauer, John Stewart Service and Owen Lattimore deserved his colleagues' "most serious attention." Mrs. Brunauer, a long-time State employee, had, according to McCarthy, sponsored several pro-Communist youth meetings and served as Alger Hiss's first assistant at the

San Francisco conference to organize the United Nations. Service, who was depicted as "one of the dozen top policy makers in the entire State Department," had been trying for years to topple Chiang Kai-Shek because he believed that "the only hope of Asia was communism." China-expert Lattimore—"one of the principal architects of our Far Eastern policy"—was nothing short of a spy.

In addition to his nine public cases, McCarthy submitted ninety-nine other names to the Tydings Committee in executive sessions. The Committee's interim report, which was issued in mid-July, cleared both the State Department and the individuals concerned. "Starting with nothing," it read, "Senator McCarthy plunged headlong forward, desperately seeking to develop some information which, colored with distortion and fanned by a blaze of bias would forestall the day of reckoning." In fact, the cases which he had submitted had all been culled from the files of a House subcommittee which had investigated—and cleared—each one in early 1948. By presenting "old and stale" cases, the honorable gentleman from Wisconsin had been guilty of perpetrating a "fraud and a hoax" on his brethren on both sides of the aisle.

Instead of being dismayed by the Tydings report, McCarthy retaliated by trumpeting loudly—and colorfully—that it was nothing more than "a green light for the Reds." He could well afford to take the offensive. Although he had not been able to prove that there was a single subversive on the State Department payroll, he had created a public image of a vigorous anti-Communist who was more interested in results than methods. The start of the Korean War several weeks before the release of the interim Tydings Report had made many people feel that the problem of internal security called for something more than the Marquis of Queensberry rules. "McCarthyism," which had been coined by cartoonist Herb Block of the *Washington Post* as a derisive term, quickly became the call to arms of those who demanded sterner measures in ferreting out homegrown subversives.

As supporters rallied to his banners during the summer of 1950, McCarthy decided that the time had come to teach his fellow Senators a lesson and, at the same time, to nullify the Tydings Report. Tydings, who had been a fixture in the upper House for more years than anyone cared to remember, was running for reelection in Maryland. His defeat would, at one and the same time, vindicate the man from Wisconsin and serve notice that anyone standing in his way was fair game for the same fate. The fact that Franklin Roosevelt had failed miserably in 1938 to accomplish the same end did not deter McCarthy, and he threw his weight behind John Marshall Butler, Tyding's Republican opponent.

With the invaluable aid of a composite photograph which gave the impression that Tydings and Earl Browder, the former head of the Communist Party, were hardly incompatible, McCarthy succeeded in convincing the Maryland electorate that it could no longer afford the luxury of its patrician Senator. "I have been vindicated," he gleefully told reporters the morning after Butler's surprising upset had become a reality. With Tydings out of the way, his committee's findings became academic, and even its final report the next summer that no instance of erroneous or improper loyalty and security clearances had been uncovered could resuscitate them.

McCarthy was off and running. It was a rare day that he was not Page One news. He accused Anna Rosenberg, Truman's nominee as Assistant Secretary of Defense, of being a Communist. General George C. Marshall was "an instrument of the Soviet Conspiracy"; Adlai Stevenson "would continue the suicidal Kremlin-shaped policies of the nation"; Dwight D. Eisenhower was no more anti-Communist than his predecessor, and he eventually apologized to the American people for having supported him in 1952. High and low, no one was immune from attack, and Presidents fared no better than innocuous Voice of America translators.

The Eisenhower sweep in the fall of 1952 had given the Republicans a majority in the Senate. Although running considerably behind the national ticket, McCarthy had been returned to Washington by a comfortable plurality. In the reorganization of the upper House, he was named as chairman of the Committee on Government Operations, and immediately installed himself as the overseer of its Permanent Subcommittee on Investigations. "We've only scratched the surface on communism," he told the eager press as he began to build the kind of staff he needed to continue his rooting.

For chief counsel, he selected twenty-five-year-old Roy Cohn, the son of a Bronx political chieftain, who, as an Assistant United States Attorney, had been involved in some notable anti-Communist prosecutions in New York City. G. David Schine, whose father was rapidly building a sizable hotel and theater empire, needed little urging to become the subcommittee's unpaid consultant-in-chief. Apostate J. B. Matthews, a one-time Methodist missionary and erstwhile fellow traveler, had a short-lived career as staff director, being forced to resign when he wrote an article in the *American Mercury* impugning the loyalty of a sizable segment of the Protestant clergy. He was succeeded in the early summer of 1953 by Francis P. Carr, the supervisor of the FBI's security section. In addition, there was a small army of investigators, the most significant of whom were Don Surine, an unfrocked FBI agent, James Juliana and George Anastos.

With Cohn as its booking agent, the subcommittee, usually manned by only its chairman, started off with a rush. Before it was two months old, it had, with the *sub rosa* assistance of some disgruntled employees, completely discredited the Voice of America. Then it was the turn of the overseas libraries of the International Information Administration. Prefaced by a whirlwind inspection junket by Cohn and Schine to most of the capitals of Western Europe, the investigation forced the now thoroughly cowed State Department to bowdlerize its foreign book shelves and to dismiss several key officials.

In early September, McCarthy turned his sights on bigger game. He announced to the press that he had found "a disturbing situation" at the Signal Corps Center at Fort Monmouth, New Jersey. With the eager cooperation of Robert T. Stevens, the Secretary of the Army, the Senator turned his minions loose among the radar and electronics laboratories that dotted the rolling Jersey landscape. In November, when Stevens squealed that two months of investigation had revealed "no evidence of current espionage" at Monmouth, the Senator blackjacked him into stating that what he had meant to say was that his department had "no proof of espionage."

While the members of his staff were still swarming over Fort Monmouth, McCarthy began to gnaw another—and possibly juicier—bone. It had come to his attention that one Irving Peress, a New York dentist with left-wing affiliations, had been commissioned a captain in October of 1952, notwithstanding his refusal to answer any questions about his political background. A year later, after Peress had been promoted to major pursuant to the provisions of the Doctor Draft Law, the Army, with one eye on the havoc at Fort Monmouth, decided to discharge him.

On January 30, 1954, the dentist appeared before the Permanent Subcommittee and invoked the Fifth Amendment as to any question about his politics. Four days later, despite the fact that McCarthy had demanded that he be courtmartialed, Peress was honorably discharged at Camp Kilmer, New Jersey. The Senator's rage knew no bounds. Even a highly conciliatory letter from Secretary Stevens promising to investigate the incident was brushed aside as "double talk" and "Communist jargon."

The Senator retaliated by directing Brigadier General Ralph W. Zwicker, the commanding officer of Camp Kilmer and a hero of the Battle of the Bulge, to appear at the United States Courthouse in New York City on February 18. On the appointed day, McCarthy, after asking the general a series of questions based on hypothetical cases, proceeded to castigate him for discharging Peress. As Zwicker later recalled it, "the Senator then stated that I was unsuitable as an Army officer, that I was shielding traitors and Communist conspirators . . . that I was a disgrace to the uniform, that he couldn't understand how the Army would ever select a person like me to be a general officer . . . that I was either stupid or deliberately trying to protect Communists."

After Zwicker had refused, on the strength of an Army regulation, to testify as to the circumstances of Peress' discharge, his inquisitor ordered him to return on February 23. When Zwicker complained to Chief of Staff Matthew Ridgeway about the treatment he had received, the latter pleaded with Stevens to intervene. The Secretary immediately instructed Zwicker not to return to New York and informed McCarthy of his decision. "I cannot permit the loyal officers of our Armed Forces," he wrote, "to be subjected to such unwarranted treatment."

On February 24, Stevens abruptly reversed his field. Following a secret fried chicken luncheon with Senators McCarthy, Dirksen, Mundt and Potter, the four Republican members of the Permanent Subcommittee, he agreed to a "memorandum of understanding" which gave the Wisconsinite everything he wanted. "The Secretary," it read, "will give the committee the names of everyone involved in the promotion and honorable discharge of Peress and . . . such individuals will be available to appear before the committee." As for General Zwicker, he, too, would be made "available" if needed. Significantly, it was not until Stevens had returned to the Pentagon that afternoon that it dawned upon him that chicken was not the only bird he had eaten that day.

The gnawing realization that he and the Army had been badly taken was the spine-stiffener that Stevens needed. Two weeks after his capitulation, he released a "chronology of events" in which he accused McCarthy, Roy Cohn and Frank Carr of persecuting the Army because it had refused (1) to give Dave Schine a commission before he was drafted as a private, and (2) to show him preferential treatment after his induction. McCarthy reacted by proclaiming that Stevens was holding his staff member as a "hostage" in order to bludgeon the subcommittee into discontinuing the Fort Monmouth investigation. At long last, the issue had been joined.

On March 16, the full Permanent Subcommittee met in executive session to consider just what it ought to do about the charges and countercharges. After announcing that "I am inclined to think that I should not sit as chairman during any of the discussions of this," McCarthy appointed Senator Mundt as acting chairman. The South Dakotan promptly indicated his appreciation of his new responsibilities by suggesting that perhaps some other committee ought to handle the matter. His fellow Senators responded by voting unanimously "to investigate the controversy which has arisen." All hearings were to be public and the acting chairman was authorized "to employ such course and staff as he deems necessary."

The hearings were scheduled to begin on Thursday, April 22. But it wasn't until ten days before the hearings that Mundt was able to announce that the subcommittee had found itself a lawyer. Its first choice, Boston's Samuel Sears, came an early cropper when it was revealed by the press that he was one of McCarthy's most devoted admirers. Finally, after a nationwide search to find some member of the bar who had not expressed himself in public about the junior Senator from Wisconsin, the subcommittee settled on Ray

H. Jenkins, east Tennessee's most active criminal lawyer. The tall, lantern-jawed barrister with a voice that seemed better suited to enticing hogs than juries, was rushed to Washington on April 12.

The day after his arrival, the Army filed with Mundt its statement of charges against McCarthy, Cohn and Schine. In the main, they alleged that, starting on July 8, 1953, and continuing to February 16, 1954, the Senator and his two aides had "sought by improper means to obtain preferential treatment for one Pvt. G. David Schine, formerly chief consultant of this subcommittee." Containing twenty-nine specific instances of misconduct, the lengthy document was signed by one Joseph N. Welch, who listed himself as "special counsel."

The senior member of a highly respectable Boston law firm, the sixty-three-year-old Welch was singularly without political experience. A tall, portly man with the face of a bemused leprechaun, he had been born in Iowa of English immigrant parents. After working his way through Harvard Law School, he had remained in Boston, where he quickly acquired the reputation of being able to cajole Hub juries into returning favorable verdicts. Strongly addicted to vests and sombre bow ties, he was as dissimilar to the sleek Roy Cohn as the roll-top desk he used in his State Street office was to the latest Swedish import.

Late on the afternoon of April 20, a bulky envelope was hand-delivered to Mundt's office. Signed by "Joseph McCarthy, Chairman," it contained "what we consider to be pertinent details concerning the attempt by two Army civilians, Mr. Robert T. Stevens and Mr. John G. Adams, to discredit the Investigations Subcommittee and to force a discontinuance of our hearings exposing Communist infiltration in their department." After disposing of the Army's charges as "without basis of fact ... [and] wholly unfounded," the statement proceeded to accuse Stevens and Adams, the

Army's legal counselor, of placing "every conceivable obstacle . . . in the path of the subcommittee's search for truth." Forty-five specific instances of obstructionism were set forth.

In passing, McCarthy leveled broadsides at both Mr. Welch and H. Struve Hensel, Assistant Secretary of Defense and General Counsel. The former, he charged, was a parvenu who had "no personal knowledge of the matter." Besides, one of the Bostonian's associates who was assisting him in this investigation had once "belonged to an organization found by the House Un-American Activities Committee to be the 'legal bulwark' of the Communist Party, and referred to by the Attorney General of the United States as the 'legal mouthpiece' of the Communists." As for Mr. Hensel, not only had he assisted Adams in discrediting the subcommittee, but he had, while with the Navy Department in the forties, been handsomely rewarded by a private ship-supply firm which was doing a substantial amount of business with the Government.

Two days after the delivery of McCarthy's formal charges, the promised public hearings began in the multicolumned Caucus Room on the first floor of the Senate Office Building. Over the week end, the stately room had been converted into a giant television studio, complete with Klieg lights, cameras and microphones. At ten o'clock on Monday morning, when the more than seven hundred spectators, some of whom had been waiting since sunrise, surged into a chamber that had never accommodated more than half that number, they were steered by perspiring guards around the tangled network of wires and cables that cluttered the oaken floor. As they scrambled for seats, they sideswiped cursing television directors who were shouting last minute instructions to a battery of cameramen and technicians who perched precariously on a scaffold which had been erected in front of the scarlet curtains that bordered the chamber's only windows.

Shortly before ten-thirty, Chairman Mundt, with the aid

of several Capitol policemen, led his six colleagues through the crowd to a long counsel table at one end of the room. As the Senators filed in, reporters noticed that stolid Henry C. Dworshak of Idaho had been pressed into service to retain the GOP majority which had been lost by McCarthy's withdrawal. McClellan, Symington and Jackson, the three Democrats, who had taken French leave of the subcommittee the preceding July after a dispute with its chairman over the hiring of staff members, followed their Republican counterparts into the room. As they took their seats, several of the Senators nodded to McCarthy who, flanked by two FBI guards, was already ensconced at the far left end of the table.

Mundt, who was puffing furiously at a pipe that refused to stay lit, waited for his cue from one of the shirt-sleeved television directors. Promptly on signal, he announced that "the hearings will now come to order." As the hubbub in the packed chamber began to die down, the South Dakotan warned the audience that he would tolerate no demonstrations of any kind. "You are here as our guests," he pointed out, "and we want nothing to occur to disrupt the decorum of the committee." He was sure that the ground rules adopted by the subcommittee would permit it "to conduct these hearings with a maximum degree of dignity, fairness and thoroughness."

After McClellan, speaking for the Democrats, had, in his doomsday voice, seconded the chair's remarks, Mundt turned to the expectant Ray Jenkins. "Our counsel . . . will now call the first witness," he said. But it was to be ten minutes before the emtpy chair in front of the counsel table was filled. As Jenkins glanced down at his witness list, McCarthy's voice boomed out. "A point of order, Mr. Chairman," he barked. He had noticed that Messrs. Stevens, Hensel and Adams had signed their charges on behalf of the Department of the Army. He hoped that the Chair would instruct these "Pentagon politicians" to list themselves as "individuals who are here to prove that a private in the Army got special consideration."

Mundt suggested that the objection be held in abeyance until Mr. Stevens took the stand. McCarthy shook his head. "I maintain," he insisted, "it is a disgrace and reflection upon everyone of the million outstanding men in the Army to let a few civilians who are trying to hold up an investigation of Communists, label themselves as the Department of the Army." As Mundt again directed Counsel Jenkins to call his first witness, McClellan wryly observed that the statement of charges filed by the distinguished Senator from Wisconsin "on behalf of himself, Mr. Cohn and Mr. Carr . . . is signed, 'Joe McCarthy, Chairman.'"

The first of more than twenty witnesses who were to make the late spring of 1954 so memorable to some twenty million television viewers, was a tall, distinguished-looking officer who, in 1953, had been the Army's Chief of Legislative Liaison. At Senator McCarthy's request, General Miles Reber had gone all out for Dave Schine in July and August. His first step had been to call Roy Cohn and ask him to send Schine over to the Pentagon to fill out an application for a direct commission. After the Chief of Transportation, the Provost Marshal General and the Chief of Psychological Warfare had informed Reber that McCarthy's consultant was not qualified for commissioned service in their branches, he had tried unsuccessfully to find a place for him with First Army, the Navy and the Air Force.

Under the subcommittee's rules of procedure, every witness was first to be examined and cross-examined by Jenkins. Then each Senator and the various attorneys were to have consecutive ten-minute rounds until no one had any further questions to ask. When Reber had described his persistent efforts on Schine's behalf, Jenkins turned devil's advocate. Was it not common practice for congressmen to call him "with reference to the inductees, draftees, or those about to

become so?" It was. And did he consider Senator McCarthy's
call on the subject of Schine improper? No, sir, he did not.
But he did feel that Mr. Cohn, who had telephoned him two
or three times a day, had been "persistently after me."

After Reber had agreed with Jenkins' somewhat irrelevant
observation that no subversive person should have been employed at Fort Monmouth, the latter turned him over to
Mundt for the first go-round of questions. The chairman had
only a few. Did the general feel that either Senator McCarthy
or Mr. Cohn had tried to intimidate him into giving Schine
a commission? "No, sir," he answered, "I was not intimidated
or anything like that." Senator McClellan wanted to be certain that McCarthy had acted for himself and not for the subcommittee. Reber, who was anxious to please all men, assured
him that he knew "of no committee action as such."

Suddenly, it was Mr. Welch's turn. His announcement
that he had only three questions for Reber was inaudible at
the counsel table. Mundt suggested that he use the general's
microphone but, even amplified, his high-pitched voice was
difficult to hear at twenty feet. Had the general been "acutely
aware" of Mr. Cohn's position as counsel for the subcommittee? Yes, sir, he had. And had that position increased
"the interest with which you pursued the problem?" Reber
was sure that it had.

Q. Do you recall any instance comparable to this in which
you were put under greater pressure?
A. To the best of my recollection, I recall of no instance in
which I was under greater pressure.

McCarthy spent his first ten minutes establishing that
Reber often received requests from members of Congress for
information about direct commissions. But there was one
difference, the general explained. "These specific calls were
impressing me with the necessity for speed, and for favorable
action." Jenkins was back on stage. Had the Army ever in-

vestigated Fort Monmouth? It had, in the spring of 1953. "Was that after Senator McCarthy had initiated his investigation?" the subcommittee's counsel asked. Reber thought for a moment. "I believe it was," he replied. "Yes, sir, I believe it was."

McCarthy's second pass began quietly. Why had the general told Mr. Welch that he was "acutely aware of the fact that Mr. Cohn was chief counsel for the committee?" Because he "inferred" that the young lawyer would have "a great deal to do with the Army." The Senator's voice hardened. Wasn't it because Samuel Reber, the witness' brother, who had been Deputy High Commissioner for Germany, had "repeatedly" attacked Cohn and Schine when the two young men had descended upon Western Europe the preceding spring? The exchange was brought to an abrupt end by Senator McClellan, who reminded McCarthy that he was giving testimony. "I do not want you testifying unless you want to take the witness stand," the Arkansan insisted. "Then I do not mind your saying it under oath."

McCarthy roared back to the attack in the afternoon. Wasn't it true that Reber's brother had been forced to resign because he was "a bad security risk"? Jenkins suddenly remembered his rules of evidence and ruled the question out of order as "wholly irrelevant." When the Senator from Wisconsin persisted, Jenkins promptly backtracked. "If the Senator will embrace those facts in his question, I will withdraw my objection because . . . those facts would make it a perfectly legitimate question on the issue of motive on the part of this witness." Reber's answer was anticlimactic. "I do not know and have never heard," he said, "that my brother retired as a result of any action of this committee. The answer is 'Positively no' to that question."

Welch tried to repair the damage that had been done to the absent Sam Reber's reputation. Would the general tell the committee why his brother had retired? Another anguished "point of order" emanated from McCarthy's corner. "I think that is a completely unfair question!" he roared. Jenkins, followed closely by Mundt, sustained the objection. Senator Jackson leaped into the breach. "Mr. Counsel," he argued, "may I say that the statement has been made in this room and is apparent to millions of Americans, that General Reber's brother was dismissed as a security risk." The fracas came to an end with the witness' simple statement that his brother had retired "as he is entitled to do by law upon reaching the age of fifty."

As Reber left the Caucus Room to return to his post in Kaiserslautern, Germany, as the Commanding General of the Western Area Command, Jenkins called out the name of Robert T. Stevens. The Secretary of the Army, a round-faced, bespectacled man who would not have looked out of place in a Madison Avenue advertising agency, perched himself gingerly in the red leather chair that Reber had just vacated and stared myopically at the seven Senators in front of him. He was to sit there for twelve straight days, responding to a barrage of questions, the answers to which made him, at times, look like Washington's biggest fool and, at others, like a latter-day Job.

Stevens had first learned of McCarthy's interest in the Army in September 2, 1953, when he had read of the initial Monmouth foray in a Montana newspaper. He had immediately wired the Senator that, upon his return to Washington after Labor Day, he would call "to offer my services in trying to assist you to correct anything that may be wrong."

Q. Did you receive any reply to that telegram, Mr. Secretary?
A. I learned after I got back that Senator McCarthy's office attempted to contact my office, I believe on the same day, which was September 4.

On September 8, he had visited McCarthy in the latter's office and again assured him of his desire to cooperate in any investigation of Army facilities. In addition to McCarthy, Dirksen, Cohn and Schine had been present at the conference. "My recollection is," he told Jenkins, "that we spent the time in discussing the cases that he was interested in."

From that day on, the Secretary was at the subcommittee's beck and call. Eight days later, he was summoned to meet McCarthy in New York at the Waldorf Towers suite of Schine's parents.

> Q. Will you please now tell this committee in detail what if anything was said to you on that occasion by Senator Mc-Carthy, G. David Schine, or any one else present, with reference to G. David Schine?
> A. Yes, my recollection is that Senator McCarthy on this occasion asked me for a commission for David Schine.

On October 2, Cohn and Carr had called on him and demanded that he order General Kirke B. Lawton, the commander of Fort Monmouth, to give subcommittee investigators free rein at the Signal Corps post. Stevens had telephoned Lawton at once and directed him "to make available those people at his installation that the properly accredited representatives of Senator McCarthy wanted to interview."

After the call to Collins had been completed, Cohn said that, if Schine were actually inducted, he would like him stationed in New York City so that he could attend to subcommittee work in that area. The Secretary had replied that Schine would have to undergo the regular sixteen-week basic training program, but that he "would cooperate . . . in making [him] available for committee work, providing it did not interfere with his training." As he remembered it, there had been "a degree of insistence" in Cohn's voice when he discussed the subject of Schine. No, Frank Carr had not joined in the conversation.

On October 13, he and John Adams had gone to New York to sit in on one of the subcommittee's executive hearings involving Fort Monmouth personnel. After the morning session, he had invited McCarthy and his staff to have lunch with him at the Merchants' Club.

Q. Was anything said at that luncheon between the respective parties to this controversy with reference to Schine?
A. I don't recall anything significant.

That evening, he had attended a dinner party given by Schine's parents in a private dining room at the Waldorf Astoria. The next morning, Dave Schine had picked him up in a limousine and driven him to the United States Courthouse where the Monmouth hearings were being held. During the ride downtown, Schine had told him that the Army was doing "a good job in ferreting out Communists," and suggested that, if the Secretary would appoint him as his special assistant, he could "go a long way in the field."

Q. And you told David Schine what?
A. I pointed out to him that I had served, my sons had served, and we all think we got a great deal out of it in addition to having the opportunity of serving our country.

A week later, at Stevens' invitation, McCarthy, Cohn and Adams had accompanied him to Fort Monmouth for a tour of the post. When the group arrived at one restricted laboratory, the Secretary had refused to let Cohn enter because he wasn't sure of his security clearance. The lawyer had become extremely angry and shouted, "This is war! I am cleared for the highest classified information. I have access to FBI files when I want them. They did this just to embarrass me. We will now really investigate the Army." At a box lunch that afternoon, the worried Secretary of the Army apologized to the still smouldering Cohn for having excluded him from the laboratory.

On October 27, Cohn had called to inform him that Schine

was to be inducted on November 3. Would Mr. Secretary ask Allen Dulles of the Central Intelligence Agency whether he could use Schine? He would. "With what result?" asked Mr. Jenkins. "Negative," replied Stevens. Then Cohn had requested that Schine be given a furlough as soon as he was inducted so that he could finish up his committee work. Stevens thought that a two-week tour of temporary duty with First Army in New York could be arranged.

> Q. Had you been advised that Mr. Schine's work with the committee was in reference to investigation of the Army?
> A. Yes, sir.
> Q. And that it was regarded as essential, and that he had reports to make on his investigations which had not been completed?
> A. That is right.

Three days after Schine's induction, Stevens invited McCarthy to a luncheon at the Pentagon so that the Senator could meet General Matthew Ridgeway, the new Chief of Staff, and several other high-ranking officers. The Secretary had suggested to McCarthy that the latter's investigation "had served its purpose" and that the Army ought to be allowed to clean its own house. "I wanted to stop the hammering and the headlines of the press of the country against the Army, which was creating the impression that there was widespread espionage at Fort Monmouth, which was not the case." McCarthy had responded by saying that it was important to the subcommittee to have Schine available so that he could complete his reports.

The next morning, he had received a telephone call from the Wisconsin Senator which, like all his incoming calls, had been monitored by his appointment clerk. McCarthy had asked him not to assign Schine back to the subcommittee after his induction. "Now in that conversation Senator McCarthy said that one of the few things that he had trouble with Mr. Cohn about was David Schine. He said that 'Roy thinks that Dave ought to be a general and operate from a penthouse on the Waldorf Astoria,' or words to that effect. Senator McCarthy then said that he thought a few week ends off for David Schine might be arranged, or words to that effect. Perhaps for the purpose of taking care of Dave's girl friends."

Jenkins, who was panting to introduce the monitored version of this conversation, deferred to Mr. Welch, who asked "the protection both of the subpoena and of a committee vote ordering [Stevens] to produce." After John J. Lucas, Stevens' appointment clerk, had testified that, except for occasional unimportant omissions, his notes accurately reflected any conversations he had reported, the subcommittee unanimously adopted McClellan's motion that "all notes of monitored conversation as between parties in this controversy . . . be subpoenaed and brought here."

However, much to the disappointment of the press corps, Lucas was not to read his notes aloud that day. No sooner had Jenkins asked him to do so when the Senator from Wisconsin, who had previously called the Army's policy of selective eavesdropping "one of the most indecent and dishonest things I have ever heard of," cut him off abruptly. Unless Lucas would swear that this was the first recorded conversation between any of the principals in the hearing, he objected strenuously to its being read. As a flustered Jenkins tried to extract this information from Lucas, Mundt hurriedly approved McClellan's suggestion that the witness be excused until he could "arrange all of those monitored conversations in order."

When the hearings resumed on Monday, Stevens, looking noticeably refreshed, was back in the witness chair. On November 13, 1953, he had informed his press conference that, the Army had "no proof of espionage" at Fort Monmouth. Three days later, Cohn and Carr had burst into his office, complaining that Senator McCarthy "felt that I had double-crossed him, and that he did not believe my statement to the press was a correct one." The next day, the Secretary had flown to New York where, after another luncheon with Mc-Carthy at the Merchants' Club, the two men had held a joint press conference at which Stevens indicated that what he had meant by his statement of November 13 was "that I knew of no current espionage at Fort Monmouth." Later that afternoon, he had flown McCarthy and Cohn to McGuire Air Force Base near Fort Dix so that they could see Private Schine.

On December 10, Stevens had lunched with McCarthy, Cohn and Carr at Washington's Carroll Arms Hotel. During the meal, the Senator had asked him "about three times" to assign Schine to New York City at the end of the first eight weeks of his basic training.

Q. What were your replies to the Senator?
A. I told him that David Schine, like every other boy, would have to finish his sixteen weeks of basic training.

The following January 14, despite the fact that, twenty-three days earlier, the Senator had written to the Secretary that he had "an unbreakable rule that neither I nor anyone in my behalf shall ever attempt to interfere with the Army in its assignments," he had again urged Stevens to transfer Schine to New York City when his training was completed. "He persistently asked me," the witness somewhat petulantly complained to Jenkins.

By the time that Jenkins, who apparently experienced lit-tle difficulty in making the shift from advocate to adversary, had finished his cross-examination, the pink in Stevens' plump cheeks had turned to pallor. Yes, he would agree that Senator McCarthy had accelerated the suspension of some security risks at Monmouth. No, he didn't want the subcommittee's investigation stopped, only the type of hearings that were being conducted. Yes, he thought that Senator McCarthy had presented "a greatly overexaggerated situation" as far as Monmouth was concerned. No, he had never asked the Senator to go after the Air Force or the Navy and leave his department alone.

Before turning the perspiring Secretary over to the subcommittee, Jenkins handed him a photograph and asked him whether it was a picture of himself and Private Schine, taken at his insistence. After studying it for a moment, Stevens identified it as a photograph taken at McGuire Air Force Base on November 17, 1953, but denied that he had ever asked Schine to pose with him.

Q. Isn't it a fact that you were being especially nice and considerate and tender of this boy, in order to dissuade the Senator from continuing his investigation of one of your departments?

A. Positively and absolutely not!

Schine, the Secretary assured Jenkins, was treated "like every other private in the Army."

When the hearings resumed the next morning, Mr. Welch rose to what he termed "a point of something." His face a choleric purple, he held up a large, glossy photograph. "My point of order," he said, "is that Mr. Jenkins yesterday was imposed upon, and so was the Secretary of the Army, by having a doctored or altered photograph produced in this courtroom as if it were honest. I show you now a photograph in respect of which I charge that what was offered in evidence yesterday was an altered, shamefully cut-down picture, so that somebody could say to Stevens, 'Were you not photographed alone with David Schine,' when the truth is he was photographed in a group."

As the Senators at the head table studied Welch's photograph, Jenkins was all apologies. The original picture had been given to him by "an adverse party of interest to Mr

Stevens," and he had not been informed that it had been cut down. "I presented it in good faith, as authentic evidence," he protested. With Mundt's permission, he interrupted Stevens' testimony and asked Roy Cohn to take the Secretary's place. Exhibiting brilliant open-field running, McCarthy's chief counsel denied that he had tried to buffalo Mr. Jenkins with a cropped picture. He had been asked to furnish a photograph of Secretary Stevens and Private Schine together, and he did not know that there had been at least two other people * in the original print.

After some delightful, but hardly conclusive, sparring between Cohn and Welch, Jenkins asked to be sworn. The Tennessean, whose discomfiture was almost embarrassing, said that Cohn had informed him that Stevens had, on several occasions, expressed a desire to be photographed with Schine. "He told me that he had documentary evidence to substantiate that charge. Mr. Cohn advised that there was in existence a picture of the Secretary and Mr. Schine. Nothing was said to me, I am sure, about the photograph being altered, changed, edited or otherwise. I accepted it at its face value. I would not under any circumstances present to this committee a spurious document." It was 1:10 when Jenkins finished his apologia. Mundt fought his way out from behind the cloudbank his pipe had created to announce a recess until 2:30.

The ordeal of Robert Stevens began in earnest on the afternoon of April 27. From 2:40 on that day until 4:37 P.M. on May 10, he was, with rare exceptions, constantly in the witness chair. Doggedly, he tried to assure his persistent questioners that he had not coddled Communists in the Army, that he had not used Schine as a hostage to sabotage the subcommittee's investigation of Fort Monmouth, and that he had tried wholeheartedly, even at the expense of his dignity and his pride, to cooperate with the Wisconsin Senator and

* A Col. Bradley and Army Counselor Adams.

his minions. McCarthy and Cohn, like hungry jackals stalking a wounded wild beast, flustered him with a barrage of questions that brought him to the brink of collapse. Jenkins and the subcommittee members were hardly less rapacious.

By noon of April 29, it was apparent to everyone in the Caucus Room that the Secretary could not go on much longer. At one point, Welch pleaded with Jenkins, who had thrown all restraint to the winds, to show "ordinary courtesy" to the exhausted witness. "I am informed, Mr. Jenkins," he said, "that you have tried many murder trials, and with great success, but may I remind you, my friend, that this is not a murder trial, and that you are examining the Secretary of the Army." Jenkins gulped twice and then, sustained by Mundt's observation that "all witnesses must appear in this committee room at the same level," continued his rapid-fire interrogation.

After the luncheon recess, however, he asked the chair's permission to excuse the Secretary and call Private Schine to cast some enlightenment on the McGuire Airbase photograph. "It is evident," he reminded Mundt, "that he is somewhat exhausted." Mr. Welch wanted it clearly understood that his client was asking no quarter. "Mr. Stevens wanted me to make it entirely clear that he is a member of the Army, and that he would go forward if the committee required him to." Although McCarthy was reluctant to let his quarry have any respite, he was willing to withdraw his objections if Jenkins insisted on calling Schine.

The most famous private in the history of the United States Army settled himself deliberately in the chair vacated by his ultimate superior. A tall, sleepy-eyed youth of twenty-seven, he had first come to McCarthy's attention in the fall of 1952 when he had written an anti-Communist pamphlet for distribution in his father's hotels. Obviously delighted by the horde of newspaper photographers who were scrambling over each other to snap his picture, he answered Jenkins' question in a calm, deferential voice. Yes, it had been he who, at Cohn's request, had gone to New York to pick up the original snapshot of himself and the Secretary of the Army. When he returned to Washington, he had turned it over to George Anastos.

Schine had no trouble holding his own with his interrogators until McClellan opened his first ten-minute round. Wasn't it true that he had spent the evening of April 23 at the Colony Restaurant with members of McCarthy's staff? The witness looked suddenly perplexed. Yes, he had been at the Colony that night. McClellan's tone hardened. "Did you at that time, with the others, have some pictures there examining them?" he demanded. Schine's voice was almost inaudible. "I may have, sir," he replied.

Q. What picture was that?
A. This was a picture of members of the staff, Senator Mc-Carthy and General Lawton.

Although he was certain that Cohn, Carr and Juliana had been present at the Colony, he couldn't remember whether Anastos was with the group. "I do not recall, sir," he answered McClellan. "I do not think he was."

When, as Mundt put it, it was Jenkins' "turn of the wheel" again, the committee counsel pounced on Schine's inability to recall who had been in the Colony party. "I am asking you about a single event," he roared, "a meeting of some five or six men, one week ago, and when you said you didn't remember whether or not George Anastos, who happens to be the man that you delivered this New York photograph to, was present or not, I felt that I should explore this subject further, and I still feel so."

Q. If you have an explanation I am sure the committee would like to hear it.
A. I am a private in the United States Army, sir.

Q. That does not affect your memory, does it?
A. I think I have a fairly good memory, sir.

Five minutes later, the witness' memory had improved to the extent that he was now able to fix the Colony meeting on April 26, instead of April 23, and to say definitely that Anastos had not been present.

It took almost all of the hearing's seventh day to trace the peregrinations of the Schine photograph from April 22, when the private had brought it to Washington, until it was delivered to Jenkins four days later. George Anastos, who confirmed Schine's testimony that he had not attended the Colony meeting, had handed the photograph, which was wrapped in brown paper, to Jim Juliana. The latter had turned it over to Don Surine, Cohn's assistant counsel, with instructions to have a photostatic blow-up "made of Secretary Stevens and Mr. Schine." On Monday, April 26, Juliana had asked Mrs. Frances Mims, the subcommittee's secretary, to take the enlargement to Jenkins' office.

Juliana took full responsibility for cropping the photograph. "It was my understanding after talking with you and Mr. Cohn about this picture," he told Jenkins, "that you wanted a picture of Secretary Stevens and Private Schine." But, he assured McClellan, it had been done "without any malicious intention whatsoever."

"Do you also take full responsibility for withholding from counsel, Mr. Jenkins, any knowledge or reference that this picture of Mr. Schine and Secretary Stevens was taken from a group picture?" the Senator asked.

"I do, Senator McClellan," was the sheepish answer.

Welch, whose courtly manner cloaked a natural bent for in-fighting, had the last word. Why hadn't Mr. Juliana merely delivered the group picture that had hung on the wall of Schine's New York office instead of producing a new version?

The witness disclaimed any knowledge of Schine's wall decorations.

"Did you think this came from a pixie?" Welch asked wryly, holding up the original framed picture.

McCarthy bestirred himself. "Will counsel, for my benefit, define—I think he might be an expert on that—what a pixie is?"

"I should say, Mr. Senator," Welch replied softly, seeing his opening, "that a pixie is a close relative of a fairy." As a nervous titter began to sweep the Caucus Room, Mundt cut it off sharply. "Counsel may proceed!" he snapped.

After an unsuccessful attempt on the evening of May third to end the hearings with the testimony of Secretary Stevens and Senator McCarthy, the subcommittee prepared, as Mr. Welch quaintly put it, to "plough the long furrow." The next day, with Stevens well into his ninth day on the firing line, McCarthy showed him a two-and-a-quarter-page document, purporting to be a copy of a 1951 letter from J. Edgar Hoover in which the FBI chief had warned the Army of the subversive backgrounds of some civilian employees at Fort Monmouth. Had the Secretary ever seen the original of this letter? He couldn't remember. Would he check his files? He would.

The next morning, Stevens reported that he had not been able to find the original of the FBI letter in the Pentagon. He was followed by Robert A. Collier, one of Jenkins' young assistants, who had spent the previous evening interviewing J. Edgar Hoover about the letter. Mr. Hoover had told him that he had not written the two-and-a-quarter-page document bearing his name, but that someone must have extracted it from a confidential fifteen-page interdepartmental memorandum which his office had sent to Major General A. R. Bolling on January 26, 1951. "Mr. Hoover advised me that the substance of the two-and-a-quarter-page carbon copy contained information relating to the same subject matter, and that in some instances exact or identical language appears in both documents."

> SENATOR JACKSON: I take it from the witness that Mr. Hoover has denied the existence of this letter. Is that correct?
> MR. COLLIER: This letter is not a copy of any document prepared by the FBI.

As Collier left the stand, Jenkins brought the reporters to the edge of their chairs with his pronouncement that he desired "to call as the next witness, Senator McCarthy." As he settled himself in the red leather chair, the Senator from Wisconsin had only one request to make. He wanted Roy Cohn and Frank Carr to sit beside him. "It isn't exactly counsel," he explained. "I just want the two young men with me." When Welch asked for permission to shift to the Senator's vacated seat at the counsel table so that he could hear better, the witness demurred. "I don't want Mr. Welch examining my notes over there," he told Mundt. "Come and take my chair, Mr. Welch," offered Frederick P. Bryan, Hensel's attorney, who was sitting a few feet away from McCarthy.

The Senator was only on the stand long enough to refuse to reveal the source of the two-and-a-quarter-page document. He would go no further than to admit that it had been given to him by "an officer in the Intelligence Department." "I will not under any circumstances," he told Jenkins, "reveal the source of an information which I get as chairman of the committee. I want to make it very clear that I want to notify the people who give me information that there is no way on earth that any committee, any force, can get me to violate the confidence of those people." Even the redoubtable Mr. Welch, who taunted the witness about "some fifth or sixth amendment notion" to withold the truth, was unable to shake the name of his informant out of him.

Faced with an obvious dead end, Mundt released his colleague and Stevens wearily returned to what Mr. Welch liked to refer to as "the hot seat." He was to remain there for the better part of the next three days while Cohn and McCarthy alternated at asking him questions, many of which had a familiar ring to the Caucus Room regulars. Finally Welch, who had become increasingly concerned over Stevens' health, could stand it no longer. "I suggest that it is time the country heard this simple thought: that the Senator is now engaged in a filibuster by the device of cross-examination." Chairman Mundt was not impressed. "Now you are testifying, Mr. Welch, not raising a point of order."

On May 12, Stevens' ordeal came to an end when a dapper, well-groomed man in his early forties took his place in the witness chair. John G. Adams, who had spent the last seven years in a variety of middle-echelon government legal positions, had been named Counselor of the Department of the Army on October 1, 1953. Two days after his appointment, Secretary Stevens had asked him to act as liaison between the department and the McCarthy Committee.

At first, relations with the Senator and his staff had been cordial. In fact, Adams had gone out of his way to keep them that way. It had been at his suggestion that the Secretary had publicly apologized to Roy Cohn for excluding the latter from a Signal Corps laboratory. On November 6, 1953, he had invited the subcommittee to lunch at the Pentagon so that "a slight irritation" which had developed regarding the Army's press releases about the Fort Monmouth investigation could be nipped in the bud.

> Q. At whose instance was the luncheon given, Mr. Adams?
> A I think it is fair to state that it was at my instance more than anyone else's.

But, in spite of all his efforts, his personal entente with Cohn & Company had foundered on the subject of Dave Schine's Army career. Starting with mid-November, 1953, Cohn had called him almost every day regarding a New York

assignment for his drafted friend. "As the month wore on
. . . and during December, they got more difficult to handle.
And Cohn became more and more expressly insistent." Never
in his five years of dealing with congressmen had he ever been
subjected to such awesome pressure.

In early December, General Ryan, the commander of Fort
Dix, where Schine was receiving his basic training, had asked
for authority to terminate the latter's weekday passes because
they were interfering with his instruction program. The
Secretary had agreed with Ryan's recommendation, provided
that Schine's week ends were free for committee business.

> Q. As a result of that decision, did you hear any more or
> receive any protests from either the Senator, Mr. Cohn or
> Mr. Carr?
> A. Yes, sir.

As soon as Cohn learned of Steven's action, "he was very put
out . . . and considered this a double cross, an Army double
cross, of a commitment already made." When Adams had
complained to McCarthy about Cohn's attitude, the Senator
"stated that he felt it was improper, and that he would write
a letter to the Secretary of the Army about it, and tell us there
would be no further interference."

A few hours later, Cohn had telephoned him and said that
"he would teach me what it meant to go over his head." When
Adams asked, "Roy, is that a threat?" the chief counsel had
shouted, "No, that is a promise!" The relations between the
two men reached a new low several days later when Cohn, in
a series of telephone calls, bitterly protested that Schine's
week ends had been shortened because he was being forced
to train on Saturday.

> Q. Mr. Adams, was there any abusive language toward you
> used at that time?
> A. These telephone calls . . . were extremely abusive, and
> they were very obscene.

Even Senator McCarthy had been unable to control his young assistant. When the subject of Schine was brought up at a New York restaurant on December 17, "Mr. Cohn became extremely agitated, became extremely abusive. He cursed me and then Senator McCarthy." As the luncheon wore on, Cohn had become increasingly bitter. He blamed the Army for not giving Schine a New York assignment, and McCarthy for not supporting him in his efforts to obtain this concession. At first the Senator had tried to pacify the lawyer, and "then he more or less lapsed into silence."

On January 13, Adams had dropped in to see Cohn in the Senate Office Building to alert him to the possibility that Schine might be sent overseas. If that happened, Cohn had told him, "Stevens is through as Secretary of the Army. We will wreck the Army." When Adams remonstrated with him, he had flown into a rage. "We have enough stuff on the Army to keep investigations going indefinitely," he had warned Adams, "and if anything like such-and-such double-cross occurs, that is what we will do."

That afternoon, the Army Counselor informed Cohn that he had just learned that Schine had been classified as an investigator and was about to be sent to the Provost Marshal School at Camp Gordon, Georgia. Five days later, he had received a call from Cohn, who was vacationing at one of the Schine hotels at Boca Raton, Florida. Was it true, Cohn wanted to know, that Dave was going to be sent to Camp Gordon? When Adams assured him that it was, his caller had become very upset and hung up. The next morning, the witness had been requested by Mr. Carr, who explained that he was following Cohn's orders, to have certain members of the Army Loyalty and Security Appeals Board appear before the subcommittee for questioning.

Since Stevens was on an inspection tour in the Far East. Adams had contacted Hensel, who had recommended that he get in touch with Attorney General Brownell. On January

21, Adams had attended a meeting in Brownell's office at which Sherman Adams and Henry Cabot Lodge were present. The Army Counselor was advised by Adams to prepare "a written record of all the incidents with reference to Private Schine," and to prevail upon the Republican members of the subcommittee to prevent the summoning of the Loyalty Board members. Later, he learned that Senator Dirksen had persuaded Cohn to quash the subpoenas.

In early February, at Carr's recommendation, Adams had called columnist George Sokolsky. The latter had suggested that, if Schine were permitted to attend a certain Course 95 at Camp Gordon, he would see "if I can't withdraw, soften this pressure on the Army which is coming from Senator Mc-Carthy." When Adams relayed this conversation to Stevens, the Secretary "issued an instruction to me . . . to see to it that Schine completed his eight weeks of basic before anything happened to him, which would positively preclude him from entering Course 95."

In all, Adams spent most of five days answering questions. Before he was excused late on the afternoon of May 24, he admitted that he had "no enthusiasm" for the McCarthy hearings, but maintained that he had gone to the extent of human endurance in cooperating with the Senator and his staff. He had drawn a map of the nine main Army areas for Cohn and Carr, not to divert them into investigating the Air Force and the Navy, but to point out where his department was worried about a homosexual ring at a southern post. Although he had accepted small favors from Roy Cohn, such as theater tickets, he had never seriously discussed forming a law partnership with the committee's chief counsel, as Mc Carthy had charged.

Adams was followed on the stand by a succession of Army officers whose testimony indicated that G. David Schine was undoubtedly the most influential private ever to fill a khaki uniform. General Cornelius Edward Ryan, the harassed commanding officer at Fort Dix, told of the volume of special passes which the new inductee had received. Lieutenant John B. Blount, the general's *aide de camp,* testified as to Cohn's efforts to relieve Schine of kitchen police duty. Colonel John T. Murray explained the markings on a chart which had been prepared by a Pentagon draftsman to show how many days Schine had been absent from Fort Dix during his basic training period.*

When Schine reported to Fort Dix, on November 19, 1953, he had been assigned to Company K of the 47th Infantry Regiment. He had not wasted any time in making his presence known to Captain Joseph J. M. Miller, its commanding officer. On his first day at Dix, he had told the officer that he could help him "if I ever wanted to make a little trip to Florida." Four weeks later, Miller had found Schine, who was supposed to be on the firing range, sitting in the cab of a truck which was parked in front of the company mess hall. "I asked Private Schine what he was doing . . . and Private Schine said he was studying logistics. I instructed the driver to take Private Schine immediately to the range."

Later that morning, Miller had visited the range. There, he had found Schine deep in a conversation with the first field sergeant. "I came up to them and determined that Private Schine was trying to get placed in an earlier firing order so that he might be finished early." Since Schine had been warned on his first day in the company not to ask his noncoms for any special favors, Miller had castigated him for disobeying orders. "He asked me if it might not be possible to lower my voice . . . he put his hand on my shoulder in an attempt to draw me aside. He told me . . . that he did not like to have instances of the kind occur that happened earlier in

---

* From November 10, 1953, the day he reported to Fort Dix, until January 16, 1954, when he was transferred to Camp Gordon, Ga., Schine was issued thirty-five passes. For the same period, the typical authorized absences of an average trainee undergoing basic training were twelve.

the morning and had just happened, that they were embarrassing to him. He thereupon told me that it was his purpose to remake the American Military Establishment along modern lines. It seemed a little ridiculous to me."

Miller was the last witness to buttress the Army's charges and, at 2:30 on the afternoon of May 26, Jenkins "very happily" announced that "we have concluded with the Army's case." Seconds later, Senator Dworshak had the floor. He moved for the dismissal of the charges against both Struve Hensel and Frank Carr "because the proof and testimony . . . are wholly insufficient to sustain said charges." Dirksen promptly seconded the motion. Despite Mr. Welch's fervent plea to retain the charges against Carr "until the evidence is in," the subcommittee voted, on straight party lines, to exonerate both men. The Army's counsel looked stricken. "May I say sadly, gentlemen," he piped, "that it seems strange to me that these Republican lips of mine, Republican for sixty-four years, can convince only Democrats, my natural enemies, and that the Republicans, whom I love and cherish, find my words are dust and ashes."

Roy Cohn was the first witness for the McCarthy team. In general, he maintained that first Adams and then Stevens had tried to halt the Monmouth hearings. In fact, they had stopped at nothing that might throw a monkey wrench into the subcommittee's investigation. They had threatened to relieve General Lawton of Fort Monmouth as "a reprisal . . . for his cooperation with the committee." The map which Adams had drawn had been part of a deliberate attempt to shift McCarthy's attention to the Air Force and Navy. Finally, when all else had failed, Schine had been used as a hostage to force the subcommittee to use its energies elsewhere.

On the third day of Cohn's appearance, Jenkins got around to the eleven memoranda which had been distributed to the press by Senator McCarthy the day after the Army had released its "Chronology of Events." Dated from October 2,

1953, to March 11, 1954, they seemed to substantiate Mc-
Carthy's charges that the Army had used every dirty trick in
the book to stop the Monmouth hearings. Four of the documents had been prepared by Cohn, six by Frank Carr and one
by McCarthy. It was Cohn's opinion that all eleven had been
dictated to Mrs. Mary Driscoll, the Senator's personal secretary.

Jenkins thought that it was about time to call Mrs. Driscoll. McCarthy gallantly volunteered to fetch her, if Mr.
Jenkins would give her a half-hour "to comb her hair and put
some powder on." Thirty minutes later, he escorted a badly
frightened middle-aged woman into the Caucus Room. Speaking in near-whispers, she stated that she had typed all of the
memoranda and filed them in a jacket marked "Investigating
Committee." When the Senator had asked her to get any
memoranda from Cohn or Carr concerning conversations
with Stevens, she had gone unerringly to this particular file.
"How did you know where to go to look for that file, Mrs.
Driscoll, when you were called upon to produce it?" asked
Jenkins. "I can't tell you that," she replied. "That is my way
of filing."

When Welch finished with Mrs. Driscoll, there were very
few people in America who did not share his doubts that the
memoranda were "the real McCoy." Since they had been
typed on several machines, he wondered what kind of a machine she used for each one. She couldn't recall. "A typewriter is a typewriter," she told him, "and I don't pay any
attention to the type of typewriter." Besides, she was in the
habit of wandering around the office and using any machine
that was available. She didn't know which girl on the Senator's secretarial staff had made the copies that were given to
the press on March 13. With ten girls in the office, she
couldn't possibly remember who had typed what. Her rout
was complete when she admitted that she hadn't turned the
jacket over to Frank Carr, although his last memorandum

indicated that he was "searching the files" for the very material it contained.

> Q. Well, did you say to him, "Mr. Carr, look no further. I have got them in the slickest little package here you ever saw"?
>
> A. Absolutely not.
>
> Q. Did you tell him his search was silly?
>
> A. I am not going to tell Mr. Carr that his search was silly or that I have all of them. Maybe I have overlooked one.
>
> Q. But you had what you got here together, did you not?
>
> A. I couldn't tell you that. I don't know.

As Mrs. Driscoll marched back to the safety of McCarthy's office, Roy Cohn resumed the stand, only to run afoul of the indomitable Mr. Welch. By a series of taunting, often sarcastic, inquiries, the Army's counsel rapidly cut Dennis the Menace, as Vermont's Ralph Flanders had labelled him, down to size. As the Caucus Room rocked with laughter, Welch, by a staccato series of what Chairman Mundt called "rib-tickling questions," succeeded in reducing the once suave, self-possessed witness to a stammering youth who suddenly had found himself way beyond his depth.

Welch started off by asking the subcommittee's chief counsel whether he had "enlisted some pretty high-powered people" in his efforts to obtain a commission for Schine. He looked surprised when Cohn objected to the use of the term "high-powered."

> Q. Do you think any little old guy off a farm in Iowa who would like a commission now could manage to have a conference between a Senator and a general and you?
>
> A. Sir, I don't think—
>
> Q. Just answer yes or no. Do you think a little boy from the farm can get away with that?
>
> A. My answer to you, Mr. Welch, is I think Iowa might exclude me. If a person from Iowa contacted Senator Hickenlooper, I am sure Senator Hickenlooper or someone in

his office would call General Reber or someone on his staff and see that the application was given prompt attention; yes, sir.

The expression on Mr. Welch's face was inscrutable. "It is a wonder we haven't got all officers and no privates in our Army, isn't it, Mr. Cohn?" he asked quizzically.

As the questioning went on, the Bostonian attempted to ascertain Schine's role on the subcommittee's staff. "By the way," he asked, "were you his boss, or somebody else?" Cohn explained that he didn't think "anybody has a boss except the chairman of the committee."

Q. Does everybody just romp around on their own?
A. Sir, that might be amusing, but the boys down there, as I have explained, don't romp around.
Q. I don't mean to be amusing. Who gave Schine orders?
A. Sir, I would like to answer you.
Q. Just tell me who gave Schine orders. That will be an answer.
A. No, sir. I would still—
Q. Won't you answer that? Who gave Schine orders?
A. Sir, before I do that, my—
Q. I don't care what you do before. You can do it afterward. Who gave Schine his orders?
A. May I answer? I think it was three questions back. I was in the middle of an answer.
Q. I will waive any question that is three questions back and now ask you, who gave Schine his orders?

Although Chairman Mundt broke in and ordered the witness to answer the question, Cohn insisted on keeping the record straight. "I would like in fairness to complete the answer to Mr. Welch's questions before he cuts in and starts with another," he said.

"If we have anything pending, I am surprised," Welch replied. "Are you still bothered about that question about romping around? Does that bother you?" Mr. Cohn nodded. "It does, sir."

Welch sat back in his chair and folded his hands over his paunch. "Now make a speech if you will, subject: 'Romping around,' " he said resignedly. The spectators, who had had great difficulty in keeping straight faces during the interchange, broke into loud laughter. Mundt, who was smiling as broadly as the audience, suddenly remembered his role. "The chair will have to ask the audience to be a little careful," he said. "I don't expect you people to sit there grim-faced throughout all the interrogatories, but I do ask you to chuckle quietly to yourselves, if possible." As the laughter subsided, Cohn tried to explain that the subcommittee staff worked "much harder than they have to to earn the pay which they get."

Welch pressed on. Did Mr. Cohn believe that there was any connection between the case of dentist Irving Peress and the Fort Monmouth investigation? He did not, but he was sure that Mr. Welch understood that any Communist in an Army camp was dangerous because he might indoctrinate other soldiers.

> Q. Now, whatever you say about indoctrinating other people, it wouldn't be too happy a way to try to drill it into people with a dentist's drill and an aching bicuspid, would it?
> A. It might be an effective way, sir.
> Q. Well, you don't have the guy's attention very well, if his tooth hurts. Isn't that right, Mr. Cohn? Let's pass it fast.
> A. Well, Mr. Welch, it is hard to pass it fast. You have this situation. You have a man with an open record as a Communist.

"What I am saying to you," Welch persisted, "is that if you want to catch a young soldier and make a Communist out of him, one pass in a dentist's chair isn't much of a pass, is it?"

Cohn's answer was less than responsive. The subcommittee had been unable to find out whether Peress had been recruiting soldiers into the Communist movement because the dentist had claimed the protection of the Fifth Amendment.

When Welch heard Cohn complain that the Army-McCarthy hearings had prevented the subcommittee from exposing some 130 Communists who were working in defense plants, his eyebrows shot up a full inch. "Will you not," he demanded, "before the sun goes down, give those names to the FBI and at least have those men put under surveillance?" No, sir, that would not be necessary; Mr. Hoover already had the names. Mr. Welch looked unconvinced. "Just for the purpose of safety, for fear something could be missed somewhere, would you mind, as a patriotic American citizen, sending the 130 names over to the FBI tonight?" There was a long minute of silence. "I wouldn't mind it at all, sir," the witness finally blurted out.

If Cohn was speechless, McCarthy was not. Mr. Welch knew as well as he did that the FBI had no power to get rid of any civilian employees. That was up to the heads of the various executive departments. "So let's not make the mistake, Mr. Welch," he bellowed, "of trying to lead the American people to believe that the FBI can do anything beyond getting the information." Cohn joined in to assure his interrogator that the bureau had every one of his 130 names. Welch smiled innocently. "Then what is all the excitement about," he asked quietly, "if J. Edgar Hoover is on the job chasing these 130 Communists?"

During the third week of the hearings, the White House had ordered Stevens to refrain from testifying as to interdepartmental conversations and communications, or to produce any such documents or reproductions. Because of the Eisenhower directive, none of the calls monitored by the Secretary of the Army were introduced until the afternoon of June 4, when they were limited to conversations between Stevens, four members of the subcommittee and McCarthy's staff.

There were no fireworks as three Pentagon stenographers read their notes into the record until Symington's calls to Stevens were introduced. As the conversations unfolded, it became apparent that, by the beginning of 1954, the Senator from Missouri had become the Army's confidant. Besides urging Stevens to keep his back up, Symington had suggested to the Secretary that, if he felt he needed legal advice, Clark Clifford, Truman's ex-aide, would be a good man to consult. "I would suggest two things to you, old fellow," he had advised. "1) let's counterpunch this stuff and not lead; 2) I think your people over there are pretty harassed and I don't blame them, but maybe some of them can't see the forest for the trees."

McCarthy's face gradually turned purple as he listened to Symington's calls. Finally, he could stand it no longer. "A point of personal privilege," he barked at Mundt. If it had been the Democratic Senator from Missouri who was responsible for "trying to wreck our attempt to expose Communists who had infiltrated the Administration," then he ought, in all decency, to disqualify himself from the subcommittee and take the stand himself. Symington, with a superb display of self-control, recommended that the honorable gentleman from Wisconsin would do better by agreeing to put his own calls in the record instead of making speeches. "Let's get on with the hearings," he concluded, "and not with the diversion."

After some three dozen monitored conversations had been recorded for posterity, Roy Cohn was back on view. Welch continued his probing of Schine's official duties, the Fort Monmouth investigation and the subcommittee's skirmishes with Stevens and Adams. As Cohn began to squirm under an unrelenting barrage of questions that made McCarthy's staff look like a pack of errant Boy Scouts, the Senator decided to apply the brakes. Mr. Chairman, he exploded, did Mr. Welch know that Frederick G. Fisher, one of the young men in his law firm, "has been for a number of years a member of an organization which was named, oh, years and years ago, as the legal bulwark for the Communist Party?"

The Army counsel looked crushed. "Until this moment, Senator," he said sadly, "I think I never really gauged your cruelty or your recklessness. Little did I dream you could be so reckless as to do an injury to that lad. It is true that he is still with Hale and Dorr. It is true that he will continue to be with Hale and Dorr. It is, I regret, to say, equally true that I fear he shall always bear a scar needlessly inflicted by you. If it were in my power to forgive you for your reckless cruelty, I will do so. I like to think I am a gentleman, but your forgiveness will have to come from someone other than me."

Fred Fisher, Welch explained patiently, had originally been selected to assist him in preparing for the hearings. However, when he had volunteered the information that he had, as a Harvard law student, briefly belonged to the National Lawyers Guild, he had been sent back to Boston. "Let us not assassinate this lad further, Senator," Welch pleaded, with tears in his eyes. "You have done enough. Have you no sense of decency, sir, at long last? Have you left no sense of decency? If there is a God in heaven, it will do neither you nor your cause any good." As a spontaneous burst of applause filled the room, the junior Senator from Wisconsin muttered to no one in particular, "What did I do? What did I do?"

The hearings were to drone on for five more days, as first McCarthy and then Carr manned the dikes. But, after Welch's outburst, there was nothing more to be said. For millions of Americans, the spectacle of one man, who had come to represent sanity and good sense, rising to protest in the name of common decency an unwarranted attack on the reputation of one of his young assistants, had ended the reign of terror. Cohn, Schine, Stevens, Adams, Hensel and even

McCarthy had, in a matter of minutes, lost all significance. A moral principle, as old as time itself, had been dramatically reaffirmed on the flickering screens of twenty million television sets.

At 6:32 on the afternoon of June 17, thirty-six days after they had started, the hearings ground to an end. Just before Chairman Mundt banged his gavel for the last time, Mr. Welch had a few words to say. "Would you, Mr. Chairman, bear a personal note? I alone, I alone came into this room from deep obscurity. I, alone, will retire to obscurity. As it folds about me, softly as I hope it does quickly, the lady who listened and is called Judith Lyndon Welch * will hear from me a long sigh of relief. I am sorry that this play had to take place in the fretful lighting and ominous roll of noises from Indochina and around the world. It saddens me to think that my life has been lived so largely either in wars or turmoil. I allow myself to hope that soon there will come a day when there will, in this lovely land of ours, be more simple laughter."

On August 30, the subcommittee issued a majority, a minority and two individual reports, all but one of which stated, in so many words, that its ex-Chairman had been guilty of improper conduct in his *auto-da-fé* with the Army.† One month earlier, however, Ralph Flanders had introduced a resolution asking his colleagues to censure McCarthy for conduct unbecoming a United States Senator. After three days of spirited debate, the Senate voted overwhelmingly for the creation of a nonpartisan Select Committee to look into Flanders' charges.

The six-man panel, chaired by Utah's staid Arthur V. Watkins, began its hearings on August 31. When the orderly, un-

* Welch's first wife and the mother of his two sons. After her death on December 21, 1956, he married the former Agnes Rogers Brown.

† The exception was that of Senator Dirksen which adopted the conclusion of the *Washington Star* that the record of the hearings was not one "which reflects pressure, improper or otherwise, in any significant degree."

spectacular sessions were concluded, its members recommended that McCarthy be censured for 1) his conduct toward the Subcommittee on Privileges and Elections which had, in 1951 and 1952, investigated the Tydings defeat, and 2) his abuse of General Zwicker. On December 2, the full Senate, by a vote of 67 to 22, "condemned" the man from Appleton for his treatment of the Privileges and Elections Subcommittee as well as for his sneering characterization of Watkins and his five associates "as the 'unwitting handmaidens,' 'involuntary agents' and 'attorneys in fact' of the Communist Party."

Mr. Welch was never to return to the obscurity for which he so fervently yearned. His star rose as fast as McCarthy's had fallen. No sooner had he returned to Boston than he found himself besieged with requests to lecture to women's clubs, preside at moot court trials, sign advertising testimonials, author magazine articles and fill television guest spots. In 1959, at the request of Otto Preminger, who knew a good man when he saw one, he accepted the role of Judge Weaver in Columbia Pictures' *Anatomy of a Murder*. The millions of moviegoers who testified to Preminger's good judgment, were happy to see that the years had not erased the disarming grin, the incredulous arch of the eyebrows and the sprightly voice that still retained a hint of its Iowa origins.

Within six months after the end of the Army-McCarthy hearings, it was obvious to his colleagues and the Capital press corps that the Wisconsin Senator's health was failing. He had begun to walk with a decided limp and was often seen dozing in his seat during Senate debates. On April 28, 1957, he entered Bethesda Naval Hospital, suffering from what his wife described as "an old knee injury." At 6:02 on the evening of May 2, after receiving the last rites of the Catholic Church, he died of "acute hepatitic failure." He was forty-eight years old. Mr. Welch, who was vacationing in New Smyrna Beach, Florida, was asked for a comment. "McCarthy was so controversial a figure," he said, "that only time can dictate what is his place in history."

Welch himself had only a little more than three years to live. In the spring of 1960, he had been forced by a heart ailment to retire from the active practice of law. He had moved to Hyannis, Massachusetts, where he quickly became a familiar sight on the streets of that resort village. On October 6, 1960, sixteen days after his seventieth birthday, he died in Cape Cod Hospital of heart failure. The erstwhile adversaries had one thing in common, at last.

# Index